Art, Origins, Otherness

Art, Origins, Otherness

Between Philosophy and Art

William Desmond

State University of New York Press

Published by
State University of New York Press, Albany

Printed in the United States of America

For information, address State University of New York Press,
90 State Street, Suite 700, Albany, NY 12207

Production by Michael Haggett
Marketing by Jennifer Giovani

Library of Congress Cataloging-in-Publication Data

Desmond, William, 1951–
Art, origins, and otherness : between philosophy and art / William Desmond.
p. cm.
Includes bibliographical references and index.
ISBN 0-7914-5745-1 (alk. paper) — ISBN 0-7914-5746-X (pbk. : alk. paper)
1. Aesthetics. 2. Art—Philosophy. 3. Other (Philosophy) I. Title.

BH39.D4535 2003
111'.85—dc21

2003057266

10 9 8 7 6 5 4 3 2 1

Πᾶσα ἀνάγκη τόνδε τὸν κόσμον εἰκόνα τινὸς εἶναι

—Plato, *Timaeus,* 29B

Lovers and madmen have such seething brains,
Such shaping fantasies, that apprehend
More than cool reason ever comprehends.
The lunatic, the lover, and the poet
Are of imagination all compact.
One sees more devils than vast hell can hold;
That is the madman. The lover, all as fanatic,
Sees Helen's beauty in a brow of Egypt.
The poet's eye, in a fine frenzy rolling,
Doth glance from heaven to earth, from earth to heaven;
And as imagination bodies forth
The forms of things unknown, the poet's pen
Turns them to shapes and gives to airy nothing
A local habitation and a name.

—William Shakespeare,
A Midsummer Night's Dream, V, i, 4–17

To Urbain Dhondt

Contents

Preface ix

Introduction 1

1 Mimesis, Eros, and Mania: On Platonic Originals 19

2 The Terror of Genius and the Otherness of the Sublime: On Kant and the Transcendental Origin 53

3 The Otherness of Art's Enigma—Resolved or Dissolved? Hegel and the Dialectical Origin 87

4 Gothic Hegel: On Architecture and the Finer Enchantments of Transcendence 115

5 Art's Release and the Sabbath of the Will: Schopenhauer and the *Eros Turannos* of Origin 131

6 Eros Frenzied and the Redemption of Art: Nietzsche and the Dionysian Origin 165

7 Art and the Self-Concealing Origin: Heidegger's Equivocity and the Still Unthought Between 209

8 Art and the Impossible Burden of Transcendence: On the End of Art and the Task of Metaphysics 265

Index 295

Preface

I have been asked more than once why I do not write, or have not written, a philosophical aesthetics, somewhat along the lines of the metaphysics of *Being and the Between,* or the approach to ethics of *Ethics and the Between. Philosophy and Its Others* does have a chapter entitled "Being Aesthetic" which might be seen to contain *in nuce* what could be amplified more fully, as the chapter entitled "Being Ethical" might be seen as being an ethics *in nuce* that flowers into *Ethics and the Between.* While this present book is not that work, and though behind it lie some systematic reserves, it does represent an engagement with the importance of art for philosophy, a concern which has been continuous for me, and not separable from the importance of religion for both art and philosophy. The themes of otherness, origin, art have also been a continuing preoccupation of mine, not only in my first published books,[1] but in other essays since then. Some of these essays supplied earlier drafts for parts of some of the reflections to follow and I am happy to acknowledge that here.[2]

I do not preclude writing an aesthetics in a somewhat more systematic manner, but there are reasons for a certain diffidence in our time, among

1. *Art and the Absolute: A Study of Hegel's Aesthetics* (Albany: State University of New York Press, 1986), abbreviation, *AA; Desire, Dialectic and Otherness: An Essay on Origins* (New Haven: Yale University Press, 1987), abbreviation *DDO.* Other books here refered to are *Being and the Between* (Albany: State University of New York Press, 1995), abbreviation, *BB; Ethics and the Between* (Albany: State University of New York Press, 2001), abbreviation *EB, Philosophy and Its Others: Ways of Being and Mind* (Albany: State University of New York Press, 1990), abbreviation, *PO.*

2. A version of some material in sections 2–6, chapter 2 appeared in "Kant and the Terror of Genius: Between Enlightenment and Romanticism," in *Kant's Aesthetics,* ed. Herman Parret (Berlin: de Gruyter, 1998), 594–614; a version of some material of chapter 3, "Art, Origins, Otherness: Hegel and Aesthetic Self-Mediation," in *Philosophy and Art,* ed. Dan Dahlstrom (Washington: Catholic University of America Press, 1991), 209–34; in chapter 4 I added to "Gothic Hegel," in *The Owl of Minerva,* 30 no. 2 (spring 1999): 237–52; a version of some material in sections 4–6, chapter 5 appeared in "Schopenhauer, Art and the Dark Origin," in *Schopenhauer,* ed. Eric von der Luft (Lewistown, NY: Mellen Press, 1988),101–122; a version of some material in sections 5–9 chapter 6 appeared in "Rethinking the Origin: Hegel and Nietzsche," in *Hegel, History and Interpretation,* ed. Shaun Gallagher (Albany: SUNY Press, 1997), 71–94. Most of this material has been extensively rethought and rewritten.

which the following have given me pause. Art has become immensely pluriform, though it is no different in this respect than the forms of being religious. But sometimes one fears a certain thinness to the ethos within which reflection on art occurs, and indeed the spiritual milieu which supports its long-term seriousness. Too often it is the boring outrages that seem to attract publicity rather than the more enduring excellences that have to struggle incognito to maintain their place. I mention a particular nadir: some years ago we witnessed the obscenity of millions being paid for a van Gogh painting—van Gogh who earned not a penny in his time, and then that purchase at least partly motivated by the calculation of "parking excess yen." The press whooped with glee at the high price, but what was prized? The art had become almost invisible. Was something rotten in the state of Denmark?

Why do we now seem to ask so little of art where once we asked so much? My suspicion is that we have spent too long asking too much of it, and in the wrong way. Deflation follows inflation, as the bubble bursts, and recovery may take time. For we have treated art as a surrogate for religious transcendence, but this aesthetic god too has died, and now we hawk the bones. I found this offensive, as would anyone imbued with a little piety. But despite the boring outrages that are the *parodia sacra* of this dying religion—and this I stress—it is the immense importance of art that I still found inspiring—importance metaphysically and indeed in terms of a truer spirit of being religious. In the face of affronts, in the face sometimes of obscenities or even blasphemies, one shows truer respect by remaining silent.

There was also the fact that art, religion, and philosophy belonged together, and the spiritual health of one could not be entirely divorced from that of the others. This belonging together I do not mean in Hegel's sense of absolute spirit. There can be something of ultimate moment about each, though this is inseparable from their common inhabitation of the ethos of being, and their different responses to what is most worthy of articulation there. Instead of alertness to what is of ultimate moment, what do we find?

Post-philosophical philosophy after the so-called "end of philosophy": a philosophy that does, and does not, want to call itself philosophy. Would you recommend that a thoughtful young person dedicate her life to that?

Art after the so-called "end of art": the "interesting" affronts to sense that do, and do not, want to call themselves "art." Would you advise a sensitive and imaginative person to spend his life on that?

Being religious after the so-called "death of God": a religiousness that does, and does not, want to call itself religious. Could one expect a person touched by reverence to take that seriously, if one was so feeble in one's endorsement of religion's porosity to ultimacy?

I do appreciate the equivocity of our condition; I do appreciate that all three are in question; but a serious addressing of the equivocity must come from sources beyond the enfeeblement itself. I think we need what I call a metaxological philosophy, one attuned to our intermediate condition, our "being between," and one with mindful finesse for all of its equivocities. I do not think we need post-philosophical philosophy. We need philosophy—philosophy with a memory longer than the "thought-bites" of immediate relevance, philosophy with a thoughtfulness lucid about the elemental perplexities of our condition of being, perplexities that recur as long as we are what we are. We also need art and religion as imbued with an analogous sense of spiritual seriousness.

What animates this work is affirmative of the metaphysical significance of art, with repercussions for the practices of philosophy and religion. In pursuing this matter, I offer a number of direct philosophical engagements with thinkers, each as provoking perplexity about the fundamental questions. My aim is to engage the questions themselves. Some exposition of thinkers is needed and given, but a report of scholarly findings is not the primary focus. I have read more extensively than might be evident, and I well know that professors love footnotes, some even first turning to the bibliography of a book, as if that provides the surest index of its excellence. I honor the spirit of philological earnestness but my interest falls on the themes themselves and engaging them with important philosophers. The engagement is philosophical. I am not doing art criticism, or literary criticism, though in matters of philosophical style, we need not be shy of the image or the metaphor, and indeed the possibility that sometimes the boundaries between art, religion, and philosophy become themselves porous.

Where I refer sometimes to my own works, I mean this not monologically (save me from narcissism), but as a sign to the *reader* that there is more to be said on a particular point, and in some instances I have done so elsewhere. I am sensitive to the matter of "reinventing the wheel" with regard to what I written elsewhere. Some readers may ask for more here or less. Some will be familiar with (some of) my other works, some will not be, so it is a judgment call as to what to presuppose, and what to explain anew.

I want to thank John Hymers for his great help with some of the references, as well as with the index. Thanks are due here also to Renee Ryan, Jason Howard, and Daniel Murphy. Warmest thanks to Jane Bunker, philosophy editor at SUNY, for her unstinting and much appreciated support over the years. Sincere thanks to Michael Haggett for exemplary professional work in the production of this book, as well as some earlier books of mine. Unreserved thanks to my family, Maria my wife, my sons William, Hugh, Oisín, without whom by now I probably would be at least half-mad. I want to thank Professor Urbain Dhondt for his wise steadiness, for friendship, for wide-ranging conversation, and for his patience in my child steps in Dutch. I dedicate the book to him.

Introduction

Art, Origins, Otherness

Our time is often said to be postreligious and postmetaphysical, but is it not true that *art* has become for many the happening where some encounter with transcendence continues to be sought? With art, it will be said, some important communication of *significant otherness* happens. With art, it will also be said, we find ourselves thinking in terms of perhaps the *exemplary* expression of human *originality*. Indeed, here it may also be said that art's otherness and originality often leave us with an enduring insinuation of enigma, such that we are given to wonder if great art privileges us with some intimation of an even more *ultimate origin*. Even in a time of abundant kitsch, the sustaining power of art to offer *more* is not yet dead. What are we to make of this situation? What are some of the philosophical considerations arising in connection with art, origins, otherness? The studies in this book deal diversely with such questions, and with how some major philosophers might shed light on them.

Art, origins, otherness—but why bring philosophical reflection to bear on these three concerns together? The connection may not be immediately self-evident. The themes of otherness, origin, art may have been a continuing preoccupation in some of my previous works, but what of the matter itself? First, questions concerning origins have marked a set of essential perplexities for philosophy since its beginning. Then, questions about art have contributed to new forms of perplexity, not least since philosophy has taken on new questions about its own tasks, especially since Kant. Finally, questions about otherness have assumed an evident prominence in our time, witnessing to our sense of distance from former, seemingly less self-lacerated practices of philosophy.

Why then ask about art, origins, otherness together? Because what we discover may well tell us something important about the following questions. First, why does our perplexity about origin not disappear, despite its being banned from "legitimate" thought by some practices of philosophy? Second, why does art continue to matter, despite the hara-kiri on spiritual seriousness it seems intent on performing in recent times? Third, why is the question of otherness less some novel discovery of postmodern discourse as an abiding worry surviving uneasily, and perhaps sometimes too recessively, in the tradition of philosophy? Has art something important to tell us about that otherness, and the enigma of the origin, as well as something about the continuing tasks of philosophical thought, tasks now more plurivocal in nature than univocal?

Great art has always drawn its admirers by its power to renew our astonishment before the mysterious happening of being, not of course in such a seemingly generalized way, but by an aesthetic fidelity to the inexhaustible singularities of the world, human and nonhuman. In its being true to these singularities, it recharges our sense of the otherness of being, and so it offers a gift and challenge to philosophy. The gift: here something of replete moment is opened or released. The challenge: now think *that!* We philosophers fail here more than we succeed, not least because we think of the singular as just an instance of the neutral universal, and *there* we feel more at home. What if philosophical thought were to renew its community with art and what art communicates? To say the least, it would have to rethink what singularity and universality mean. And what of origins? The theme of "originality" is one of the major preoccupations of Romantic and post-Romantic culture, and in an exemplary form with reference to art. Yet this preoccupation has often hidden metaphysical presuppositions that constitute incognito lines of connection to the longer philosophical tradition, and its concern with origins, and the meaning of original being. Art matters for this preoccupation, no less than for the issue of otherness, and these incognito lines of connection. If there is something exemplary shown in and through artistic originality, perhaps it may be of singular help in aiding us to philosophical mindfulness of origin or original being.

The word "metaphysics" is often thoughtlessly used to refer to some naïve and fantastic resort to an otherworldly transcendence. Call this the cartoon version of "Platonism," or "Christianity," a cartoon that is one of the poisoned chalices offered us by the postidealistic inheritance. We are said to have left *that* behind us. But how often we are still captive to some variation of the scheme of Comte: first theology, then metaphysics, then, alleluia, positive science. I know now many no longer shout "alleluia" at this third. We have grown used to, tired of, disillusioned with the "positive," as our deconstructive, postmodern age finds itself—despite our liberation from seemingly everything in preceding centuries—still in chains, our originality stifled or wounded or merely sullen. But then again, beyond the "scientism" of the positive, does not the saving power of the "aesthetic" still make an appeal? Suddenly, as if reacting to some hidden cue, we buck up.

My question: Is there not something self-serving in all of this? In our progress beyond "metaphysics," do we not drag metaphysics with us? This is what one would expect if there is no escaping the fact that to be human is to be shaped by fundamental orientations to being, and by implicit understandings of what it means to be. Then to be post-metaphysical is still to be metaphysical. "Overcoming metaphysics"—that game of philosophical leapfrog we

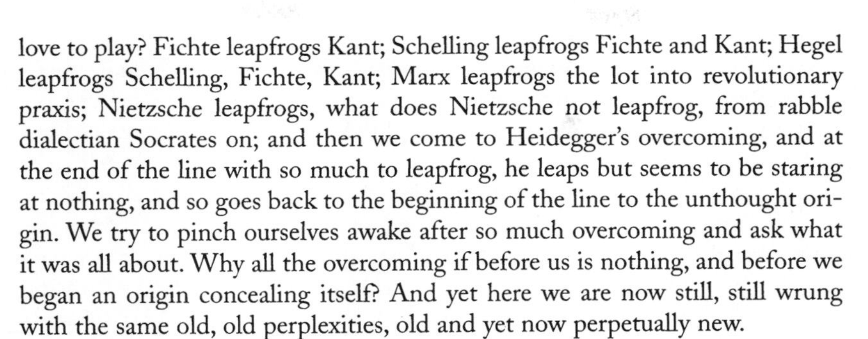

love to play? Fichte leapfrogs Kant; Schelling leapfrogs Fichte and Kant; Hegel leapfrogs Schelling, Fichte, Kant; Marx leapfrogs the lot into revolutionary praxis; Nietzsche leapfrogs, what does Nietzsche not leapfrog, from rabble dialectian Socrates on; and then we come to Heidegger's overcoming, and at the end of the line with so much to leapfrog, he leaps but seems to be staring at nothing, and so goes back to the beginning of the line to the unthought origin. We try to pinch ourselves awake after so much overcoming and ask what it was all about. Why all the overcoming if before us is nothing, and before we began an origin concealing itself? And yet here we are now still, still wrung with the same old, old perplexities, old and yet now perpetually new.

And one could well ask too: Would being "post-religious" perhaps not also mean still to be "religious," though that word be locked behind seven seals of silence? And suppose that the appeal of art also hides a yearning for transcendence that cannot or will not now name itself as before it did, as "religious," or in close communion to it? We are in a very ambiguous situation, to say the least. And perhaps also we drag along with us the "metaphysical" when we heed the appeal of the aesthetic. My hunch is that concern with origin has migrated to art, where it seems to be without metaphysical presupposition or religious commitment, though reflection will show that this is not at all univocally the case. In an equivocal way, not only are surrogate forms of the religious not absent, but our entire ways of thinking about art, origin, creativity are shot through with unnamed metaphysical presuppositions.

Art and the Metaphysics of Origin

Perhaps it will help to say something about origins, and show how this leads us along many pathways, not least towards the metaphysical importance of art. First, if the question of origins marks an elemental human perplexity, it is not foisted on us by "onto-theology," or the "metaphysics of presence," nor actualizing the philosophy of fascism, as Adorno says, with Heidegger in his sights, nor necessarily guilty of the sins of "foundationalism" or "nostalgia." We ask: "Whence?" Sheer whence? The question seems indeterminate. Not whence this, or that, or the other: but whence? The question of a sage or the gaping of an idiot? Yet we often are stunned by the sheer "that it is at all" of the world and of ourselves. Not by this, not by that, not by anything in particular, but by the given thereness of what is, in a more than determinate sense: that it is at all and not nothing. Why, whence? This is the old and ever recurrent question of metaphysics. It names an archaic metaphysical perplexity.

To invoke metaphysics, whether to praise or depreciate it, is to start somewhat too late. Good metaphysics, I think, always knows it starts late, hence knows its indebtedness to an other origin it does not itself initiate. It occurs already on the way, or under way. To live as human is always to be porous to being struck by this astonishment and perplexity about origin. And this not only in the more domestic sense of needing some knowledge of where we come from to comprehend where we now are, who we now are, and where we are to go; but in a more fundamental sense that is imaginatively figured in the stories, representation, practices of being religious. Religious myths are stories of origin in as ultimate a sense as particular peoples or communities seem able to voice. It is within the articulations of religious stories that most humans have gathered some sense of origins, and found some alleviation of the elemental perplexity. And of course, the birth of philosophy was itself in a displacement from origins figured in religious myth to origins reconfigured as the fundaments of being, approachable now in terms of the power to give a logos—*logon didonai*. Philosophy arises as a development, displacement and refiguring of the religious imagination of origins, itself answering in mythic story and practice to the elemental human perplexity before the astonishing givenness of being at all, and most especially the mysterious being of the human.

Does this make metaphysics a merely disguised "theology"? I confess that this question, as usually formulated, seems more and more nonsensical to me. Philosophy is, in one sense or other, a disguised something. It arises in the reflective transformation of life, which is the matrix of elemental perplexity, which itself can be addressed in a multiplicity of ways, including philosophical ways. Philosophy arises in the matrix of the between, even if it reflectively transforms other ways of being mindful there. It cannot live without its being in relation to these others, including the aesthetic and religious images that shape and express our sense of the ultimate. The real issue for us, whether as philosophers, or simply as thinking humans, is what are the fundamental perplexities, and how can we honestly voice what they communicate. Philosophy is to be the mindful safeguarding of fundamental perplexity.

To dismiss "metaphysics" as "disguised theology" surely should entail also dismissing "post-metaphysical" philosophy as "disguised something or other," be it "disguised science," or "disguised economics," or "disguised grammar," or "disguised whatever." And why not "disguised art"? I would reformulate the whole matter in terms of this view: to be something is to be in relation to something other. To be philosophical is to be mindful of what is it to be, but always in relation to significant others, such as science, art, religion. Good philosophy is not merely "disguised something or other," but honesty about the inescapability of *being in relation to what is other in the very being of itself.*

I cannot dwell further on this than to say that above "dismissals" follow from a self-conception of philosophy that wants to enact the so-called autonomy of thinking, rather than the task of thinking by being in relation to the others of philosophy. This is a very modern ideal of philosophy in which it asserts its will to enlightenment by wanting to free itself from entanglement with theology, or art, or some other "domain." This ideal of autonomous self-determining thinking can be severely criticized. Another practice of philosophy is defensible, and has been enacted, in which its being in the matrix of perplexity, and in communication with others, is needed. I call this a metaxological practice of philosophy: a being in the between in which our thought is with the view to a logos of the *metaxu*. The *metaxu* is the milieu of being, but also the field of communication between thought and what is other to thought, between philosophy and its others. Indeed the very happening of the between calls for thought, striking us diversely into perplexity about its giving origin. How respond to the perplexity? Among other answers, by being open to religious and artistic sources that help us to name that perplexity, both in terms of what addresses it and what it addresses.

Origins, Otherness, Being Religious

We are perhaps most familiar with the claim that God as creator answers our perplexity about origins, and the marvel of coming to be. But in some ways of thinking there is no address to the happening of being in terms of *the that it is at all*. The basic elements of the ontological situation are simply taken for granted, as being already granted. The classic instance, I suppose, is to be found in Plato's *Timaeus*. The origination of a *cosmos* is not a *coming to be,* but a *coming to form*. It is a making rather than a radical originating. This is the demiurgic view: the maker imposes form on chaos or matter, but chaos or matter already are, as well as forms of intelligibility, and necessity; these are woven by the maker into the unity of a cosmic art work. The world as come to form is a cosmos, a thing of beauty, as well as an ordered whole, because the maker has imposed form on matter. Even if there is some bending of necessity here, there is no radical contingency of the happening of being. The process of origination is one of fabrication or art, in the sense of *technē:* the imposition of a form on perhaps recalcitrant matter, that is worked up into a more beautiful intelligible presence. But notice the crucial community of the mythic or religious and the aesthetic. Contra Nietzsche's view of Plato as depreciating the world of the aesthetic, the cosmos itself is an aesthetic god, a sensible divinity that images the intelligible (*eikon tou noētou theos aisthētos, Timaeus,* 92c): the most beautiful possible. Deeply interwoven here are metaphysics, aesthetics, religion, and ethics (in an ontological sense pointing to the goodness or worthiness of what has come to form). Nietzsche says that only as a work of art is the world justified, and he sets himself against Plato. But Plato offers a kind of aesthetic metaphysics in the myth of the demiurge; and indeed an affirmation of the ontological good and beauty of this cosmos, not any nihilistic depreciation.

The idea of God as creator suggests, by contrast, a more recalcitrant notion of origination. I call creation a hyperbolic thought, in that it exceeds all determinate intelligibilities.[1] For within the world, what we know are more

1. "Hyperbolic Thoughts: On Creation and Nothing," in *Framing a Vision of the World: Essays in Philosophy, Science and Religion,* ed. Santiago Sia and Andre Cloots (Leuven: Universitaire Pers Leuven, 1999), 23–43.

or less determinate processes of becoming. What of the original of such a world in process? It would entail a coming to be in excess of determinate being, which would be the issue of this more original origin. We often mistake demiurgic making for creation in this hyperbolic sense. Heidegger seems to conflate them: if he did so ignorantly, this ignorance is astonishing; if he did so willfully, it is unforgivable. In *Genesis* are there demiurgic overtones, since the spirit of God moves on the waters? Perhaps, but I am not a Biblical exegete. I am interested in the metaphysics of origination and the relations implied therein. Most basically, there is the *transcendence* of the divine: an *otherness* to the origin that cannot be assimilated to any worldly process of becoming; and yet, notwithstanding this otherness, there is an *intimacy* of the creator with the world, and a hyperbolic "yes" to the goodness of what has been brought into being ("It is good, it is very good"). There is the difference of origin as (one might say) creating as creating and the world as creation created, and the difference of origin and world not only names the otherness of the former, but releases the latter into its own being for itself. This offers an affirmative image of finitude and the goodness of its free being for itself. And yet there is the uniqueness of the divine originality: there is nothing like this unique bringing into being that is constrained by nothing, a giving source infinitely creative in excess of everything finite and nothing. Everything else is making or made—something is already granted to be, and then from it something is made. The radical sense of origin in creation (here creating as creating, not the creation created) claims that nothing determinate is presupposed to be, since the origination is the coming to be of finite determinate beings. Hence the hyperbolic uniqueness of the divine.

The human being is said to be in the image and likeness of the divine. We come across a theme we must revisit, namely, the relation of image and original. But if there is this hyperbolic uniqueness to the original here, how can there be *any image* of it? For an image to be an image, there must have some likeness with the original, and hence a sharing in something of the original. How then can the original be hyperbolically unique? If the original is absolutely other, how then any relation between the origin and what is created? The traditional answer, such as we find in Aquinas, is that creation is a one-way relation which effects the creation but not the divine origin; it is not a motion, I would say not a "becoming," but a "coming to be," which effects what comes to be, but not the origin of coming to be. Does this entirely satisfy? If the creation is other to the origin, and yet an image of it, is there not something in the creature that mirrors the original, and hence refers it back to its origin?

The problem is complicated by the following consideration: How is it possible to think of the human being as original in itself, *a finite origin that images a more primordial origin?* In premodern theories the ascription of uniqueness to God seemed to preclude claims of creativity to humanity. Such claims seemed to usurp the divine prerogative. And yet if the image images the original, why should not the image also shows its own originality, especially since the very origin gives rises to something that itself, as created, is radically *new?* The newness of the creation itself seems to testify to its difference, its originality, even if derived from an ultimate origin, and hence the impossibility of being "reduced" to a precedence in which what it is for itself and in itself disappears. (What could "reduce" mean here?) This is another way of speaking about the peculiar character of the *that it is at all* in terms of the contingency of finite happening. This contingency is not only a creation but in its newness suggests its own *promise of creativity*. The promise of creativity: have we not thus arrived at one of the great concerns of modernity through very unmodern pathways? Can we think of the creativity of the finite but not deny an origin that cannot be reduced to finitude? Theologically: can the radical origination as divine and the finite originality of the human be held together?

While this sounds like a very unmodern question, I hope to indicate that something like it keeps getting resurrected in masked forms in modern and postmodern thinking. I also hope to offer some suggestions about the nature of the *masking*. This is not something merely random, but reveals the development and consolidation of certain patterns of understanding that make something essential recessive, even as they make something else, itself essential in its own way, more forthright. What I mean here is this.

There can be something at *odds with itself* in the metaphysics of original and image, when that metaphysics is formulated in fixed dualistic terms. These terms are easily secreted by univocal claims for radical transcendence: if the origin is radically other, its relation to the finite seems to be no relation: the origin as other becomes a beyond, whose entry into relation with finitude compromises just its transcendence. The original is original and that is that; the image is image and that is that; the two are radically other. But this makes nonsense of an image; it could not be an image without relation to an original, even granted that they are not identical. What is the character of that relation, and how does it effect how we speak of the two "sides" in original communication? We try to fix the original univocally, and we end up making the relation of original and image equivocal; and then not only do claims about the image also become equivocal, but also those made about the original.

Shaftesbury had something right when he said: "We have undoubtedly the honour of being originals." Unfortunately, we often are self-satisfied with what we take as the complement to our esteem in our being called originals, and we forget that we are thus *honored*. We do not first honor ourselves, we are first honored, and we honor ourselves the more truly in granting that the honor first is granted from sources that are not determined by us. Shaftesbury also spoke of the artist as a "just Prometheus under Jove."[2] We have thrilled

---

2. For Shaftesbury's remarks, see *Philosophies of Art and Beauty,* ed. A. Hofstadter and R. Kuhns (Chicago: University of Chicago Press, 1976), 252, 240.

too much to the Prometheanism, and have overlooked the qualification of the creative Prometheus by justice, and the supremly important order that the human creator is under Jove. Our being original is expressed by Shaftesbury in terms of pagan myth, but in any event we are not the source, the ultimate original that grants the honor, and offers it the supreme measure of justice. The paganism of a Nietzsche has proved more infectious to many when he exclaimed: No God above me, and no man either! What do we dishonor in thus honoring ourselves?

We have to address the above returning equivocities with more finesse. These are some of the questions we have to ask, and will ask in the chapters to follow. Can we think of the relation of original and image in other than dualistic terms? In dialectical terms? In more metaxological terms? Do eros and mania contribute significantly to reformulating this space between them? Does transcendental thinking help us? Do more post-transcendental forms of erotic thinking, for instance, as embodied in Schopenhauer's will, or Nietzsche's Dionysian will to power? Or does the origin as such, remain unthought, as Heidegger claims? Does he too leave that origin unthought? Or do we need to think an agapeic origination that releases finitude into its own being for itself, which can communicate in relation to finitude without any loss of otherness, think a communication that possibilizes finite creativity and its promise, and that requires a philosophy beyond holism as well as dualism? For as there is a dualism of immanence miserable with itself, there is a holism of immanence satisfied with itself; and neither freed into consent to the creative promise of finitude that is already granted in the hyperbolic "It is very good" of the origin.

Art and Displaced Transcendence?

These questions and more concerning origins and otherness will occupy us, questions also that relate to art. Consider further the dualistic way. This way seems strongly to uphold the transcendence of the origin, but can it also end up *undermining* that transcendence, and thereby occasioning a *migration* of radical transcendence to immanence? Do we not find this when the human being claims *to be* transcendence? But does not this metaphysical migration bring on problems *within immanence* of a sort analogous to the previous form with metaphysical and religious transcendence? I mean: we assert that the origin is the absolute other; if so, the world is also absolutely other to this absolute other, and hence voided of traces of the origin; so we accentuate the world as being for itself as separate, and instead of the community of creator and creation, we have their opposition; but we still are perplexed by the question of origin. The dualistic way leads us either to an impasse, or back to our own world and ourselves. What have we learned from seeking the other origin and returning? Nothing of the origin, except it is absolutely other, but of ourselves we have learned the *passion for transcendence,* and indeed discovered ourselves as transcending. How account for our powers of transcending? But *our originality* seems on this side of the gap separating us from the absolute other. Why not redefine the meaning of transcendence as what is given to us on this side? For what is given is not merely a set of finite objects; it is that and more; it is the human self as transcending original in itself.

In a word, a certain understanding of the origin in terms of dualistic transcendence produces a migration of transcendence towards immanence, and transcendence comes to reside in us. The image becomes an original for itself. It begins to define itself in terms other than mimetic; it is creative in its own right. Our claim *to be transcendence* may have been overtly stated in the twentieth century by such as Jaspers and Heidegger, but the migration is as old as the epoch of modernity. They followed Nietzsche, who himself echoed and redoubled, sometimes unwittingly, themes sounded by precedent thinkers, especially since Kant. Earlier, the human being as transcending, habituated to dualism, may have continued to conceive itself over against the other, be it nature or the divine. Later, as in our time, it may try to unweave its habituation to dualism, but it may not at all have shed its acquired addiction to thinking of itself as transcendence.

There are deep equivocities in all this, not only with regard to the otherness of origin, but to the *immanent otherness* of originality in us. And what if this addiction creates its own toxins? One might try to purge oneself, but the purge looks like a worse fever, and one is tempted back to the consoling toxin; and then even in the act of weaning oneself from the addiction (call it "deconstruction"?), one suddenly finds oneself breaking out again in that old song of self, and we get some small relief or consolation. And then the sweats come on again.

But surely, you say, there are sobrieties still available to us? And, yes, one might defend the turn to the human as the reference point for defining what is other to us. We are not passive before what is other, we are original, and hence our art, our creativity mediates not only that other to us, but ourselves to ourselves. (The industrial version of this is Marx's philosophy of work.) Our art becomes the source of access to the origin, but what is this—our own originality, or some source as much transhuman as immanent in human creativity? We celebrate the artist as the place where transcendence comes to manifestation; there original power is most "divinely" figured forth in the creative artist. But if we push this to a limit, do we not lose astonishment before the otherness of, say, the generative powers of nature that can make us wonder about a source of original power even more primordial than ourselves and nature natured? Everything to which we relate seems mediated through ourselves and all we see there in otherness is our own faces endlessly reflected back to us. First we celebrate this as confirming the release of our "creativity" but soon we grow bored with our own face, and come to suspect we are our own cages. But then does not the sense of *our own otherness* return with renewed force and the face of our own claims to originality assume a new enigmatic character?

The sustainable significance of this migration to art of our concern with origin is our worry. Art seems to stand forth with unprecedented autonomy, but is it, how is it, standing in as surrogate, or incognito for a transmuted metaphysical origin, or a muted religious sense of transcendence? Does the gain of autonomy for creativity find itself threatened by the loss of its roots in a more primal creativity, previously named religiously? Does a culture of "autonomy" always communicate a loss of this rootedness in primal creativity, if to be autonomous is to insist on oneself over again the other? Is one in danger of blocking access to sources of creativity in the self itself that requires more a *passio essendi* rather than a *conatus essendi,* a passion of being rather than an activist endeavor to be? Does not our creativity find itself beholden to a *primal porosity* of being in which is offered to us sources of origination we could not produce through ourselves alone? Are not the truer ways of being religious intimate with this primal porosity? If one fakes the *passio essendi,* does one not also then produce a fake image of originality? The ancients knew, as did the poets, that one must *woo* the muse. One cannot force this. There is something about wooing beyond our self-determination, and beyond our will to power. What does *that* will to power woo?

One of the intriguing feature of modernity and postmodernity is the upsurge of sources of creativity that can hardly be attributed to the so-called autonomous self; and yet we have got into the bind of wanting to insist on calling ourselves autonomous. Creativity seems to involve the shattering of the pretensions of autonomous self-determination. If this is true, the seemingly overcome otherness begins again to haunt us, not it seems from "above," but from the very immanent abysses of the human self itself.

The absent transcendence of God seems to produce the dedivinization of nature in the sense of the obliteration of any traces of the divine there. And if there is a migration of transcendence to man, and in some circles the temptation to a certain divinization of man, now announcing his final autonomy of all subordinating otherness, alas these names "autonomy" and "transcendence" are difficult to weave seamlessly together. There is a deep tension between them. I would say there is an antinomy between them that is unsurpassable in terms of our own autonomy. The deeper we explore immanent transcendence, the more the dedivinization of man shadows his divinization. The apotheosis of the human is also the inauguration of nihilism, and we end up not with genius, or the *Übermensch* but the last men. Worse: last men who have read all about genius and the *Übermensch,* and take themselves to be the glorious fulfillment of time. The worse mimics the best: counterfeits of completion who desire no more, for they have no desire for more than themselves.

This result, I think, cannot be detached from our loss of the origin as other. The happening of originality in art forces us to acknowledge the qualification of our autonomy by a communication of transcendence that cannot be accounted for in terms of our own self-determination. Something in excess of our autonomous self-determination comes to expression. In that expression, we are newly opened to the immanent otherness of our own original being, as well as to a more original origin, as sourcing our own accession to the finite power to create.

An Overview

To do systematic justice to some of these claims requires drawing on the resources of the metaxological philosophy I have tried to develop, most extensively in books like *Being and the Between* and *Ethics and the Between*. The present studies engage the thinking of important philosophers, and in a manner that reflects some of these systematic considerations. These studies are explorations of art, origins, otherness in dialogue with these thinkers. With the exception of the first and last chapters, they focus on Kant and his successors, Hegel, Schopenhauer, Nietzsche, Heidegger. I try to see things as they did, but I do not see things as they tried to do. I want to understand their philosophy, but I want to understand the matter itself, and that asks both fellow travelling and departure from them as the matter dictates.

In chapter 1, I begin with a reflection on Platonic originals because the matter is much older than modernity, than transcendental, and posttranscendental philosophy. Plato is for many the bogeyman, but I find something inspiring in the companionship of his elusive thinking. Of course, the issue of dualism takes form there with reference to art and mimesis. Not only do we need to look at what a metaphysics of image and original means, we must ask about other resources to deal with dualism, and transcending in the *metaxu*, such as Plato discussed in terms of eros and mania. Variations of the latter concerns reappear in Kant and post-Kantian aesthetics, in discussions of, for instance, the rupturing powers of creativity, or in the idea of the genius, in the notion of original willing as erotic self-transcending, such as we find in Schopenhauer and Nietzsche. Platonic mimesis answers the question of originals in terms of Ideas that cannot be reduced to human constructions. The mimesis, whether an artifact or the human actor, is subordinate to a paradigm that transcends the mimesis and that cannot be reduced thereto. While there is an irreducible otherness inscribed in the mimetic way, eros and mania are different ways of *traversing the middle space between originals and images*, and have a suggestive power by no means exhausted. My own efforts to develop a metaxological philosophy tries to articulate those spaces of difference without rigidifying them into dualistic oppositions. This means doing justice *both* to the immanent powers of origination of the human being as transcending itself in the between *and* to a sense of transcendence more than human self-transcendence. A dualistic philosophy cannot do justice to the doubleness at play, not to the redoubling of the human being as it reaches beyond itself, not to the communication of what is other as it offers itself to the responding human. Eros and mania also have to do with what I called above the porosity of being, and with our being a creative between or medium. Dimensions of this view will recur throughout the book.

In chapter 2, I turn to Kant's aesthetic thought, in light of his efforts to mediate the dualisms of modernity in terms of a transcendental, rather than transcendent sense of originals. While the between is initially accepted in terms of a different dualism of subject and object, more deeply it is reconfigured in terms of the original mediating power of the transcendental self. Nor can we disconnect this from a morality of autonomy, and its hardly hidden complicity with the possible originality of the human being. That originality seems to give us the mediating power that defines the intermediate space between itself and what is other. If it is original, what is other, mediated by it, is an image of what it determines it, as other, to be. What begins to happen then is: The spaces of intermediation are reconfigured as the milieu of human self-mediation. Kant consolidates this and begins a new movement with transcendental imagination, concretized aesthetically in the genius.

What interests me here is the dissolving of self-mediating power at the limit where it seems most to come into its own possession of itself. Also intriguing here is the continued need to refer to Ideas, not Platonic perhaps, but in Kant's aesthetic idea certainly symbolic of something "beyond" determinate concepts. Shadows of eros and mania also begin to gather again, and turn from shadows into newly living powers of origination. Kant's approach to genius and the sublime, in light of his transcendental approach, is very instructive about his *wavering* domestication of recalcitrant otherness and a darker origin; and this despite the fact that Kant also grants something here finally unruly to the rule of human autonomy.

There is a caution to Kant that makes him both shallow and profound. Shallow in pursuit of this darker origin; perhaps profound in his guardedness about the dangers possible here. He is diffident about the demand of bolder thinkers for a more unrelenting pursuit, diffidence buttressed by a doctrine of metaphysical limits. Fortunately, his philosophical eros was sufficiently impassioned so as not to stick rigidly with his own prohibitions: the "beyond" of determinate concepts is named in qualified, roundabout, that is, devious ways. Kant is important, I think, for the opening of inwardness in its otherness, but he is more fully an Enlightenment thinker than his successors who suspected more than him the vacancy at the center of Enlightenment reason.

Hegel seems to be a bolder thinker than Kant, but oddly enough his boldness serves a more complete domestication of unruly otherness, origins, art, within a system that claims to be the speculative comprehension of original being. Hegelian courage is a species of knowing that seems *self-certain* from the outset, and hence one finally wonders: What really does Hegel risk? Hegel wants to have it all, or have all that matters within the inclusive grasp of his speculative concept. In chapters 3 and 4, I look at the aesthetic expression of Hegel's dialectical origin, and how its self-becoming necessitates for Hegel the final solution of art's secret. Nothing secret, he believes, can resist his knowing. Hegel's origin, like his Idea, is self-articulating, and in terms of the structuring process of his dialectical logic. He may initially genuflect before the otherness of art, and the transcendence of the religious, but when knowing comes into the enlightened maturity of its own self-determination, it now sees how these have served as moments towards a philosophical self-certainty assuring itself, assured in itself, of its own absolute truth. Knowing this, art's otherness and religious transcendence can no longer quite captivate us. We may play before that otherness, and act as if we believed, we may even believe we believe, but the robustness of otherness and transcendence are gone. They are lost in being so found.

Or perhaps betrayed? This is my question. Does Hegel's version of philosophy's *conatus essendi* so win out over the *passio essendi* of art and religion, indeed of philosophy itself, that the original porosity of our being in the between is closed into a circle of thinking at home with itself alone? A circle of thinking that mimics that porosity but closes us off from the ultimate origin? Does Hegel's dialectical origin give us speculative counterfeits of otherness and transcendence? Hegel's tart comment about Schelling's absolute is famous: the night in which all cows are black. But are there stings in the tails of those cows for Hegel's own absolute: not the night, but the *light* in which all cows are black? Excess of light can make us blind. Plato knew this, Pascal knew this. Solid Aristotle knew we might be like the bats in the sunlight, but this means we must hew true to the middle regions of being, the between, otherwise we cannot even *see* what is *above* us. In being above himself and these middle spaces, Hegel seems to see everything but perhaps he sees nothing, nothing of what is most important about the otherness of art, and the mystery of religious transcendence. Their night is turned from the light, and turned into his counterfeit light.

In chapter 4, the Gothic Hegel, as I will call him, will be shown to present the silhouette of a double face. Hegel two-faced despite himself: charmed by a certain transcending, called out and up by the Gothic Cathedral, yet inoculated to its excess by his dialectical logic which would recall us earnestly to the worldly prose of bourgeois modernity; scornful, but perhaps secretly terrified by a different truth to transcendence as other to human self-transcendence. Perhaps Hegelian courage is not so courageous after all.

Thinkers after Hegel will enter into that secret terror, and sweat. They will seek therein to be more intimate with the darkness of a more primal origin that mocks, from the dark side of the moon, the reflected light of idealistic thought thinking thought. In chapters 5 and 6, dedicated to the erotic origin of Schopenhauer, and the Dionysian origin of Nietzsche, we will explore these darker visions in terms of the creative power of art to throw light on what remains other to full conceptual enlightenment. Schelling is a thinker whom I would have liked to discuss more fully, but he is worth mentioning as important for drawing our attentions to the otherness of nature and the unconscious, and to the power of art to concretize their togetherness in the great work. The great art work does this in a way more fulfilling to the human being than the concepts of philosophy. Contrary to Hegel, art makes a claim on absoluteness more fulfilling than philosophy. Schopenhauer and Nietzsche follow Schelling here, as do they also in returning us to an ontological darkness more original than diurnal reason.

Schopenhauer dips into this primal darkness of the origin in terms of his notion of the will. There is here a continuation and radicalization of the Kantian will, now no longer a good will of pure practical reason, but a will *prior to* goodness and reason, in fact, at times more like an evil will that takes on diverse forms in the world of phenomena, and revealing its insatiable self-insistence in *our* will or eros. There we are immediately intimate with the origin in its otherness to phenomenal reality and the law governing there, namely, the principle of sufficient reason. Schopenhauer spends his inheritance from Kant by breaking free from him in the name of a return to the *ontological underground* of Kantianism and rationalistic idealism. Yet there is something also in-between about him, and this is evident with regard to art. For here again the ghosts of Plato and the Ideas come back, now to save us from the horrors we face in that ontological underground, which is known most intimately in the immanent otherness of our own erotic desire. *We are the unruly underground* where the dark original will erupts, living us as self-insistent desire, that drives us more than we direct it. If we need Ideas and art, we need them to *save us from* this despotic eros, not in order to fulfill eros, as with Plato. The unruly underground will of Schopenhauer is an *eros turannos,* not an *eros uranus*. There is no heavenly eros in Schopenhauer, and in that respect the darkness of his origin anticipates, in a prototypical way, many of the philosophies of the absurd we have come to know since his time. We are not bats in sunlight but, so to say, bats in perpetual darkness, driven round the caves of night by an engorged eros deluded about itself. Art, Schopenhauer says, offers us a release from that eros turannos. We must ask: if the metaphysics of the origin is unremittingly posed in terms of erotic *lack,* can art, can anything, even offer such release? Does Schopenhauer, in naming the release of art, also counterfeit that release?

Nietzsche, discussed in chapter 6, has antennae that are almost hyperactively alert to such counterfeits. He seeks to substitute a "yes" to will for Schopenhauer's "no." And yet there is much in him that never breaks with the underlying metaphysical presumptions we find in Schopenhauer, and not least in relation to the darkness of the origin. The mythic name for the origin is the vegetable god Dionysus: rooted in the earth but growing up from it, and above it bearing fruit in the sunlight; rising from underground but offering above ground to humans the gift of wine and a diviner intoxication. Art has everything to do with that Dionysian intoxication. While Nietzsche is officially anti-Platonist, the Platonic themes of eros and mania take on here a life that has appealed to many. In this regard, he is more an antagonist of Enlightenment reason (be it Kant's or Hegel's) than Plato, though his own will to power is inseparable from the modern opening up of the inward otherness of the self that develops out of transcendental philosophy, and not least in its aesthetic concretization. The origin is other and dark, and tragic wisdom, not dialectical philosophy, he holds, is both more honest about that dark otherness, and more full of the promise of redemption.

The promise of redemption: what I find here noteworthy is the promiscuity of art and myth in Nietzsche, that is, the equivocal ferment of religious promise, meaning here pagan possibilities, in his Dionysian origin. It is the *saving power of art* that is crucial. Hyperbolic hopes are invested in art, hopes one might normally invest in the religious. Is there too much of the *conatus essendi* in Nietzsche's will to power, not enough of the *passio essendi* that grants intimacy with the porosity of being religious? And what does the "saving" of art portend for Nietzsche? It is, on one hand, the "saving of" an elemental "yes" to life, in its ontological worthiness to be sung. But it is, on the other hand, a "saving from" the horror of the origin as understood by Nietzsche. Surface appearances notwithstanding, Nietzsche never adequately freed himself from Schopenhauer's stylization of the erotic origin as ultimately, and irredeemably dark. And struggle gloriously as Nietzsche might, one wonders if his "yes," his "redemption" through art, must also be finally engulfed by the horror it can only *seem* to transcend. There is much that is appealing in Nietzsche's desire to say "yes," but if the origin is as he describes it to be, this "yes" must be *despite* its darkness, and a "yes" *despite* is not quite the "yes" Nietzsche desired. It is the darkness again, and horror before being more than joy.

These and other claims await their fuller justification. But in chapter 7, I remark on Heidegger's origin of the art work. Admirers of Heidegger have often erected this essay into something *sui generis,* something almost holy. While Heidegger's singularity is not in doubt, overstated claims by his admirers, and hints of his own exceptionalness signaled by the master himself, cannot be granted, especially when we consider the subtlety and complexity concerning art, origins, otherness, we find bequeathed by the above thinkers. I do not belong to the tribe of Heidegger's hagiographers nor to the school of his mere debunkers. I do think it is a disservice to the matter itself to totalize the previous tradition as something like "onto-theology," or with his deconstructive successors "metaphysics of presence," for we then underestimate the *original otherness* of some of these precedent thinkers. I contextualize Heidegger differently with respect to precedent thinkers dealing with art, origins, otherness. Heidegger clearly continues the line in which the origin is darker than idealistic thought thinking itself can comprehend. This darker origin becomes a self-concealing origin, even in its showing. These are important considerations which do turn away from the overblown claims of comprehensiveness made in the acme of German idealism. Heidegger wants to dismantle the concepts of traditional aesthetics that seem to cover over a more originary communication of the origin. Thus we might try to think the unthought origin. I find something very indeterminate about the hints Heidegger seems willing, or is able, to give us about the origin. One wonders if the articulated thoughts of the above precedent thinkers might not be of more aid to us than these hints allow. The question of will and will-lessness is important to a longer tradition, evidently so after Kant, but suggested in the earlier and different idioms of eros and mania, insofar as they hint at what I have called the porosity of being and the *passio essendi*. And then there is the "saving power" of art. Is there a disguised equivocation here between the artistic and the religious that ought to engage our more candid mindfulness? Does the unthought origin remain, in the end, not thought? Is Heidegger's own not thinking of the origin connected with the fact that the between also remains relatively unthought?

My final chapter is a reflection on the "saving power" of art and the impossible burden of transcendence that has been laid upon it since around the time of Kant. I turn again to look at the migration of transcendence into art, and the accompanying equivocation on the religious, for this we can now get more into lucid focus. I ask what the so-called "end of art" portends for the contemporary task of metaphysics. Too much has been asked of art in such a way that now almost nothing is asked of art. One manifestation of this (there are others): high modernism asking too much, postmodernism asking not much at all. We expect too much from, then give up, the ideal of pure aesthetic perfection in favor of "anything goes."

It happens thus that art sometimes mimics less eros as sex, and without the woo of love: everything first expected, at the last nothing much asked. Our path to a paradise of sensuous show turns into a vertiginous descent from more importunate gratifications, thence by degrees into the flat shamelessness of pornography, and the last pleasure seems the self-justifying outrage. We still find ourselves enmeshed in the equivocity of show, but when the show does not show, a violence on the body seems needed, as if the intimate must be forced, whipped to the surface. Transfiguration and disfiguration make a pact, but the show that does not show breeds disappointment. But then again, aggression is the lagging child of disappointment that is eager to make wicked amends for its previous infatuated faith. The promise of a feigned paradise fulfills its emptiness in ravening. We are reminded of a kind of spiritual torture: everything seems shown, nothing is shown. This showing is something more paradoxical than a show of counterfeits. It is a counterfeit show.

As idolatry is to religion, pornography is to art. True, idols can be dazzling and seductive but for reasons that will become clear art cannot be *the* exemplary manifestation of transcendence, if the practices of philosophy and religion have themselves been enfeebled relative to origin and otherness, and if indeed the ethos of human life groans under the tyranny of instrumentalized life, the dominion of serviceable disposability. Everything then even hinting of an other transcendence is refashioned into a means for instrumental self-mediation, and even artistic creativity has to struggle against being press-ganged to serve this dominion of serviceable disposability. The art work serves human freedom but it is not thus disposable. It serves to dispose us towards a freedom beyond instrumentalized life, and indeed beyond moralized autonomy, though its "beyond" here treads in a hazardous domain where it now most needs what it seems now most to despise. I mean the porosity of being religious, or reverence for the agapeic origin that sources our own access to finite creativity, or offers us, as a happening that defines us and that we do not first define, its unmerited gift. And what would a philosophy be like that dared to think *that?*

1

Mimesis, Eros, and Mania

On Platonic Originals

Philosophical Imagination and the Middle

Vico's inspiring work reminds us of the importance of what he called the imaginative universal. An *imaginative* universal, of course, would strike many rationalistic philosophers as very odd. It will not so strike the person with even minimum exposure to the revelatory power of art. Vico not only gives our imagination wings, as Joyce said; he also had more wings than not a few philosophers. Think, for instance, of his opposite in spirit, Descartes. Or perhaps Hegel, whose version of speculative reason, one fears, betrays this intimate strangeness of being. One might say: a properly winged *philosophical* imagination knows this intimacy and this strangeness.[1] Can the name "Plato" stand for that philosophical imagination? This too will seem odd, since Plato is taken as the implacable foe of the poets. But who has endowed the philosophical tradition more richly with its philosophical images, such as the Cave, the Sun, the winged soul, and so on? Do not these images present some of the imaginative universals of philosophy itself, to which thinkers return again and again, and not because they are deficient in speculative reason but

---

1. The admirable work of Donald Verene helped open my eyes to the importance of the imaginative universal in Vico. Verene has also awakened us to the philosophical importance of images in Hegel, and especially his *Phenomenology*, in *Hegel's Recollection: A Study of Images in the Phenomenology of Spirit* (Albany: State University of New York Press, 1985). Verene offers us a more winged Hegel, but this is a "Hegel" to whom, as I will show later, Hegel himself came to *play false*. On the intimate strangeness of being, see my "Neither Deconstruction or Reconstruction: Metaphysics and the Intimate Strangeness of Being," in *International Philosophical Quarterly* (March 2000): 37–49.

because something offers itself for thought that is in excess of the concept, even Hegel's. What Hegel would take as their conceptual deficit may well be a surplus of significance through which the philosopher is endowed with winged thought.

Today for many, the name "Plato" is synonymous with "metaphysics," or the "metaphysical tradition." And, of course in our superior times, these things have been left behind, overcome, deconstructed. Richard Rorty will speak of Plato in terms of big P Philosophy; by contrast, he desires small p philosophy. One may be inclined to say with such small desires: Rorty can have his small p. But other philosophers with bigger desire are worth noting, not least Nietzsche. Has not Nietzsche won the polemos in the minds of many, even when the name "Nietzsche" is anathema?[2] I mean that even those who pride themselves on their analytical sobriety, or on having their ordinary feet on the everyday ground, are often at one with the dithyrambic Nietzsche in thinking the metaphysical flights of fancy of "Plato" are simply incredible in these enlightened times.

There are many reasons for this, among which I would include: a defecit in finesse for transcendence as other; lack of attunement to the sense that the given world might be a sign of something not immediately given, something divined through the given as imaging something beyond itself; the postulate that we are autonomous, and hence under no need to make reference to an ultimate good as other; the feeling that Plato is committed to a truth already there at work, not the product of our activity, one to which we must consent or submit. We do not think of ourselves as submissive; we think of ourselves as creative; we want to consent finally and only to what we claim is our own. Here again the Nietzschean inheritance seems decisive: the law is not given; we give the law, and then forget that we have given it. We wake up to the truth when we wake to ourselves as the true originals, in a world itself devoid of inherent truth, or form, or value. If we are originals, the name "Plato" seems to stand as metaphor for the metaphysical father whose spell for millennia has kept from us this our proper inheritance.

While there are many issues at stake here, I will focus on what might be said about Platonic originals. Does reference to Platonic originals entirely undercut what today might be said to fall under the rubric of "creativity"? Is Plato more complex than an exclusive "either/or" between submission and self-activity, a simple dualistic opposition between, say, mimesis and creativity? Or does what is genuinely original about the human being find itself lost in an unintelligible labyrinth if it short-circuits its reference to originals that

2. I qualify this: with some postmodern currents of thought Levinas seems to have supplanted Nietzsche: some kind of ethics of the other seems to have superseded the self-affirming will of Nietzschean aesthetics; though, unlike Levinas, one notes a diffidence about God; could one speak of atheistic Levinasians? And who does Levinas himself cite? Plato! See "Neither Deconstruction or Reconstruction."

are not the product of its own self-activity? Plato's image of this labyrinth is, of course, the Cave. But in the Cave we are nót just seeking ourselves, though we seek self-knowledge; and the light by which we seek, is not our own. Can we offer an approach to Platonic originals that frees "Plato" from the cartoon versions of transcendence that we have inherited too uncritically from thinkers like Feuerbach and Nietzsche?

I think we can, and indeed already we find a seasoned consideration by Plato of elemental energies of being intimately tied to human originality, and in relation to originals not produced by human originality. I mean, of course, the energies of eros and mania as intimately present in the Platonic outlook on origins. Since the time of Romanticism these are often taken to chime in with the ethos of unprecedented originality claimed by, say, aesthetic modernity. True, Plato was important in a more positive sense for thinkers like Schelling and Schopenhauer, and poets like Coleridge and Shelley. True also, eros and mania have variously been resurrected in aesthetic modernity, indeed postmodernity, with respect to artistic genius and creativity. But then, more often than not, this is usually in a context that tends to look on "Plato" as a repressive father that kept these our original powers jealously under wraps, keeping for the gods the dangerous nectars, while throwing to us mortals the safer bones of "imitation."

Indeed normally, when we come to think of art, and hence "creativity" in a Platonic outlook, we immediately turn away to imitation, and give an account of mimesis that easily fixes into dualism, and with consequences for our understanding of human self-transcendence, as well as transcendence as other to us. I think the situation is more complex, indeed plurivocal. Mimesis, eros, and mania go together, each as different but complementary ways of approaching what is original, and this in both a human and other than human sense. One might even say that eros and mania suggest a *second underground,* more intimate to the soul than the first Cave, and in which the soul, so to speak, is under-grounded in what exceeds itself, an exceeding that, in turn, incites the soul above itself, beyond itself and the first Cave. This second underground will return diversely throughout our considerations to come of Kantian and post-Kantian originals.

What I offer is not a textual study of Plato on these matters, a study that might be coincident with the basic themes inspiring Platonic thought. On the whole I prefer Plato as a companion inspiring thought rather than an "object" of research production. So I offer a reflection on Platonic originals in the spirit of a metaxological philosophy. What I mean by metaxological philosophy I have variously tried to define in many works, but it will suffice for present purposes to recall that the word itself has Platonic origins referring us back to the notion of the *metaxu* in the *Symposium,* where eros is called a metaxu or a between. A metaxological philosophy sees philosophy as seeking a logos of the metaxu, an intelligible account of what it means to be between or intermediate. It is a philosophy of "mediation," but not just of self-mediation, more a philosophy of plurivocal intermediation. Much hangs on how we understand the "inter" that is mediated, and how it is mediated. I will say that this "inter" is diversely mediated by mimesis, eros and mania, and diversely intermediated because of the nature of the originals as other, as well as of human originality as participating in a more ultimate original. Nor does a philosophy of the metaxu exclude consideration of what ruptures or exceeds our self-mediation and intermediation.

Plato is a metaxological thinker; he is not just univocal, but plurivocal. I mean that while we find a commitment to the legacy of Socratic elenchus, namely, the search for definition in terms of essence, there are also other voices at play which cannot be reduced only to the rational search for univocal definition. Often today the quest for total univocity is seen, rightly, as the great enemy of art, for art cannot be univocalized. Socrates recognized this last point when he tells us that the listeners to a poem often seemed to be in a better position to gave an account of it than its makers or rhapsodic performers (*Apology*, 22b–c). The question of creative otherness is at stake in the quarrel of poets and philosophers: poets, so to say, articulate what cannot be articulated: they speak a meaning that to some philosophers lacks meaning since it resists complete encapsulation in conceptual terms. At a minimum, there is a tension between the otherness of the creative act and any philosophical ambition to bring all otherness into the light of explicit logos. "To give an account" *(logon didonai)* for the philosopher here means to state determinately what the poem means, what it means intelligibly, beyond the equivocity which intrinsically seems to mark the poetic speaking itself. It might seem that this equivocity is something inherently negative, to be dispelled by a univocal definition of the sort acceptable to the rational requirement of the philosopher. I will come back to this again, and certainly a commitment to determinate univocity is part of Platonic thought. But the question is: Is that all? Is the search for univocity the ultimate quest? Are there other voices just as essential, and that perhaps relativize any absolutizing of the univocal?

One must answer, yes. Yes, because of the context in which the search is undertaken; yes, because of the dialogical character of that search; yes, because of the often aporetic character of the end of that search, since success or failure just in terms of univocity bring us to a limit where *more* than univocity seems also needed; yes, because at that limit *other ways of saying* are ventured, especially of a more mythic sort; yes, because to get to that limit we have to grant the *dynamism of passing* through context and through dialogue—this dynamism is erotic and perhaps more than erotic; yes, because at the limit something other may be granted that communicates energies of being that come from the source sought—this communication is mania, and mania may be divine, though it may be not. All these factors are interwoven in a metaxological understanding of Platonic originals.

Originals and the Middle: On Univocity, Dualism, Participation

First, what of the ethos of thought of Platonic originals? There is the obvious fact that the context of Platonic thought is the world of *doxa*. The everyday has to be taken with great seriousness. We must have finesse for the ambiguities of the everyday and to read the signs of intelligibility in what often seems to be lacking in it. The context of doxa is an ethos of communication, and in that respect a world of intermediations. The ordinary words we use, the *logoi* towards which Socrates turned, articulate communications of putative intelligibilities; and so, if we examine these words, we can come to a more explicit understanding of these intelligibilities. The everyday ethos of thought is an implicit metaxu: a space of communicative interchange in which intelligibilities are at work, but in a manner that is taken for granted. But if taken for granted, how are they granted originally? The search for more univocal intelligibility in that equivocal ethos addresses this question.

This search is connected with the nature of Platonic originals, now here understood as eidetic units of intelligibility: the ideas or *eidē*. This does not mean that such originals *as found* are identical with the searching *as seeking*, or with the *finding as itself communicated* to mindfulness. There is *more* in the full ontological situation than a realm of eidetic units of intelligibility. We must never forget this context of the ethos: it is the intermediated space where intelligibilities are sought and communicated, and on the basis of which is made possible the qualified intelligibilities of life as lived in human community in the polis. Must the search for originals short change what more fully is in play in the ethos of communication? We can only answer that question by trying to do justice to what is fully communicated in the ethos. This is connected to the rationale for the return of the philosopher to the Cave. Only this way is justice more fully served.

I call the ethos of being the between: this is the ontological milieu within which we find ourselves, such that all philosophizing begins "in the midst." From the midst, the sometimes extreme questionings of philosophical thought take form. We reach down into the depth of the midst, or up and out from it, but we are always within this milieu. There we awaken to what I called the intimate strangeness of being: so intimate we often have to struggle for the distance of thought in order to be mindful about it; yet strange, in the sense of striking us as astonishing, and in more troubled thought, as perplexing, as very hard to comprehend, as ever recalcitrant to our intelligibilities. This intimate strangeness is that before which we wake to wonder, or *thaumazein*, said by Plato to be the *pathos* of the philosopher (*Theaetetus*, 155d3). Wonder, we might say, wakens up the *passio essendi* of the philosopher in a new, or renewed porosity of being—porosity become an astonished mindfulness of being. Notice that this original *thaumazein* cannot be completely univocalized, even if it sets off a search for univocal intelligibility. The communication of "more" than univocity is at play from the origin. From this our initiation in overdetermined astonishment, more determinate forms of thought and articulation come to be shaped, as we seek the intelligibilities of what is there at play in the milieu. Once again this is all "in the midst," even though here a vector of transcending in thinking itself seeks to comprehend what is not articulately known by us as at play in the between. Philosophizing "in the midst," as faithful to that energy of transcending and what is communicated to it, is metaxological: it seeks a logos of the metaxu.

Suppose we think of the metaxu, the middle as a complex community of being that allows for a plurality of "mediations" (we could also say "communications") between beings, between self and other. This is to put the point in slightly more "modern" terms. Why do so? Because in modernity we find the predominance of the self as trying through its own original power to define the middle. The Platonic rejoinder would be: irrepressible otherness is resurrected again and again, even in the most hyperbolic efforts to assert such a dominance of the active self. Why is it resurrected? Because the complex nature of intermediated being cannot be reduced to the mediations of the self. Just as Platonic mimesis cannot be reduced only to a representational univocity, such as we are more likely to find in the modern mathesis of nature, so eros and mania bring about ecstatic unsettlings of the human soul that the modern *cogito,* clear to itself and self-certain, tends to shun. (How even "postmodern" can Plato seem to sound, if we understand thus this "premodern" philosopher!) How the point works its way out will become for us more evident in aesthetic thought: art is an extremely rich event, a crucial comportment towards being in which we try to approximate some open "wholeness" with respect to selving, and some ultimacy with respect to otherbeing. The ontological, metaphysical basis of art is at stake. What does art tells us about how humans conceive of being, and of themselves as participant in the process of being? The practice of art, as well as the philosophical reflections of superior minds, is extremely instructive here. Plato provides an essential contrast between more pre-modern and modern responses. There may well be some truth to the claim that a repeated temptation to dualism has immensely affected western culture throughout the Christian era. There may also be some truth to the claim that in response to otherworldly dualism, we find the onset of modern intraworldly dualism, as in Descartes between self and soulless nature. But how fair is the blanket charge that the "tradition" or "Plato" are to blame for such otherworldly dualism? If "Plato" is a metaxological thinker, if philosophy seeks a logos of the metaxu, the situation must be more complicated.

We might see something of this complexity first by, so to speak, *turning around* this issue of dualism in relation to the question of otherness. Return again to being in the midst. There in the milieu of being things are not univocally fixed. As existing in a process of becoming, they both are what they are and are not fully what they are: to become themselves, they cannot be fully coincident with themselves, but yet must be themselves in order to become themselves. In short, things seem double and equivocal, with a kind of wavering indeterminacy that makes it hard to fix their intelligibilities. They appear but appear not fully; hence they as much suggest something withheld or perhaps lacking, as something present and given. How respond to this double condition of equivocal appearance? Perhaps the most immediately plausible response is what one might call the univocalization of the manifestation: fix it as determinate, make it to be this and not that, hold its flux still for mindfulness to get a stable vision of what it is, that is, if it is anything that can be so stabilized at all. In a word, reduce the wavering indeterminacy of equivocal appearance to univocal, determinate form.

There is where we find *one version* of Platonic originals. The equivocal appearances are not originals, for an original, it seems, must have a stable and reliable nature, relative to which the images of it gain whatever intelligibility they possess. An appearance is an image which both shows and does not show fully its original. Equivocal appearance suggests and withholds: suggests what it shows, and withholds just what is shown as *other* to complete appearing. The originals are other to appearing, even as they appear in the image. Did they fully appear, the images would no longer be images but originals. Did they not appear at all, the appearances would also not be images, for they would image nothing, and hence nothing would be appearing. The otherness of the original is interpreted by the univocalizing mind as pointing to the unchangeable stability of the originals. They are not sensuous or aesthetic, but eidetic; to be reached as other by dianoetic and noetic movements of mind; and they are mono-eidetic, uni-form in that they have a reliable and constant oneness, relative to which appearances appear to be plural, multiform. I do not need to develop the point further. There is a complex logic, more persuasive than granted by its antagonists, that leads from the double nature of equivocal appearances or manifestations to the so-called forms: univocal units of eidetic intelligibilities, indeed eternal units. These, it will be said, are the Platonic originals.

Consider now the dualistic way the point is often put, with relation to what is thought to be a major problem of the Platonic schema, namely, *participation*. We are all familiar with Aristotle's tart dismissal of participation as a mere metaphor. Should Aristotle have tried a bit harder? The problem here is put in essentially dualistic terms. The *eidē* are eternal unities that nevertheless are universal, and relative to which the features of generality we find in temporal things are to be explained. They are defined in terms of a contrast that veers towards an opposition of two discontinuous ontological orders. The problem is the following. The philosopher is concerned to make intelligible sense of what appears, to save the appearances; one of the ways is by understanding the general features that bind a plurality together into a similarity. Even stronger, a plurality seems to exhibit a certain unity across difference or diversity; there is a certain general sameness across the diversity; to give an account of that sameness is to make rational sense of the things; it is to try and answer the question "What is X?" But what if the sameness across diversity cannot be the same as any one individual, precisely because it obtains across a plurality? Then the "factor" of binding sameness, in fact, is marked by an *otherness* to any one individual: in order to apply to a diversity, this sameness must be other to each and every instance of the things comprised by this diversity. Already the dialectical play of sameness and otherness is complex.

Platonic originals would seem simply to accentuate the difference: the otherness seems to be turned into an opposition. Were this so, the difficulty now would be that this very opposition would *undercut* the proposed solution to that very problem which resort to the forms was intended to solve. That is, we appeal to the forms as an intelligible otherness to make rational sense of the things given to us; but when our appeal to otherness takes the form of a dualistic opposition, intelligible otherness cannot be related to those things which it was supposed to make intelligible. Our solution repeats the problem, which is just one of intermediation, not dualism. Participation is a name for trying to mitigate this dualistic opposition and hence allow the forms to function as intelligible principles, that is, to be intermediating in the requisite manner.

Aristotle's criticism implies that the forms as radically other are ontologically redundant to explain the things of genesis.[3] It implies that participation simply renames the problem, pushing it back one step further. I would rather say: the point of his criticism is directed precisely at the space *between* the originals and the image, the forms and the things. He is correct to return us to this space of the between. But the implication now: if the extremes of this between are defined by a dualistic opposition, the forms are *not* what the things are, otherness is a gulf that allows no mediation, hence the "between" itself, understood in terms of the mediation of "participation," remains as only a new name for the old problem. Even if one agrees with Aristotle on the necessity of some immanence of form, as Plato himself clairvoyantly did in his own *Parmenides,* the issue persists concerning the manner of this immanence, and the mode of manifestation proper to it. A critique of dualism does not do away with the otherness implied in the happening of immanent manifestation; certainly not if manifestation is always also a reserving of what is showing, and hence its continued otherness, even in the show of appearances.

If many of Aristotle's points hit the mark with regard to a certain dualism,[4] nevertheless, if the context of thought is the ethos of the metaxu, Platonic thought *inevitably brings us back to the between.* Let us think of Plato pri-

3. Obviously, this discussion could be expanded in detail to take in other criticisms, such as the third man argument, the issue of ontological duplication, the question whether a form can be a cause, not to mention the knowability or unknowability of form.

4. See *DDO,* chapter 4, on the problems of static eternity; also *Beyond Hegel and Dialectic* (Albany: State University of New York Press, 1992), chapter 1, on time and eternity (abbreviation *BHD*).

marily a thinker of the middle where we discover complex intermediations of self and other. This middle is revealed as dynamic, especially if we take notice of human eros. Suppose we say: all being is a participation in the middle. Suppose we then say: individual things go to comprise the middle, but they do not exhaust it. How could they, if they already are in communication, *are at all* in being intermediated? Let us say that individual things exhibit a certain commonness, a certain community. How do we explain this community? Even if one of our resorts is to appeal to the forms, notice we have not left the middle. Will this begin to satisfy Aristotle? Obviously more must be said.

Notice that, whether we hear "yes" or "no" from Aristotle, we can *still say* that these forms are never univocally identical with any one individual. If they were, their communal character, and the happening of community, would be impossible. In the middle itself, we have to say that any nominalistic reduction of being to a collection of particulars does not make sense finally. We could say that the forms are themselves possibilities of "being together" that also arise in the middle. They are other to the individual things as more than determinate particularities, but they essentially name the fact that the individual itself is not exhausted by its particularity; its individuality as a member of the middle community points beyond bare particularity. The individual in the middle is beyond itself as a member of the community of being. Universal form names this sur-particular participation in the "beyond"—a "beyond" of itself which is its "being together" with others, more proximately with others of its own kind, more mediately with all other beings. And this "beyond" is, nevertheless, also right here and now in the middle. (A sign of this doubleness of the "beyond" might be seen in the way the word *"meta"* can mean both "in the midst," and also "over and above.")

Note also that now the issue is not quite how individuals participate in the forms; the deeper issue is that *both* are modes of participation in the middle. Universality and particularity are modes of participation of individual things in the community of being. That community of being is the middle, but the issue of making sense of the middle for the philosopher can be exhausted neither by the enumeration of a collection of particulars, nor the abstraction of a set of general concepts. Universals themselves might be said to be nonparticular, sur-particular modes of participation in the middle. Does not this escape the stricture of Aristotle, even though more might still be said?[5] If someone still were to say that participation remains a metaphor, perhaps one can only direct attention to the experience of *participation in community we actually do have in the middle*. It may indeed be the case that there is a metaphorical extension of human community to being beyond the human. But this does not undercut the suggestion, though it does ask us to explore further the nature of the communication, which is plurivocal. And it may be

5. See *BB*, chapter 9, on intelligibilities as modes of being together in the between.

that such metaphorical speech is not a logical defect but the fundamental way we have of making sense of being in community. For human community, and communication, are carried by an eros of likening in which we know, not univocal identity or difference, but the inseparability of unlikeness and likeness. It may also be less that we metaphorically extend human community to being beyond the human, but that *to be at all* is to be in metaxological community, and that this is *constitutive* also for human community, apart from any metaphorical extension. Perhaps also such metaphorizing (notice again the *meta* and its ferrying power) is itself possibilized by metaxological community. There are many large issues I cannot take up here (on communities, see *BB*, chapter 11).

To mitigate the questionable consequences that follow from a univocalizing dualism, my suggestion is that we *turn around,* in a metaxological direction, the significance of participation. We can then acknowledge that there is a strain in the Platonic philosopher who, as a thinker of the middle, is yet driven to the extremes. Philosophical eros is for the ultimate; a sense of the otherness of being emerges in the middle; eros is drawn on by the presentiment that being in the full is not exhausted by what is shown in doxa, whether shown univocally or equivocally; as oscillating between equivocity and univocity, the world of doxa can lend itself to a reduction of the promise of the middle; what we make of being is sometimes pitifully poor in relation to that promise. Some will see this view as objectionable: the "Plato" who throws to us the bones of the feast. One could well say the opposite: there can be a dogmatism of doxa that asserts itself as the measure of being, as if it were on a par with the ontological richness of the middle. It is this dogmatism that lacks a feel for the feast. It would have us live from the thin gruel of the taken for granted middle, while prescribing any eros for otherwise filling food. But did not Plato in the *Laws* (see 796) recommend that life be lived as if it were the play of a kind of divine feast day? Did not the Athenian Stranger there suggest (828b) that there be 365 feast days in the year?

Perhaps driven by the contrast between different ways of dwelling with the middle, by a radical eros, Plato had a tendency to pit the extreme against the middle, as more ordinarily domesticated. The extreme can be dangerous, of course, just as eros and mania can, and the middle can be differently domesticated, and not always by commonsense, but perhaps too by philosophy. That contrast between extreme and middle can result in the otherness of being now being reformulated in terms of a dualistic opposition. This can happen if we stress the *reserve* of the intelligible in sensuous showing. One can also understand why it might happen in dialogues of limit situations, most especially in *Phaedo,* where the extreme looms up in radically negative form, namely death. It is surely understandable why this sense of otherness is articulated in stronger dualistic terms in this context of limit situation, and entirely compatible with less pronounced dualistic forms in other dialogues where such a extremity is not directly before one. In that regard, Platonic dualism is made more understandable as a response to the different kinds of otherness that emerge in the middle. That said, the forms as originals, and participation as a communication of the originals, are susceptible to a more nuanced understanding that preserves their otherness without fixing on a univocalizing dualism.

Below I will suggest that is it this dualistic otherness that easily comes to the fore when treating of *mimesis:* we are tempted to spread the middle out in a spatial, geometrical structure, univocally emphasizing the extremes as set in opposition to each other. I will suggest a more nuanced view of mimesis, since both *eros* and *mania* undercut this univocal "spatialization" of the middle. One can think of Platonic originals in terms truer to the middle and the dynamic energies of being that emerge there—whether it be the energy of ambiguous showing in mimesis, or the original energy of self-surpassing emergent in the soul with eros, or the original energy of being erupting from the other in mania and overpowering the self of quotidian consciousness. But before turning to these points in detail, one final consideration, relative to the larger setting beyond Plato.

As is well recognized, some version of Platonic dualism has been extraordinarily influential in determining the shape of ontological, metaphysical vision in the west. One does not have to be a Nietzsche or Heidegger to realize that. Nor does one have to denounce Platonism as nihilism. This is now altogether too crude. I will say: premodern metaphysics did not emphasize active selfhood in the modern way because its participation in the middle was marked by a strong sense of the otherness of being. You might put this down to terror before the unknown in nature, as some debunking modern enlighteners have done. Again this is entirely too simplistic, though not without a touch a truth. Premodern humans lived, like us, in the middle, but the middle in its otherness communicated its perplexing enigma as much as the self asserting itself. This can take an affirmative, celebratory form, as in a kind of reverence that has ontological roots, as well as a terrified and even nihilistic form.

I will not dwell on this except to say that we moderns are sometimes shamed by the joy pre-moderns took in the *beauty of the cosmos.* And that on the part of those Platonists who allegedly had nothing but the "evil eye" for beauty and the superlative worth of being. One has only to think of the *aesthetic cosmogony* of the *Timaeus,* where the Demiurge, while forming matter according to geometrical forms, is most concerned to make the world the best and most beautiful possible. The coming to form of the cosmos is an *aesthetic act* that affirms the *ontological good* of what comes to be. Not the horror of being, but the worthiness of being to be affirmed—this is what, one might almost say, is *sung.*

Dualism is a manageable, because *crude* way of dealing with different senses of otherness. Philosophical views that are influential in the wider culture cast their spell in their cruder forms, and only because they lend themselves to formulation in a coarser version (think of Hegel's afterlife in Marx). One might say as much about "Plato" with regard to dualism. But one is the victim of a self-incurred obtuseness, if one neglects the joyful participation in the beauty of the middle that often marks pre-modern humans. One has only to look at some of the art to see this joy. The Greek celebration of the human body is witness enough to this. But even in the seemingly miserable Middle Ages, we are often stunned. Look, for example, at the serenity of being of those extraordinary faces carved on the door of Chartres Cathedral. Joy in the cosmos involves a kind of metaphysical *aisthēsis,* though these serene faces communicate something even beyond that immanent joy.

My point is not to defend dualism. As I indicated, in the long run dualism undermines the otherness it ostensibly defends; but in a certain sense, it is almost unavoidable that the senses of otherness be formulated in its terms. Something like Platonic dualism may have been carried forward into Christianity in the contrast between the herenow and the hereafter; and at the end of the Middle Ages, perhaps ambiguities with this theological dualism come to pitch the human being back into the middle as a "nature" divested of communications of the divine. Dualism and otherness are identified with and consigned to the other world, while the active human self comes on the scene of a nature that is progressively stripped of its enigma and worth. The seeming eclipse of the divine as other, the atomistic contraction of the singularity of things, nature as a valueless mechanism, homogenous quantity, the human self contracted into the self-expanding expression of its own will to power, these together shape a new dualizing of the middle. The middle is not the ontological milieu, aesthetically astonishing, holding together selfness and otherness. Univocalizing power pulverizes the plurivocal middle. Otherness becomes the externality of a dead nature to be exploited by a self that, to feel itself participant in the middle, now asserts its own original power over against any claims of heteronomy.

Consider the sense of otherness in the middle conceived of as a Cartesian mechanism. The Cartesian dualism is far more insidiously destructive of the sense of significant otherness than is the Platonic dualism. Certainly the sense of otherness carried by Platonic *eidē* is gone. One might be tempted to say: we now have mere things; but do we have things at all? We do not have the community of being. And there is no participation because in the homogeneous continuum there is a sameness which reduces all differences. Participation demands an intermediation of sameness and otherness, an interplay of likening and unlikening. In the indifferent continuum of the Cartesian "middle," there emerges only the self-assertive self which, to protect its own vanishing into the continuum, sets itself in opposition to the rest of being. This is an astonishing change, not least because it signals the dying of astonishment. Astonishment before being is overtaken by its counterfeit double, a hubristic curiosity that slyly lurks in doubt.

Let us be clear. This is essentially a degenerate relatedness in the middle and to the middle, for implicit in it is a degenerate relating to otherness that seems to spread all over modernity in the succeeding centuries. Where find room for ontological joy in nature, or reverence in the Cartesian world? Who could write a poem to Cartesian nature? What eros is aroused there, what mania there to inspire? What could one love there? The answering silence is revealing. The shadow of an ontological nihilism is cast. The shadow is less dispelled by the light cast from a reason uprooted from the ontological milieu, as it is lengthened the more the light broadcasts itself. Of course, certain thinkers (Kant and post-Kantian) did wrestle in different ways with the senses of otherness, and not least with reference to the ontological significance of art. Their struggles can best be seen as trying to do more justice to the middle, despite the danger of disfiguring its promise. Indeed a relation to Plato, or Platonic themes, and a recurrence of eros and mania, as we shall later see, will figure significantly in such thinkers as Schopenhauer and Nietzsche. Nor will our trials with the underground be lacking.

Mimesis, Originals, and the Middle

I now turn to mimesis, eros and mania as essential illuminations of our participation in the between, as well as ways of addressing dualism. Mimesis is inseparable from a metaphysics of image and original in which a *double* attitude towards the image seems unavoidable: the mimesis proves to be both revealing and concealing of original being. This perhaps lights up something of the paradox of Plato as a thinker: most critical among philosophers concerning the status of images; greatest genius of the philosophical image, his similes still fresh for us. Indeed his image of the divided line itself is a mimesis of our ontological and cognitive ethos: the lower mimics the higher but is also bound to it; likewise ascent and descent, as up and down a continuous and discontinuous ladder, are made possible through truer energies of being and knowing released in the soul. We will come to these energies with eros and mania, but one can see how the doubleness of mimesis, as a kind of creative equivocity, can be frozen into a metaphysical dualism. Dualism, as we saw, may be a way of guarding otherness but it also can lead to aporiai: it can undercut otherness in the defense of otherness. Rather than a dualistic spatialization of otherness, the interplay of the mimetic relation needs to be understood plurivocally.

Mimesis is also one of the great concepts in the tradition by means of which art's *grounding relation* to originals is articulated. Mimesis has a range wider than the aesthetic, with ontological significance with respect to beings themselves as images, and with ethical meaning in that we become good by imitation of those already good, as Aristotle reminds us. Mimesis has had a long dominance as the key aesthetic notion, relative to which more modern notions like "creativity," despite their current pervasiveness, have a much shorter history, perhaps emerging with strength in Renaissance humanism, and gathering to unprecedented influence from the time of Romanticism.

First we need to say that mimesis is more nuanced than any merely facile copying. This last notion follows a univocalization of mimesis, indeed a univocalization of being, in which image and original are congealed into a too fixed one-to-one correspondence. Mimesis is a relation, and hence has a *dynamic of relating* at work in it. The complexity of the relation has to do less with some univocal visual mirroring than a balanced relativity between an image and an original. That relation is double rather than univocal, indeed plurivocal in that an openness is necessarily inserted *between* original and image. There is a showing *and* a reserve of the original, and both the showing and the reserve are themselves ambiguously shown in the image.

Consider: The image imitates the original, and in that respect *shows* the original. Take the actor who mimics. I mimic your voice and make you present in my presentation of you: I am you as other; I represent you, not in a simply visual image but by dynamically making present something of the reality that is you, as other to me. And so the mimesis shows my ability to be other than myself: I must transcend myself to imitate you; but your otherness is not absolutely strange, since your life as other-being takes up a guest residence in the welcome of my imitation. My transcending to you in imitation bridges a gap between us, and also shows that your otherness is not so other as to be unbridgeable in an absolute dualism. Mimesis is a complex intermediation in which sometimes the representation of what is other to the image is paramount. At other times, the very power of the image to present and show takes on something of its own life, and seems to stand there in terms of its own achieved creative accomplishment: I mimic you so well, I seem *to be you!* I do it so well, I make you uncomfortable, I seem to have stolen your life.

An adequate account of mimesis cannot reduce it to facile copying, since then one might ask, why bother to copy at all? Given that we seem already to have the original in itself, why duplicate it? Thus the further point: if the otherness is to be shown, in one sense, it must be absent, in another sense, available for manifestation. The imitation is an agent of a manifestation which, as intermediating, communicates across a gap, and indeed may carry its own power, yet it never entirely destroys that otherness as other. Were it to do so, the mimetic relation would be destroyed: and we would have to speak of something more like self-creation *simpliciter*. I think it is important that the insights about originals present in Platonic thinking want to guard that sense of nonreducible otherness. Only when that safeguard is discarded, when indeed otherness as other is felt as a curb on human freedom or "creativity," does the deeper rationale of a mimetic relation become corroded. That does happen in post-Romantic modernity. Imitation is suicide, says Emerson.[6]

---

6. *Emerson's Essays* (New York: Thomas Corwell, 1961), 32. I have discussed the contrast of mimesis and creativity in a number of places, for instance, *PO,* chapter 2; also in "Creativity and the Dunamis," *The Philosophy of Paul Weiss: Library of Living Philosophers,* ed. L. Hahn (Chicago and LaSalle, Ill.: Open Court, 1995), 543–57.

Despite the above complexity, there is a recurrent temptation to simplify mimesis into a univocally proportional relation in which we insist on a one-to-one correspondence between image and original. Such a univocalizing of mimesis easily closes down the open transcending latent in the activity of relating mimetically. Then, with this closure, it will seem we have two *fixed* orders of reality: the image and the original. The original is univocally fixed; the image is a more or less wavering counterpart of the fixed original; and the best imitations are the most univocally correct reproductions of the fixed original. The doubling here is to be fixed, in the best case, to a univocal one-to-one correspondence between the original and the image. Needless to say, no such univocal correspondence is possible on the terms of mimesis; for otherwise the difference would be undercut, and you would have something like a version of Leibniz's identity of indiscernibles—you could not tell the difference of the original if the image is absolute and exactly like the original. There must be difference for an imitation to work—you need the unlikeness of the image, as much as the likeness. One could say that the image, to be true, must be false, if truth means univocal correctness. But if the image is true by being false, there must also be a "being true" that *takes the equivocity of appearing* into account, that does not sidestep this equivocity.

I think the premoderns were never so literalist in their univocalizing that no allowance was made for this openness of the mimetic relation. This we see, for instance, in Plato's discussion of the difference of an *eikastic* and *phantastik* image (*Sophist,* 235d ff.). To appear as a true image, a phantastik image must depart from the exact proportions of the eikastic and be proportioned to the viewer: in a certain sense, to be true, it must be false to the original, and only by being false does it appear as true. This, I would say, is an *affirmative sense* of the equivocity of the image. Only with an uncompromising univocalizing of the mimetic relation, does insensitivity to these nuances become more pronounced. Here I find it revealing that modernity's quest for univocity (proximately in science and mathematics, more generally in relation to being as such) *paradoxically releases, in its relation to art, a glorification of equivocity,* and not least with respect to "creativity" and its indeterminacy. One wonders if the diminished prestige of imitation for modernity goes as much with this univocal inability to understand a nuanced mimesis, as with our impatience with any relation to an other that puts a curb on our vaunted "creativity." The aesthetic glorification of equivocity seems to compensate for the pulverization by univocal reason of the plurivocity of other-being.

I would say that when the univocal tendency is in the dominant in Plato, then the *negative vision of mimesis* comes more to the fore. The difference of the original and image, the ontological distance never absolutely abrogated, is seen to cut us off from the truth of the original. Then the difference is not stressed as, so to say, the condition of the possibility of the appearing of the original in the middle. This second affirmative difference in inseparable from the showing of the truth of the original. And since the univocalizing tendency is one of the strains in Plato, we repeatedly find different forms of a certain ambivalent relation to what exceeds such univocal determination. I mean that the double evaluation, the positive/negative relation to "art," will also appear with respect to eros and to mania. Now it seems we are dealing with something divine, now with something delusionary. Do we perhaps always deal with *both?* If so, there is no absolute evasion of the equivocity of the situation. Sometimes this equivocity will be condemned, if it is taken as only as *failure* of the univocal test. But it will come in for a different praise when an other sense of being true beyond univocity is allowed to enter consideration, let us say, when philosophical *finesse* is granted its freedom beyond geometry. For philosophical finesse is just what we need to tell the difference between the delusionary and the divine.

A certain univocal fixation of the between easily turns the mimetic relation into a (failed) quasi-mathematical grid of structural relations. The gap between the image and the original is fixed by that structural grid; and we can freeze into a posture of dualistic opposition between this world and the other, between images and originals. As I said, this is a perennial temptation; but it cannot be true to mimesis itself. The dynamic of relating immanent in the mimesis is evident with an investigation of the relation itself. This becomes more evident when we more explicitly take account of other energies of that dynamic. I suggest that erotic transcending and manic inspiration have much to do with naming that *happening of criss-crossing between image and original* that is present also in mimesis but too easily forgotten and frozen with the dominance of univocal mind. It is not so easy to univocalize eros and mania. One might even wonder why the image of the *bed* was chosen to discuss mimesis in the *Republic.* What are beds for? For sleeping, for resting, no doubt; but also for love. What would the divine idea of the bed then be? What kind of sleep would come over one, what kind of love would waken, on *that* bed? Nor should one forget that it is the couch of seductive luxury, so to say, that is being purified in the *Republic.*

Before turning to eros and mania, I conclude these present reflections with a remark on mimesis and the dynamic between. Mimesis *can* lead to a more static spatialization of the milieu of the middle. Then the ethos of the between is fixed in terms of certain relata, themselves fixed in their difference, and hence to be mediated by some *subsequent* relation of correspondence. But what if the middle is *already alive with correspondings?* Say: beings are, as already in response to each other; each is hence both itself and beyond itself; each shows itself and shows something more and other than itself; each is double in its appearing, appearing as itself, and also as showing its being in response to what is other, and even in its showing also reserved. Looked at this way, we dynamize the between, now seen as a network of dynamic respondings: a network of communication between one and the other, between same and other, between identity and difference.

From this point of view, it is not at all surprising that *music* is said to be the most imitative of the arts; for just that responsiveness, immediately at work, is alive here. Music takes us back to the original plurivocity of the between, where the voices of being are being formed, and sound together in original resonance, and without being fixed in one voice alone. And if the soul is taken out of itself by music, as the Pythagoreans knew, it is also the most mathematical of the arts. Is not music then somewhat like the making of the Demiurge who weds in matter cosmic aesthetic discernment with geometrical form? This most imitative of the arts, music, is the most resounding: equivocal and needing finesse, yet structured by univocal form; appealing to depths of responsiveness in the psyche, while avoiding destructive formlessness. This preeminence of music as mimetic fits neither with modern logocentrisms which so emphasize univocity that geometry overwhelms finesse; nor with postmodern anti-logocentrisms, where finesse often is overcome by a formlessness that is the counterfeit of creation.

Is it not perfectly understandable that Nietzsche here would derive the origin of tragedy from the spirit of music? The original formlessness gives birth to the high civilizing form of tragedy, where art, religion, philosophical vision, ethical wisdom pass into each other in a manner at the opposite extreme to their modern division. The spirit of music seems the opposite of mimesis, but when we are transported by music it is just our *being re-formed* though the energies of music that make us *be other*. Kant hated the involuntary aspect of this transport. I would speak of the original formlessness as a primal porosity of being. I would speak of the transport as a dipping down into and release of the *passio essendi,* and it has to do with an idiot wisdom.

Eros, Middles, Originals

We know that there are many discussions of eros in Plato. Its nature and presence is a focus in many dialogues: *Symposium, Phaedrus, Republic.* And in these dialogues, different faces of eros are shown, and not least in the *Symposium,* where we must take seriously the *plurality* of possible interpretations offered, and not think too univocally that we can identify simpliciter Plato's views with those expounded in Socrates's contribution to that dialogue. The great myth expounded by Aristophanes, and here presented with such power, not least, must make us consider that Plato wants us to consider these many faces of eros; wants us to consider the archeology of eros, as much as the teleology (Socrates). One recalls the story that Plato, on being asked by Dion as to what the Greeks were like, is said to have sent the works of Aristophanes in reply. There is also the story that found under the pillow of the dead Plato were the works of Aristophanes.

Eros gives expression to the porosity of our being, mingling, often in a fertile equivocity, the passion of being with our endeavor to be. Patience and striving mix there. The plurivocal, if not protean character of eros asks us to be ambiguous between celebration and caution. Some of Plato's dialogues, (e.g., the *Republic*) seem more to offer an image of eros as needing discipline and purification; others, such as the *Symposium* and the *Phaedrus,* seem less guarded about the indispensable affirmative powers of eros, though even then the equivocity between *eros uranos* and *eros turranos* is never forgotten.

My concern cannot be with all the subtle intricacies of Plato, even if one could ever be sure what Plato thinks, even did we seem to master all the details of his dialogues, not forgetting either the dramatic nature of these dialogues, and its indispensable role in the showing and communication of truth. These dialogues are images of philosophy as a living dialectic between singular humans, each giving voice to his understanding of truth, none possessing it completely, yet each contributing in the play of voices to the furtherance of the search. Philosophical dialogue plurivocally mimics the possible pathways to truth in the middle, as indeed also some of the possible departures from the path, also in the middle. Dialogue: a middle of plurivocal *logoi,* each seeking to be true to what is coming to articulation in the spaces of questioning and answering between thinking human beings.

Surprisingly also, I think that dialogue commands that we pay *attention to surfaces*. Surfaces are the interfaces of communication. Philosophy must be a mindfulness of surfaces as places of showing. Plato gives us a philosophy of surfaces by offering us the drama of human showing. For words can be the richest showings: articulated surfaces that can be the communication of the deepest hiddenness. It is not accident that we speak of eros surfacing: the incarnate human is aroused, inspired, besides itself. The surfacing promises an intimacy of communication to the one who loves or is loved. One might say that art is a happening where surface and depth coincide. The hypersensible shows itself as sensible. The intelligible shines. (Aristotle said (*De Anima,* 426b4–5 that *aisthēsis* too is a kind of *logos.*) The Platonic dialogue is a drama of surfaces, of words as the surfacing of souls in the between and in communication with each other.

What might be said about eros and the metaxu, in light of previous discussion of originals? Let me put the point about the energy of eros in terms of different views of "being true," relative to our fidelity to what shows itself in the between.[7] One might correlate mimesis with a more *correspondence* view of truth, in that an other original seems given to which the imitation is to be likened. We have already seen the difficulty of trying to fix a univocal one-to-one correspondence between original and imitation: there is openness in the correspondence, giving likeness in unlikeness, unlikeness in likeness. Correspondence points in itself to more that fixed univocal correlation: the dynamic of *passing between* the two sides of the mimesis, between one and the other.

I would situate eros here: eros reminds us of self-surpassing, eros is itself the dynamic of self-surpassing. "Being true," in this instance, is fidelity to the

7. On "being true," with references to the different senses of being, see *BB,* chapter 12.

movement of self-transcending in relation to truth as (originally) other to us, other because we do not possess it through ourselves alone. Indeed we are self-transcending to the extent that a call is made on us by what we do not possess: we are driven beyond lack as much by that lack, as by what we lack. The *passing between* is here to be discerned. But there is a temptation analogous to the temptation to fixity of mimesis: this is not now the fixing of an external original as ultimate; the temptation is rather to *intoxication with the self-transcending itself as original.* For eros seems to release something original in us, showing us to be more than mere passive images. If there is a passion of eros, it is a powerful passion, and hence as power is more than passion. So we are tempted to conceive of ourselves as originating the self-surpassing movement through ourselves alone. We might even then hold that truth, or "being true," is a matter of being self-constructed, self-determined.

This, I think, can be but a reversal of the above temptation to univocal fixation, but like the latter, it has its own equivocity, in that the lack within self remains enigmatic, as does the plenitude of power that immanently energizes the movements of self-surpassing. *We first find ourselves in them,* we do not construct them ourselves. Whatever construction there is comes after this first finding. "Being true" must include fidelity also to this first finding, and not just to the subsequent constructions or self-determinations. Fidelity to "being true" may come in self-exceeding towards a limit, but there is an already given relation to the truth in the movement of self-exceeding. There is also a limit where we might well find ourselves visited with a *reversal,* relative to any complete claims to self-construction. Something is given and shown from the other sought, but now it is granted as communicated to self—from beyond self.

Is it not here that one might situate the happening of mania: something is communicated enigmatically to the soul from beyond itself, but it enters most intimately into that soul, so its strange transcendence is also intimate immanence? It makes us at home and not at home with our own "being true," and with true being as other to ourselves. There is here neither univocal clarity nor certainty, nor complete self-mastery and self-possession. We seem rather to be possessed with a truth more *revealed* than simply found or constructed. Such a revelation would be neither an univocal foundation nor an equivocal construction. It would be a plurivocal *passing between* the passionate soul and the communicating origin. The soul must be porous to let be that passing.

I will return to mania, but consider further the point about correspondence: think here of eros as the coming to mindfulness in the soul of its being as *responsiveness.* (The word "soul" here is more resonant than the modern word "self.") The soul *is* in *co-responding,* where response is always to or with something other to itself. Eros reveals an energy of self-surpassing in which the soul is more passionately energized in itself, while at the same time it reaches more extensively beyond its own limits: more intensively aroused, more extensively self-transcending. We know this from eros: something more fully comes alive in us and also some presentiment of desire for what is beyond us also comes alive, as the sense of need or lack relative to which we must seek beyond. Thus the seeming paradoxically character: *innerness most aroused,* most passionately taken hold of, perhaps even besides itself so overpowering is the energy, and yet more fully itself in this being besides itself; and yet also the soul is *most driven out* to seek what it is not, besides itself because in itself it cannot be complete but must seek what is besides it, what is more than it, in order to be at home. *Being besides itself:* the double face of "besides": intensive arousal of itself, extensive exceeding of itself to what is other or above.

If there is a temptation to univocal structure and correspondence with mimesis, with eros it becomes more explicit that there is something *beyond structure:* there is the dynamism out of which structure comes to shape. Beyond fixed form there is forming, structuring. If we fix mimesis to a structure of relation, eros more fully reminds us there is a structuring in the relation, indeed that there is something that exceeds structure. Indeed this excess is necessary if the form of *relation as a relating* is to be possible at all, relating *between* terms that are like and unlike, as are the image and the original in the relation of mimesis. There is a passage from one to the other: there is a movement between them; for the image images the original, and hence something passes between them; just as the original is such as to be imagible in the images, and hence again something passes between them. How make sense of this passage between? Participation and mimesis point to this between, eros does so more dynamically relative to the movement of the human soul itself.

Proximately we seem to be turned to the dynamism of being in the self, but there is something unmastered about this. This is related to what I have called the *passio essendi.* We are passions of being before we are endeavors of being *(conatus essendi).* With eros the passion of being arouses itself, or is aroused in us, in a desire that knows itself as a restlessness called out beyond its own confines. The call initially is the opposite of mastery; perhaps it will enter some mastery of itself; but this will always be qualified by its being sourced more originally in the *passio essendi.* There is also an excess within. This might be called the inward otherness: eros beyond absolute mastery by us: the power in us that draws us, drives us beyond. We discover our own beyondness as in search of a more radical beyond. Eros is participant in the dynamic bridging of the gap.

Eros shows its sources in the sensuous body, this being its *aesthetic* happening. It is also more than aesthetic happening, since we also find the self-structuring power of an inward otherness, a power not confined to its own self, but moved to the transcendence of inward otherness in the direction of an other otherness: not its own beauty, but beauty as other, beauty itself. Any dualism of "in here/out there," or of "up/down" breaks down. There is a plurivocally intermediated middle—metaxological, not univocal, not equivocal. Eros "bridges" the metaphysical dualism from our side, though it is not just us doing the "bridging." The process of overcoming originates in our bodies, in the idiotic recesses of the flesh, our aesthetic being, but it reaches out of those recesses to beauty in a plurivocal number of forms, from the elemental flesh to the hyper-aesthetic beauty of *to kalon* itself.[8]

If eros traverses the metaxu, it does so out of sources in the soul that are double, full and empty, excessive and intensive, seeded in the intimacy of the soul, yet growing through the forms of the body and aesthetic being, to what is outside the body in actions, customs, communities, to what is above aesthetic being. Eros reveals immanence most rich in search of transcendence as what calls immanence to its own height.[9]

Thus eros lets us understand that the metaxu has a vertical as well as a horizontal dimension. Eros tells against dualism; in surpassing in and through the metaxu, it binds up the whole, as Socrates says. Such a whole is nothing like Hegel's self-mediating totality. Differences are preserved in it but the kinds of differences are such as to include reverence for the excess of transcendence itself. Dialectical thinking, in Hegel's mouth, makes its own case too easily, when it sees itself as transcending dualism, identified with oppositional difference to be overcome. Here in Platonic transcendence, any immanent wholeness is always qualified by the beyond of the Good, *epēkeina tēs ousias* (*Republic*, 509b9). Ecstasis towards this other transcendence is not something that Hegelian holism is at all at home with, just because there is an acknowledgment of an *unsurpassable limit, and on the heights*. Something remains more than immanence, and more than us, and brings the philosopher to a humility before what exceeds his categories. (I return to this and Hegel in later chapters.)

Just for that reason, our speaking has to resort to other means, not least the mythic, and the artistic, if it is to venture some speaking of what is beyond. This is not a defect, but an effect of our finitude and the too muchness of what is beyond. This effect may be entirely positive relative to our finitude, in that the most fitting way for us to speak of what is beyond cannot dispense with an imagistic dimension. The image itself is an equivocal carrier of eros. Much might be said here of Plato's own *philosophical art*.[10] I confine myself to this.

---

8. Martha Nussbaum in *The Fragility of Goodness* (Cambridge and New York: Cambridge University Press, 1986) goes in an opposite direction with a developmental view of Plato, moving from asceticism to eros. Clearly there are places where an ascetic dualism is to the fore, as in the *Phaedo;* but if one considers the dramatic context, one would hardly expect dithyrambs to sexual eros on the eve of death. The *Symposium* then is a drinking party: *in vino veritas:* there is here no Plato lite as might suit more moderate tastes. In *Phaedrus* a kind of divine madness inspires the speech about eros, but this is visionary excess and sobriety in one. This is the doubleness as richly equivocal, not as simple dualism. The redoubled excess of the human being cannot be simplistically univocalized; if the soul has no fixed *eidos,* it cannot be univocalized.

9. On the double parentage of eros, in terms of feast and want, see *BHD,* 329–30.

10. See my "Plato's Philosophical Art and the Identification of the Sophist," *Filosofia Oggi,* 11, no. 4 (1979): 393–403; also below, pp. 170–72.

Since eros is itself equivocal between seeking a sovereignty on the heights and openness to what transcends such sovereignty, it must be suitably qualified by philosophical mindfulness which guards against its own daimonic possibilities. By daimonic I mean now the sense in which the excess, the inward otherness, can exert its power over us, and hence no longer be eros uranos, but eros turranos. Just as above we saw these double possibilities with mimesis, so here also with eros. This reflects nothing other than the equivocity of the human being, and the need of philosophy as that mindfulness of the bewitchments, the bondages into which we are liable to fall through this half-light, half-dark power. And perhaps it is less dualism, as this unruly half-and-half equivocity that is reflected (in the *Phaedrus,* 246a, 253d) in the powerful images of the dark and white horses.

Mania, Originals, and the Middle

Mania is intimately related to the pathos of originality, but it is fraught with dangerous ambiguity, both in itself and in Plato. Is all talk of "divine madness" mere florid hyperbole, or can we find a deeper truth to the hyperbolic? There is madness and madness, and mad madness is not easy to discriminate from divine madness. For how discriminate except in terms of reason? But what is at play in madness is both more and less than reason. Hence reason has to face what is recalcitrantly other to it, and with means not always sympathetic or useful in discerning what the madness might communicate. Yet again the point cannot be a simple dualism of madness and reason. We must rather recall the problematic middle space between them; and this between, while it might be mediated in some measure, cannot be *entirely* mediated by reason alone in the ascendancy of its diurnal sobriety. Reason, to be reasonable, might have to descend into, or find descending on it, a nocturnal intoxication or dishevelment.

Postidealistic excess, such as we find in Schopenhauer or Nietzsche, and postmodern excess, such as we find in Bataille, and each following in the shoes of Romantic excess, emerge in the wake of Enlightenment reason as an other exceeding thought thinking itself. All signal the emergence of an equivocal transcendence hinted at in its own way in Platonic mania. Romantic and postidealistic mania make reference to the original self. Nietzsche, by contrast, seems situated somewhere between Romanticism and postmodernism whose mania seems to be originality without origin or originals. Hence as mania, it risks madness *without* the divine. How again distinguish this from mad madness? If for no other reason than this, we should be attentive to the double response Plato solicits: skeptical guardedness, suspicion, fear even; openness, fascination, suspicion in another sense positive, namely, a presentiment that something of ultimate moment may here be communicated. Mania is both: on one hand, a defection from univocal reason; on the other, our being effected by what cannot be effected by self-determining reason. We are asked for both these: critical skepticism towards mania; acknowledgment that nothing of great excellence seems possible without it, even in philosophy. (We will come upon a *differently guarded attitude* of Kant to unruly genius, in the next chapter.)

Mania is clearly a sister or brother of eros. Both testify to the porosity of our being, one striving beyond this porosity, the other receiving from beyond it. Think also of the fact that it is a mantic priestess, Diotima from Mantinea, who instructs the younger Socrates in the truth about eros. Mania, one might divine, is the mistress of eros. In both, there is a "being beside oneself," but the stress is distributed somewhat differently in each. I mean in mania the stress is less on the self-surpassing of restless desire towards the ultimate as other, even in the most intensive energizing of the longing soul; more, it intimates something of the communication of the ultimate as other which is offered to the soul as a medium of its communication and receipt. Mania names an offering to us, rather than a seeking by us. Not that we open ourselves, but that we are opening, being opened. We are not just an erotic lack seeking completion, but an opening into which a surplus original broadcasts something of its creative plenitude. Then we are indeed besides ourselves, but besides ourselves because what is other to us has communicated its transport to us from its own otherness. We are transported; we are not self-transporting. There is an ecstasis in both mania and eros but the directionality of the ecstasy comes from down up in one case, and from up down, in the other. And if what we know of eros finally derives from prophetic communication, offered by a source like a mantic priestess, the way up for us would presuppose the way down, and the way down not just effected by us.

I take all this to be a sign of the unavoidability of both eros and mania, and the necessary complementarity of each as modes of ecstatic transport and communication in the metaxu. There is a traversing of the between, but there is a traversing towards us, as well as our traversing towards what is other to us. There is this difference: the erotic way from down up seems driven, at least in part, by a lack seeking fulfillment in more beyond itself; while the manic way from up down seems the descending communication of an origin that is more than lack, a "more" that communicates to our lack from itself as surplus source. This "more" is an original in excess of formal structure, in excess also of the erotic formlessness of the soul over which it comes. The soul as opening is overcome.

I take all of this also to be a sign that the *verticality* of the metaxu is being stressed, in that mania as well as eros refer us to dimensions of height. They also refer us to the dimension of depth, in that the communication of either ecstasis can erupt from the reserved ontological intimacy of the soul itself. The soul is deep as well as high. As Heraclitus said (fragment 45): you could not search out its furthest limits, even if you traversed all of the ways, so unfathomable is its logos. We find a similar thought in Plato (see *Phaedrus,* 246): One would have to have a divine speech to say what the idea of soul is; only a god could tell it; humans can only speak of the soul in figurative terms, and what it resembles. The Platonic dialogue may well be an iconic drama, a mimesis of Socrates and others. We are given images of Socrates: stingray, gadly, midwife, Silenus figure. But to the original there is something still more and other. Socrates is "in-between" and *atopos* (*Symposium*, 215a2, 221c2–d6), but no one knows Socrates (*Symposium*, 216c7–d1). A certain "silence," so to say, or reserve, about the original, generates the need for many images. Something similar might be said above the silent reserve of Plato himself in all his writing. "Plato before, Plato behind, in the middle a chimaera"—so said Nietzsche.[11] But the chimaera, this middle is also a monster.

Of the soul, there is no absolutely direct univocal account. We need the image which imitates, showing likeness and unlikeness. Images draw out the soul in speaking of it in figures, configure its native sleeping. Thus the figure of the winged soul. The gods did not call eros the winged one but the giver of wings (*Phaedrus*, 252). We find a figure of height, as well as of possible falling. The winged soul shows less the simple dualism of white and dark as the soul's own internal equivocity, flying from below to what is above. The internal equivocality makes it at odds with itself and hence liable to fall as it rises, and even to rise as it falls. Just the tension of this strife energizes the ambiguous going beyond or falling below. The depth can refer to disturbing darknesses in the soul, and hence the dangerous daimonic aspect of both eros and mania. (Recall my remark above about the underground of the Cave itself, and not just the Cave as itself underground.) Depth and height are not finally separable. They are *"altus"* in the Latin sense, which can mean both "deep" and "high." This recalls my earlier point about the word *"meta"* as meaning "in the midst" as well as "beyond": most intimate and most transcendent; most our own, most other and not our own. The words we need here are dialectical, though in a metaxological sense rather than Hegelian: the togetherness of the extremes, the "opposites" together, and together because of the interplay to and fro, back and forth, in and out, up and down, in the between. The between

---

11. *Twilight of the Idols*, §190. Diskin Clay, in his thoughtful *Platonic Questions: Dialogues with the Silent Philosopher* (University Park, PA: Penn State Press, 2000), 8, points out how this is in imitation of *Iliad* 6, 181, where Homer describes the chimaera: "A lion in front, a snake behind, in the middle a goat." Of course, Plato showed himself intimate with the monstrous. I cite two examples. There is the famous image in the *Republic* (588b ff.) where we are given a three-dimensional image *(eikon)* of the soul: first a many-headed beast, likened to the Chimaera or Scylla or Cerberus, second a lion, third the figure of a man, and all these three wrapped together into one and enclosed within the external mold of a human being. We are that extraordinary and explosive mix, often at war with itself, capable, however, of justice and harmony with itself under the reconciling reason of the human in us. A second example is the well-known perplexity of Socrates in the *Phaedrus* (229e-230a): Am I a monster more complicated and swollen with passion than Typho or a more gentle and simple creature to whom nature has given a divine and lovelier destiny? This question, rather than scientific speculations about nature, must first be answered, and to meet the Delphic injunction: know thyself! Besides Typho who made war on the Olympians, Socrates refers also to other monsters: the Chimaera, Hippocentaurs, Gorgons, Pegasus, and "multitudes of strange, inconceiveable, portentous natures" (229d).

is a site of criss-crossing, and the dimensionality crossed is as much vertical as horizontal, indeed more vertical than horizontal. Perhaps this ineradicable verticality leads more univocalizing minds into its fixation into a simplistic dualism of a this-world and a beyond-world. If rather we think of the eros and mania as in a dynamic field of interplay, relating, responding, co-responding, then this univocal stabilization does not suffice. When we stress this dynamic milieu of being, the issue of static dualism seems less of a problem than in more traditional formulations of Platonic thought.[12]

What has mania to do with this milieu and the question of originals? The *Ion* here helps. There the description of the poet refers to him as *entheos*—in the god, enthusiastic. This is "being beside oneself" as given to one. The familiar doctrine of inspiration is sister. To be inspired is to be breathed upon. The breath might be stormy or delicate; and yet it is as if life from a truer source had entered both intimately and transfiguratively into what otherwise would be unmoving and uncommunicative. Inspiration brings up the thought of extraordinary beginnings. Think of the *humus:* the breath of divine life is breathed over and in it; and the humus becomes human: moving, living, minding, communicating, seeking. What is suggested is a moving source that communicates movement to a recipient, who then takes on some of the characteristic of being self-moving. In the ancient understanding, self-movement was taken to be the character of soul. But notice here there is something *prior* to *self-movement:* there is first a *being moved.* I do not first move myself; I am moved first, then I move myself. If we think of the human soul as first thus a recipient, we would have to grant a *passio essendi* as first, and then a *conatus essendi.*

And even were we to speak of the overcoming of a gap between the human and the original source of life, this overcoming the soul does not first effect, but *finds itself effected,* and from the side of an otherness beyond oneself. (Recall Socrates' veneration for the ancients, the *palioi, Phaedrus,* 235: ideas seem to have been poured into his ear, though how he has forgotten. He is a hearer, a recipient from original sources, exactly how and who remaining

12. The themes of genius, madness and inspiration are important in Romanticism and in thinkers like Schopenhauer. One thinks of Coleridge: indebted to German idealism, especially Schelling and Schlegel, there is a genuine feel for Platonic originals in him. One of his obsessions was to find that space of connection in which inwardness in its most intensive self-searching communicated with, entered in to knowing rapport with, so to say, "outness" and indeed "upness" (in the sense of the depth dimension). I have made some remarks on Stanley Cavell and Coleridge, also on the theme of "being besides oneself" in Cavell, Emerson, Nietzsche, in "A Second *Primavera:* Cavell, German Philosophy and Romanticism," in *Stanley Cavell (Contemporary Philosophy in Focus),* ed. Richard Eldridge (New York and Cambridge: Cambridge University Press, 2003). Richard Eldridge's writings are very impressive in bringing philosophy and Romanticism into fruitful dialogue, both renewing a dialogue that once was, and making available its truth for our own time. I have learned much from our conversations, and on the present theme especially from his *The Persistence of Romanticism: Essays in Philosophy and Literature* (New York and Cambridge: Cambridge University Press, 2001).

unclear.) Moving oneself, even upwards to the heights, comes subsequently to being moved by what comes down to us; comes subsequently to what comes up in us, moving us up, beyond ourselves. If the divine is this other source, as source it is original by being originative: it initiates, it opens a porosity, it sets in motion, it enlivens, it communicates, it makes the soul also be besides itself, empty yet porous and full with a power that is most intimate and yet is not of itself alone. What is most my own is not my own.

The manner in which here we have to speak begins to border on paradox. Because of this, the living otherness of the original might seem to be a mere mad madness to the solid competencies of sober everydayness. Philosophers—banner carriers for sober reason—are themselves wary of this disturbing otherness. To Plato's credit he is not reluctant to acknowledge the importance of what resists logical encapsulation. Even in the quarrel of poets and philosophers, the power of the poets must be granted. What kind of agon would it be were the advantages stacked massively to one side? Plato knew something of how this beyond in its otherness erupts, disrupting our more domesticated equilibriums. The unmastered, unpredictable sources of such eruptions will inspire Nietzsche in anti-Platonic directions. Under the banner of Dionysus, he will march to war against the middling rationality of the last men, and against the philosophical tradition as the historical nursery of these last men.

Here I just make this point: the issue is not quite the quarrel of poetry and philosophy. While this is a genuine quarrel (as well as conversation and affiliation), there is an issue at a level deeper than this difference and affiliation, namely, with respect to the original that is the radical other to poetry and philosophy, without which both would be dead. If we must say that great poetry and philosophy are impossible without the gift of divine mania, they both, even in their quarrel, are subtended by a more radical origin, of which they provide each a kind of erotic mimesis, albeit differently qualified. Philosophy and poetry are both formations of middle mindfulness, though they each may take us to the extremes; and while their ways of seeking and saying may differ, each at the best gives form to the original energy of being disturbingly communicated in both eros and mania.

Of course, there is an entire typology of different forms of divine madness in the *Phaedrus,* prophetic, purificatory, musical, philosophical (244b–245c, 249d, 265a–c). Let me here confine myself to how the image of the charged magnet in the *Ion* (533dff.) is instructive. Though the point bears on mania, it is also instructive with regard what I called an erotic mimesis. For does not mania, in the surplus sense above delineated, point to a prior source or original which, it now seems, makes possible both eros and mimesis? Consider: The poet is inspired and inspiring the rhapsode; the rhapsode is inspired derivatively in performance, and then inspiring those who participate in properly listening to the performed words. This is not the more or less static mimesis of the *Republic:* idea of bed, real bed, painted bed. In mania there is an energy passing from the original to the first mimesis (the poet), itself energized originally in its derivativeness and inspiring another (the rhapsode), and so on. We are offered an image of this *passing energy* (the charged magnet), and that we are offered an *image* is again not incidental. An image carries power, mimetic power in its likening capacity, but also erotic power in that an image can crystalize and give form to desire. The lack of univocal fixity in the image calls to the openness of desire itself. Hence the pedagogic indispensability of the image, as well as its danger (this doubleness is crucial to the dialectic of the *Republic*): an image can crystalize the erotic shape of the soul before the soul comes to know itself or enter into its own self-appropriation. And there may also be something beyond self-appropriation, both in the origin and in the end.

The image of the charging magnet suggests an energy beyond containment by self-mastery, even though the rhapsode is a kind of master. He certainly is singular in being gifted with the power to receive the communication from the more divine sources. The magnet charges the various rings, which themselves as charged communicate further the charge to other rings; and all the rings *hang down* from the charged magnet from which they get their own charge, as well as the power to be in communication with the source that now enlivens them. Take away the magnet and they fall to the ground.

There is a relation here, and you might think the rings need the magnet as much as the magnet needs the rings, in that the magnet seems to need these others to show its power to communicate and charge. The most important point seems rather the *asymmetry* in the relation: without the magnet the rings would be lifeless and unmoving; they do not charge the magnet but by a contagion they come alive with a life that is communicated from beyond them. This asymmetry is important: since either as poets or rhapsodes we are rings, we will always be in a position of *being recipient* of the gift of inspiration.

Socrates is quite clear about it: poets does not produce through *technē,* but by means of a kind of divine lot. Socrates, of course, is very much an admirer of *technē*. Does he not in the *Apology* seem to place higher than the poets the ordinary artisans who at least have a *technē* that they can teach to others, while the poets seem constitutively incapable of giving an account or explicit *logos* of what they have produced. This unease or discomfort with what cannot be more explicitly univocalized is present throughout the *Ion,* making commentators wonder to what extent Socrates is approving or disapproving in granting that the poets create through a divine lot rather than through *technē*. Socrates calls Ion a veritable Proteus in being able to assume every shape and so to elude Socrates' grasp (*Ion,* 541e8–10). I detect sarcasm, though not too harsh. Proteus puts one also in mind of the porosity of being: liquid metaxu through which erotic and manic energies stream. Overall, I think, the ambiguity of Socrates' attitude is persistent, which does not mean his affirmative admiration is feigned, nor his guarded diffidence unreal. Both sides are entirely appropriate, though our discernment of the appropriate cannot be given an entirely technical form. The judgment of *fittingness* requires a discernment more like *phronēsis* than like *theōria;* and an *intermediate sophia* that would include just that discernment of singular happenings that cannot be neutrally universalized in a univocal generality. (Remember the *phantastik* image as showing the fitting, as proportional to a viewer.) Indeed does not the Socratic art as midwifery (another image of assisting generation) indicate just that attention to the singular, and discernment of the signs indicative of fertility, conception, and impending birth? As discernment of the fitting with respect to the singular happening, midwifery is more an art than a technique, even though general guidelines need not be entirely eschewed.

As in the communication of contagion, as in the excitation of the derivative by the original, the muse charges the poet, the poet in and through the poem charges the rhapsode, the rhapsode—in this case Ion—charges the listeners: all are drawn beyond themselves, not just by their immanent eros but by their being caught up by a power beyond them, that comes down on them. Since the original power comes down on them, there is a *reversal* of the directionality of eros, even though the excitation is equally experienced as a being besides itself of the soul. Some might think that eros can be drawn more fully within our complete control, though this is an illusion. The calculative eros at the beginning of the *Phaedrus* addresses just this will to control—that is to say, its treason against the truer power of eros to take us beyond ourselves, the power of love to subvert even the most well-planned calculation of our own "rational" self-interest. "Treason" is perhaps a fitting word, for as Socrates says about his first feigning *logos* about calculative eros: Was it not all "foolish and blasphemous; and what could be more terrible than that?" *(Phaedrus,* 242). Socrates covers his head when making that first speech (his recantation is with head bare, 243b). There is only one other place where Socrates covers his head, and that is in the moments before he dies.

When Socrates delivers his second inspired speech about love as a divine madness, the sun stands at its height at midday. Shadowless noon may be the demonic hour when gods show themselves to mortals, but the moment of maximal light is also the moment of the happening of mysterious communication. How far we are now from the static spatialization of the between that can tempt a too univocal mimesis! How elusive the notion of inspiration is! From where does it come? (Nietzsche, great anti-Platonist, testified to his own inspiration in terms redolent of *theia mania.*) Having come, to where does it go? A poet or philosopher puts something down in words, and may suffer energies at work that he or she hesitates to attribute univocally to himself or herself alone. One might be deceived in this, as many the writer has discovered in the ashen light of the day after, when the visionary glow has gone. But you might also find this: you return to what you once did, and you are startled to have to ask: Did I do *that?* How could I do *that?* I could not do it now; that is, I could not simply decide here and now to *reproduce* something like *that.* Surprisingly, you are surprised that what is your own is not your own, and there seems something there that you cannot say how it got there. And yet there it is, and yes I did *that;* but no, I did not do that alone. But what then was that other power that companioned the energy that still continues to live on there in that?

Or consider the old idea that the poet has a muse who must be *wooed.* Wooing evokes the power of Mnemosyne, mother of the muses. Memory would require a study to itself, but it too is an essential mode of mindfulness in the between, involved in intricate affiliations with imagination, mimesis, eros and mania. One recalls the striking story—beautiful and poignant—in the *Phaedrus* about the singing cicadas. The cicadas once were men before the birth of the Muses, and when the Muses were born and music appeared some of the men were so ravished by delight that they sang and sang, forgetting food and drink, and they died. From them the cicadas arose, gifted by the Muses, and so overcome with the boon of music that they simply forgot to eat or drink. Such is the excess, such the madness, such the ecstasy: being sick with love. On death the cicadas go to the Muses and tell of men to them, tell also of those who pass their lives in philosophy, and for whom the thought and music of heaven is the sweetest.

What is it to woo? You cannot force the response of one you woo. You cannot demand it. There is a courtesy, and a coaxing perhaps; but the initiative does not entirely lie with the one wooing; the one wooed has to come into the middle space and come freely, and this cannot be dictated, though it can be called. What if the one wooed also calls us? Our wooing may be itself a being wooed. Certainly there is no method or *technē* by means of which the one wooed will be forced to show herself. Of course, one might seduce, in the sense of seeming to love; but would the showing then not be tainted by the treason to love? Love would have been instrumentalized, and in that fact bent from its freer truth as being given to us. Seduction would here be force by guile or wile; not free communication in the metaxu. The communicative power of truth would be distorted, indeed it would *be feigned:* it would look like a communication but in fact be closed to communication.

Some modern ideals of truth which suggest the image of juridical torture are at the opposite extreme of the wooing of truth (Bacon: putting nature on the rack; Kant: make her answer questions of our devising); though perhaps there are torturers who themselves have learned to use a counterfeit of wooing to loose the tongue of those they want to ensnare. Wooing intertwines mimesis, eros and mania. Wooing is a ritual of love, but as such it is a kind of erotic mimesis, and more, it is a kind of musical mimesis which is willing to wait patiently for the resonance of a co-responding from the beloved, from the ofttimes incognito muse. For often we do not know what we love, and we must wait to know, wait on the other. Wooing we are at the opposite extreme to any will to power with pretensions to complete control.

Wooing awaits in love and the sweet kiss that answers may inspire from the very roots up of our mortal *passio essendi.* Thus, for example, listening to the Cello Suites of Bach: the music is heard as a gift, passing through its composer, and played through its performers, from a source that is loved in its namelessness, once the music is heard. And if it is heard as a gift, our hearing is attendant to a wooing that is there in the music itself; for the gift performs the wooing itself, though the gift answers the wooing of the artist; and we hearers are in the midst of this wooing and gift, between our coursthip of the origin and the origin communicating beyond itself, in its courting of us. And it is not at all unlike the elemental porosity of a kind of praying.

If wooing is a kind of willing, or being willing, it is not will to power. It awaits something other being given. Think of the deliberate will to create a poem, according to what appears a reasonable formula. Surface appearances may indicate a well-wrought poem, but the result may well be so as a corpse is still well-wrought, though lifeless. One might say that calculative *technē* alone produces the counterfeit double of the original, not a true image or mimesis of the living original. The true mimesis lives with the life gifted of the living original. Beyond calculative control, we touch on the issue of the original as other. Socrates acknowledges this: philosophy cannot capture this, yet it needs it. Admittedly, one wonders if philosophy's need of mania is acknowledged a bit grudgingly by Socrates (after all he is said to be envious, jealous in the *Ion,* 530b–c). And yet there is something entirely fitting that the *Phaedrus* concludes with Socrates' *prayer* to Pan and the other gods of the place. Be that so, there is the justified diffidence which knows the *danger* of this "beyond" of mania: there is mad madness and divine madness, as we said, and we still need the discernment to see the difference. Socrates aside, I think we have to grant that Plato is not thus grudging, and perhaps just in his hint to us that there is sometimes grudging in the philosopher's respect for the poet and the rhapsode. He does not say this; he shows it.

One has to grant a kind of search for balance and measure in Plato, even when eros and mania cause the soul to be besides itself and communicate something of the extremes. There are rebukes to hubris. There is the restraint of the intelligibility of the *eidos;* the restraint of the Good; the restraint of the divine as a source superior to humans. While the danger of eros turranos is always granted, the modesty on the heights of eros uranos is also invoked. The ethos of the metaxu communicates intelligibility, beauty, worthiness, indeed a kind of piety called to reverence of transcendence as other to our self-transcendence. These are made problematic in modernity with the loss of what I call the agape of being. Eros risks becoming tyrannical, mutating without rebuke into will to power. Mania drives then towards its own (self-)divinization—but without the divine. Instead of wooing the presentiment of the agape of being in the between, we court the nihilism of the valueless whole. But, of course, we cannot live with that, so even those who take themselves to be within a valueless whole have to struggle against it. But to fight it is to lack what we seek most: the "yes" to the good of the "to be."

God is not jealous: this is the famous refrain of the *Timaeus,* here spoken with reference to the divine Demiurge, and echoed down the centuries by thinkers as diverse as Aquinas and Hegel. Not to be jealous: this is a mark of a true original. Jealousy, being envious, is a name for a grudging withholding of communication, communication of the good of being. God is not thus grudging. When we think of the divine, the image of *the great feast* comes to mind (*Phaedrus,* 247; 256b). That mania as enthusiasm happens means that the showing is given, the manifestness happens—even if it happens to be also that we as recipients, as its hearers or readers, as hermene, do not understand completely what has been shown or communicated. What kind of original would an absolutely nonenvious original be? What would be the communicative being of such an original? Do we then come, in the end, to a question at the limit of Platonic originals? For would not such an original have to be more than an erotic original? Would the divine madness it gives not make us wonder if it must be more like an agapeic origin?

Demiurgic Making and Origin beyond the Between

What of this suggestion of an agapeic origin? Here is a concluding remark. This suggestion points us towards a surplus source of origination that gives out of surplus, that gives for the good of the other originated, gives not for a return to itself, but to broadcast generously the good of the other-being that comes to be originated. I am not saying that Plato offers a notion of the agapeic origin, but some hints are suggested by his image of the Sun as the Good, in that the communication of its light is the giving of being, intelligibility, truth, and the good of becoming, to the things that have come to be in the interim of time. The Good seems to be an unoriginated original that yet is communicative of other-being as originated. Is the Good itself good? We love the Good but does the Good love us, or the beings that come to be? If the Good were an agapeic origin, would its being not be something like an unconstrained love of the "to be" that gives being beyond itself? Can one think this giving as original, radically originative? Is it possible to think this thought? Do we find the resources in Plato to address the issue of agapeic origination as a coming to be of being as good for itself? A radical coming to be from a surplus origin of goodness?

Certainly we find much that draws our attention to a divine festivity that cannot be described in terms of an economy of lack, nor in terms of forms of desire and transcendence that are driven dominantly by the sense of lacking. The double parentage of eros itself is suggestive, as are many other indications. How does the question look with respect to the theme of originals? We have seen more senses of Platonic originals than those named by the stability of the ideas, for energies of origination arises in us with eros, and are communicated to us with mania. Both these showings of original energy are dynamic and beyond final fixation in terms of form alone: the forming that gives form is in excess to form, even if it finds expression in form. But is there still here a tendency to think in terms of formations that do not full justice to the surplus good of agapeic origination? Let me make the point about Platonic originals with reference to demiurgic making.

The making act of the Demiurge is not a radical origination: the Demiurge works on what is other to it, already given, and works on it in the light of forms of intelligibility that guide the act of making as aesthetic design. The matter to be worked is taken as given; and the working on the matter is done with the forms taken as the intelligible paradigms of what is to be wrought in the given matter. The doublet of forming and matter is effective here. Demiurgic forming is bound by both the givenness of the matter and the forms as eternal standards: it is not an origination limited by nothing but its own giving. An agapeic giving would be more like a giving (as) giving; pure giving; not bound by something already given; for what is given is originated by this giving (as) giving.

There is more, of course, with the Demiurge. He is guided not only by the geometry of the ideas, but by the vision of the good, and by the love of the beautiful: the work of art to be wrought is the world as cosmos: a work of beauty, whose aesthetic harmony sings of the intelligible order of the ideas, but which brings forth energies that are not just geometrical, but communicate love of the good. The Demiurge makes the cosmos to be the best possible, the most beautiful, but also the most worthy: it is the good of the "to be" that is affirmed and sung in this aesthetic act of making. This aesthetics of world-making is also inseparable from an ontology of the good, in that the sensuous cosmos is the material incarnation of the affirmed good of the "to be." The Demiurge sings: this is good to be, and beautiful.

Perhaps it is in these latter registers that some hints of the agape of being are more to be found, more so than in the geometrical order imposed by the Demiurge on the matter. The cosmos arouses something of the appreciation, perhaps even reverence, we experience before great works of art, whose greatness humbles and exalts us at the same time. The aesthetic act as ontological is a religious praise. And so the cosmos, the *Timaeus* tells us, is an aesthetic god. And is there not also the crucial claim that the divine persuades necessity? There is something higher than necessity: the love of the good as the properly fitting, what accords with the good. Is this not love of the finite as finite? Why otherwise the desire to make the cosmos the most worthy and beautiful possible?

Heidegger is not entirely wrong to see the sense of origin as "production" present in the Western tradition, but he seems not to do justice here to this most essential point which is beyond geometry and *technē,* and having everything to do with the giving of the being there of the cosmos as good, and the religious praise and reverence for the worthy beauty of the gift wrought. I return to this matter in Heidegger. Demiurgic making does stress the imposition of form on matter, the kneading of a primal chaos into an intelligible cosmos. That granted, there is still the exceeding of these by the shine of the Good, for this shine is not a making, or a form, or a chaos, or an intelligible. It is in the dimension of the hyperbolic. It exceeds them all, even if it is what makes all of them worthy to be. And is not this power even hyperbolic to what is shown as hyperbolic through mimesis, eros, and mania?

2

The Terror of Genius and the Otherness of the Sublime

On Kant and the Transcendental Origin

Disturbances of the Middle and the Transcendental Origin

Kant is famous for claiming a Copernican revolution in philosophy by initiating what he calls a transcendental philosophy. "Transcendental" here means something other to what it means in premodern thought, namely, the utmost universals which are presupposed by all intelligible articulations of being, and which make those articulations possible. The premodern transcendentals are what one might call the hypercategorial universals, pre-eminent among which is "being," but including also "one," "truth," "good," and in some enumerations also "beauty." These "transcendentals" one might call ontological originals, in the sense that without them the truth, the intelligibility, the goodness, the very being of the "to be," could not be articulated. As is well known, "transcendental" philosophy for Kant signifies an investigation not of the objects of knowing, but of the knowing activity itself, and by implication also of the relation between that activity and the known object. Heidegger might claim that Kant's transcendental philosophy is preparatory for something like a new fundamental ontology closer to Heidegger's own sense, but he has to strain Kant to make this point. There is a touching innocence on Kant's part when it comes to some of the more disturbing ontological and metaphysical perplexities with respect to origins, otherness, the between.

Kant implied that one could understand another philosopher better than he understood himself, specifically understand Plato better than Plato understood himself. This general hermeneutical principle is perhaps applicable to philosophers of the second rank and lower; but it is dubious, not to say fatuous, with respect to Plato, of all thinkers, the enigmatic, masked philosopher par excellence. Kant was himself often a masked and tortured thinker, whose deeper intent was not at all immediately evident. Did Kant sometimes draw back from directly uttering the heart of some of his philosophical views, and not in the sense meant by Heidegger? It may seem a strange coupling, but I often think of Kierkegaard's indirect communication (Plato, like Socrates was a master of indirect communication) when considering the very form in which the Kantian project is articulated. Is the real truth, one wonders, perhaps elsewhere, perhaps other to what seems to be said overtly? There is a striking and perhaps just irony that Kant's own successors saw themselves as understanding Kant better than he understood himself: the generation of idealists for one, Schopenhauer for another, all claiming his heritage and mantle, though there was much in all these that would have made Kant recoil. As he said himself with regard to Fichte: save us from our friends, our enemies we can take care of ourselves! Did Kant here have to contemplate the *nemesis* of his own hermeneutic principle?

I find something equivocal, at the outset, in his claim to inaugurate a *Copernican* revolution. Copernicus is celebrated for proposing we make the *sun* the point of reference in our calculations. Heliocentrism turns us away from fixation with earth, and our earth-bound standpoint as the center of reference. In what way is Kant "heliocentric"? Surely it is Plato who is "heliocentric": all being, intelligibility, becoming and truth are ultimately defined with reference to the Good, imaged in the imaginative universal, the Sun. The Kantian sun is not *that* "Sun." Far from it, his turn from known objects to knowing subjects, from an ontology of other-being to an epistemology of self-being, is anti-Copernican. The shock of heliocentrism is the dislocation of a *heterocentrism*. Kant sought to *restore stability* after the shock. His so-called Copernican revolution offers oddly equivocal stability, for it seems *autocentric* through and through. At the center of this autocentrism we find Kant's will to unconditional autonomy. And restoration of stability via *that* will lead to a descendence that is, and descendants who were, more radically destabilizing. Pure reason does not leave behind so easily its own underground.

This too has repercussion for a Kantian understanding of origins, otherness, and art. This interests me. Make no mistake about it, there is still a *sun* in Kant, and it is not a Platonic original, nor for that matter the creating God that is communicated through the monotheistic religions. It is the very same self that is the condition of the possibility of knowing, now named with an appellation from which, for some, sparks of ultimacy seem to fly: the transcendental subject. That subject raises questions for us about what looks like a radical autocentrism: radical in the sense that what looks like an ultimate center is a radix, a root, an originating source from which is generated the diverse, determinate intelligibilities that occupy us, say, in mathematics and the natural sciences. If this transcendental root is a condition of the possibility of determinate intelligibilities, such as we find in the particular sciences or mathematics, or indeed of the possibility of morality, then as center, this condition of possibility also seems unconditional. It seems autonomous: as original, what is other may derive being or significance from it; but it does not derive from them, but rather, it seems, originates from its own immanent resources of self-activity.

There are large issues here, but here are one or two remarks on the ethos of Kant's thought, as this has bearing on the theme of origins, art, otherness. What of the between as ethos of being? This in Kant in not like the (Platonic) metaxu. It continues the line of reconfiguration in which objects are over against subjects, such as we find from early modernity onwards with thinkers like Descartes. The dualistic latencies in a certain interpretation of mimesis spatialize the middle in such a way that it is reconfigured as, on the one hand, an aggregate of objects that are merely there, and, on the other hand, discrete subjects that have to work to reimpose some intelligibility, indeed value, on this mere thereness of externality. Relative to nature as other to us, as the environment of other-being, we are not participants in it quite. It has rather been subjected to a mathēsis much more radically univocalizing of the ethos than can be found in premodern thought. The mathēsis of the natural middle yields a given thereness that is stripped of inherent value: there, just there, without origin, or end, it seems, sheer neutral ongoingness without finality and originality.

If we find ourselves in it, we find ourselves as over against it, and are tempted to *elevate ourselves* as over above it. And all this perhaps to defend ourselves against what seem to be an ontological thereness, in itself lacking in inherent intelligibilities, lacking that is, till we impose our sense of intelligibility on it. Other-being must lose all claims of originality in that situation; and we must be the origins. A mathēsis of the middle becomes, so to say, a rampant geometry of being in which the will to univocalize all equivocal thereness asserts itself. Such a mathēsis of the middle makes impossible the more finessed mimetic relation to originals as other, such as can be found in a properly understood Platonism. For why imitate *that* valueless, stripped down thereness of other-being? Indeed that valueless otherness finds its metaphorical expression in nature as *machine*. If nature is a machine, why imitate that? Any imitation would itself be mechanical; it could not be the original mimesis that is possible if nature, as other-being, were a different kind of originating matrix. In such a context of the univocal fixation of nature as machine, the fertile possibilities of mimesis must themselves be lost, and imitation be reduced to a univocal one-to-one copying or representation of an otherness already fully determined in its own absolute univocity.

In such a scheme there is no room for freedom, nor any proper human originality, and hence no moral distinctiveness either. If we see Kant's turn to the transcendental self as original as thus situated in such a univocal mathēsis of the middle, we can also see more clearly what is at stake in his efforts to retrench intrinsic value in moral autonomy, and his own praise of the human as an end in self, the only one in nature we know. What then of art and originals? Light can be shed on this too. But remember these crucial points: nature as machine signals a diminution in the sense of other-being as itself an *aesthetic metaxu;* and yet something of this aesthetic metaxu is inescapable for us, since our own elemental being given to be is always within this aesthetic milieu of being. Kant no more than any other human being can finally evade this, and so we find, I believe, a resurgence of an *equivocal hesitation* with respect to the other-being, a hesitation most evident when we consider his aesthetic doctrine. The sense of nature here cannot be reduced to the univocal mathēsis of mechanism or valueless thereness. What of this other sense of nature? Is there a sense of nature as original, in a sense going beyond mechanism? These question bear on the sublime, as also on the genius, as putatively the favored of nature.[1] A machine is nothing sublime, though it be monstrously gross. And a machine cannot *favor* anything or anyone, and even less *grace* them with the sublime powers with which some great artists are gifted. In a word: *other-being as original must come back to haunt us, even in the extremities of the univocal mathēsis of nature.*

There is *more* when we consider the turn to self. A similar haunting by original being as other occurs, but now in the *ontological intimacy of immanent selving itself.* I said the turn to transcendental origins is a certain turn to self, indeed the self even might make claim *to be the middle.* After all, if it is the center as radix, it is not just one side merely of the relation between itself and what is other. Quite to the contrary, it seems to be the active power that determines from itself qua center the form of the middle between itself and what seems other. It is the active power to mediate the difference between itself and what is other. We will later see Hegel developing this point and claiming this center as a dialectically self-mediating origin. But we can see how this turn to self seems consistent with claims made for humans to be determining of what is other, and thus so, because finally they are the *power to be self-determining.*

This is one of the implicit sources of the historical influence of Kantianism: its appeal to this latent sense of human self-understanding which feels itself as free, and hence in some manner as original of itself. In an ontological milieu of a devalued ethos of other-being, such as the mechanization of nature, it is not surprising that this should rise to the surface more insistently, sometimes defensively against the devalued ethos, sometimes offensively as more radically self-assertive, despite this environing valueless ethos. My point is not to deny this freedom or originality, but to underscore the problem of how we are to understand it, and how inseparable this understanding is from an appreciation of the milieu of being, of our intermediate condition of being. Over against the devalued otherness we might think *our* intermediate being is to be radically mediat-

---

1. Concern with teleology and nature in the second part of *The Critique of Judgment* is, of course, very important. I confine myself more directly to the theme of art, otherness, origins. It is very evident in the second part of *The Critique of Judgment* how all directions in nature lead to the human being as the only end in self in nature, an end chiming in perfectly for Kant with his moral doctrine. In the text I will refer to *CJ,* in the Meredith English translation, plus the paragraph numbers.

ing of this otherness, and hence to refigure it in terms of our mediations, and this finally with the aim, now recessive, now defensive, now assertive, now excessive, of determining ourselves as self-mediating, or mediating ourselves to ourselves as self-determining. The high purpose again seems a radical autonomy, in which the human is master of itself and its own original powers.

Here's the rub. We are visited with disturbance, just in connection with the otherness of the origin that great art seems to reveal. Our powers of self-mediation, or self-determination, claiming originality, seem haunted by an elusive, often overwhelming power of origination that does not seem to belong to us univocally. In the very heart of self-determination a *strange immanent otherness* seems to arise again and again. We univocalize nature, and something more equivocally other still haunts us. We determine ourselves, and seem to be at one with ourselves, and yet something other, in the most radical *intimacy of being creative,* disturbs our being at one with ourselves. Our self-mastery seems to emerge from a deeper origin we do not master but that itself make self possible, possible as this original self. This, I believe, is the issue touched on in Kant's treatment of genius, touched on, but also run from. And yet there is no place to where we can flee. If we flee to nature as other, we encounter the sublime; if we flee to ourselves, we bring with us the immanent otherness we try to flee. In the immanent origination claimed by genius, an *other sense of origin* breaks up the pretension to complete self-mediation and self-determination. This breaking up brings terror, but the terror has ontological importance as opening what Kant, and indeed the transcendental ego, could not conquer. What is reappearing is not unrelated to the *eros* and *mania* that we found unavoidable in our discussion of Platonic originals, and that come back to disturb us, even when the milieu of nature has been mathematicized, even when we seem to leave behind us a mimesis contracted by our univocalizing of being, and stake our claim to a more radical originality. Genius is also bound up with the question of the *daimon,* and our being between. Let us look more closely.

Kant between Enlightenment and Romanticism

Kant's *Critique of Judgment* exercised an important, if perhaps improbable influence on the Romantic movement, with its sanctification of originality, its apotheosis of the creative artist, its repudiation of the cold, lifeless abstractions of the scientific Enlightenment. Kant's work itself gives all the appearances of a scholastic treatise; there seems to be nothing Romantic about it at all. Indeed we know that Kant was unfriendly to the *Sturm und Drang* movement and what passed as Romanticism. His work is organized in a purportedly architectonic way; it seems intended to complete a system of philosophy whose center, many commentators think, is not in art or the aesthetic, but in morality, with its strict call of duty for duty's sake. Moreover, the aesthetic sense of its writer seems somewhat restricted in its range, with a definite penchant for the formality of abstract design. In a word, it carries many of the characteristics of eighteenth century Enlightenment.

A certain ideal of rational intelligibility is paramount, as is reflected in the work itself. The younger Kant had felt that the aesthetic could not be made into a science or subjected to a rigorously systematic rendition. The adage says: *De gustibus non est disputandum,* and the earlier Kant concurred, seeing nothing in the aesthetic that might raise it to the level of scientific universality. He came to believe otherwise: one could have a critique of taste, though not a science. A certain type of universality might characterize the aesthetic, not certainly the rational necessity characteristic of physical science expressed in Newtonian mechanics, but a kind of necessity nevertheless. Why then did the Romantics take wing on reading this ostensible exemplar of Enlightenment thinking? A full answer would have to include Kant's desire to go beyond the dualisms of his earlier writings, and to present what might be called a more holistic vision of things. But some of Kant's utterances about genius fell on ears ready to hear them, and to hear them with ears *differently attuned* than Kant himself. They heard some of their own inarticulate longings in what Kant said, and so he appeared as a liberator that, like Moses, brought them out of the land of bondage, where cold mechanism and soul-less reason held the human heart in thrall.

They heard something unequivocal in Kant's remarks about genius that answered their felt need for liberation from the mechanistic view of nature, self, society, indeed God. But what Kant himself said about genius is much more *equivocal.* The glorious liberation of human creativity was heard by many of the Romantics, a liberation that might restore wholeness beyond mechanism, in self, nature and society. Kant is much less sanguine. There is what I will call a certain terror about genius. This I will more fully elaborate, but I now merely state that for Kant the genius always harbored the danger of *transgression:* the genius often initiates a break with precedent norms and standards; and indeed, the genius may be exemplary in giving the rule to art, but just in this, there may be something about the genius that is *beyond* rules.

This possible transgression and transcendence to complete rule-bound determination seems to me to have struck a certain trepidation into Kant's rational mind. For the Romantics it is just this transcendence and transgressive originality that augured a proper release and fulfillment of human freedom. I put it thus: Kant's remarks on genius implicitly contain everything that the Romantic artist desired; but what the Romantic artist required, Kant did not want to endorse unequivocally; to the contrary, just what they willed, he feared; and hence Kant tries to hedge the potential unruliness of genius with renewed Enlightenment strictures.[2]

---

2. When Kant says that genius is the favorite of nature we might pass on, since the phrase is a commonplace; we will not make too much of it. What concerns us here is that Kant is quite

This equivocal attitude to genius can be stated in terms of a related equivocation that has significance beyond Kant. This is the second equivocation: In one strand of Kant's thinking, it is the *self* who gives the rule to nature; in another strand, however, it is *nature* that gives a rule to art through the self of genius. In one strand, nature is passive to us; in the other, we are passive to nature. How can nature be both: Given the law and yet law-giver? How can the self be both: Giver of the law, and agent of the law-giver as other? If we give the rule to nature, how then can nature out of itself give rules to us? Are we just giving rules to ourselves, and so simply using nature to relate just to *ourselves?* Or is it the opposite: Is it nature that is using us all the time, all the time we confidently think of ourselves as supremely autonomous? It seems to me that we in late modernity have become uncertain how to answer. We would think of ourselves as autonomous to nature; yet we are nagged by the suspicion that such autonomy is empty, and that a more encompassing process, over which we have no control, has the last word.

The terror of genius is again relevant. With genius the curtain seems to be drawn back briefly, to reveal, just in our seeming creative sovereignty, the pretentiousness involved in any such claim to mastery. Something other to the mastering self seems to laugh at the illusion of such claims to creative autonomy. These are not things Kant says. Yet, I think, Kant drew the curtain back a little, but he quickly closed it again. In that respect, he was *between* Enlightenment and Romanticism. But he named what he saw, albeit ambiguously, and that naming was enough to encourage others to draw the curtain back more violently. Enlightenment is driven to draw back the curtain. But when it draws back the curtain on the self, the risk is that its rationalistic idols will stand revealed as straw dogs.

We might say that Romanticism is the truth of Enlightenment relative to the self: it sees that the self cannot be rationalized in the same way as a supposedly mechanistic nature. Inevitably, the question will arise as to whether the self can be rationalized *at all?* Romanticism may be the truth of Enlightenment, but there may be a *darkness* in this truth that serves to show that Enlightenment is untrue. Kant might be seen to oscillate cautiously between these two, though his successors are far less inhibited in letting loose the seemingly darker truth of Romanticism. We are the heirs of Kant in that

---

disparaging of the excess of genius. John Zammito's helpful *The Genesis of Kant's Critique of Judgment* (Chicago: Chicago University Press, 1992), 137–42, sees the discussion of genius as ironical. Yes and no. Kant is more sharply sarcastic in places, but that is not all. The commonplace phrase has important repercussions. While there is a side to his discussion attacking some of his "Romantic" contemporaries—Herder has been suggested in particular—there is more at play in his views. This "more" embroils him in some dilemmas from which he would escape and for which he would severely chastise others. That despite his hostility to the movement of *Sturm und Drang,* he yet influenced artists like Goethe and Schiller and others in the Romantic movement, indicates something of this enmeshment, or involuntary promiscuity with his others.

regard: we oscillate between these two, often bewildered as to how to escape, now driven to one extreme, now back to the other.

The matter has to do with the ultimate privilege we give to human originality, and with the relation between nature and that originality. Where is the stress to fall: On human originality as something essentially other to nature? Or primarily on nature as itself the origin of humanity, and hence the origin of human originality? Is human originality completely within the mastery of the human being, or does human originality reveal its source to be in something other to the human, and so as always beyond complete capture? Or must we find *other* terms again, that is, think the ultimate origin differently, in order to deal adequately with the perplexing equivocations of creative freedom? Must we rethink the original ethos of being as a metaxu?

TRANSCENDENTAL EQUIVOCATION, MIDDLE ORIGINATION

Let me further develop the equivocation. We must first take seriously the transcendental character of Kant's *entire* critical project. As suggested above, we must especially bear in mind the priority granted to self in mediating the relation and interplay between self and other: as an active source of intelligibility the self has undoubted primacy in shaping that relation and interplay, in terms of the complex transcendental "machinery" outlined in the *Critique of Pure Reason*. This, of course, determines how we think of nature, and most importantly, of nature as *other* to the self.

In Kant's writings nature is defined in a way some have considered revolutionary, the so-called Copernican Revolution. Traditionally, it was held that there were a set of more or less ready-made objects, already out there, awaiting in full determinacy the approach of the knower. The knower conforms to the pregiven determinations of nature as being-other. Consider mimesis here as susceptible to an interpretation of the knower as (pre-)determined in terms of a univocal representationalism. There was the complexity that in post-Cartesian epistemology mind and nature were defined as essentially opposite substances: neither could be reduced to the other; only mind could interact with mind, only matter with matter. How then was knowledge of nature possible? Various answers were proposed, though, in the main, a representational model of mind tended to prevail. Our ideas, which were "in here" and of the mind, somehow represented, imitated the reality that was "out there," material and other. The great difficulty was in articulating the conjunctions of these two. The mental representation served to mediate mind's access to being-other. Moreover, being-other was defined in terms of the essentially mechanistic nature that classical Newtonian physics had formulated. Kant agreed that modern science revealed a world that answered to Newtonian physics, but he tried to alter the terms of answering how our representations related to this being-other. Very simply, the intelligible order we come across is not a pregiven determinacy; it is rather the outcome of a process of determination that the mind itself performs. Nature as being-other is determinately intelligible because we have determined it to be intelligible. The knowing self is an origin of intelligibility. The latter is not pregiven to knowing, but imposed on what otherwise is lacking in order and structure. *This* Copernican Revolution is questionably Copernican, since there is nothing essentially anthropocentric about Copernicus's Copernican turn.

What is important for our theme is that nature is essentially defined in its intelligible order because *we* have *imposed* such an order on it. As far as we can say legitimately, nature in itself is unknown. Yet if our determination of its intelligibility is the only truth we have, nature seems to have no inherent intelligibility of its own, before we go to work on it, as if it were a kind of ontological magma. Thus Kant will say: the order in the appearances we entitle nature could not be so, did not we ourselves, or the nature of our mind, not already introduce them there. We could say: mind gives the rule to nature.

A plethora of citation on this score could be adduced from the *Critique of Pure Reason*.[3] The problem emerges when we place side by side with this certain suggestions made in the *Critique of Judgment*. Remember that this work falls within the architectonic of a transcendental philosophy, with all that this implies about the synthetic, mediating power of active selfhood. It is quite clear that Kant's determination of the judgment of aesthetic taste is consistently thought in terms of the subject: namely, the discovery of a transcendental a priori relative to the delight in the beautiful, which we can impute universally, not in relation to an object as beautiful, but in relation to the responding subject.

Suppose we now take a second approach, this time with respect to Kant's acquiescence in the view that *through genius nature gives the rule to art*. But first it may help us we recall some important points about genius. In modernity genius has progressively come to be seen as the epitome of creativity and originality. In premodern views the human being was a mimesis of what was other to itself. Man, say, as *imago Dei* might mirrored the divine life, but was not viewed as genuinely creative in its own right; only God was creative in a radically originative way. Aquinas emphatically says that creation belongs to God alone. Not so with the modern conception of genius: the great artist takes to himself many of the attributes formerly reserved to deity. He is someone *sui generis,* not defined through another, marked by extraordinary power, both in making and in vision, a superabundance of overflowing energy that irresistibly finds its mark, perhaps even having a status beyond the law, beyond good and

3. A representative citation from the *Critique of Pure Reason,* B xiii: Reason "must not allow itself to be kept in nature's leading strings, but must itself show the way with principles based upon fixed laws, constraining nature to give answers to questions of reason's own determining." This way "the study of nature has entered on the secure path of science," B xiv.

evil, as Nietzsche would have it. Kant's account of the knowing subject already has traces of this apotheosis of self-activity: the knower imposes form on the formless, determines the intelligibility of being-other, is dynamic activity, not passive representation or imitation.

Genius seems to give the rule to nature, in being nature's exemplary manifestation. But this is not enough. Genius seems to depart from any ideal of decorous moderation: genius seems to be the epitome of creative transcendence in human existence. Marking that transcendence, there is something over and above, something excessive. The transcendent other may be put in clouds, or indeed placed on ice by the Enlightenment, but the need and exigence of transcendence does not vanish. Quite to the contrary, the genius becomes an image of transcendence as immanent, as actually coming to manifestness in human existence. It seems we do not have to look to a "beyond" for a sense of the transcendent: genius brings the "beyond" into the here and now. Here we might have creative transcendence incarnate.

Kant does not use this language, yet his more staid scholastic language should not shield us from some of the implications at stake. His contemporary readers immediately saw something revolutionary in his elevating of the knower's self-activity into the primary determinant of nature's intelligibility. This promised something of the hope of autonomy: the human being, no longer supine before nature, beyond it as free, and free clearly in its putative power to determine the intelligibility of other-being. It is no surprise that the Romantics could be enthusiasts of a writer, ostensibly so severely unromantic. The apotheosis of the self undercuts all surface appearances.

Of course, this apotheosis is not the end of the matter, and here the ambiguity of genius appears. This self can be elevated to a higher status, not simply in virtue of its human-all-too-human being, but in virtue of something excessive coming to manifestation in it. Genius suggested the revelation in the human being of something other than the human, something perhaps greater and more fundamental, more originary and more ultimate. This is where we find the suggestion of another meaning of nature in Kant, as when he defines genius as he *through* whom nature gives the rule to art. Nature here cannot be Newtonian mechanism. How could it be? How could such a machine give rise to creative transcendence? There must be another more original meaning to nature. Certainly that was how the matter was seen by Kant's own Romantic contemporaries.

In the earlier picture of nature in the *Critique of Pure Reason,* the self gives the rule to nature. Now, in a reversal, it seems that nature is giving the rule, and through the genius. This is all the more interesting in that we would expect genius to be the *most forceful rule-giver,* as the most creative, energetic and elemental power. Yet Kant does not quite say this. What he says implies that *something other* is working through genius. This other is called "nature." But how can this other nature compare with the first sense of nature considered above, namely, nature in itself as lacking proper intelligibility until we impose form on it. This latter nature lacks the inherent original power to impose form on itself, must less to determine a rule and give it to art through the genius. Kant's transcendental view of nature, in the first instance, makes it passive to the active subject; it has no inherent original power to determine itself through itself. Then the second view of nature, suggested by genius, is significantly other: nature seems originative, a source of giving that *in itself* is an author of order, moreover, an order that creatively transcends the mathēsis of lifeless mechanism.

This is the equivocation, then, rather a double equivocation. First, the equivocation of genius: the self as self-activity; the self as something of a gift, patient to the gift of nature. Second, the equivocation of nature: nature as passive to the self; nature as (actively?) giving the rule to art.[4]

What follows from this? What follows is the complete *destabilizing* of Kant's so-called Copernican revolution. We set out to construct a new philosophy in which the intelligibility of being-other is to be defined as a subordinate function of the self's active making of intelligibility. To effect this goal, nature has to be degraded. But in elevating the self into primacy we eventually move in the direction of genius as exemplifying everything supposedly creative about the self. The revolution seems to be complete in this sanctification of genius. But lo and behold, what then happens looks a complete reversal of the first beginning. For the genius to be genius it must reveal a sense of *original being-other* to the human. For the genius to be the manifestation of transcendence, he must be given the power of transcendence by something other to himself. Nature in the latter sense breaks free of complete determination by the self. There is something in excess, in excess even of the excess of the creative genius.

---

4. With respect to nature there may be inconsistencies between the *Critique of Pure Reason* and the *Critique of Judgment*. As not a few commentators have wondered, in the latter Kant seems to speak in a manner not entirely in accord with the critical strictures of the former. This may perhaps be inevitable if the *Critique of Judgment* serves to mediate the troubling dualisms that remain after the *Critique of Pure Reason* and the *Critique of Practical Reason*. Yet Kant does insist on the *transcendental standpoint* in the *Critique of Judgment*, and hence implies the deep inner, if not surface, coherence of the entire project. Kant was not the kind of thinker who could tolerate the dissonance of even the mildest self-inconsistency. He would not have his project be otherwise, given too his various hymns to the spirit of thoroughness. With respect to his architectonic ambitions, clearly evident in the first introduction to the *Critique of Judgment*, he would have held most surely this spirit of thoroughness to be at work, both in the *Critique of Judgment* and *between* the third and the previous two critiques. I am not interested in nit-picking with respect to inconsistency, such as might stem from an incidental slip. I am interested in an inherent instability that one senses in Kant. One's concern for this is magnified, given the history of readings of Kant that are offered by both his idealistic (e.g., Schelling and Hegel) and anti-idealistic successors (e.g., Schopenhauer, and with qualification perhaps the later Schelling). The entire matter concerns the precise metaphysical place of nature, nature conceived other than mechanistically and in relation to creative art, and all this in light of Kant's putatively radical turn to the active and synthesizing self of transcendental philosophy.

I am not saying that Kant will accept this line of argumentation. Not at all. Quite to the contrary, he would want to domesticate every such manifestation of excess. And yet one can claim that a consistent unfolding of the primacy of self-activity, such as Kant as transcendental philosopher recommends, leads just to this outcome. Such an outcome, however, leads to the undermining of the form of transcendental philosophy, such as Kant recommends.

The Terror of Genius

Why speak of the *terror* of genius? What is this terror? The terror of genius must be situated in relation to a certain expectation of intelligibility that was so strong in the Enlightenment. Some of the relevant considerations are these.

First, there was a certain tension, often extending to unrelenting conflict, between the claims of scientific reason and those of religion. Claims made by religion about transcendence are particularly important, since if they are taken seriously, there may be a sense of divine otherness which ruptures the self-sufficient circle of rational autonomy. Kant's vehement contempt for any suggestion of *submission* to God is indicative of his Enlightenment prejudice: he pours vitriol on this as "cringing and abject grace-begging" (for instance, in the analytic of the sublime, *CJ*, 126). In *Metaphysical Principles of Virtue* in the section "Concerning Servility," Kant says:[5] "Kneeling down or grovelling on the ground, even to express your reverence for heavenly things, is contrary to human dignity." The self-assertion of scientific reason as autonomous is coupled with resistance to claims of otherness and transcendence that must call into question such autonomy.

Second, coupled with the claimed autonomy of reason, there was the expectation of progress. The expectation was: If the intelligibility is now not there, it *will come to be, or be brought to be* through a progressive dynamic. There is a *task* set here for the progressive rationalization of all being. Kant's own remarks on the progressive nature of science, as opposed to the works of genius from which we can expect no further progress, Newton versus Homer, indicate his clear judgment that science is superior.

Third, there is the crucial social character of all this, most especially evident in the rational cultivation of humans away from a prior condition of barbarity: perfection of social cultivation is always future, and in the process of being progressively perfected; hence what is past carries inevitable stains of regressiveness, the dark origins of a more primitive heritage. Kant's own cultivation of himself as a cosmopolitan thinker, even though he never left Königsberg, Kant's own submission to what he calls the discipline of taste, is indicative.

---

5. English translation of *Metaphysical Principles of Virtue* is to be found in *Kant's Ethical Philosophy*, trans. James W. Ellington (Indianpolis: Hackett, 1983), 99.

Kant was heir to all of these considerations, though obviously he has complexly qualified views of each. The terror of genius surfaces relative to the emergence of some power that does *not fit* into this way of thinking. As I have indicated, genius was viewed as the exemplar of human creativity, and one might be inclined to see this as entirely consonant with the implied apotheosis of human autonomy, suggested by the above considerations. And yet, genius seems to erupt into the self-sufficient circle of self-defining autonomy, as a kind of emissary of something *other*. Not surprisingly, genius was often invested with a quasi-religious significance, as if the genius were the given incarnation of a creative transcendence whose ultimate source was other.

One thinks of Schelling's view of art and genius as revelatory of the absolute, and with respect to the very task of philosophy. One thinks of Nietzsche's transsubstantiation of genius into the *Übermensch*—he who *will be*, or *wills to be*, the exemplar of creative transcendence in a world deprived of divine transcendence. Moreover, this emissary and eruption is not at all *progressive*. The emergence of genius is beyond our control; it is episodic, hence unpredictable. There is not a progressive movement from one genius to another, with the successor more a genius than the predecessor. Kant recognized this, and comparing it to scientific development, judged it inferior, precisely because he thinks the limit had been already reached with genius, whereas the potential progress of science still harbored possibly unlimited advance.

Of course, it may be entirely misleading to define genius relative to progress, whether social, scientific, or whatever. The episodic, unpredictable nature of its eruption may be just its most important message, namely, that progressive, activist autonomy breeds a basic distortion when it is absolutized. The eruption of the episodic may be the smashing of this idol. In that smashing, an uncomfortable sense of what is other to rational autonomy may be intimated, forcing us to rethink what is other to all our Enlightenment mediations.

With respect to sociality, there is an undoubted disruptive aspect to genius, and this because the rules come *after*. The genius is said to give a rule, but if so, genius is originally beyond rule. The giver of the rule is not itself a rule. And hence there is something that escapes encapsulation—a creative freedom that is beyond the law, potentially lawless and therefore a potential scandal to the norms of civic cultivation, the canons of received taste. Kant sensed this dark side of genius. From it he also recoiled.

In so far as Kant was *between* Enlightenment and Romanticism, one understands his recoil, especially since Enlightenment intelligibility deems it necessary to place a constraint on the excesses to which Romanticism seemed prone. Yet in offering a philosophy of autonomy, whether moral or aesthetic, Kant is implicated in equivocations he never escapes. His successors who insist on the autonomy of the aesthetic in a way that exploits, in a non-Kantian way, the ambiguities of Kant's description of genius, do not escape either.

Aesthetic modernity is caught and twisted in something like the following dilemma: It wants to affirm the freedom of creative origination; it wants to do this to an extreme which rejects any interference from anything other to creative freedom itself; but in affirming this freedom, it inevitably comes to see that the very power of creative origination has something about it that is not in the complete self-mastery of the creative self; something other and over and above appears, and yet at the same times escapes beyond control. We begin by asserting our creative superiority, and end by wondering if we are the plaything of powers outside our control. We stand above nature, and end up as enigmatic productions thrown into being by a nature, now more enigmatic than ever before, and even filling us with a darker unease about something more sinister underground.

I do not think the dilemma is a historical curiosity, for we still live between Enlightenment and Romanticism. The first is taken up by scientific and technological development. The second takes the form of the cultivation of the expressive self—all pervasive in aesthetic modernity—in richer and more vulgar forms. Sometimes, we find a *war* between these two, when the second reacts to the spiritual emptiness of the first, or the first denounces the potential for soft emotional mush of the second. At times, there can be an *oscillation* between these two, in which Enlightenment and Romanticism play back and forth less antagonistically. At other times, there can be an *interpenetration* of the two, especially where technology serves self-expression. In sum, the tension emergent in Kant's time is still with us, though since him we have seen a variety of possible relations between the two, including efforts to define that very "between." The immediately succeeding generation to Kant addressed itself courageously to some of the major dilemmas constituted by this "between." The problem is not at all confined to the nineteenth century, and is still with us as we enter, in a supposedly postmodern mood, the beginning of the twenty-first. In good part, what names itself as the postmodern only rebaptizes the dilemma.

We deal with an unstable mixture of elements which allow a plurality of combinations. I stress a major one relevant to the present theme. This is it: Kant's transcendental philosophy opens up subjectivity as an entire world unto itself; but the world thus opened up proves to have reserves, indeed excesses that Kant did not suspect, or where he did, he was very wary. This is very evident with genius: there is an excess to subjectivity itself, or an excess emerging in subjectivity itself. Schopenhauer, and indeed Nietzsche will make much of this. This excess is intimately tied up with the self's power of transcendental origination: source of differentiation, source of synthesis, source of construction, but also source of deconstruction, indeed destruction.

This excess of subjectivity can easily become, and often did, an excessive subjectivity. The formalism of Kantian beauty proved no match for this excess emergent in inwardness itself. The beautiful in its pleasing formality failed to provide an adequate "objective correlative" to what may emerge in this inward otherness. The inward otherness surpasses the form of the beautiful object, because there is about it a kind of creative formlessness. And given the shift to active selving in transcendental philosophy, it is this creative indeterminacy that asserts itself as the primary determiner of the relation of self to an external other. Nothing other in externality, beautiful though it may be, will answer to the excessive indeterminacy emergent in selfhood itself.

As the full consequences of this are unfolded, there will be an *eclipse of the beautiful,* for the surge of self-transcending passes beyond itself, and ceases to find itself at home in the beautiful object. There is a certain infinite restlessness in selving, and the finite whole of formal beauty cannot contain this surge of its surpassing movement. The equivocal position of the beautiful in modern art follows. "Equivocal" is perhaps too mild a word, for at times we find the very destruction of just those ideals of beauty dear to Kant's heart: deformation of harmony, exultation in dissonance and the ugly, even the deliberate cultivation of the emotion that for Kant is alone absolutely taboo, namely, disgust (*CJ,* §48, 173–74). The freedom of the artist runs to an extreme, and the extreme here is the identification of its creativity with the *revolt against or destruction of the beautiful.*[6] One wonders what Kant would make of the ironical gesture of Piero Manzoni who a few years before his death in 1963 canned 90 samples of his own excrement and called these works "Merda d'Artista." Cans, I mean works, have been bought for impressive sums by the Museum of Modern Art in New York, the Pompidou in Paris, and the Tate Gallery in London. Also ironically, and due, it seems, to a fault in the design, since their first creation about half of the works, I mean cans, have exploded. Kant, one does not doubt, would have been horrified, but read in a certain way, are the seeds of the excess already dropped in his writings?

What of First Originals?

The terror of genius is related to what might be called the question of *first originals.* Let me elaborate in relation to genius and taste. Kant states that the comportment of genius is not *imitation* (*CJ,* §47, 169). He stresses originality; there is to be no aping; the products of genius are to be exemplary (see *CJ,* §49, 181–82). Inevitably one thinks of the distinction between reproductive and productive imagination. Reproductive imagination might be correlated with "imitation," while productive imagination might be linked with

6. See *AA,* chapter 6; also *PO,* chapter 2. In his recent Carus Lectures, delivered at the American Philosophical Association, December, 2001, Arthur Danto spoke of the revolt against beauty in contemporary art, as well as the cultivation of the revolting and the disgusting. He tells of a person's reaction to maggots breeding in dead flesh which was to exclaim "How beautiful!" This was exactly the reaction that was *not* wanted, since the point was not to show maggots or dead flesh as beautiful but rather, it seems, to *play with our revulsion.* Of course, if we are excited too much with outrage or satiated with disgust, soon it all becomes just passé. What would Kant make of *art cannibal* (Flaubert), or vagina monologues?

"creativity." Certainly some such a contrast is widespread in Kant's Romantic successors, and is deeply ingrained in the self-understanding of contemporary aesthetic culture.

We could see in Kant the *return* of a certain kind of mimesis with respect to the discipline of taste. We have to learn from the precedence of great exemplars. Even genius must be educated by looking in their direction if it is to have a cultivated taste, or its production are to be polished and rubbed free of the traces of the barbaric. Mimesis of the exemplars will provide guidance, form, stability, and a freedom from mere idiosyncrasy. Kant will speak of following a model, not imitating, but, suitably qualified, "following" can be understood as a kind of mimesis, at least in a sense closer to the more nuanced view discussed in the last chapter.

Kant wants to subordinate originality to the discipline of taste and the discernment of judgment. In one way, he is entirely correct: "sheer creativity" will not amount to anything significant, if it is divorced from the disciplined shaping of productive energy into a formed and harmonious product. Without emulation of models (i.e., a kind of mimesis), originality would be in a vacuum, hence be empty, hence not be originative at all. We would have energy without direction, dissipating itself into futile formlessness. In Nietzschean terms, we would have Dionysus without Apollo; but Dionysus needs Apollo to rescue it from merely amorphous vehemence. After all, an art work is a *work* of art, with all the toil and struggle, the need for control and concentration, directedness and discipline involved. Conversely, pure form would be empty were it not enlivened by energy, a mere rubric, an outward show without spirit. It would be harmony that is no harmony, for it would be a dead structure. One need not dispute the obvious need of discipline, more obvious in our time than in Kant's. Unbridled "creativity" turns into destruction and negativity—the easiest way to get an undisciplined charge of energy. Result? Perhaps the boring outrages that are now recommended to us as advanced aesthetic excitement.

In practice, the issue is perhaps one of the interplay, perhaps now and then the equilibrium, of originality and form. But *philosophically,* and this is the issue here, the question concerns that of *priority,* ultimate priority. Kant's successors will see in Kant the encouragement for giving *originality* the priority to form. For originality is the *forming power* that is prior to form: the primordial forming power that itself produces form, and that hence is *more than any form.* Kant's doctrine of the transcendental ego can be understood to point in this direction: the transcendental unity of apperception suggests original dynamic activity prior to all categorial intelligibility. Admittedly, even here Kant is equivocal, vacillating between original power and logical form (see *DDO,* chapter 2).

An analogous equivocation turns up with respect to genius: the source of form and rule, is other than, in excess of, form and rule. And while form and rule are necessary, they would be *nothing at all* without the prior source. Hence this source is transcendentally more ultimate than form—closer to the ultimate origin, so to say. Kant's successors will exploit the greater transcendental ultimacy of this seemingly formless power more ultimate than form. They will exploit it in some cases to *deconstruct* form. While Kant sensed this and protested against it, he cannot stem the tide, since his own philosophy has *opened up* this prior originative source. So again, the issue is not one of denying the importance of discipline and form, but of an account which prevents form from being swallowed by formlessness, if what produces form is prior to form, as Kant ambiguously suggests.

In invoking the discipline of taste relative to precedent exemplars, does Kant direct us to a kind of "tradition of originals," as we might call it? If so, do we not find the following tension between "imitation" and "creativity," reproductive and productive imagination? The second is ultimately more primal, if we are to take our sights from the *Critique of Pure Reason*. Transcendental philosophy testifies to a power of synthesis that is prior to the determinate order we find in experience. Imagination in this non-reproductive sense is transcendental, a condition of the possibility of all experience, including the experience of art. Without it there would be no ordered experience at all, and hence indeed no basis for any imitation or reproduction. But we cannot give a complete account of this prior power of synthesis in terms of any of its derived products. There is something original to it that exceeds every determinate production that comes out of it, or that is shaped and originated by it. The discipline of taste, as looking to a "tradition of originals," is itself, in the end, a production in a history of this more original source, a source that is itself in excess of the "tradition of originals."

Kant does not really think this problem through at all. He thinks of the discipline of taste as clipping the wings of genius. But, in fact, the tradition of originals or the discipline of taste would *not be at all,* were it not for those wings and their soaring! The tradition of past originals will be used to clip, ground, domesticate the soaring eagles of present genius. The very break of these past originals with tradition, their own excess to domestication in terms of precedent rules, is now conveniently forgotten. We honor dead originals after all, not the living genius who threatens our canons of taste. Indeed the danger is that we use the dead originals as a club to curb the ambiguous flight of living originals. Kant has all but nothing to say about the very origin of a tradition of originals, and hence of the discipline of taste itself, origin relative to its being first the product of exemplary human origination—that is of "genius," or whatever you want to call it.

There is always, relative to this tradition of originals, a difficult perplexity generated by the problem of the first originals. It may be true that every genius who turns out to be an original has first to look to the accomplishment of the already adept, and imitate, repeat his work, discipline itself thus to shape its own initial formlessness. It may be, indeed it is true, that every creator who turns out an original begins his journey to perfection as a humble imitator of *another,* who exemplifies something already achieved of the perfection now sought anew and differently. If one only becomes an original through the mimetic following of originals, these prior originals, in turn, need their exemplars, and so on and on. Where then do we get the first originals? Is the genius a mimesis of a mimesis and so on back to nothing? If so, do we then deconstruct the genius into a hall of mirrors reflecting nothing, for there is no original to reflect. Originality becomes an image, but an image of an image and finally an image of *nothing*. And with this, originality as meaningful also vanishes into nothing.

The doctrine of imagination does suggest some way beyond this. The mimetic chain seems to offers us a series of reproductions of originals, themselves reproductions of other originals, and so on, such that the whole process is the reproduction of reproductions. But if there is a productive imagination, the series of reproducing reproductions is ruptured decisively. That is, reproduction or mimesis has its origin in a prior production, and this prior production has greater claim to be called original. So the first originals are not those who simply mimetically follow another, but in some sense they *exemplify* a creative power immanent to their being as humans. In their work they are exemplary expressions of this original power of creative imagination. They bring to manifestation something of the promise of the human being. They do not merely image themselves, for they give expression to something essential of this human promise, and this need not be merely idiosyncratic. They struggle to rescue human promise from its formlessness; they follow less mimetically an external model as exemplify the original power of being at first just slumbering in us; original power that would still slumber in many of us, were not these exemplars emergent to trace a richly significant trajectory for human self-transcendence.

If so, it seems we have to say that, relative to the discipline of taste in a tradition of originals, the first or preceding originals were also "geniuses." But these are involved in founding acts that help inaugurate a tradition. And such acts are not completely subject to the discipline of the tradition; they break with a previous tradition, in their efforts to begin an other tradition. Whichever way we look at it, the discipline of taste, if tied to a tradition of originals, is dependent on something in *excess* of that discipline. In a word: Taste is derivative from that which it is supposed to discipline. We risk having here, as it were, the cultivated offspring chastising its own mother for an uncultured fecundity, without which the offspring itself would not be. Colloquially this is known as biting the hand that feeds you—all in the name of higher culture, of course!

If the first originals, and founding acts and inaugural events, are themselves indispensable sources of what subsequently will be the discipline of tradition, the first originals seem to augur a *radical freedom,* not yet rule bound. And this freedom beyond rules is itself presupposed by determinate rules, just as determinate syntheses, say, great works of art, presuppose a prior original synthetic power, let us say the creative power of the great artist.

What is this creative freedom? Might we not say that it is at work in *imitation itself,* imitation as implicitly original (see *PO,* 88–90)? Do we not have to think beyond any simple dualism of imitation and creation? Kant is rightly aware of the indispensability of a certain "mimesis," as well as the dangerous ambiguity of a certain originality. Yet he does not get us to the proper point beyond their dualism. Indeed he bequeaths crucial equivocations to German Idealism, and hence also to succeeding anti-Idealistic strands of thought. That is, despite his trepidation before unconstrained originality, just because of the legacy of transcendental philosophy, the inherent promise of mimesis as a *relation to the other* is subordinated to or subsumed into a "creativity," understood in terms of self-defining self-relation or original *self-activity.* We need to think self-relation deeper in its inseparability from the relation to the other implied by imitation. Otherwise, the *negative* definition of the other, implied by dominant self-relation, will cause "creativity" itself to degenerate into an excessive subjectivity, asserting itself against the other, lording it over and violating otherness.

Genius as Intermediate

Let us return one more time to the view that genius is nature's favorite through whom she gives the rule to art. There is a certain *intermediate* character to genius as thus described. On the one hand, the genius, as it were, puts one root deep into nature; there is a reference in this human self to something other than the human. On the other hand, from this root, and with this exemplary self, there emerges a significant articulating power. On the one hand, we have a power that retreats into opaqueness; for the root in nature is, as it were, below ground, and hence not directly available to the light of rational inspection. On the other hand, this exemplary power serves just the bringing of significance into the light of expression. On the one side, the inarticulate origin; on the other, the genius as an intermediate originating power that gives rise to articulation. Between enigma and emergent expression, the genius is an original spontaneity that arises from another origin, about which we cannot be absolutely determinate. Indeed as thus intermediate, genius seems suggestive of the unknown root of the two stems that constitute the powers of sensibility and understanding (*Critique of Pure Reason,* A15, B29). It is also suggestive of the schematism, as an art concealed in the depth of the human soul (*Critique of Pure Reason,* A141, B180).

We might say that the origin of genius is lost in the enigmatic originality of nature itself. If genius is a mediator with respect to nature, once again nature cannot be understood as a Newtonian mechanism. This is most evident in that there is no prediction of genius: it is outside the calculation of an absolute determinism; if we were able to predict its emergence, it would not be genius at all. We find the implication of a *genuine newness* that is not the mere reorganization of prior determining powers. There is the appearance of a free power of articulating. If genius gives the precedent, something about it is without precedent. If nature gives the rule to art through the genius, the origination of rule is outside the rule.

We encounter something that resists complete determination. About genius there is a free indeterminacy. If it gives the law, there is a sense in which it must be outside the law. This, I think, secretly terrified Kant. One thinks of his desire to completely rationalize freedom in terms of the categorical imperative. Though Kant retreats before this terror to the safeguards of the Enlightenment, these safeguards will be less and less respected in the centuries to follow. The threat and promise of Romanticism appears here: freedom beyond mechanism indicates, as Kant puts it about genius, freedom "running to wildness." This wildness was to be celebrated by the Romantics against the scientistic mathematicization of the world, but this is not a cause that Kant will endorse. Genius finally has to be reined, domesticated, civilized in terms of the norms of taste.

We have previously referred to Kant's position between Enlightenment and Romanticism in his view of the relation of taste and genius. We need to return to this. Taste has to do with judgment which, among other things, concerns the capacity to discern the fit and the appropriate. There is something public, and implicitly universal about the requirements of taste, Kant holds. There is a discipline that goes to constitute a person of taste. There is then a *sensus communis,* which perhaps may not be subjected to a mathematical measure, but nevertheless it is subject to measure. Taste is the very decorum of aesthetic measure. Taste has to do with the education of feeling, but ultimately the education of feeling is a moral education. The discipline of taste, in the end, is inseparable from the discipline of moral feeling.

By contrast, there is something *beyond* measure about the spontaneous eruption of genius. Compared to the more general and public norms of taste, there is something singular about genius: genius cannot be made an instance of a genus. Kant will praise the true genius for making aesthetic ideas "universally communicable," yet the danger is always that genius will lay claim to a singularity that is lawless or wayward relative to the *sensus communis*. Even if we admit something exemplary about this singularity, Kant gives no license to genius to run rough shod over the decorums.

The excess of genius can also be seen in terms of what he originates, what Kant calls aesthetic ideas (*CJ,* §49). Remember we are not taking about inarticulate genius, but the emergence of exemplary articulation. Concerning the faculties of mind that constitute genius, Kant invokes *Geist,* which again is correlated with the power to present aesthetic ideas. He understands them as representations of the imagination which occasion much thought without any definite thought, that is, concept being adequate to them. They cannot be completely compassed or made intelligible by language. They are the counterpart to the rational idea.

Kant invokes the imagination *as productive,* as very powerful in creating *another nature* of the material which actual nature supplies. Surely this "actual nature," we ask, cannot be the quite the same "nature" that gives the rule to art through the genius. If it were, we would have to say, with Nietzsche, that nature is a work of art giving birth to itself. Such productive imagination exhibits freedom from the laws of association, in so far as imagination goes to work on the material supplied by "nature"—this is "nature" as passive again, is it not?—to produce something different that surpasses nature. Consider: Nature gives the rule to art in genius; genius works on nature to produce another nature in excess of nature. Does not this mean that nature works in and on itself through the genius to produce itself in another form, namely, as human art? If we follow this line of argument, it is only a little step to genius as agent of nature's own creative transcendence, creative self-transcendence. Nature as a work of art giving birth to itself; humanity as nature's genius creating itself. But such a view of nature and humanity is obviously impossible to comprehend on the terms of the Newtonian, mechanistic paradigm.

One might claim that aesthetic ideas are products of our creative self-transcendence that strain to be images of transcendence. For Kant aesthetic ideas, as representations of imagination, are *ideas* because they surpass the bounds of experience, seeking to approximate the presentation of rational ideas, giving them the appearance of objective reality. "The poet ventures to realize to sense, rational ideas of invisible beings, the kingdom of the blessed, hell, eternity, creation etc., . . . and to present them with a completeness of which there is no example in nature" (*CJ,* §49, 176). I find it significant that the images Kant invokes show aesthetic ideas as imaginatively transcending towards the *ultimate extremes*. Looked at in light of the above reflections, is this nature producing (through genius) images of transcendence that point beyond itself, beyond nature itself? Does nature's productive power in the aesthetic ideas, themselves inseparable from the animating power of *Geist,* offer us vectors to transcendence as other?

One might even wonder if Kant would have been helped by an understanding of eros here. Aesthetic ideas are, after all, a kind of conjunction of opposites: the sensible and the hypersensible. Aesthetic ideas recall to mind my previous invocation of Vico's imaginative universals. And does not Plato with eros, and indeed mania, have quite a differentiated response to the space between the aesthetic and the idea? We are reminded of a deeper/higher release of powers of the soul with respect to deeper/higher powers of being as beautiful, as good, as worthy to be loved. The space between the aesthetic and the idea is traversed by eros and mania. One might say: the eros of genius is rooted in the cosmos, or nature as the aesthetic happening of being; while with mania, something is given or received, some inspiration from below, from above. Plato is more focussed on the dynamic of traversing the between. This is not Kant. He is too dualistic, without clear resources to articulate what is not one, not the other, but one and the other. His aesthetic idea implicitly names this "being one and the other," but eros is already aesthetic idea in this sense: the soul transcending in the flesh, and more.

To be fair to Kant, he is very suggestive here. Thus he speaks of imagination (*CJ,* §49) as serving to enlarge and enliven, and bring into movement, the understanding. More thought is aroused than can be determined in a concept or captured in words. Aesthetic ideas generate an enlivening of the mind, but in a manner that cannot be reduced to clear concepts. I take from this the point that aesthetical ideas show themselves to be in *excess* of determinate intelligibility. One might claim that the project of Enlightenment, in its scientific form, is to make being completely intelligible. To make being completely intelligible is to make it completely determinate; for, in line with an old ideal, much older than Enlightenment itself, to be intelligible is to be determinate. The Enlightenment claim will also be that only relative to such complete determinate intelligibility can we be free from error and falsity, and mediately free in an individual and social sense. The irony, not to say outright contradiction, is that this freedom could not be completely determined at all. So the whole project of complete determination, relative to freedom, already runs up against something beyond complete determinacy. The purpose of Enlightenment thus is not amenable to complete statement in the same Enlightenment terms. The purpose of its putatively complete light is itself not a light, in the same sense of being a completely determinate intelligibility. The real point of determinate intelligibility is not itself completely a determinate intelligibility.

Kant does see something positive in aesthetic ideas. Even if they exceed the measure of completely determinate intelligibility, they are not absurd. They release the powers of mind, both in their harmonious interplay, and especially in their quest after a maximum. They are both determinate and indeterminate, neither sheerly definite nor indefinite. They are in between, and yet are provocative in sending us in quest of something that exceeds the bounds of complete determination. In that respect, aesthetic ideas send us beyond Enlightenment, understood as bound up with the ideal of completely determinate science. Aesthetic ideas are *ideas,* and this signifies for Kant a transcendental use. Kant had barred any transcendent flight of the human mind, such as was beloved of the old metaphysics in search of soul, world, God. And yet one senses that something of the old urge for transcendence is resurrected in aesthetic ideas: the search for something "more," something over and above, something that yet is deeply significant for our being here and now. As inciting mind into self-transcending beyond finite limits, aesthetical ideas seem to assume something of this old metaphysical purpose. When Hegel and Schelling, Schopenhauer, Nietzsche, and Heidegger variously saw art as absolute or as having deep philosophical significance, they were heirs of Kant's suggestiveness. The aesthetic has metaphysical significance—it intimates the sensuous manifestation of transcendence. Kant himself may not be bold enough to come straight out and transgress the limits he had imposed on metaphysics elsewhere, but he is certainly *flirting* with such transgression.

But flirting is only flirting, and all such coquettish games must come to an end. After the ball is over, Enlightenment wins out over Romanticism. In the end the transcending surge of genius must be sacrificed to taste, if that transcending looks like it is getting out of hand. In some respects, Kant's views here are quite reminiscent of Socrates in the *Apology*, or of Plato in the *Ion:* we find rational caution mixed with chary fascination concerning something that passes beyond controlled logos. If I am not mistaken, the philosophical eros of Plato was more bold and audacious than Kant's, though also, interestingly enough, more porous and receptive to the ingression of transcendence as other to human self-transcendence. To cite an intriguing instance from the *old* Plato: In the *Laws* there is an extended discussion of the right uses of drinking parties, and a justification of the gifts of Dionysus (see 672a ff.). This is not altogether unlike Kant's discipline of taste. But where are the drinking parties in Kant, and their homage to Dionysus in the wise formation of ethical excellence? I know that the *younger* Kant held ritualized dinner parties, but young or old, one divines that Kant always wanted to be in control: never to be beside oneself or to lose self-possession. This is evident in his praise (*CJ*, 124–25) for the highest possibilities of Stoic *apatheia*. "Such a stamp of mind is alone called noble." What honor to Dionysus here? What mutation of eros and the *passio essendi?*

Recall how in the *Apology* Socrates castigates the poets for not being able to account for themselves, for not being in command of an explicit account of their work's meaning; a passerby could do a better job. The poets may have an inspired vision, but they fail to provide the explicit knowing Socrates sought. Perhaps Socrates asked the wrong question, even a stupid question, expecting of poets what, of course, they could not deliver. This is the "ancient quarrel" of the poets and the philosophers, or as Nietzsche puts it: "Plato versus Homer—this is life's great antagonism." But Kant too is participant in this quarrel, though with him it is the divergence of *Newton and Homer* that is cited (*CJ*, §47, 170). Still he is a son of this logotechnical Socrates here, in that we can see his discussion of genius as putting art below science. As I mentioned above, we may expect progress from the latter, not from the former. Even if Kant still speaks of genius as nature's elect, in a vein like Plato's view of inspiration, the implied superiority of science comes from its potential for unlimited progress. We are also reminded of Descartes with respect to "genius": at most perhaps we need a exemplary originator of method, but once originated the method can be used by anyone; we can then dispense with "genius."

Plato does not seem to be quite so hostile, as Kant does, to powers beyond rationality, such as eros, mania, enthusiasm and so on. Kant (*CJ*, 128) connects mania with fanaticism, which he ties with "rational raving"; he relates enthusiasm to delirium. Mania is "profoundly ridiculous." In enthusiasm the imagination is "unbridled," in fanaticism it is anomalous. The first may be a transitory accident, the latter is an "undermining disease." Kant has little of Plato's irony and finesse about eros and mania. His stern earnestness was exasperated by them. Think of the playfulness of Plato in the *Timaeus* (71a–72c) speaking of the liver and divination: in sleep arise prophetic dreams, but in the morning we have to subject them to rational discernment and judgment. But Kant has a deaf ear for Plato's ironic playfulness. His solemnity is edified by work, such as he finds in Aristotle, not by Platonic play. Plato is critically wary, but not as *rationalistically fanatical* as Kant is in his opposition to them. Though Kant on the surface keeps himself under control, one detects that, at another level, *he is beside himself* at what he considers to be the ravings of the *Schwärmerei* and the *Sturm und Drang*. His reasonableness hides a passion that echoes the passion he chides in others. Hatred of *Schwärmerei* is still hatred, even when it congratulates itself on having pure reason on its side.[7]

THE SHADOW OF MADNESS

If Kant is given to sarcasm at the excesses of "genius," there are ironies in what he says that boomerang on him, and produce ironies at the expense of his whole system. These stinging ironies are particularly evident if we couple genius, aesthetic ideas and the productive imagination. Kant did not aim to call spirits from the vasty deep, but they came nonetheless, and possible monsters among them. Like the sorcerer's apprentice, it is hard to stem the flow of water, some pure, some bilge, once it pours out from that bottomless well. Kant, after all, initially did suggest that the whole so-called Copernican revolution be undertaken as a *Versuch,* a *trial* or *experiment* (*Critique of Pure Reason,* B xvi–xvii), but its far reaching implications Kant neither fully understood, nor could master. It is not clear if these implications have yet been understood or mastered. One might even think of it as a kind of hyperbolic "supposition." We start a magic story with "suppose, suppose. . . ." But what do we let loose? Kant is the sorcerer's apprentice of transcendental philosophy, and what flows from the well is the power of subjectivity, in excess of Kant's desire for mastery. The self-assurance of the architectonic is haunted by its shadow, desperation.

Nor is there any use just to command the genie to go back into the bottle. Consider Kant's scorn for those who fancy themselves as original—even granting that originality is essential to genius. They do so by throwing off "all academic constraints of rules, in the belief that one cuts a finer figure on the back of an ill-tempered than of a trained horse"(*CJ,* §47, 171). The choice of

7. As I indicate below, Kant has difficulty to give us an ultimate philosophical basis to discriminate divine madness and mad madness. And even if it proves extraordinarily difficult to provide that basis, divine madness, relative to the excess of genius, may be just what we need to rethink. See Kant's polemic against "Plato" in "On a Newly Arisen Superior Tone in Philosophy" (1796), recently translated in Peter Fenves, *Raising the Tone of Philosophy: Late Essays by Immanuel Kant, Transformative Critique by Jacques Derrida* (Baltimore: Johns Hopkins University Press, 1993). One also finds very revealing remarks on "fanatical mystagogues," and on genius as "breaking your neck" in the section on humor in *CJ.*

metaphors is revealing. We find the contrast of wild nature and tamed domestication. It is quite clear that "nature" without the culture of taste is an ill-tempered beast! How does one tame such a beast? Restraint, not to say violence, may be necessary. Even though Kant grants that the rule in art cannot be determinable in concepts, and even though mechanical and fine art are distinct, there is always something of the mechanical in fine art. This is one way in which discipline can be exercised. In line with this, genius is said only to provide rich material, but it needs form, and form requires "a talent academically trained . . . to stand the test of judgment"(*CJ,* 171–72).

Kant is quite forthright: To give scope to imagination at the expense of the critical faculties is be an impostor, a mere tyro, gulling the simple-minded public (*CJ,* 171). Elsewhere (*CJ,* §50, 183) he speaks of the danger of imagination's freedom in its abundance and originality; this can lead to lawless freedom and nonsense. Again there is need of judgment.

> Taste, like the judgment in general, is the discipline (or corrective) of genius; it severely clips its wings, and makes it orderly and polished . . . it gives it guidance, directing and controlling its flight, so that it may preserve its character of finality. . . . And so, when the interests of both these qualities clash in a product, and there has to be a sacrifice of something, then it should rather be on the side of genius; and judgment . . . will more readily endure an abatement of the freedom and wealth of the imagination, than that the understanding should be compromised. (*CJ,* 183)

Does this mean then that genius *in itself* is blind?[8] Is its energy perhaps like the blind striving of Schopenhauerian Will? It may need reason to guide and discipline it, but if this energy is, in fact, more *ontologically primordial,* why should it submit to that discipline? One is tempted again to think of Nietzsche's Dionysus and Apollo, or indeed Schiller's *Stofftrieb* and *Formtrieb,* as analogues to genius and taste in Kant. Nietzsche has a kind of aesthetics analogous to Kant, but reversed with respect to Dionysus and Apollo, genius and taste. When Nietzsche gives the primacy to Dionysus over Apollo, genius over taste, in a way he is being a more consistent Kantian than Kant, and a more metaphysically honest thinker in facing the consequences of what is more ontologically primordial.

In illustration consider Kant's different attitudes to poetry and music. He thinks of poetry as the supreme art (*CJ,* §53, 191). One suspects a "logocentrism" in his judgment, although he has granted the excess of aesthetic ideas

8. One recalls what Kant says of the power of imagination (*Critique of Pure Reason,* A78, B103)—"a blind but indispensable function of the soul, without which we should have no knowledge whatsoever, but of which we are scarcely ever conscious."

to complete articulation. "In poetry," he says (*CJ,* 193), "everything is straight and above board. It shows its hand." The words of poetry are subject to some public scrutiny; they can be made more or less determinate; they seem relatively controllable. The extent to which this is true is another question. But consider now his attitude to music. Perhaps music is the romantic art par excellence, at least some have thought so, including Hegel. But Kant condemns music to inferiority. There is something about it that is beyond our control.

Kant uses a very revealing image: he compares music to a dandy pulling a perfumed handkerchief from his pocket—the smell of the perfume spreads everywhere indeterminately and one has no choice about being subjected to it (*CJ,* §53, 196). I find very touching what Kant says about "the singing of spiritual songs" in a delicious footnote here: "they inflict a great hardship upon the public by such *noisy* (and therefore in general pharasaical) devotions, for they force the neighbors either to sing with them or to abandon meditations." It seems Kant lived close to a prison where the prisoners had to sing hymns, and Kant, forced to listen, must have been beside himself. Or perhaps if the footnote speaks true, there is comedy in this—Kant forced to join in, to sing along with the spiritual songs of convicts! (Has irreverent imagination got the better of me?) Music comes upon us, as it were. It *moves us* without asking our reason or our will. We find ourselves caught up and moved. It is beyond rational will. Music communicates to and with the *passio essendi,*[9] the passion of being which, like *eros* and *mania,* is responsive prior to and exceeding the sway of determinate reason. Kant sees only an *intrusion* in this involuntary responsiveness of the *passio essendi,* and does not like it. He does not see the spontaneous surgence of transcending that is powerful, precisely as other to our rationalized and willed mediations. This power of music will be very important for thinkers like Schopenhauer and Nietzsche: it will be evidence of something other than human all-too-human will. It will be the singing of transcendence; it will be a metaphysical revelation of something other, named by them as will or will to power. Nietzsche revealingly confesses on occasion that his life would hardly have had a point, were there no music: it is his *consolatio philosophica.*

Kant's negative judgment on music suggests the same supreme will to be in control that we noted above. There is an indeterminacy about music—it is only *fleeting,* he says (*CJ,* 195)—you cannot pin down or fix univocally why it so deeply moves us, and yet it does. Or Kant has a fear of flying, whether it is in clipping the wings of genius, or bringing back to earth the dove of metaphysics that tries to soar high into the heavens.

Again in the end Enlightenment must rule Romanticism, and the potential wildness of genius be subjected to rules. On what basis are we to accept this

9. On what I mean see, for instance, *EB,* chapter 12, "Released Freedom and the Passion of Being."

relative subordination? I cannot see an ultimate basis for it in Kant, whichever way we look. If we look in terms of the active self, why should this self be such a respecter of rules, even if we claim that the rules are self-imposed? The tale of post-Kantian aesthetics and culture is a progressive radicalization of the power of active selfhood to claim itself as the source of rule, law, intelligibility. It asserts itself always as beyond the law. The Nietzschean philosopher will even set himself up as the legislator who *dictates* the law. Genius also pays its homage to "the splendid blond beast." No doubt, Kant had no intention of letting a wilder ego out of its cage, but once out, it won't go back in.

Alternatively, if you say, that nature dictates this subordination, where is the basis of the restraint? Newtonian mechanism? But why respect this? Properly speaking, even in Kant there is no basis in nature itself for any such respect. Kant will say that only in morality do we find the rationale of respect, but here the whole horizon of consideration is defined by the primacy of moral *self*-determination, and this primacy of self-determination, whether aesthetic or moral, is precisely what is in question.[10]

Or indeed if we say something other gives the rule to the self, then either there is an inward otherness to selfhood which is beyond complete autonomy, or the self is a manifestation of something more primordial, and what is more primordial is not itself lawlike, and ordered and regular: the primordial is beyond the law. This also means that the so-called sovereignty of the self is illusory: when self proclaims its complete autonomy, it is only masking from itself its issue from something that is not reasonable, or intelligible, or morally benign. Again Schopenhauer, and Nietzsche, and their numerous followers come to mind. I need hardly emphasize that many post-Kantian thinkers took some such route: the inward otherness impels the self to its own internal limit, and what it finds there is not the rule of Kantian taste or decorum. More often it is wildness, frenzy, the primitive, the ugly, the excremental, the senseless, and now the disgusting (see note 6). Genius and madness become indistinguishable. And we seem hard put to discriminate between divine madness and mad madness. Or indeed between art and Merda d'Artista!

You might say that this proves that Kant was right after all. Perhaps in a pragmatic sense. One might issue the command: Do not open that door because hell is there. But if one is dedicated to honest Enlightenment, and the truth of genius is only tolerable under the condition of its domestication, and if the untamed truth of genius is indistinguishable from madness, Kant's defense measure against excess by means of the discipline of taste is mere whistling in the dark: it is metaphysically dishonest. This Enlightenment survives by plucking out one of its eyes. There will be others who will pluck out the other eye—the eye of scientistic rationalism. And ultimately there is no ultimate reason in Kant, or in Enlightenment, why this should not be done.

---

10. Do Kant's references to the "supersensible substrate in us" match similar equivocations in his philosophy of God? This would require another study.

Sublime Disturbances

The topic of the sublime is large, and the focus of renewed interest in recent decades. I cannot do justice to all the sides of Kant's view nor dwell on the different forms of the sublime, in art, in nature, the mathematical, the dynamical sublime. My interest is in the sublime power of nature relative to our overall theme, and how this fits with the determination of nature in the *Critique of Pure Reason*. Is it not the exact *opposite* in some ways? In the latter "nature" seems to want in determinate intelligibility till we knowers determine it. With the sublime, nature's power as other shows itself to us as *beyond* our determination. And if so beyond, is there not something questionable about the epistemological pretension to impose on it categories of our own devising? In the *Critique of Pure Reason,* I repeat, nature seems to be passive to us, outside of the intelligibilities we construct and impose on it. Nature's intelligibility is in the measure of our determining; whereas sublime nature is incommensurable with us, hence beyond our measure, perhaps beyond our intelligibility. It is all very well to suggest that perhaps Kant here is talking about nature in itself, as thing in itself. Apart from the fact that this is already a trespass against the strictures of the *Critique of Pure Reason,* namely, that we cannot know anything about the thing in itself, there are more difficult consequences, even if we forgive Kant his trespass. For if the sublime reveals the power of nature as thing in itself, then this power suggests the *pretentiousness* of the entire transcendental project whereby we knowers essay to be the measure, if not master of nature, phenomenal or otherwise. If the sublime *shows* the power of nature, the sublime appears; it is in some sense given, it presents itself; what is beyond phenomena is phenomenal; the thing in itself appears. If what appears is beyond the measure of our determining power, the epistemological claims of the *Critique of Pure Reason* are exposed to the suspicion of mere posturing before an excess which finally will defeat all our efforts to reduce it to the intelligible determination of our categories.

The point is suggested if we reflect on Kant claiming (*CJ,* §45) that art must look like nature, that is, "as free of all constraint of arbitrary rules as if it were a product of mere nature." This nature can hardly be the nature of Newtonian necessity, for if art were to be a mimesis of Newtonian mechanism, we would *deaden* art's power in terms of a spiritless necessity. What kind of natural necessity could it then resemble? While clearly Kant was seeking beyond spiritless necessity, he did not want to attribute *objectively* to nature a different necessity. Would one have to think a necessity communicated in nature and art in excess of "objective" nature? Clearly with respect to teleological judgment, Kant was moving beyond mechanism, a movement his idealist successors claimed was not thorough enough in bringing spirit and nature into a proper unity. Is a *spiritual* necessity then needed? But there is something double-edged here. Perhaps a sense of nature more primal than Newtonian mechanism opens into a dark abyss, and not into the reassurance of spirit that Kant would not dare to assert constitutively, though the idealists had no hesitation. The boldness of his successors, idealist and anti-idealist, moved in opposite directions out of Kant's cautious middle, one up, the other down. Hegel will move up to a constitutive teleology, rather a self-constituting teleology with the purposeful self-becoming of *Geist*. Schopenhauer will move down into the ateleological will in and behind nature, with its purposeless self-insistent *conatus*. Nature as original may be dark, on the other side of idealistic reason. Hegel will find this excuse enough to pronounce the *impotence* of nature with respect to spirit. Schelling and Schopenhauer thought otherwise, in terms of an other power. The Kantian and Hegelian consolations will not be original enough.[11]

Kant, in his own way, is not untrue to the sublime in terms of phenomenal appearing. The real problem lies in the philosophical interpretation of appearing and of what appears. Something excessive is appearing. Its very excess is frightening. Beyond appropriation, it potentially destroys the whole project of pure reason. Beyond encapsulation, it mocks the architectonic ambition of the system, always remaining beyond its determination, hence wounding the system, or visiting on it a hemorrhage of ultimate ground in which its claims to completeness drain away. The claims are consumed by their own consistency in going to the limit, and finding at the limit what they cannot take in.

Kant knows the terror of the sublime: there is both attraction and repulsion; there is a kind of vacillation or tremoring *(Erschutterung);* "that which is excessive *(das Überschwengliche)* for imagination . . . is, as it were, an abyss *(Abgrund),* in which it fears to lose itself" (*CJ*, §27). There are statements that imply a presentation of the supersensible substrate of nature. If the supersensible is presented, it is not, properly speaking, absolutely supersensible: it is manifest, or shows itself, or appears. The dualism of phenomenal and noumenal cannot be upheld at this point. With the breakdown of this dualism, or its traversal by a show of excess, there is the terror of the incommensurable.

The very otherness of this is something from which, in the end, Kant retreats. Like the imagination staggering before the sublime, he names and recoils, feels the terrible attraction and yet secures himself against it. The *moralizing* of the meaning of this show of excess is consistent with the will to preserve the human in its own autonomy. The sublime is not to threaten us, since our exposure must be from a position of safety. The show, if you like, becomes just a show—a spectacle in which the threat to the roots of our ontological being is domesticated. We play with the show of excess from a safe distance.

---

11. Kant, of course, did think there was something impermeable about matter—in *Metaphysical Foundations of the Natural Sciences* (*Metaphysische Anfangsgrunde der Naturwissenschaften* [Franfurt: Suhrkamp, 1980]) by its nature, matter is *undurchdringlich*—impermeable, but perhaps also unfathomable; something that on its own is impossible to grasp. "Absolute impenetrability is in fact nothing more or less than [a] *qualitas occulta*" (53–54). The basic forces of matter *(Grundkrafte der Materie)* are inexplicable (68). Newton seemed to believe this too.

Kant is not primarily interested in any *aestheticized* sublime: the aesthetic show of what exceeds show. While the presentation of the supersensible is weakened in its otherness, primarily this is to serve as a reminder of *our* supersensible destiny as moral beings. The retreat from the sublime as excessively other to us Kant converts into an advance, in the name of our higher moral ideality.

What if there were no such retreat? The pretension of self-sufficient moral autonomy might be ruptured, not perhaps to deprive us of an ethical destiny, but perhaps to rob it of any pretension to being, through its autonomous self-legislation alone, the measure of the good. The good itself as other may disrupt us in this rupture to our moral autonomy. If I might put the point in religious terms, either horror or the enigma of God as transcendence itself is lurking in the shadows, or else intimated in a silence that, even as it tries to stifle the name of God, finds that name escaping its muzzled lips. The Psalmist sung: The glory of creation proclaims the Lord! There is precious little of the glory of creation in Kant's nature, even if he does talk about the starry skies above, and in the *Critique of Judgment* in almost exactly the same words that he famously used at the end of the *Critique of Practical Reason*. Just as he recoils from the *inner otherness* of genius by means of the discipline of taste, to say nothing of a secret retraction when his autonomy clings to the moral law within, here the ontological terror before nature's "too-muchness" in its sublime otherness is mitigated in terms of the supersensible destiny that elevates us to self-assurance about our moral superiority. The supersensible granted is the supersensible in us, in moral form. *We* then, qua moral beings, are *the superior*—even though we preach against the newly arisen superior tone in philosophy.

If the sublime offers the presentation of what transcends sense, does it not remind us of aesthetic ideas as exceeding determinate conceptualization? If something other coming to manifestness also exceeds manifestation, in a completely determinate presentation, these excesses of the sublime and the aesthetic ideas are other to complete conceptual determination, and also augur a breach of aesthetic form.[12] Kant acknowledges this breach, but draws back from its ominousness to the security of an unshaken moral destiny. Why does he repeatedly refers to us as *being safe,* in the face of nature's might. What saves us, what keeps us safe? Is there any saving power beyond ourselves? The sublime might seem to humiliate us as natural beings, but it serves mediately

---

12. Lyotard and his admirers seem to move in some such direction, seeking to offer an "other" Kant to the Kant of Enlightenment taste and culture. This other Kant may be other despite himself. I would say: There may not so much be an other Kant, as that the matter at issue may be other to what Kant would have it be, and that in dealing with this matter (e.g., the sublime), Kant reveals its potential for *dissidence* with respect to the Kantian schema. Certain "virtualities" emerge *equivocally* in Kant's account, that just in their equivocality allow of different options of interpretation, not all of them coherent with or acceptable to Kant himself. The question remains how we are *philosophically* to interpret this equivocality.

to awaken us to our higher destiny beyond nature. This is the "beyondness" of our moral being. But does not this confirm further what I said at the outset about the human being as the mediating center, and the end in itself in the otherwise valueless otherness?

The sublime does not here communicate the ontological power of other-being, terrifying to us yet gloriously prodigal in the ethos of the between. The *seeming otherness* of the sublime really serves as a *mediating detour back to ourselves* and the self-confirmation of our sense of moral superiority. Is not this just what is implied by the logic of what Kant calls *subreption?* Kant says: ". . . the feeling of the sublime in nature is respect for our own destination, which, by a certain subreption, we attribute to an object in nature (conversion of respect for the idea of humanity in our own subject into respect for the object)" (*CJ,* §27). What this implies is that, though nature's otherness to self is recognized, it is also undercut and set at naught, by being subordinated to the superiority of the idea of humanity and the (moral) self. Subreption embodies a logic that was to be endemic in all idealistic philosophy, and even, I think, in philosophies that defined themselves in protest to idealism. This I would call dialectical self-mediation through the other. There is a relation of self and other, and there is a mediation of the two, but this their interplay is always defined in terms of the priority of the self. The other serves a self-mediation. The sublime in Kant ultimately serves moral self-mediation. But there are speculative self-mediations through the other, and the movement of will in self-mediation through the other, and there are Dionysian self-mediations, and self-deconstructing self-mediations that mediate still a self, albeit eclipsed and self-lacerating through the other.

In sum, the suggestion of the transgression of rule in genius, the suggestion of transcendence of determinate concepts by aesthetic ideas, and the threat of rupture to aesthetic form by the sublime, all testify to Kant's equivocal uneasiness, finally laid to rest by reinstatement of the Enlightenment paradigm of rational, autonomous self-determination, and supremely in its moral form. The solicitation of transgression, transcendence and rupture to rule-bound self-determination that struck trepidation into Kant, for the Romantics augured an originality that would be the release and fulfillment of creative freedom. What they welcomed, he dreaded. Is this why, reading Kant, one thinks one hears, with a second set of ears, a cry of secret terror barely stifling its urge to cry out: Why if *that* were true, then our moral being might *come to nothing,* might amount to nothing, in the end?

Kant's enlightened safeguards will be less and less respected by those following him. Kant would have defended his account of the sublime as entirely consistent with a philosophy of culture, if we understand the highest cultivation as really moral cultivation (thus beauty as symbol of the moral). Any interruptive otherness or transcendence is to be subordinated to moral autonomy or self-mediation. We can still think of Kant as between Enlightenment and Romanticism, but in this "between" Enlightenment reason holds sway, and many seeds of Romanticism are not watered or allowed to sprout. But if we think of the manifest otherness differently, the Kantian coherence becomes fragile, and all the more so, given that his successors were *emboldened* by his *Critique of Judgement*. Their boldness extended to different interpretations of the "supersensible substrate," whether in us or in nature. Hegel will name it the Idea or *Geist,* and give us a speculatively excessive absolutization of reason. Schopenhauer will name it Will, and in this process incite a palace coup that dethrones the moral sovereign. Nietzsche's naming of the excess in terms of will to power will complete the *demoralization* of the sublime. Aesthetic ideas will be creative productions of Dionysian will to power, and in the sublime innocence of becoming, beyond good and evil, the security of any moral order will be dismantled. But there is a kind of logic of *subreption* in Nietzsche's philosophy (also in Hegel and Schopenhauer), except that the self that projects itself will *exult* in that transgressive transcendence, the thought of which gave Kant the sweats.

Do you think I am joking when I mention the sweats? But it was no laughing matter for Kant. We know the story: on his constitutional, that afternoon walk that fixed the image of Kant as fixated on ordered routine, Kant would *stop* if he had the presentiment that a sweat was coming on. *Stop*. Lest *that* break out. What? Not the noonday but the *after*noon demon? Not afternoon delight in any case. And unlike Socrates at shadowless noonday, Kant was not inspired to sing a *second* speech praising eros as divine madness. Safe under a tree from the heat of the sun, he would wait till the threat subsided, and then he would resume his measured walk.

Nietzsche is only one of the most extreme who will contemplate the "supersensible" in us, and sweat. What if we substitute the "hyperbolic" for the "supersensible"? Even if we say nothing about an outer otherness as sublime, there may be an *inward otherness* to the subject, in excess of all autonomous self-mediation, and that is hence, against Kant, at best *equivocally* moral. The inward "sun" will also makes us sweat. When Kant implies a certain indeterminability to the supersensible, that very indeterminability invites determination, and other thinkers will not determine it in the predominantly moral terms Kant recommends. And why should they? The sublime and the aesthetic art of genius will be both transcendent to and transgressive of this moral ideal. But the equivocities that Kant's successors will determine differently are already ingrained in Kant's own determination of the matter. The Enlightenment thinker in Kant would have been vehemently opposed to, not to say shocked by, the exploitation of the same ambiguities by those inheritors. But they carry his genes.

Origin, Breakdown, Breakthrough

I ask metaphorically: What are the sweats? I answer, asking imagination: Advance signs that there is offered to us a reawakening of the primal porosity of our being. We can misread or refuse the portents; we can forestall the reawakening offered. If we allow the porosity, there can be a breakdown—breakdown of a too insistent *conatus essendi* or self-determination. There may also be a breakthrough—breakthrough again of the energy of the *passio essendi*, and in its intimacies with the fertile equivocity of both eros and mania.

In the face of the sublimity of nature, Kant faces a breakdown. He comes to a limit which is, in truth, the Golgotha of every logic of self-mediation. Self-determining is broken down and potentially broken open. Kant does not learn this lesson. The otherness of the sublime does not really count, for nature properly speaking is not sublime but just our attitude or frame of mind. His "subreption" is a playing with the otherness of the sublime—a playing false that counterfeits the sublime. Instead of the truth of the sublime being granted as the limit of subjectivity in an otherness beyond even transcendental subjectivity, there is a reversion back to moral subjectivity, and perhaps a perversion of the sublime in this. This reversion is invested with the transcendence that is other, and we as supersensible, as morally autonomous beings are elevated into a position of unshakable superiority to all of nature. This reversion is implied by the logic of subreption which, when known as such, requires us to subordinate the otherness of nature qua other to what we supposedly have invested in it. For Kant the reversion brings home the dividend on the investment, which dividend is only *ourselves* in our moral superiority to nature.

The breakdown reverts us to ourselves, and Kant is not wrong in calling attention to a reversion. Does he pervert the reversion by not acknowledging here the negative moment of a breakthrough into acknowledgment of something other and in excess of self-mediation, but as a detour to a consolidated, indeed elevated (moral) self-mediation? There is no real breakdown, and hence no breakthrough into a release of the excess of transcendence, or release towards the excess of transcendence as other to us. There is a short-circuiting of the energies of the sublime into the circle of subjectivity at home with itself in the self-satisfaction of its own superior moral destiny. Is this not to fashion a *counterfeit* of the fuller promise of the release?

One can appreciate why Kant would retreat from the breakdown. It potentially destroys everything he held most dear. Briefly one touches a boundary, and dismay passes into one that faith in one's moral superiority amounts to nothing. One is nothing. One is swallowed up in the immensity of other-being. One is humbled, not just as an animal; one is humbled to the very ontological roots of one's being. One is as naked as Job, whether on the day of birth, or the day of death, or the day the flesh is afflicted with curse. Kant smothers the horror of such shatterings, and so delivers still-born what might otherwise be a new child of humility. For the shattering might augur the possibility of a breakthrough of something other, just in that new humility. The circuit of subreption short-circuits this shattering and breakthrough, neither of which is subject to the determination of our autonomous self-determination. Kant held on, could not let go, and hence warded off the promise of a release towards the glorious excess of the sublime, glorious just in its otherness to us, glorious just in its excess to all our secure self-mediations.

There is a common view that with Kant, art, properly speaking, is finally *born,* as a purely aesthetic phenomenon. It is not so simple. What "art" here means must remain equivocal, and not only because of Kant's own negotiation of the terrain between art and morality. Something is born, yes, but perhaps something is also still not born, or stillborn. Should we not ask: suppose the sublime communicates a de-aestheticizing of the aesthetic? If so, have we not then transcended art as inextricably tied to intimate union with its sensuous form? Does this then lead, not to the birth of "art," but rather to a kind of *end?* "End" less as a finish than as a transcendence than can never be fully contained in a finite, sensuous form. Suppose there is a transcendence beyond the whole, though communicated equivocally in the works of wholeness great art creates? Transcendence may exceed the form of beauty, though it may still be sublimely beautiful. Such an exceeding would not simply be the birth of art but the work of the *religious.* The sublime in its excess to form may tell of transcendence in a sense that is not reducible to either aesthetic self-transcendence or to moral autonomy.

If, to end, we ponder on the virtualities of Kant's description of the sublime, it might suggest rather the birth of the *equivocal* religious. I do not mean the making of art into a quasi-religion, the inheritance of which is still with us. I mean rather a deep ambiguity, sometimes in the form of a vacillation, sometimes in the form of an evasion, sometimes in the form of a hostility, towards divine transcendence. Queries for later: are the different forms of the equivocal religious in Schopenhauer, Nietzsche, and Heidegger all connected with different *counterfeits of release?* What could a counterfeit release be? What has it to do with the "saving" power of art?

Kant mentions with praise the refusal of the Jews to fashion graven images. But he still insists on complete security for autonomous self-determination. Hegel will connect the sublime with what he calls the Oriental world generally, and with the sense of divine transcendence in monotheistic religion, and especially in Judaism. Hegel will even praise the Psalms for the majesty of their sublime poetry. I would say: they sing the glory of creation. But this sublimity for Hegel is only a symbolic beginning whose indeterminacy will be conquered by the dialectical progress of reason. Hegel will carry through the logic of self-mediation through otherness even more thoroughly than Kant, and finally here too, there will be a domestication, albeit dialectical, of the excess of transcendence. The glory of creation will be dimmed into spirit in its alienation. There will be no sublime, no glory of creation in such spiritless exteriority. That is Hegel's problem.

I would say: The seeming birth of art as equivocal religion will threaten a different death to the religious, and perhaps a different death to art too. I would also say: The sublime excess of transcendence may have to be resurrected for thought, beyond the logic of self-mediation; and beyond the new bewitchment with ourselves that arises when we think we have freed ourselves from the bewitchments of allegedly naïve subreptions.

3

The Otherness of Art's Enigma— Resolved or Dissolved?

Hegel and the Dialectical Origin

HEGEL BETWEEN ENLIGHTENMENT AND ROMANTICISM

In this and the following chapter, I offer two explorations of Hegel on art, origins, and otherness. In this chapter, I deal with whether Hegel resolves or dissolves art's enigma, in light of his overall aesthetics. We will see that Hegel's understanding of origin cannot but end by including art's otherness within a purportedly more inclusive conceptually self-mediating whole. Then in the following chapter, I look at what is revealed by his treatment of architecture, in some ways the most primitive art for Hegel, because most under the weight of matter's gravity. Here Hegelian spirit finds it hard to soar. Why then does Hegel soar, or seem to, when discussing the Gothic cathedral? This art of beginnings also has something to teach us of Hegel's dialectical origin, of yet undissolved otherness, of transcendence. But first some situating remarks.

Hegel is a thinker who, like Kant, moves between Enlightenment and Romanticism, though he does so differently. I note some opposite reactions to Hegel. Some see him as a betrayer of Enlightenment reason, the grandiose last metaphysician who seemed to learn nothing from the critical strictures of Kant. The acknowledgment of finitude at the heart of Kant's best thoughts is brusquely brushed aside in an intellectual impatience to surpass all limits. And so for such defenders of Kant's affiliations with Enlightenment reason, Hegel is in philosophy what his contemporary poets seemed to be in art: given to Romantic wind. This Hegel, we might say, *sweated too much*.

By contrast, there is the opposite evaluation: more uncompromisingly than Kant, Hegel is an heir of Enlightenment reason, in that he had undisguised contempt for Romantic wind, a contempt that found systematic expression in his conceptual mutilation of the mystery of religious transcendence, his excoriation of philosophies of faith or feeling, and his pronouncement that art, on the side of its highest destiny, is for us a thing of the past, for us, that is, we natives of the home and dry age of absolute reason. This Hegel, we might say, *did not sweat at all.*

How could such opposite evaluations arise? The simple answer is that there is some truth in both. The problem is that if we do not balance these truths properly, we end with a falsity, and make the truth of both views also untrue. There may also be an immanent equivocity here. Hegel only seems not to sweat because he is, so to say, *sweating within himself.* But then are we quite so home and dry in the age of absolute reason?

To the first: Hegel repeatedly criticizes Kant, claiming that the only coherent completion of Kant's philosophy of limit lies in the surpassing of limit; otherwise we could not determine limit itself, and by implication state the full implications of Kant's way of thinking. This is logic, not Romantic wind. But it is logic that is shaped originally in the feeling for the self-exceeding becoming of the human being. And so, even in the logic, the silhouette of Romantic striving shows itself. To be is to be beyond oneself, hence beyond limit; but to be thus beyond is to find oneself again, and hence not to be beyond. So we end with a philosophy of immanence in what looks superficially like a resort to transcendence as other. Romantic transcendence (Platonic eros too) is systematically brought within the boundaries of Enlightenment immanence.

To the second: Hegel did begin his philosophical odyssey as much under the influence of Romantic themes as Kantian. One might say that Hegel participated in the same equivocations as his contemporaries in their reading into Kant of Romantic concerns with art, and genius, and the sublime, and so on. We know that his collaboration with Schelling, the so-called "Prince of Romanticism," was important in his formation, but more indelible was the intimate influence of Hölderlin. But where the Kant of Pure Reason became more open to the importance of the aesthetic, Hegel moved in a somewhat opposed direction, that is, from Romanticism to a more and more systematic claim of the supremacy of reason. His drive for system demanded he overcome earlier Romantic equivocations, and oddly then he seems to be a more thoroughgoing heir of Enlightenment reason than even Kant. The two turn out to be far closer than surface appearances lead one to believe.

Can one then say that Hegel is *both:* Enlightenment thinker and Romantic dreamer? Yes, but with these qualifications. I mean that for him the dreams of Romanticism must become themselves Enlightenment. They must be woken from their aesthetic and religious slumbers by the cocky cry of reason, a reason even higher that the merely analytical understanding *(Verstand)* marking the standard Enlightenment, a reason *(Vernuft)* higher in fact just because it can appropriate to its own concepts *(Begriffen)* the dreams of art and religion. Enlightenment will dialectically embrace the sleeping rationality of Romanticism, and then it will no longer sleep, and there will also be no enigmas or mysteries hidden in sleep anymore. These dreams will then lose the bewitchments they cast previously because of the allure of a false, because secret, otherness. Philosophy will wake us from these dreams and bewitchments but fulfill them more satisfactorily in the supreme wakefulness of philosophy's absolute knowing. A higher enlightenment will satisfy both Enlightenment and Romanticism and we will not longer waver equivocally between these two.

Why no longer waver? I would say because Hegel's version of this higher reason claims to have the measure of this between, indeed of all betweens, and the between. Does this bring us back to Plato and philosophizing in the metaxu? Not quite. Rather Hegel offers an idealistic reconfiguration of the between in terms of a certain philosophy of *mediation*. This dialectic is not the dialogical dialectic of Plato that keeps the intermediate open as a space of interplay between self and other, or the transcending soul and the transcendent Good. Rather it continues the line defining Kant's reconfiguration of the between in terms of the self-activity of the knower as *the* mediating power between itself and what is other. This is absolutized as the self-positing, self-alienating, and self-returning absolute. It is not that otherness is not acknowledged by Hegel. It is mediated, hence acknowledged, but acknowledged as the other for self (the "self" of the "absolute"), and hence the medium in which a more inclusive, more absolute "self" can overreach *its* other, and thereby prove itself *at home with itself in its other*. But then, with Hegel's absolute, there is no other as other, no otherness that is beyond the reach and overreaching of the process of self-mediating reason. If there is a "middle," it here turns into an absolute whole, inclusive of all otherness, and hence is no genuine "middle" between one thing and an other, except in the now disingenuous sense of the medium of the absolute whole's mediation with itself. If this is true, then for Hegel between one thing and another finally there is no otherness as other, hence no between. It is all "between" the absolute and itself, in its own otherness.

What of eros and mania? They too are overreached, overtaken by a knowing of self fully lucid to itself, and in its own satisfied immanence absolutely freed from any transcendence as other to it. Home and dry in the epoch of absolute reason, what place then for the otherness of art, and transcendence of religion? What place for mimesis? What would be the Hegelian original? Would it not be one he claims is an absolute self-mediating origin? An origin "imitated" in the media of finitude, but in these finite media only *self-imitating,* and hence an origin again self-mediating? (An interesting thought: the absolute *mimicking itself in finitude,* as if it were *making faces of itself.*) But would not this too be the death of mimesis, and its religious sister, representation (Hegel's word, *Vorstellung*)?

The End of Art and the Dialectical Origin

Consider now that famous theme for which Hegel's aesthetics is known: the "death" of art. This is an extremely complicated issue in Hegel himself, with religious, political, historical, and ontological dimensions. It has been called to our attention in our century by thinkers as diverse as Heidegger and Danto. For Heidegger this "death" is related to the oblivion of the origin in *Seinsvergessenheit*—in the evening of the west we must await the dawn of a new origin. For Danto one wonders if a secularized world spirit has at last found a comfortable post-Hegelian resting home in New York art circles. Hegel himself never uses the term "death," though he does talk of art's dissolution *(Auflösung)*.[1] Can we understand the "death" of art without understanding the sense of dialectical origin, implicit in Hegel's aesthetics and continuous with his entire system? I think not. Claims about the end cannot be disjointed from understandings of the origin. This should not surprise any close reader of Hegel. Origin and end are not two separated extremes; finally, they are one, since both are mutually implied moments of a circle that traverses only its own circumference to constitute itself as a self-articulated whole.

The aesthetic importance of the issue is evident in post-Kantian culture where a sense of origin predominantly gets articulated in terms of notions like "originality," "creativity." This is explicit in Shaftesbury's utterance that I have quoted before and that, suitably modified, might be seen as a manifesto for aesthetic modernity: "We have undoubtedly the honour of being originals." I say modified, since Shaftesbury also calls the artist "a just Prometheus under Jove." The qualification is essential, since it subordinates human originality to a more ultimate power and hence hearkens back to the Platonism that Shaftesbury also maintained.[2] Later aesthetic modernity will hold that the honor of being an original demands that the creative self imitate *nothing other than itself:* it images, indeed originates itself alone. Again to invoke Emerson's pertinent saying: "Imitation is suicide."[3] Prometheus will refuse to be under Jove, indeed will claim to be self-creative. I think of Marx and Nietzsche as two such modern Prometheans. Marx stresses man's social self-creation through historical production; Nietzsche's artistic *Übermensch* is the individualistic hyperbole of Promethean self-creation.

---

1. G. W. F. Hegel *Vorlesungen uber die Ästhetik,* vols. 13–15 of *Werke,* ed. E. Molderhauer and K. M. Michel (Frankfurt: Suhrkamp, 1969–1971), vol. 14, 220 ff. where Hegel speaks of *die Auflösung* (dissolution) and *das Ende* of the Romantic artform; *Hegel's Aesthetics;* trans T. M. Knox (Oxford: Oxford University Press, 1975), vol. I, 593 ff. Hereafter I cite the German as VA, and the English as HA. Arthur Danto speaks of the end of art in *The Philosophical Disenfranchisement of Art* (New York: Columbia University Press, 1986); M. Heidegger in "The Origin of the Work of Art" in *Poetry, Language, Thought,* trans. and ed. A. Hofstadter (New York: Harper and Row, 1971) notes the still unmet challenge of Hegel's remarks about the end of art. The same translation appears in *Philosophies of Art and Beauty,* ed. A. Hofstadter and R. Kuhns (Chicago: University of Chicago Press, 1976), and I will refer to that translation. The German is "Der Ursprung des Kunstwerkes," in *Gesamtausgabe,* Bd. 5 (Frankfurt: Klostermann, 1977).

2. For Shaftesbury's remarks, see *Philosophies of Art and Beauty,* 252, 240.

3. *Emerson's Essays* (New York: Thomas Corwell, 1961), 32.

We confront again the relation of the "creative" self to otherness. The original the modern aesthetic self aspires to be is, as we saw, often associated with Romantic genius, understood as the artistic concretion of the active constitutive subject of Kantian transcendental philosophy. The significance of what is other to us is not intrinsic to otherness as such but is constituted by us as actively originative. Such a *subjectification of origination* has met with much criticism. What passes under the protean banner of postmodernism is only one more recent expression of this criticism, claiming to deconstruct such a self. Hegel's sense of origin, though articulated *within* the context of Romanticism, also claims to be beyond any such subjectification. Many aspects of his aesthetics make him still contemporary on these issues.[4] But his understanding of origin in terms of a *dialectical interplay* between self and other, in the end makes him a modern: this dialectic comes to rest in a complex *self-mediation* in which otherness is included as one of its necessary moments. Otherness is necessary to self-mediation, yet within dialectical self-mediation there is no final otherness that is recalcitrant to conceptual incorporation.

These general considerations have a bearing on his aesthetics, for the grounding logical structure of his thought percolates into his most challenging statements about art's importance and vocation. Dialectical self-mediation through otherness define both aesthetic origination and ending, each of which have important consequences for how we hermeneutically view the history of art and interpret its present dilemmas, for whether its present is an exhaustion or still promises a future of renewal. Hegel should be situated in the longer aesthetic tradition, if we are to be clear about his dialectical origin, both at the individual level in terms of genius, and at the historical level in terms of the forms of art, the symbolic, classical and romantic. We will then be in a position to grasp crucial difficulties at the "end" with Romantic art when all otherness seems for Hegel to have been aesthetically overcome. Dialectical self-mediation fits perfectly with Hegel's view that the radical turn to inwardness of Romantic art produces art's dissolution and transcendence of sensuous otherness. By contrast, I want to stress how otherness reappears in an even more recalcitrant form within this culture of "inwardness." The sweats break out again. At the so-called end of art, an inward otherness, inwardness as itself other and recalcitrant to dialectical encapsulation, remains reserved and dissident, signaling a silenced sense of origin in excess of dialectical self-mediation. Facing again the otherness of the origin, a *different* sense of the metaphysical importance of art is intimated, an intimation pursued by important post-Hegelian thinkers.

---

4. On Hegel and postmodernism, see *AA,* especially chapters 5 and 6. Also my "Art and the Absolute Revisited: The Neglect of Hegel's Aesthetics," in *Hegel's Aesthetics,* ed. William Maker (Albany: State University of New York Press, 2000), chapter 1.

Hegel's Origin: Beyond Platonic Originals and Kant's Transcendental Origin?

The question of origin cannot be confined to aesthetics, conceived of in a post-Kantian way, but has unavoidable metaphysical dimensions that cannot be divorced from our being in the between or from our relation to being as a "whole." The Hegelian form of this is evident in art being claimed for absolute spirit, together with religion and philosophy. We should favor Hegel with the company of post-Hegelian philosophers on this score: thinkers such as Schelling, Schopenhauer, Nietzsche, and Heidegger, philosophers for whom the relativity of origin and artistic origination is at issue. Perhaps origination in art communicates, even exemplifies a more primal sense of original being, not to be confined to art as some specialized domain? Does the great art work communicate something significant about the meaning of being as such? If it articulates a rapport with being at its ultimate, the philosopher must give due weight to what it reveals, even if this means having to contemplate the *breakdown* of his categories. This is not something Hegel contemplated about *his own categories,* which does not mean he did not think the categories of *others* might be inadequate to art, again as given residence by him in absolute spirit. But it is important to get clear that this feel for art is impossible to fit into post-Kantian aestheticism.

Reconsider Plato. It is impossible to think of his "aesthetics" in terms of any putative self-sufficiency of *"l'art pour l'art."* This would be to distort his concerns with a foreign superimposition. His "aesthetics" are "metaphysics" in the relation of image to original being, be it *eidos* or the good. His "aesthetics" are "psychology" and "ethics" with reference to the significance of erotic self-transcending, and the manic communication of inspiring power. We make Plato a moralistic thunderer against the seductions of passion to which art supposedly panders. But the ethical is grounded in relation to original being, in that the good human being is a mimesis of the good. As aesthetics and metaphysics cannot be divorced, neither can ethics and metaphysics.

Recall some salient points from our previous discussion. If the art work is a mimesis, it participates in a relation to original being, whether identified with the *eidē,* or some still more transcending source. Though it is an image, the art work nevertheless is a sensuous intermediation of intelligible being, considered as original and other. There is a participation that paradoxically brings near the intelligible otherness, without destroying our distance from it. The aesthetic pertains to what is sensuously presented to us, but the intelligible otherness so presented cannot be reduced without remainder to sensuous manifestation. There is a difference which brings home to us the *untruth* of claims to the mastery of original being. An otherness remains unmastered. And while an aesthetics of imitation can set up an incompletely bridged dualism of image and original, eros can intermediate the gap between image and original in terms of desire's movement beyond present partiality, while mania can intermediate the gap by the ingression from beyond of a powerful inspiration beyond our complete rational control. A similar point holds for philosophy. There is no complete, conceptual overcoming of this otherness of image and original. At the limit of *logos* Plato must perforce resort to *muthos*. The infamous denouncer of the image gives us the most powerful philosophical images.

Modern thought offers us less than this pluralized Platonic intermediation by singularly turning to the human self as mediating from itself its own dualistic opposition to nature, now reduced to an ensemble of objective things or a homogeneous *res extensa* (Descartes). Eternity as transcendent otherness is bracketed by philosophical reason or offered to religious faith for its safekeeping. No eternal Ideas mediate our relations to things (nominalism); things are just things, neutrally there. The upwardly directed motion of Platonic eros is redirected towards inwardness, since the search for original being finds no ultimacy in the external ensemble of soulless objects. The modern epoch originates, as it were, with the *epochē* of Platonic eternity and ends with its Nietzschean eclipse. Hegel stands somewhere between, as does his sense of origin and end.

In post-Kantian aesthetics the sense of origin is consonant with this turn to self. Large tracts of post-Kantian aesthetics depend on aesthetic reformulations (some covert, some overt) of Kant's doctrine of transcendental imagination. Aesthetic genius is the exemplary creative self who serves as the standard for less concentrated forms of human creativity. While Hegel breaks with the subjectification of the origin, his dialectical philosophy retains the crucial emphasis on self-mediation through the other. Art is understood as a form of dialectical self-mediation through sensuous otherness. His idealistic thinking cannot be innoculated from what is troublesome with all transcendental philosophy: does emphasis on the active constituting subject at the least attenuate, at the worst make impossible, true recognition of otherness as other? Does the mediating self so dominate the relation of self and other that all otherness is redefined as a *mediating detour* to our own self-appropriation? What else is entailed by Kant's *subreption?* Or think how today the language of "project" and "projection" is quite pervasive. If so, is otherness significant only in so far as it is *for* a self? This little word "for" can hide or silence a host of perplexities.

I name this one: even if the "for" acknowledges a relativity, even co-relativity of self and other, does the "for the self" inevitably place the other in an ultimately subordinate position in the intermediating relation as a whole? The "for" then covertly signals the project of the self to stamp its own self on the relation as whole, not only vis-à-vis the origination of the relation but also its final determination or consummation. Aesthetically this must mean that art becomes a form of self-mediation through which we always only mediate with ourselves, even while seeming to mediate with otherness. The image of the art work becomes a mirror in which we only see our own face. At best art becomes a mediated, if sensuous form of *self*-knowledge. If otherness remains, it too will be mediated, and the human being will only see *itself* again in that mediated otherness. No mystery, no enigma, no riddle will remain, or be allowed to remain, to mock our mediation.

Anxiety of the System: Origin as Other

Hegel's aesthetics points in this direction: *Humanus heisst der Heilige:* humanity is now the holy. But lest we too quickly take issue with this, we should consider the full dimensions of the matter, and remember how a concern with origins permeates Hegel's whole system. Hegel's obsession with beginnings is linked to the desire to make philosophy a presuppositionless science. This concern is pervasive in modern philosophy, extending from Descartes' view that philosophy requires a radical new beginning to Husserl's claim that phenomenology was an unprecedented philosophy of transcendental subjectivity. Hegel's worry is clear from his *Logic*. Why be surprised when one the most debated question is the legitimacy of Hegel's starting point? Hegel dwells on the question "With what must science begin?" yet a remarkable fact is that, at least in one interpretation of the entire system, it is the task of the *Phenomenology* to provide the beginning for genuine philosophical science. The task is to provide natural consciousness with the ladder to absolute knowing which allows us to *begin* to philosophize, properly speaking. It is to articulate the dialectical unfolding of consciousness from the immediacy of the natural standpoint to the entirely mediated self-knowing of philosophical science. Any genuine beginning, it seems, cannot be simple but must be inherently complex or mediated. We cannot simply begin or begin simply; to begin is already to be under way, to already have begun.

But if we always have begun, then we have never begun, and then where does our being on the way go? Does it go away? I would say we are always in the between, where we are given to be, before we begin to be self-determining and give ourselves our own determinate forms of being. But the ideal of presuppositionless science demands, it seems, that absolute knowing be entirely self-determining, that is, absolved from the original being given to be. Hegel must reconfigure this original being given to be, and this original giving, beyond self-determination, if it is to conform to the ideal of absolute self-determination, be it in knowing, or in being itself. Hegel's origin is, indeed, always too late, but too late not necessarily in the sense he intends.

I cannot pursue these issue further here, except to highlight the connection of origin and otherness. Hegel systematically cuts out what I call the primal agapeic astonishment before being as given in the between (see *BB*, chapter 1). Here we are given the marvel of the overdeterminacy of being: the mysterious too muchness of glorious givenness. This agapeic astonishment is the most primal source of the festive creativity of the human in art, as well as the celebrating reverence before the divine of the religious person and community. But Hegel begins with a derivative erotic perplexity that contracts this overdeterminacy into a mere indeterminacy: a lacking given that must be dialectically converted by negation into more and more determinate form, all the way to the truest form of determination which is absolute self-determination. The oblivion of the overdeterminacy in this beginning always effects the form in which the middle, or the intermediation of the between, is formulated by him. The whole he will claim is a whole that is emptied of all that, and so it is not the absolute whole he claims it to be. It is a counterfeit whole.

I have amplified these points in other places, but perhaps I have too quickly moved to proposing some countering reflections. Let me just say that the telos of Hegel's entire thought is implicit in his thought of beginnings. The telos is that thought become absolutely self-mediating, and so fulfill philosophy's desideratum, as Hegel saw it, namely that it be self-grounding, self-determining knowing. This is significantly different from the self-understanding of philosophy as intermediate or metaxological. The intermediacy of being has been converted into a philosophy of dialectical self-mediation in and through the self's own otherness. This *seems* to close the gap between the finite thinker and the ultimate origin. It also means that the Hegelian origin is only known as origin in so far as it mediates with itself. The development or unfolding of Hegel's origin is simply *its own dialectical self-mediation in its own otherness*. Moreover, since what is implicit in the origin is only known in and through this self-developing mediation, the full nature of the origin is only truly known in the completed end. The end is the origin, in so far as the end is the completed dialectical self-mediation of the immediacy of the putative first. For Hegel there is no radical origin as an *absolutely immediate first*. Rather the immediate first is always the undeveloped. Though in one regard we are always beyond the first immediacy, nevertheless the process of continuation, hence ongoing origination, does have a determinate character. For Hegel this recurring dynamic structure is again dialectical self-mediation in and through the self's own otherness, in which the end of the process fully realizes what was only implicit in the beginning, and in which the beginning is impoverished if asserted in its simple immediacy. All otherness is progressively appropriated by a process of dialectical self-mediating development.

Hegelian "Creativity"

A second apology to those who are not Hegelian adepts for risking lostness in the dialectical labyrinth of Hegelian enlightenment! Fortunately, there is an *aesthetic* manifestation of this view at which we can now look more closely. Hegel is committed to the view that the structure of the logical concept is the structure of being, the logic of dialectical self-mediation in and through its other will also appear in the unfolding of the logic of the aesthetic, and this will be so not only in concept, but also in "reality," that is, in human history.

Does Hegel have a notion of "creativity"? If he does, it entails a break with the subjectivism that was taken, rightly or wrongly, to be entailed by Kant's transcendental origin. Hegel speaks of self-generating Idea, self-articulating *Geist*. Hegel, I see, as navigating a course between Platonic and Kantian emphases. (Schopenhauer, as we will see, steered a course guided by the Platonic Idea and Kant's notion of freedom, but with decidedly different results.) The Hegelian Idea as original tries to unite the Platonic *eidos* and Kant's transcendental ego. With the Platonic *eidos,* it shares an ontological character and emphasis on determinate structure. With the transcendental ego, it underscores the active subject as self-articulating and self-relating. But here are the differences. Hegel's Idea articulates itself in *time,* hence we must transcend the Platonic dualism of time and eternity. History tells of the emergence of *Geist* which becomes free in its dialectical overcoming of otherness: spirit becomes at home with otherness by recognizing *itself* in otherness. This also defines the difference with Kantian "aestheticism" as demarcating the aesthetic as a self-contained realm. Hegel calls attention to a certain dialectical *porosity* of art, religion, philosophy, history. Gadamer rightly praises Hegel for this,[5] though, as we shall see, the porosity understood metaxologically is not the same.

First let me dwell on *origination as individual* to illustrate dialectical self-mediation in otherness. An art work is the production of an artist and as such it is something other to and external to its maker. We might here be tempted to insist on a *dualism* of creator and creation, but Hegel's dialectical way will undermine any such dualism. Creator and creation cannot be abstracted from each other and fixed as poles of an opposition. Both participate in a larger process in which each plays an indispensable role, though in mutual implication rather than separation.

Suppose one were to take the creative artist as an original power sufficient unto itself. The genius is a godlike being in himself; he has to do nothing but be himself; it is simply his being that establishes him as an original (Picasso said as much about himself). In the preciousness of his self-sufficient inwardness, he feels his status as creator. Thus the beautiful soul *(die schöne Seele)* that feels its aesthetic and ontological superiority, no matter what it does. Indeed it might be better not to do anything, for this would be to become entangled

---

5. As trying to unite Platonic and Kantian emphases, consider the remark in the aesthetics (VA, 13, 110; HA, I, 78) that the original concept *(der ursprungliche Begriff)* itself must *invent* the shape of concrete spirit, so that the *subjective* concept (in this case the spirit of art) merely *finds* this shape and makes it appropriate to free spiritual individuality. This shape which the Idea as spirit assumes in proceeding out into temporal manifestation is the human form. For further discussion of Hegel's aesthetics in relation to Plato's and Kant's, see *AA,* chapter 6. H.-G. Gadamer praises Hegel's break with Kantian aestheticism in *Truth and Method,* translation ed. G. Barden and J. Cumming (New York: Seabury Press, 1975), 87–88; see my "Hermeneutics and Hegel's Aesthetics," in *Irish Philosophical Journal,* 2 (1985), 94–104; reprint in *The International Library of Classical Essays in the History of Philosophy, HEGEL, Volume II,* ed. David Lamb (Aldershot: Ashgate, 1998), 335–45.

in the soiling otherness, and hence to compromise one's purity. The genius floats in condescending superiority over all otherness, but remains a god within himself.

Hegel is vicious in his attacks on this view. It is the abstraction of supercilious subjectivity. Far from being originative, it is impotent. It will not adventure in the world of otherness and so give real expression to itself. Apart from its smirk of divine condescension, it is as nothing; it is not original. It is the smile of the Chesire cat that has vanished into its subjectivistic self-satisfaction. The self must *other itself* to be properly itself. This is one of Hegel's important insights: the self comes to articulate itself in the objects it originates, but those objects offer the mirrors in which it knows its own power. The object, seemly other, is the self in its otherness. The work is the mediation, the middle by which the self comes to itself and its own self-knowledge.[6]

The same point can be made if we try to assert the *art work* as something subsistent. Hegel will deny this. The work is not a given thing that is there. Even as a thing, it is already an invitation to thought or mind. The work as worked is the objectification of mind, and hence the concretization of original activity. The call of this objectified origination to a respondent is the call to actualize the promise of the work. What is communicating here for Hegel? The work in itself is a mediation of its originating self, but as self-mediating, it calls for a corresponding self-mediation by the respondent. In its seeming thereness, its very otherness as there is a call to the other.[7] The other as beholder, in responding to the call of what is there, comes to mediate not only with the work as a given externality, but with *itself*, as finding itself at home in this externality. The otherness of the work becomes appropriated as the beholder's own otherness, and hence the medium or middle in which the opposition of work and beholder is dialectically overcome. Dialectical self-mediation in otherness seems to reassert itself again.

In sum, whether we consider the creator or work, Hegel will claim that the entire process is this dialectical self-mediation in which the spirit comes through otherness to its own self-knowledge. This is not the conceptual self-knowledge of philosophy, but the sensuous self-knowledge of art. Hegel believes such sensuous self-knowing offers us a dialectical circularity that is the aesthetic counterpart to the conceptual self-knowledge of philosophy. Granted some self-knowing is afforded in the happening of art, does the circle close, either aesthetically or conceptually? And does the communication actually keep open spaces of otherness that escape the logic of dialectical self-mediation through otherness? Indeed does artistic self-mediation itself open

---

6. On individual dialectical self-mediation, see, for instance, VA, 13, 50–51, 60–61; HA, I, 31–32, 38–39.

7. In relation to the call to the other, Hegel speaks of the art work as displaying the subjective for the subject and says that the spectator is, as it were, in the art work from the beginning. VA, 15, 28; HA, II, 802. Danto quotes this passage from Hegel (*op. cit.*, 135).

a renewed rapport with an *other happening of the between* of which there are no circular closures, and whose openness can communicate the call on us to participate more agapeically in free creation and re-creation?

These questions place us at an angle to Hegel. But it is important to remember that Hegel does not think that the process of aesthetic self-mediation is defined by an individual creator or beholder. Quite the contrary: an "abstract" individualism mars the cult of the godlike genius or beautiful soul. There are no individual creators apart from the more inclusive totalities of social and historical wholes. In turning now to this, Hegel in no way abandons the logic of dialectical self-mediation in otherness in favor of an original otherness that resists our determination, aesthetic or conceptual. Far from it, the development of the aesthetic in its rich historical unfolding, indeed at the level of the absolute where Hegel places it, evidences the same story. The Hegelian origin comes to (self-)determination in a process of historical emergence, but the dialectic of its unfolding and completion concretizes the *same logic*.

The inseparability of artistic creator and concrete historical world is especially evident in Hegel's three forms of art, the symbolic, classical, and romantic. Hegel rightly rescues the idea of origination from a merely subjective form: the genius (if we retain the idea) is originative in terms of gifts given by nature, but more importantly in terms of his rootedness in a rich *Sittlichkeit* or social form of life. This is very clear with premodern artists who did not have to imagine from nothing a distinctive aesthetic content. Their content was often the already rich mythological tradition, for this was a spontaneous formation of *Geist* in its social, ethical, religious embodiment. The genius as individual was the exemplary voice of this already operative historical and cultural formation of *Geist*. Origin has to be thought of in more than subjectivist terms.[8]

Only in modernity, with its unparalleled stress on the individual, does there emerge the idea of the individual creator as a unique original in its radical difference from the social ground. Indeed a great problem in modernity is just that the individual is uprooted from such a *sittlich* ground. This results in the subjective freedom to make *any* content our concern. The difficulty with this is that the artist must imagine from himself a content that thereafter must be invested with convincing aesthetic power. And this last cannot be merely individual. By contrast, art in premodern times serves to articulate the origin in a more than individualistic sense. For the aesthetic was the sensuous manifestation of the character of *Geist* as concretized in a particular *epochal formation;* hence the religious, the ethical, the political were not differentiated from the aesthetic. There is here an interesting affinity with the Platonic notion of the "aesthetic" as bound up with the ethical, religious, political formation of a

---

8. On genius, VA, 13, 363–73; HA, I 281–88; on the Greek artist and mythology, VA, 14, 27 ff.; HA, I, 438–40. The stress on myth in the "Earliest System-Program of German Idealism" is not denied, even if perhaps qualified, by the *Aesthetics*.

society. The "aesthetic" is musical, in the more encompassing sense of the Greek *ta mousika*.

Hence Hegel's three art-formations are not just "aesthetic" categories. They are names for *Weltanschauungen* (Hegel's word), that is, names for different formations of the power of being or *Geist* at its most originary and ultimate (VA, 13, 107 ff.; HA, I 76 ff.). A consideration of these three will tell us about Hegel's *epochal* theory of art and his sense of the origin as instituting, mediating, consolidating itself in different cultural, historical formations of *Geist*. I do not mean epochal in any simplistic linear sense. Rather different epochs concretize different dominant emphases in the relation between sensuousness and spirit. The symbolic refers us primarily to the oriental world, the classical to the Greek world, the romantic to the postclassical, Christian world. Through these three epochs, the entire historical process of aesthetic formation is subject to the logic of a dialectically self-mediating origin. This process begins with an unmastered otherness, but in the long run, coming to our time, it ends in the aesthetic mastery of the first otherness. Everything of the initial hiddenness is aesthetically brought to exposure.

First Epochal Self-mediation of the Origin: Symbolic Art and Indeterminate Beginnings

The *first* formation, the symbolic is dominated by nature's otherness and mystery. Here we find an indeterminate beginning, an aesthetic origin closest to the immediacy of sensuous nature. Such immediate beginnings are hardly beginnings at all, for Hegel. One thinks of Adorno's identification of origins and immediacy and his rejection of philosophical concern with either.[9] Hegel rejects any simple identification of immediacy with origin: the origin is always mediated. Hegel does not deny entirely a moment of immediacy, but concern with pure immediacy only displaces the problem of beginning. Instead of regressing along a temporal series to an immediate, pristine first, we are always, as I said, in the middle, which is a mediation of the immediate. The origin as a mediated origin always appears in the middle. The really crucial issue is not Adorno's rejection of origins as immediacy but whether that mediated origin is to be exhaustively described as dialectical self-mediation, or whether a more articulated metaxological understanding requires a different view of middle, hence also origin.

With symbolic art the sense of beginning found in Hegel's *Logic* crops up again. The undeveloped and indeterminate character that Hegel here stresses is found in the arts of oriental pantheisms, in Jewish sublimity, in Egyptian

9. T. Adorno, in *Against Epistemology*, trans. W. Domingo (Cambridge, Mass.: MIT, 1983), 20, seems to identify fascism, immediacy, and the search for origins.

enigma. All art for Hegel expresses the Ideal: the Idea in sensuous manifestation. The Idea manifests itself historically in the different epochal formations of *Geist,* and in these self-formations, the Ideal evidences a unification of form and content, a unification susceptible of different configurations, depending on the state of development of either the content or the form. The content ultimately is the Idea, but the Idea can lack its full self-mediation. Likewise, the sensuous form in which it tries to manifest itself can possess the character of an other that stands in opposition to the content's inherent requirement to be self-mediating.

This is the case with the symbolic beginning: the sensuous stands as an external otherness that overwhelms the spirit in its rudimentary state of development. To bring together the content and form involves *struggle* rather than harmonious unity; hence Hegel calls this art the *aspiration* of the Ideal. It is an art of yearning, one in which the spirit throws itself repeatedly into bizarre shapes because it does not really know itself and because nature's overwhelming presence affords it the only occasion of self-expression. It is an art of discord, of not-being-at-home with being. Hegelian *Geist* is not first at home with itself: nature has not been subdued as a proper other for spirit's own self-mediation; it is an alienating other. Any harmony and peace is either provisional or else a diminishment of spirit (see VA, 13, 107–9; HA, I 76–77).

Surrounded by the otherness of nature, spirit is subordinated to the engulfing whole. External otherness is infinite and inexhaustible, while inwardness is frail and finite. This *disproportion* between external otherness and inwardness is nowhere more clear than in Hegel's example of the pyramids. Egypt, for Hegel is "the land of symbols" and the sphinx is the "symbol of symbols." The purpose of the pyramid is spiritual—to be the burial chamber of the divine pharaoh, a vessel to safely carry the god-king to eternity. But the very massiveness of the physical structure swamps, encases the soul of the dead god-king. Spirit is entombed in a lifeless externality. The very tininess of entombed soul is eloquent testimony that spirit has not yet properly asserted its superiority to matter. Spirit is drowned in sensuousness, though its aspiration expresses its yearning for self-mediation. It tries to mediate with itself in otherness, but it cannot adequately do it because nature's otherness and the sensuous medium of its own self-expression are not yet subdued to its spiritual shape. Thus the sphinx, "symbol of symbols," is half-animal below, half-human above, imaging the emergence of the human from nature while being still immersed in it. Only by struggling with the otherness will it develop its own power sufficiently to stamp itself on the otherness with greater mastery, and only then will its proper self-mediation be possible (on Egypt see VA, 13, 448 ff.; HA, I 347 ff.).

For Hegel spirit emerges from and wrests itself free from nature with Jewish religion, as is reflected in their sublime poetry (e.g., the Psalms). God as spirit is elevated absolutely above nature. Through God's otherness as a radical "beyond," nature as an external otherness is dedivinized. Hence the human being, as the bearer of a higher spiritual destiny, itself promised by the transcendent God, can assert its superiority to nature. If Jewish sublimity allows the human self to assert its superiority to nature as an otherness, still for Hegel there is this problem: *God's otherness* is such as to diminish the human spirit to a subordinate role. Not nature's transcendence but God's prevents the more complete self-mediation of the human spirit. Dualism is necessary for Hegel to develop our difference, but if we remain in opposition, the mediation of self in the otherness is itself stopped. The human being becomes a servile, alienated thing confronted with a godless nature over against it, and threatened above by the towering and majestic transcendence of God (see VA, 13, 478 ff.; HA, I 371 ff.).

I am not endorsing these views of Hegel. Far from it. It is dubious if every form of otherness can be subordinated to Hegel's version of dialectical self-mediation. Why should God's otherness be the problem Hegel seems to think it is? Who dictates that the goal is the complete self-mediation of the human spirit? Spirit itself? God as spirit? Humanity as spirit? Could we even *articulate* what this would mean? If so, would it not be enigmatic and perplexing, perhaps not as perplexing as God's otherness, but certainly perplexing in its *hyperbolic* character? Hegel has no answer to these questions. Did he ask them, even have an inkling of what asking them might mean? Note only now how Hegel pursues the historical working out of dialectical self-mediation in otherness with an almost appalling, perhaps lethal consistency. But if his understanding of origin is off the mark, the entire subsequent development is systematically skewed away from the truth of the issue. The perplexities that should arise never do. I will return to this.

Second Epochal Self-mediation of Origin: Classical Art and the Achieved Ideal

With classical art, epitomized by Greek art and religion, we move beyond the above dualisms and beyond the striving of symbolic art. Art arrives with classical art. Hegel says the Ideal is attained: here is dialectical self-mediation in the most consummate aesthetic form.[10] Yet even the acme of Greek art is a mediated result—it has a history of struggle behind it, where what precedes harmony has strong symbolic overtones (see VA, 14, 64 ff.; HA, I 468–75). The indeterminate symbolic origin is dialectically self-mediated and, as aesthetically articulated, here receives its greatest manifestation. Nature, and

---

10. On the classical attainment of the Ideal see VA, 13, 109 ff., 114 (there he says of the three forms: *"Sie bestehen im Erstehen, Erreichen und Überschreiten des Ideals als der wahren Idee der Schönheit"*); HA, I 77 ff., 81.

especially the human body,[11] become the body of the gods, themselves seen as personal powers, not subpersonal savage forces (captured in the Titans). Spirit emerges from nature, comes into its difference as other to spiritless nature, yet retains its continuity with the sensuous symbolic beginning out of which it emerges. This is the aesthetic *Aufhebung*. For instance, the battle of the chthonic and Olympian gods, and the latter's victory which preserves something of the former, yields an *Aufhebung* in *myth* of the symbolic into the classical (see VA, 14, 46 ff.; HA, I 453 ff.).

Hölderlin called the Greek world *Ein Reich der Kunst*. Hegel agreed. Yet he had a complex attitude, mixing enthusiasm and skepticism, respect for its achievement but cold awareness that no return was possible (see *AA*, 106–14). His enthusiasm and reservation center precisely on the Greeks as *the aesthetic people*. That is, their way of being exhibits the logical structure of the concept as dialectical self-mediation in otherness, but this self-mediation predominantly takes an aesthetic form. Hegel even calls their religion the religion of art *(Kunstreligion)*.[12] Their gods are beautiful gods, expressing a union of nature and spirit, a union that itself is spiritual and not immersed in the otherness of nature as is the symbolic beginning. Spirit comes into its own as other to nature; though it is bound to nature as a sensuous other, it knows itself to be fundamentally dealing with *itself* in its dealing with nature. Does it not then epitomize the sensuous self-knowledge we discovered above in aesthetic self-mediation?

Because self-mediation attained the full promise of its aesthetic form in the Greek world, Hegel sees art as the fundamental mode of expressing here what he calls the *absolute*. Hegel's absolute is not a God beyond the whole; it is the immanent spirit that comes to full self-knowing in immanence itself; so he says. What is now salient is the *anthropomorphic* self-mediation of original *Geist*. With their "logocentric" predilections, philosophers look to the Greek world in terms of its great thinkers. Would one not expect this especially of the "panlogist" Hegel? But in his philosophy of history, the Greeks are not the people of philosophy but the aesthetic people. In this regard, Plato seems an *anomaly* in his relation to Greek aesthetic being, as Nietzsche claimed about Socrates. In a sense, Hegel agrees with Nietzsche. I demur: if Plato is also the philosopher of the image, such as I have argued, the situation is more complex than "Homer versus Plato." And this for the *philosopher*.

For Hegel, the ancient Greeks, as a *people*, were artists, not philosophers. Hegel claims their sense of the ultimate was expressed in threefold aesthetic fashion: as the subjective work of art, the objective work, and the political work of art. First, it is expressed in the care and cultivation devoted to the

---

11. On the body as organ of spirit see VA, 13, 194–95; HA, I 146–47; also *Enzyklopadie der philosophischen Wissenschaften im Grundrisse (1830)* (Hamburg: Meiner, 1959), §§411, 558.

12. See G. W. F. Hegel, *Phenomenology of Mind*, trans. A.V. Miller (Oxford: Clarendon Press, 1977), 424 ff.

human body, the only true vehicle of spirit in nature for Hegel. Hegel speaks of the *subjective work of art:* the bodied subject shapes itself as a living organic work of art, imbued with respect for the body not void of religious reverence. Second, the Greek people objectified its sense of the ultimate powers in the statues of the gods that are beautiful spiritual individualities: the artistic idealization of the human body is also essential. By contrast with the formless indeterminacy of the symbolic, we encounter determinate, indeed radiant individual wholes. As the aesthetic people the Greeks are the people of the Ideal. In the attained Ideal, every indeterminacy seems to have been overcome. Hegel calls these statues—religious more than merely "aesthetic" figures—the *objective works of art.* (Query: In what respect are Plato's Ideas the noetic counterparts to such aesthetic wholes?)

Third, Hegel refers to the Greek polis as the *political work of art.* Here we find the ethical, legal and political self-mediation of the Greek people that articulates itself in aesthetic shape. The polis was like an ethical, religious whole, shaped by its citizens as if by a community of artists. It is self-mediating, not in terms of any solo individuality but of the community as a whole. In the assembly, the customs and laws, in the games and festivals, *the people* came to recognize itself in the social otherness. The polis overcomes the otherness of the social world for the citizen and so, like a communal work of art, was a dialectical whole wherein the people found itself again.[13]

Why not say, here we have reached a completion and a summit? Why go further? How go further? For Hegel no time or people was ever so beautiful, or exceeded in beauty. What is the limitation in the achievement? Greek absoluteness is an *aesthetic absoluteness,* a harmonizing of mediated spirit and immediate sensuousness. And just because of the *otherness* of the aesthetic immediacy, the limit of this self-mediation of absoluteness appears. Dialectical self-mediation can never be absolute for Hegel if it remains tied to a sensuous other that remains a sensuous other. But there will *always* be some such a "remainder" in the aesthetic.

THIRD EPOCHAL SELF-MEDIATION OF ORIGIN: ROMANTIC ART AND THE EXCESS OF INWARDNESS

Hegel's third art form, the romantic, testifies to a more thoroughgoing *self*-mediation but also begins explicitly to *exceed* the form of the aesthetic. With romantic art we find a more radical turn to inwardness which, when known in its immanent infinity, can never rest contented with any merely finite form, or sensuous other.

---

13. On the subjective, objective, political work of art see *The Philosophy of History,* trans. J. Sibree (New York: Dover, 1956), 241–74.

What are the important considerations here for Hegel? There is the fact that *philosophy itself* "comes on the scene" (an interesting Hegelian locution): in its elevation of *thought*, philosophy breaks with the sensuous otherness of Greek aesthetic being (again I think of Plato). Hegel singles out Socrates as the beginning of the end of the Greek world and hence as marking a rupture with classical art. Hegel actually has some sympathy for Aristophanes' attack on Socrates, a sympathy that should astonish those who charge Hegel with simple "logocentrism."[14] Yet for Hegel philosophical thought does insist more uncompromisingly on a further dialectical self-mediation, the constitution of a self-grounding knowing. Philosophy mediates for the few, not the many. For the latter, the Christian religion (passing through the Roman world) articulates and historically consolidates a sense of spirit as an infinite inwardness that can never be adequately mediated in an aesthetic way. Spirit *overreaches* all sensuous otherness, because it knows itself to be always and in principle in excess of sensuous mediation. This means that dialectical self-mediation in otherness must now take place in inwardness. Here for Hegel both religious representation and conceptual thought are more adequate than art.

If in symbolic art, the infinitude of sensuous otherness exceeds the finiteness of spirit, with romantic art the infinitude of spirit as inward is always in excess of sensuous otherness as finite. Where symbolic art was the aspiration for the Ideal and classical art its attainment, romantic art is the transcendence of the Ideal. We move beyond art as an *aesthetic* self-mediation. The opening of the depth of inwardness gives rise to a sense of the transcendence, one might said, excess of inwardness, to any sensuous manifestation. This is reflected in the Christian emphasis on the infinite worth of the individual. Here, and not unrelated to the romantic notion of original genius, individuality as individuality receives confirmation. Original individuality will, of course, only be developed further by the secularization of the Christian standpoint in modern Romanticism. But it is already contained in the Christian view of God as an individual human being—Christ. Romantic art does not present the idealized human body of classical, Greek art. We see the this body racked by this particular suffering of torment and death. Christ's agony and crucifiction cannot be idealized in an Apollonian way. What is at stake is not a beautiful sensuous other, but a deeper appreciation of inwardness, including its destined knowing of extreme suffering.

For Hegel human selfhood as thus individual is the concrete embodiment of infinite inwardness. From the end of the Greek world to our own time, the epochal formation of spirit is dominated by this sense of infinite inwardness and the working out of its implications. These implications are as much social and cultural as individual. It is not that otherness vanishes; rather its dialecti-

---

14. See *BHD*, chapter 6 "Can Philosophy Laugh at Itself? On Hegel and Aristophanes—with a bow to Plato."

cal overcoming takes place in the ethos of a different culture of spirit. Hegel details a long process to this dialectical overcoming. The Roman emphasis on the legal person's universality; the anguish of a godless world driving the self into itself; Medieval dualism as projecting this "beyondness" of the self to sensuous externality into a supersensuous "beyond"; the Reformation recovery of immanent freedom; the subsequent secularization of selfhood that transubstantiates worldly life—spirit presses forward through all these towards its final reconciliation with *itself* in Hegel's own time: the fulfilled mediation of an unsurpassable return to self.

This compressed summary of Hegel's view of historical development shows how at its end what we normally called Romantic art appears, though obviously "romantic" for Hegel has a wider connotation. Now the development reaches an end in the full articulation of all the essential aesthetic possibilities. This telos *reiterates* the structure of aesthetic origination, namely, dialectical self-mediation in and through sensuous otherness. Romantic art is the art of infinite inwardness, hence its self-mediation cannot be simply aesthetic—no sensuous otherness will ever serve as the absolute mirror in which inwardness can completely recognize itself. This is one reason why Hegel sees romantic art as *art transcending itself*. What was implicit in the beginning has at last come out of its hiddenness.

The indefinite, symbolic beginning, with its enigma, mystery, yearning for elusive "beyondness," has now been entirely mediated, aesthetically speaking. Art has fulfilled its task of entirely mediating the dialectical origin. The new disproportion between sensuous otherness and spiritual inwardness signals the completion and exhaustion of the power of the aesthetic as an absolute mode of self-mediation. This is why I said at the outset that Hegel's view of the end of art can only be fully understood if we understand his sense of origin. For this end is for him the entire self-mediation of what was implicit in the aesthetic origin and its being brought out into the light of spirit. The end is the origin again, in the sense of a return to symbolic disproportion but in an entirely new context, demanding both religion and philosophy for the truly absolute self-mediation of inwardness.

I underscore that this result, while necessary for Hegel, is fraught with ambiguity. For this end also produces the *subjectification* of origination spoken of earlier. Thus Hegel speaks of an overcoming of the *content* of art in its *otherness*. The modern Romantic artist is no longer tied to the substantial ground of a rich *Sittlichkeit*. He is a subjective creator, no longer rooted in one of the essential *Weltanschauungen*. I cite the most important passage where Hegel implies that what was implicit in the beginning has been brought to exposure out of its hiddenness. In the course of the development, he says:

> the whole situation has altogether altered. This, however, we must not regard as a mere accidental misfortune suffered by art from without owing to a distress of the times, the sense for the prosaic, lack of

> interest, etc; on the contrary, it is the effect and the progress of art itself which, by bringing before our vision as an object its own indwelling material, at every step along this road makes its own contribution to freeing art from the content represented. What through art or thinking we have before our physical or spiritual eye as an object has lost all absolute interest for us if it has been put before us so completely that the content is exhausted, that everything is revealed, and nothing obscure or inward is left over any more. . . . The spirit only occupies itself with objects so long as there is something secret, not revealed *(ein Geheimes, Nichtoffenbares),* in them. This is the case so long as the material is identical with the substance of our own being. But if the essential world views implicit in the concept of art, and the range of the content belonging to them, are in every respect revealed by art, then art has got rid of this content which on every occasion was determinate for a particular people, a particular age, and the true need to resume it again is awakened only with the need to turn *against* the content that was alone valid hitherto; thus in Greece Aristophanes rose up against his present world, and Lucian against the whole of the Greek past.[15]

The subjectification of artistic origination gives the individual creator a new, more democratic freedom, licensing him to take up any content as the occasion of the display of *his own* virtuosity. But this greater subjective freedom means for Hegel the loss of substantial grounding, and so a *loss of spiritual seriousness for art.* Thus the paradox: the deeper subjective inwardness becomes, the more its nature as spirit is developed, the greater the danger of the loss of spiritual seriousness on the part of that subjectivity. If everything and anything can now be the content of art, nothing really shows itself as aesthetically absolute anymore, except perhaps the subjective virtuosity of the individual creator. His subjective originality replaces (let us call it) the transsubjective origin whose aesthetic self-mediation is historically effected by the three formations of art.

Hegel, I believe, provides us with a hermeneutic narrative that claims to show *the necessity of that loss,* though his own vituperation against the shallowness of subjectivity in his own time show him in no way to be reconciled with its spiritual bankruptcy. (One wonders about an analogous aporia in Hegel's ethical-political views in relation to the place of subjective freedom in the modern state.) One cannot but ask: What right has he *not to be reconciled* with this loss, since he has shown us its necessity, it seems? And how dare he *preach*

15. VA, 14, 234; HA, II, 604–05; Hegel goes on to talk about humor and comedy in relation the debunking power of subjectivity. On Hegel's own harshness towards the subjectification of *Originalität,* see VA, 13, 380–84; HA, I, 294–98.

against the shallowness of that subjectivity, for has he not shown his dialectical origin as destined to that outcome? As if to say: It *must* be, but *ought not to be!* And there is nothing more that Hegel despised in other philosophers than preaching. But listen more carefully to him. Hegel too mounts his pulpit.

Does Hegel not have his escape route? I mean does he not *leap* beyond the aesthetic? And must there not be something like this, since it is the consummate form of the aesthetic that creates the dilemma that it itself cannot solve? If the language of leap is too Kierkegaardian, we could still say: Hegel claims to follow the thrust of the aesthetic in the direction of its own self-transcending; the aesthetic as romantic inwardness *itself* points to its own self-transcending. Only a more intensive inwardness and a more spiritual self-mediation will effect the solution. Ultimately only philosophy, as Hegel understands philosophy, can effect the absolute self-mediation through otherness, both in form and content. Religion and art may have the absolute content but they both lack the absolute form, since their forms are still burdened with an otherness not yet dialectically overcome.

In sum: the dialectical origin is driven by the quest to overreach all otherness, a quest that cannot be completed aesthetically. The dialectical essence of that quest is manifest aesthetically in Hegel's account of the progress from symbolic, through classical to romantic art. The symbolic is the immediate, impoverished first; the classical is the aesthetic middle; the romantic is the end which entirely mediates the sense of "beyond" of the symbolic, though it returns to a new sense of disproportion in inwardness, indeed it yields the aesthetic aporia just outlined. The aesthetic cannot complete the quest for the dialectical overreaching of all otherness; ultimately this romantic disproportion can be overcome, Hegel believes, only by Hegel's own philosophical concept as the articulation of spirit where inwardness is both the content and the form. Are we not back again between Romanticism and Enlightenment? But is it not here that the *immanent sweats* begin to break out again? Does something break in, in inwardness itself? Instead of being home and dry, does something here leave us high and dry?

BEYOND THE DIALECTICAL ORIGIN: THE ENIGMA OF OTHERNESS INTENSIFIED?

The above aesthetic aporia is very important, but our response need not be Hegel's intensification of dialectical self-mediation in religion and philosophy. Quite to the contrary: We can be surprised by an intensification of astonishment before the otherness of the origin. My remarks now open a set of issues whose fuller significance will engage us diversely in subsequent chapters. The main point now: even granting Hegel his outcome of the aesthetic mediation (namely, infinite inwardness), otherness is not in fact unambiguously overcome. Otherness reappears in an even more recalcitrant form *within* the context of inwardness. For at the so-called end of art, inwardness as itself other and recalcitrant suggests a sense of origin in excess of any dialectical self-mediation. What Hegel grants as the infinitude of Romantic inwardness suggests an inward otherness, and one wonders if it could ever be entirely mediated in a dialectical fashion. Does not Hegel have his own version of Kant's terror before genius: origin exceeding determinability and self-determination?

Suppose we grant the complex twists and turns of Hegel's dialectical self-mediation of otherness, the question is: Does the inward otherness resist such self-mediation? Is inwardness an otherness precisely because its infinitude points to a ground beyond encapsulation? Is the enigma of this ground dialectically overcome, as Hegel believes, either by religious representation or the philosophical concept, if both the latter are also the issue of, or derivative from this ground? If that origin makes self-mediation possible, is it not other to self-mediation, and other precisely as possibilizing self-mediation? Did this otherness of the origin not possibilize our original powers, there would be no self-mediation, dialectical or otherwise. One might multiply related questions. I cite Rimbaud's much cited utterance: *Je c'est un autre,* I is an other. This is a post-Romantic echoing of Augustine's great exclamation, itself spoken in the context of religious inwardness (Romantic inwardness for Hegel): *grande profundum est ipse homo.* Rimbaud's systematic disordering of the senses is very suggestive of possibilities, not least of a kind of creative eros or mania, and not all of them pointing in a merely aesthetic direction. When inwardness is seen as an inward otherness, the "self" is other to itself; it does not quite know "itself" anymore. In knowing itself, it knows it does not know itself. There is always something other to its own self-knowing, in its own self-knowing.

Does the *disproportion* of inwardness point to the transcendence of the origin to dialectic? Is dialectic itself made possible by this other original which is never exhausted by any its issue? Does this origin grant an otherness to its issue, such that these creations are not to be defined as *its own* others: finite others that are not its own self-othering, or the media of its own self-creation; others endowed with this difference, given to be as other, as true creations. This origin is not mimicing *itself* in immanence, making faces of *itself* in finitude. It is not a child that sucks its thumb and thereby mimics the whole; not a knowing that kisses its own back-side and so feels it completes the circle. Such an origin as other might originate its own self-mediation, but its self-mediation is *not the same* as its creation of what is other to it. As creative origin it would exceed every one of the derivative creations which it gives to be. Such an origin, I think, would have to be described in the language of *agapeic origination,* in which the creation is not for the sake of a dialectical return of the origin to itself, but is released into a free difference that is endowed with the power to become creative in finitude (see *BB,* chapter 6). Such an origin would be truer to the otherness of the ethos of being as a between, an ethos that exceeds all self-mediating determinations. It would be truer to the disproportion of the origin intimated in the excess of infinite inwardness. It would be an overdeterminate source of origination, not a merely indeterminate beginning, or lacking indefiniteness, as in Hegel. Something remains dialectically unmastered, namely, the originative ground of all putative dialectical self-masterings.

I conclude this present reflection with three remarks that take their cue from Hegel's triad of absolute spirit. I will speak of the aesthetic other, the religious other, and the other of philosophical logos. An understanding of the relation of the three different to Hegel's is needed.

Aesthetic otherness: A point of major interest is that Hegel *does* recognize in this infinite inwardness what I called an inward otherness; certainly other in its resistance to aesthetic encapsulation. What develops in Romantic art is a certain *excess of subjectivity,* as I call it in *Art and the Absolute.*[16] Hegel tended to see the *negative* side of this excess. Romantic subjectivity becomes an inward restlessness that crystallizes as an aesthetic version of what he called the "bad infinite"—the inability to attain any standpoint of harmony or wholeness, a voraciously discontented subjectivity that flits from one aesthetic possibility to another. It interesting that Kierkegaard and Hegel are in agreement here. Kierkegaard's figure for this dissatisfied excess of subjectivity that endlessly seeks ever new satisfactions is Don Juan. Inward otherness, of course, can take this form of negative excess. But there can also be a positive expression of the "excess," the "more." I think Nietzsche was getting at something of this when he spoke of individuals who create out of an affirmative excess, out of plenty rather than lack or poverty. The negative side is a dissolving, ontologically unanchored selfhood; the positive side is the inward otherness that creates from out of an original plentitude. Is this excess the image of agapeic origination?

If we grant this latter sense of original plenitude, it does not mean jettisoning dialectical mediation entirely, as many of Hegel's antagonists do, but acknowledging the limiting otherness that relativizes the absolute claims Hegel makes for it. Can we say that art after Hegel sometimes vacillates between these two poles of excess or transcendence? One thinks of Nietzsche's distinction between the decadent and the tragic artist, the first creating from lack, the second from a rich surplus of will to power. One thinks of Picasso saying that a painting is a sum of destructions. Picasso himself might be seen as a unity of the two: great destroyer, great creator, mixing violent disgust with being, with intrepid exploration of the labyrinth of the dark breast. One senses here something of the ancient duality of eros as a destroyer, eros as creator, *eros turannos, eros uranos.* Or indeed the perplexity of discerning the difference of divine madness and mad madness.

Hegel himself turns away from any celebration of this inward otherness in the Romantic manner, because he wanted uncompromisingly to overcome

---

16. On Romantic and post-Romantic art and excessive subjectivity, see *AA,* 114–20.

all otherness. Any Romantic celebration of otherness struck him, one might say, as a "feminine" dwelling in enigmas that a more masculine logical thought would penetrate. Certainly one of the lessons of art after Hegel points towards the above noted ambiguity in the "excess" of inwardness. Consider this example from André Breton's *Second Manifesto of Surrealism*:[17] "Let us remember that the point of Surrealism is simply the total recovery of the powers of the mind by a means none other than a vertiginous inner descent, the systematic lighting up of all our hidden places, and the progressive shading off of the others. A ceaseless promenade in full forbidden zone." This was written more than a century after Hegel, but how current its desiderata (if one can call them that) still sound. An interesting mix of the anarchic innerness and the systematic? A wild afterlife of Hegel? Not so silly a suggestion, when one thinks of the surrealists' desire for affiliation with communism, another afterlife of dialectical thought. And the "ceaseless promenade in full forbidden zone"? The surrealists were not the first to promenade, and now after perhaps centuries of such promenading the thrill of transgression is a little dulled. It is, the cool say, "no sweat" any more. If there is an *inward* sweat, why does one wonder about a sort of *forced sweat?* And where a kind of shameless confession is pursued, it lacks the religious point of Augustine's vertiginous inner descent: *reverent shamelessness* before God.[18]

Hegel saw that the excess can degenerate into the "bad infinite"—the excessive subjectivity that is despair of finding peace with being.[19] But it can also be an excessive subjectivity open to an other sense of origin as the enigmatic ground of selfhood within self. This is central to some post-Hegelian thinkers concerned with art's importance. They learn a different lesson from art than Hegel, and with implications for philosophical thought. Here begins exploration of the limits of "logocentrism," perhaps even its dismantling from within.

---

17. André Breton, *Oeuvres complètes,* vol. I (Paris: Gallimard, 1988), 791. See Ian Gibson, *The Shameful Life of Salvador Dalí* (London: Faber and Faber, 1997), 241–42.

18. One also wonders if hatred of beauty in post-Enlightenment culture sometimes conceals a contorted anti-religious religiousness. We find contempt for anodyne beauty, but what is beyond beauty? Is it sublime? Sometimes rather it is the outrage, sought to raise a pleased howl of protest, successful often enough now to have become for us the boring outrage. But perhaps we should not take the outrages too seriously (as indeed we are sometimes admonished to do), politely suppress our yawn, and exclaim, How interesting! Of course, sometimes we seem so bored that the outrage has to become more extreme to dispel the loss of interest, "beyond good and evil," you might say, as when Stockhausen marvelled at the terrorist attack on the World Trade Center Towers as *das größte Kunstwerk*. Damien Hirst congratulated this event too as a work of art in its own right, "visually stunning" albeit "wicked." He retracted almost immediately into abject apology, but something had come of it, I suppose—celebrity attention having been achieved.

19. Hegel's notion of true infinitude is always articulated in terms of a self-mediating circle whose end returns to its beginning, while the so-called "bad infinite" is the failure of such self-mediation. Perhaps, however, there is a true infinitude, which is not Hegel's "bad infinite," and relative to which Hegel's own true infinitude, and the claims he makes on its behalf, itself appears as a false infinitude, or a playing false with the openness of the infinite.

Thus in completing subjective idealism and breaking with it, Schelling was intent to preserve a sense of otherness to the imperialistic subject: the great art work concretizes that otherness in a way that resists complete conceptualization. The original or primal identity of subject-object as realized in the great art work manifests an *unconscious* as well as conscious side. This duality of unconscious/conscious will never be entirely transmuted into an absolutely singular consciousness which lucidly incorporates the unconscious as other; without the otherness of the unconscious, self-consciousness would itself not be possible. Similarly, Schopenhauer understood will as primal being, a dark origin in relation to which the deepest source of art is said to be on reason's other side. As original being, the will for Schopenhauer transcends the principle of sufficient reason and the subject-object split that obtains in the phenomenal realm. In so far as *music* is *the* metaphysical art, we are on the other side of any logicist determination of the character of primal being. So also for Nietzsche, the sense of the ultimate origin is spoken of as will to power. This is sacrally or mythically named as Dionysus whose irreducibility to the Apollonian logos signals its otherness. Heidegger points to the otherness of the origin which withdraws from manifestation even as it makes all manifestation possible. Being in its primal plenitude is other to the subjectivism and will to power of the modern era, other to the putative "logocentric" mastery of the metaphysical tradition. Even Derridean *différance* might be seen as an inward otherness relative to the absolute self-presence of Husserl's transcendental ego considered as an absolute origin.

Religious otherness: I can only mention the point now.[20] If the inward otherness and its infinity resists dialectical self-mediation, then we must ask if there is in Hegel an equivocal relation between wholeness and infinity. There is a matter here which concerns (among others) Levinas and Derrida: Athens and Jerusalem.[21] Does not Hegel always tip his hat towards wholeness because of dialectical self-mediation, hence tipping towards Greek circularity rather than the unmastered infinite whose otherness resists the Greek logos (see previous mention of Jewish sublimity)? Admittedly Hegel is ambiguous, since infinite inwardness can never be adequately understood in terms of Greek circularity. But this is true of the circle of *aesthetic* self-mediation. He does claim that in the Christian religion there is a complete return to self in inwardness, hence a spiritual, and not just sensuous, dialectical circularity, and that this inward dialectical circle is only fully closed in the philosophical *Begriff* in terms of form (itself absolutely inward) and content (always ultimately inward). In religion and philosophy, thus understood, does not dialectical self-

20. The point will be more developed in the next chapter on the Gothic Cathedral, and I return to it on a broader canvas in my last chapter. For a full study see *Hegel's God: A Counterfeit Double?* (Aldershot: Ashgate Publishing, 2003).

21. See Richard Kearney's revealing interviews with both Levinas and Derrida in *Dialogues with Contemporary Thinkers* (Manchester: Manchester University Press, 1984), chapters 2 and 5.

mediation again predominate and appropriate all infinitude and transcendence? This is a variant of the question of divine otherness put repeatedly to Hegel, in the accusation of "pantheism" in his own life, and trenchantly by Kierkegaard in relation to the intermediation of the finite and the infinite. Kierkegaard's insistence on the *final hiddenness* of religious inwardness is relevant to the issue at stake vis-à-vis the inward otherness.

Philosophy and otherness: If inward otherness, precisely as infinite, evidences a resistance to dialectical self-mediation through otherness, if the self in its inward otherness cannot be entirely self-mediated thus, the matter for philosophy is not a return to a simple, undialectical "either-or" between reason and the irrational, thought and nonthought. One can be other than dialectical without being undialectical. Kierkegaard is a classic case. The issue is not one of abandoning thought for deconstructive celebrations on the margins of philosophy, but of developing thought in a manner which does justice both to the qualified claims of dialectical self-mediation and the philosophical necessity of openness to otherness at the limit of self-mediation. Thought must not only think itself but also its other, and not simply its other in a dialectical sense only.

The question of art's beginning and end brings us back to the beginning of philosophy, as Nietzsche and Heidegger would agree. Wonder *(thaumazein)* is the pathos of the philosopher, Socrates says, and also its arche, as Aristotle reiterates. But if, in fact, otherness were entirely overcome by Hegel, this originating wonder would vanish. Hegel claims as much with reference to art and hiddenness. If we were to transpose this claim to *thinking,* philosophy would also lose its interest. Since Descartes, *doubt,* not wonder, has been said to be the beginning of philosophy. Doubt is wonder's negative counterpart. Their difference mirrors philosophically the two senses of transcendence or excess distinguished above. Hegel wanted to overcome doubt through doubt itself, as the negative that negates itself, thus looking to complete Descartes' quest for certainty. This again implies a certain subordination of otherness in that (in the *Phenomenology*) Hegel seeks the dialectical identity of truth and *self*-certainty. Hence his controversial claim that philosophy as love of wisdom, where ontological wonder is never put to rest, only deepened, at last becomes wisdom as science *(Wissenschaft),* where the negatively transcending power of doubt is affirmatively transformed into systematic knowledge.

By contrast, the great art work in its otherness to the logical concept may offers us an occasion of such originating wonder—ontological admiration, appreciation of being. If wonder at the origin is entirely brought out of its initial hiddenness by art's dialectical development, it must cease to provide this challenge to philosophy, and philosophy itself, if it cannot be challenged by originating wonder coming from elsewhere or itself, must itself atrophy.

Is it then surprising that soon after Hegel speaks of the end of art, we find talk of the end of philosophy? Or that where "wonder" survives, its astonishment is transmuted into intellectual curiosity about technical puzzles—as has happened with many analytical heirs of Enlightenment, and Hegel? Alternatively, one might react against Hegel and reassert the power of otherness, in art and elsewhere. This is what happens in many of Hegel's continental heirs—perhaps most challengingly in Heidegger, who was cognizant of the modern tendency towards the deformation of philosophical wonder into mathematicized, technicist curiosity. The danger here (deconstructive thinking risks this danger) is that in an excess of fear that Hegel's dialectical self-mediation exhausts *all possibilities* of philosophy, one leaps outside philosophy. Our alternatives cannot be only the contraction of dialectic into analytical virtuosity, or a deconstructive surpassing of dialectic into an unphilosophical "outside." Philosophy, as much as art and religion, takes form in the primal porosity of being, and can come to mindfulness of this.

The origin and end of art cannot be separated from philosophy's quest for origins, including its own origin. The resurrection of its originating wonder, agapeic astonishment, is in question, in how we think of the otherness of being and our ontological relatedness to it. If there is a sense of the original otherness of being beyond dialectical self-mediation which art (and not only art) serves to communicate, then philosophy after Hegel can only renew itself by coming again into communication with that otherness and thinking it through in terms other than Hegel's. Beyond the alternatives above, we need a riper maturing of metaxological mindfulness.

And art's ontological significance? This can bring us to the limits of self-determining knowing, and so foster the promise of metaxological mindfulness. But what if the practices of art acquiesce in the "death" that is "announced" as their destiny? Then one may have to consider reluctantly that, in such circumstances, they offer a deficient home for metaxological mindfulness. The solicitation of generous creation is held out to art too. Art, no less than religion or philosophy, may play false with the promise, and the chalice it passes on be poisoned. There is no evading the need to discern the equivocity, be it of art, or religion, or philosophy. Philosophy needs finesse, but if the practices of art themselves lack finesse, they can hinder rather than help. If ontological perplexity before the otherness of the origin solicits philosophy, philosophy may have to make good on the promise in a disturbed reawakening, beyond the sleep of Hegelian self-determination, and its too many incognito afterlives.

4

Gothic Hegel

On Architecture and the Finer Enchantments of Transcendence

Flying Up and Flying Down: Architecture and Home

An interesting light on origins, art, otherness is shed by considering the case of architecture. This is not a merely "aesthetic" art, in that it is bound up with the everyday life of a people, and the ethos of ethical value in which people go about their diverse businesses. The ethical and religious practices of a people are reflected in their architectures, how they build homes for themselves on earth. I mean "home" in the extended sense of having to do with a being at home with being, in its more immediately practical sense, and also its more extraordinary dimensions, and not least with respect to ultimate powers that transcend humans. A home includes what shelters us from the sometimes forbidding elements of nature, what gives us a livable place wherein to enact the tasks and joys of everyday life, and also the space to house our understanding of the first and ultimate things. Building a home allows us to live with the transcendence of nature, its support and its threat, with the self-transcendence of the human, in its practical and more contemplative modes, and with the sacred space of transcendence itself.

Architecture for Hegel is the most primitive art, in that Hegelian spirit is least released from the gravity of matter into its own being at home with itself. But is this "home"—this being at home with *itself?* If the origin is other to dialectical self-mediation, this "being at home with itself" is not home, but the simulation of being at home with what is other to oneself. Architecture, this art of beginnings, teaches Hegel about art's overcoming of the heavy otherness of matter. Does it fly up? How does it fly up? Because there is still yet an other presentiment of origin? Does not Hegel insist it be brought back to earth again? Why does Hegel insist on this further immanence of the human spirit?

On the whole, there is something disappointing about Hegel's discussion of architecture. I mean this primarily in a philosophical sense. I do not deny that, as always, one is somewhat astonished at Hegel's comprehensive intentions, even where these exceed his actual reach. Those of us who have long studied Hegel are often overcome with a sense of the "too muchness" of what Hegel seems to know. Even when Hegel's knowledge is sketchy one is still impressed. No, what I mean is that there are long stretches of his discussion of architecture which seem to lack an element of philosophical *inspiration*. One finds there is much descriptive work going on, even an element of quasi-technical virtuosity, say, in his discussion of elements of the Greek temple. But much of the discussion, so to say, does not take fire.

Hegel partly excuses himself in advance by claiming that something about architecture hinders more then helps the self-manifestation of spirit. The gravity which concerns architecture, the very heaviness of matter itself with which architecture has to wrestle, these present real resistance to being shaped into a vehicle for the expression of spirit. Hegel also suggests that this very materiality of architecture determines a variety of factors that resist being easily assimilated into a straightforward systematic account. Not that Hegelian system is ever straightforward. Moreover, despite these limitations, Hegel does labor to bring the recalcitrance of his own material into some sort of systematic exposition.

I find one place where Hegel seems to be more philosophically set on fire, namely, in his discussion of the Gothic cathedral. Am I superimposing some of my own aesthetic preferences? Perhaps. Nevertheless, I find that in the discussion of the Gothic cathedral there are more sustained passages of philosophical flight, and generally a sense that Hegel has been roused from the rather somnolent, albeit dutifully competent expositions of other forms of architecture. I want to look at Hegel being thus set on fire. Our question might be thus put: What is this enchantment of transcendence? Who is this one, this Gothic Hegel?

My interest is aroused by the fact that often one thinks of Hegel as given to a certain hostility to things Medieval and Catholic. I think, of course, of his discussion of the unhappy consciousness in the *Phenomenology*, often interpreted, whether rightly or wrongly, as a very disparaging picture of the putative other-worldliness of medieval religiosity. One thinks also of Hegel's picture of the Catholic Middle Ages in his *Lectures on the Philosophy of History* which borders on sectarian slander. He presents the epoch as in thrall to a patriarchal transcendence that really causes it to be sunk in spiritual corruption. And yet here in his discussion of the Medieval cathedral, Hegel seems to soar. Who then is this Gothic Hegel? Am I overestimating his sympathy? Am I underestimating what is being left unsaid?

I suggest that typically Hegelian equivocities are at work in his approach: a "yes" followed by a "no," and the "no" so qualifies the "yes" that we are uncertain what remains of it, despite all reassurances that the essential has been "preserved." Does the balance of "yes" and "no" amount to the more inclusive dialectical whole Hegel claims? I doubt it. I doubt it, just because such a language of the inclusive whole is untrue to the transcendence of the God beyond the whole sung in Gothic soaring. Something about Gothic transcendence enchants and alarms Hegel. Enchants: for this transcendence lifts the native eros of the human spirit above itself. Alarms: for someone determined above all else to make his final home here below in the prosaic bourgeois world of secular modernity, this "being above" must bring not only a fear of flying but a refusal. Or perhaps: a systematic *reversal* of flying up: a flying down, even as one seems to fly up. Does Hegel have wings enough to avoid a crash on the earth?

First, I rehearse the systematic context which shapes this flaring of the Gothic Hegel. Then I look more intently at this Gothic Hegel, with a side glance at the Greek Heidegger who, though he was a lapsed Catholic, a torn Catholic, glows with philosophical fire before the Greek temple. I want to raise a question about secular architecture. How might Hegel stand architecturally in our time of the prose of the world? Why Hegel's massive silence about more contemporary architecture? And then I come again to Hegel's equivocity towards transcendence, and the otherness of the origin.

ARCHITECTURE: AESTHETIC AND MORE THAN AESTHETIC

The major systematic components in Hegel's account of architecture are particularizations of the general requirements of the Ideal, and then further of the different formations in which the Ideal comes to definition, completion and surpassing. The Ideal is the Idea in sensuous shape. A spiritual content is embodied, such that there is a sensualization of spirit, a spiritualization of the sensuous. But there are a plurality of possible relations of Idea and embodiment. There are three formations that progressively give more adequate realization, both in terms of the truth of art and historically, to the requirements of the Ideal. These three are, as we saw before, the symbolic, the classical, and the romantic formations of art. These, in turn, correspond to the Oriental, the Greek, and the Germanic/Christian worlds of the philosophy of history. This systematic unfolding of relations between Idea and embodiment defines Hegel's approach to art, but the classification is not at all static. It articulates a dynamic becoming in which the beginning is always relatively indeterminate—for Hegel this means impoverished, and undeveloped—while it is the end that is most richly determinate and complete. The end is the true realization of the latent promise of the beginning.

The complication with regard to architecture is that Hegel sees it as an individual form of art that always and necessarily partakes of the beginning.

So architecture as a particular art corresponds to the *symbolic* form of art, realizing that form in the most appropriate manner.[1] The environment of externality it creates merely indicates the spiritual meaning: its meaning is communicated symbolically. Even when classical and romantic in form, architecture still is symbolic, since it remains at the indeterminate beginning.

As such a beginning, art is still seeking for a proper mode to express its sense of spiritual significance. In a sense, it is always a seeking of this harmony, and hence never fully realized as art. Moreover, there is the fact that architecture for Hegel is most burdened with matter, and the weight of gravity itself weighs down the energy of spirit. The work of architecture with matter has to struggle as against an obstacle, an obstacle that is always only partially conquered. Hence as the art of the beginning, Hegel places it at the bottom of the hierarchy of individual arts (VA, 14, 258–59; HA, 624).

There is the added consideration that for Hegel art has to be an end in itself. It is a free value for itself alone, and is not justified by extrinsic purposes. But architecture is so placed in the flow of life that this ideal of being an end in itself is subjected to severe strain. In one sense, the idea feeds into an aestheticism which makes the work for itself alone. But Hegel does not subscribe in any simple way to this aestheticism. Great art is the manifestation of spirit, hence also embodies the richest expression of a culture's or people's sense of what is most ultimate and high. One of the great strengths of Hegel's aesthetics as a whole, in my view, is just his refreshing freedom from this aestheticist view of art.[2] And this is especially evident with respect to the three forms, symbolic, classical, romantic. They refer to fundamental configuration of our understanding of being at its most ultimate, most fully expressed in the sense of the divine that finds representation in the mythologies and religions of different epochs and peoples.

One would think that from this point of view the non-aestheticist aspect of architecture would recommend itself to Hegel: all of human life, the spirit, is somehow manifest in the architecture of a people, and not life in its contemplative modes, but also life in the nuance of its pragmatic transformation. Architecture reveals what a people ultimately values. This strongly impresses itself on us with sacred space, be it the Neolithic burial mound at Newgrange, or the Pyramids, or the Gothic cathedral, or the Temple of Heaven at Tiantan Park. There is so much at stake in the construction of such buildings or spaces that they show the trouble to which people are willing to go, as they put up monuments not always to their own magnificence but to what they consider magnificent for itself. And this even in the age of prose where people will only

---

1. G. W. F. Hegel, *Vorlesungen uber die Ästhetik,* in *Werke,* ed. E. Moldenhauer and K. M. Michel (Frankfurt: Suhrkamp, 1969–1971), Bd. 14, 269; English translation T.M. Knox, *Hegel's Aesthetics* (Oxford: Clarendon Press, 1975), II, 632.

2. On this see "Art and the Absolute Revisited: The Neglect of Hegel's Aesthetics."

trouble to build in the image of their own search for quick convenience, or effective utility. What is loved, what is ultimately valued, is still shown.

But I need to offer some qualifications. Hegel is clearly aware of the inseparability of architecture and purpose, but what interests him is, so to say, the transformation of purpose: its transfiguration through art into being an end for itself. He looks to the creation of a work that gathers up into itself what is most rich in the life of a people or epoch, and to no falsification of what is even everyday and pragmatic in its concerns. Building can obviously rise to such a level and thereby enter the realm of art. Hegel seems aware of this doubleness of character in relation to architecture, namely, the need to serve definite purposes, and the need artistically to present a work that itself is its own purpose, and hence is beyond any one determinate, finite purpose. The need to serve a purpose may range from unrefined protection against the elements to the most sublime creation of space for entrance into the holy. None of these purposes is purely aesthetic. Is this an objection or defect? There are times when Hegel wavers here. He wants art to be for itself, and yet knows that art cannot be for itself alone; if it is to be great it must have an openness that makes a home for all the major importances of the human being. This means its openness to, and also possibly contamination by, the seemingly "nonaesthetic." This should not bother Hegel at all, I think, and yet there are times when he is not sure how the double requirement dovetails into the singular harmonious wholeness of a great work.

Another line of approach might be this. The freedom of art and especially of architecture is not that of the purely aesthetic. It is rather a freeing of the human spirit that comes to sensuous articulation in the great work of art. What is freed may include reference to the fullness of the human spirit, and indeed must do so in great works of art. The work of art is an end in itself because it is just the sensuous concretization of a certain freedom, the freedom of the human spirit as it takes on its most rich embodiments. This second line need not be subject to the disjunction of purpose, and being an end in itself. For the purpose of art is just this freeing, which in one sense has no end beyond itself. The main question then becomes the character of this freeing or release. The fact that architecture has a practical purpose may have nothing to do with the aestheticist criterion that there be nothing "extrinsic" to purely aesthetic requirements. Its purpose is just to concretize a sensuous space for freedom, a freedom that shines through the so-called nonaesthetic concerns. Art does not lie to one side of the non-aesthetic, but is a releasing transformation that works in and through the nonaesthetic, and lifts it up to its own divine freedom. Whatever one says of these suggestions, I believe they illuminate Hegel's discussion, and also the Gothic Hegel who catches fire at the end. As I will try now to indicate, this fire is smoldering in and through the previous configurations of architecture, but now the embers flare into brightness. But they were burning all along, are always burning all along.

GOTHIC HEGEL

Consider in a little more detail the three formations of art as Hegel relates them to architecture. In the symbolic formation of art there is an indeterminacy to the spiritual content and a certain predominance of the sensuous or material embodiment. In this regard, Hegel's discussion of the Egyptian pyramids, and the sphinx shows this massiveness of the material embodiment dominating the still relatively indefinite spiritual content that is struggling to emerge into the light of day. The riddling sphinx embodies this doubleness of nature and nurture: the claws of the lion, massive claws, hence powerful as nature is powerful, but capable of tearing and twisting and effortlessly killing; the breasts of the woman that give suck and gently nurture the child. These architectural structures show the spiritual condition of the people, and most especially in relation to the meaning of death.

The classical formation is an ideal form wherein an individualized and determinate unification of spirit and sensuous embodiment is found. Generally we find this in Greek art, most especially in its sculpture, but also in its architecture. For instance, the unstrained placement of the human being in nature is suggested by the way, relative to the Greek temple, one can as easily step outside, as walk within the building itself. The temple is not closed in, even though it offers a human space that is not at all immersed in nature. Moreover the spiritual is not immersed in the building as in the symbolical, but has also been attained outside the building, namely, the emergence of an immediate sense of spiritual individuality (VA, 14, 303–4; HA, 661). This latter is most concentrated in the sculpture of the god, but the temple serves to house this, but again in no sense of merely closing it in.

The romantic formation is one where a sense of the Idea begins to transcends what can be entirely incorporated into any sensuous manifestation. Like the symbolic there is here an excess but in a kind of reverse: it is the excess of spirit over the sensuous, rather than the dominance of sensuous materiality over spirit. The accent is not on the immediate harmonious embodiment of spirit, but on the surpassing of spirit, beyond every determinate embodiment. The stress is then on transcending. And thus the Gothic cathedral as the embodiment of the romantic form of architecture is transcending in massive materiality itself: the massiveness of materiality is itself made to soar. Is Hegel just parasitical on this soaring when I call him the Gothic Hegel? Or does he, as I think, get caught up by the transcending materiality itself and turn upwards?

How may we connect this with Hegel's point that architecture corresponds to the symbolic form? I think we need to reconsider the double requirement previously noted, namely, of a building as serving definite purposes, and as standing there as a work for itself. The first is served relative to the religious purpose of the building; the second is embodied there, because the point of the building is just what is contained within the building. Hegel at one stage calls our attention to what he calls "a point of supreme importance which I have not found emphasized anywhere although it is implicit in the concept of the thing and can alone provide an explanation of the varied shapes of buildings and a guiding thread through the labyrinth of architectural forms." The supreme point is to find buildings which unite the above requirements, namely serving to enclose a purpose, and yet which "stand there independently in themselves, as it were like works of sculpture, and which carry their meaning in themselves and not in some external aim and need" (VA, 14, 269; HA, 632).

This point of supreme importance recurs in Hegel's opening remarks on romantic architecture. Noting that the Gothic is the properly romantic style, and that it had been considered crude and barbaric for a long time, Hegel endorses Goethe's efforts to rehabilitate Gothic architecture, in opposition to the hegemony of the French taste, meaning, I suppose, the neo-classical. The religious function is particularly to be stressed, but not as any mere extrinsic purpose. As he puts it: ". . . the architecture which is independent is united with that which serves a purpose" (VA, 14, 330; HA, 684). Utility is transcended and the building is erected freely, independently, and on its own account. Thus while these buildings are entirely suitable for worship and other uses, their real character transcends any specific end. Thus, "as perfect in themselves, [they] stand there on their own account."

One is tempted to quote a longish passage here, since it would be hard to better Hegel himself, he says it so well (VA, 14, 331; HA, 684–85):

> The work stands there by itself, fixed, and eternal. Therefore no purely abstractly intellectual [or mathematical] relation determines the character of the whole; the interior does not have the box-like form of our Protestant churches which are built only to be filled by a congregation and have nothing but pews like stalls in a stable. Externally the [medieval] building rises freely to a pinnacle, so that, however appropriate it is to its purpose, the purpose disappears again and the whole is given the look of an independent existent. No one thing completely exhausts a building like this; everything is lost in the greatness of the whole. It has and displays a definite purpose; but in its grandeur and sublime peace it is lifted above anything purely utilitarian into an infinity in itself. This elevation *(Erhebung)* above the finite, and this simple solidity, is its one characteristic aspect. In its other it is precisely where particularization, diversity, and variety gain the fullest scope, but without letting the whole fall apart into mere trifles and accidental details. On the contrary, here the majesty of art brings back into simple unity everything thus divided up and partitioned.

When one reads passages like this one feels like saying: Hats off to Hegel!

Let me call attention to a few points. I note the very sharp sideswipe at Protestant churches, even though Hegel clearly identifies himself as Protestant.

These churches partake of the prose of the world; their box-like form embodies an architectural geometry, inspired by uninspired *Verstand*. If the pews are like stalls in a stable, this hardly means that the worshipers are like the infant Jesus in Bethlehem. One thinks more of the dumb attendant animals. I must not overread Hegel, but all this does seem to reverse Hegel's normal apotheosis of Protestantism and slander of Catholicism.

It seems to me also that Hegel's account of the Gothic cathedral fits well with what Kant ascribes to beauty, even though here we are dealing with sublime architecture, not the beautiful. I mean Kant's immensely suggestive notion of purposiveness without any definite purpose (*Zweckmässigheit ohne Zweck*, see *Critique of Judgment*, §15). Relative to the sublimity of the cathedral, I would say there is a kind of religious purposelessness that yet is peculiarly purposive, beyond every definite or finite purpose. And this purposeless purposiveness is not extrinsically imposed from above by a heavenly despot but comes to shine in the soaring self-transcending that arises out of the earth itself. It is the earth itself that is transformed, lifted up, by this purposeless purposiveness. Hegel refers to the elevation above the finite, and this phrase is redolent of his own view of religion as an *Erhebung* of the finite to the infinite. Nor is this elevation a denial of the finite, since particularities and diversity do not fall apart into an unconnected manifold. The whole building offers a home to all together. You might say that if there is a contrast of the secular and the transcendent, the contrast is surpassed in the surpassing dynamic of the building itself which transforms what is below in a kind of vertical exstasis in stone.

There are other points worth mentioning. I note that Hegel is intent on stating how the Medieval cathedral serves to recollect the soul in inwardness. This is one of the major developments of humanity in postclassical culture. Indeed we still live with its legacy, even though the sacred aura seems to have been stripped off it, and religious inwardness is lost in an omnivorous secular self. The Medieval cathedral provides an enclosure from the outside; one goes inside. Even the light allowed to filter through the stain glass windows is not the light of nature. Overall, the movement of inward recollection is the first, and then in a second movement, out of inward recollection there is a movement upwards. The process is not set out quite so boldly by Hegel. But as I thus describe it, I cannot help thinking of the description of Augustine of his own *itinerarium ad Deum: ab exterioribus ad interiora, ab inferioribus ad superiora.*[3]

One might here ask about the peculiar *intimacy of massiveness* we can experience in a Medieval cathedral. This is connected with the recollection of

3. *Enarratio in Ps.*, 145, 5; PL 37, 1887. Erwin Panofsky speaks of the Medieval *manifestatio* and *concordantia* as involving an "acceptance and ultimate reconciliation of contradictory possibilities" (*Gothic Architecture and Scholasticism* [New York: Meridian Books, 1958], 64). This has a dialectical ring to it and he even mentions the Hegelian triad (86). He all but speaks of the cathedral as an *Aufhebung* of other buildings (78–79). We, of course, cannot forget transcendence as other of which there is no Hegelian *Aufhebung*.

inwardness. But the inwardness is not any precious subjectivism. Nor is the massive meant merely to cow or quash the self. It is to lift it up to the superior, to make it feel its own community with the superior, even in the frailty of its finiteness. Why does the massiveness of some secular building emanate a sense of the sinister? One thinks of the grandiose structures dreamt of by the Nazis, by Albert Speer, for instance.[4] Without the intimacy of inwardness, and the community with the spiritually superior, massiveness becomes a fake sublime, indeed a sinister sublimity, since it really has nothing to do with the freeing of the self, with the release of its highest powers. Loss of intimacy of spirit leads, as it were, to monstrous pyramids that merely crush us with their weight; for their exploitation of the sublime is for purposes of cowing people into conformity before the surrogate superiority of the sinister. Breakdown without breakthrough of spirit. I think a question that comes out of this is how can we create large spaces and still retain something of this intimacy of being. How discriminate such spaces from their counterfeit doubles?

Moreover, this intimacy has nothing to do with isolated subjectivity at all. Hegel does not have to be told this. I particularly call attention to the what we might call Hegel's sense of the catholic character of the Gothic cathedral, in the sense of an ecumenically inclusive community. In the cathedral there is room for the entire community, Hegel says (VA, 14, 340; HA, 692). The assembly of the community is not just around the building but within it. A wide variety of interests have their place. People come and go. The most various goings on can coexist simultaneously, if there is not a high mass going on: a sermon, a sick man brought in, a baptism, a marriage, a bier. Hegel compares the people to wandering nomads. But the variety of activities are not dispersed into a dissipated multiplicity. Nothing entirely fills the building, things pass quickly. No doubt here Hegel is drawing on the contrast

4. Albert Speer, *Architecture, 1932–1942,* foreword by Albert Speer, editor Leon Krier, introduction by Lars Olof Larsson (Bruxelles: Aux Archives D'Archictecture Moderne, 1985). In his foreword of 1978, Speer says: "[M]y architecture represented an intimidating show of power. . . . It was the fulfillment of a claim to dominance over a nation. Every person, if they wanted to survive, had to submit to it" (213). He speaks of standing before St. Peter's in Rome (1936), when already he had drawn up the plans for Berlin's Great Hall. Though "the eye was unable to transmit the notion of scale here achieved, . . . the greatest church of Christendom appeared to me both familiar and comprehensible. . . . I returned from Rome dismayed. All my attempts to give my buildings the power of their vast dimensions were doomed to failure, when these dimensions could not be given a credible mediation" (ibid.). "When Hitler spoke of the effect of a building he had planned, he always referred to the power of suggestion. He would talk enthusiastically about the farmer who would travel all the way from the provinces to Berlin, enter the Great Hall, that gigantic area of 220 metres high and 250 metres diameter, and felt literally crushed by what he saw" (214). You can be sure such farmers would not hear the Angelus in such monstrous buildings. An analogous example: the mausoleum to the dead Mao by Tiananmen Square strikes one as the mimicry of the sacred; while close by, yet so far away, in Tiantan Park, the Temple of Heaven, though not now consecrated to sacred rites, still communicates, in its great spaces, and without intimidation, something of the intimate streaming of the serenity of the highest.

between transience and eternity, a contrast that itself seems embodied in the constancy of the immense building itself. It is the sublime that is here embodied and the human spirit is not only concentrated on itself and its own interiority, but once being recollected to its own infinite inwardness, it soars illimitably into the infinite.

There is more that could be said about the details of the Gothic Hegel, but those of us who have stepped out of the cathedral and read Hegel outside know that there are Hegelian silences here. We know something of what Hegel sees as the equivocities of this transcending, but these remain relatively recessive in the account here. Do I detect a slight current of contempt in the reference to nomads? After all *Geist* builds higher civilizations only when human beings cease to wander and settle down. We must not remain strangers on the earth. And does not Hegel see such strangers as trapped by the dangerous seduction of vertical transcendence?

It might provide an illuminating contrast here to cast a sidelong glance at what we might call the Heideggerian temple. In Heidegger's discussion of the origin of the art work two cited examples are notable: The Greek temple and the peasant shoes.[5] Both express a world. And of course, the Greek temple expresses one kind of world, the peasant shoes another, worlds actually at very different poles, the classical and romantic, in Hegel's nomenclature. One overhears Heidegger's resonance with the Greek temple, for its tense rootedness in the earth. Even though earth and world are distinguished, the temple is rooted in the earth, it emerges out of the earth. Hegel's account of soaring materiality does put us in mind of Heideggerian strife between earth and world. But it is the rising of the world *above* earth that is the question. The earth itself entails an element of concealedness. One thinks of the Nietzschean command in Zarathustra's diktat: Remain true to the earth, O my brothers, remain true to the earth! Despise those Christian priestly afterworldsmen, looking into the beyond![6] Hegel does not chant or rant like Nietzsche, though he does sometimes preach in the name of rational necessity, and yet he too was a brother who would remain true to the earth. Even the Gothic Hegel.

Is there not some important shift when Heidegger turns to the peasant shoes? I put aside the question of whether these boots belonged to van Gogh himself. And whether van Gogh's shoes belong to French peasants or Dutch peasants, they were Christian peasants, I suppose, not pre-Christian Greeks. These peasants belong to a more Gothic than Greek world, I surmise. Suppose we see these peasants as perhaps Lutheran peasants of Germanic roots. Even if they are French peasants, hence Catholic, their shoes are firmly placed within Hegel's Germanic world, the world of inwardness and Christianity and post-

---

5. Martin Heidegger, "The Origin of the Work of Art," in *Philosophies of Art and Beauty,* 663 ff. (shoes), 670 ff. (Greek temple). I return to Heidegger.

6. F. Nietzsche, *Thus Spoke Zarathustra,* Part I, section 3.

Christianity. What have the shoes got to do with architecture? Van Gogh was influenced by Millet and some of his paintings. One thinks of the peasant and his wife and their heads bowed at the Angelus. When the bells of the Angelus toll out from the church, it is not to the Greek temple they call us. If Hegel calls us to cease being strangers on the earth, our new rootedness would have to be as much Christian as Greek, more Christian, in fact, since there is no renouncing the call to inwardness. But is there a renouncing of the call to the superior as transcendence above us, beyond us? The Gothic Hegel must settle down and make his dialectical peace with the world. And the professor will not be wearing peasant shoes either when he makes that settled peace.

Just as we wonder why the Lutheran Hegel takes flight at the Gothic, we wonder why the Catholic Heidegger seems more rooted to the earth, and remains silent about the toll of transcendence in the world of the Christian peasant. If we stood in the shoes of the peasants what kind of elevation would we experience? They do not remain rooted to the earth. Why does Heidegger say nothing of this? Does it reflect his tortured relation to Catholicism? One finds nothing of tortured Catholicism, even in the Gothic Hegel; perhaps nothing of torture at all.

Why this serenity? Perhaps because for Hegel the Gothic has its place but it is not the last word. If romantic art and the Gothic are the third and last form of architecture Hegel treats, still we know that Hegel thinks all architecture is still symbolic, and so tied to the beginning, and its undeveloped indeterminacy. We must not be allowed to get too enthusiastic about the Gothic Hegel. There is much to come that will painfully puncture our soaring.

We have to think that the Gothic Hegel is only a passing philosophical nomad, dialectically arising and vanishing. Is not the settled Hegel the more real Hegel, the burger philosopher of the early nineteenth century? But is it not astonishing that Hegel have almost nothing to say about architecture of his own time, or even other times more contemporary to his own. Why this silence?

Is it because the fate of the poetry of the Gothic is to become the prose of the modern? And if so, then must not architecture lose much of its spiritual power, at least in Hegel's scheme? For if architecture is symbolic, then with the advent of the age of prose, we must give up the symbol, and settle down amid the transparent signs of prose that reach the limit of freedom from the sensuous medium as such. The symbolic sculpture that is the Gothic outside must be deciphered. Or if the symbol persists, it will at most survive with a subordinate function but devoid of any cultural or spiritual dominance. The prose of the world must clip the wings of transcendence. (Voila the age of information!) It will put the house of God to one side, even on a hill if it must, but there will be worldly work to do, and we must get busy. So busy, we clog the primal porosity between us and the divine. So busy, we cannot spend too much time on our buildings beyond what is necessary to make then functional and efficient. There is work to do but it is not sublime work, not even beautiful. It is utilitarian exploitation of the earth, not its *Erhebung*.

One wishes that Hegel had more to say on this score. Heidegger's meditation on technology is not silent here. Hegel hated any kind of nostalgia that was a retreat or escape from the present. And yet there is this massive silence about the present in his treatment of architecture. And then there is his eloquent song about the Gothic. Did he wander too far from his home? Then why do we feel him so at home, at home even as his thought takes wing, in the sublime cathedral? Gothic Hegel is carried by a surge of transcending, the same transcending Hegel will dialectically domesticate. Hegel, I well know, will offer us a myriad of dialectical justifications as to why Gothic transcendence must return its soaring to the earth. Dialectic will necessitate that we make our philosophical peace with the prose of the world. Well let us pretend we have settled for that peace. But who still can forget the brief flaring of that Gothic Hegel, and the haunting song beyond all prose?

HIGH BUT NOT SO DRY: THOUGHT SINGING WHAT IS OTHER

Must we close our ears to that song? Can thought sing what is other, and not just think itself? Is there a being at home, beyond our being at home with ourselves? Are there finer enchantments of transcendence that do not bewitch us but bless? Here are some observations.

First, transcendence is not at all an Hegelian word, and where there is any suggestion of it, it seems predominantly associated with a dualistic *Jenseits*. We see this in his attitude to the unhappy consciousness, but also in his attitude to the sublime and the symbolic. The unhappy consciousness? Come now and look on a different serenity to Hegel's. Look at the faces of some of those figures, carved before the entrance of Chartres Cathedral: faces of extraordinary serenity marking a door to the house of God, one could hardly credit the gargoyle faces leering out higher up. The serenity seems to come from above, and yet here it is below, marking entrances and exits, and radiating intimately from within out in these figures. The unhappy consciousness? No. Is their serenity even beyond the gods of Greece? One would have to be spiritually coarse, a philosophical gargoyle, not to see these as the faces of blessing, their shine gifted by the peace of the divine agape and its festivity.

Nor is there anything in Hegel such as I would designate as a post-Romantic symbol.[7] Transcendence as other is dialectically assimilated to a comprehensive form of self-mediating *Geist,* ultimately at home with itself

---

7. On a post-Romantic symbol, see *DDO,* 237–38, 246; *BB,* 216–22, especially 220. Properly, I should rather speak of the *hyperbolic,* and not just the symbolic, since the hyperbolic suggests our "being thrown *above*" *(huperballein)*. The hyperbolic is in the dimension of the overdeterminate, as I explain in *Being and the Between*.

through its own self-becoming in and through its own other.[8] Does one here detect some vacillation between the aesthetic and the religious? In his *Aesthetics* Hegel sometimes strikes one as somewhat equivocal about the aesthetic as "for itself" in distinction to the "religious." Is this an acquiescence in contemporaneity and art as for itself, an acquiescence that followed by others, like the Romantics, leads in directions to which Hegel could not acquiesce? His understanding of the religious exceeds potentially many of his contemporaries, though this is not the case with respect to the representation of transcendence as other. Finally, he too is a cheerleader for the cultus of self-determining being, offering a holistic logic, that eschews any thought of transcendence as other, or of a God beyond the whole.

Second, what of Hegel's dialectical qualification of the symbolic? The symbolic is said to deal with the infinite but under the form, or formlessness, of the indefinite. The teleological thrust of all Hegelian dialectic is from the indefinite to the determinate, thence to the self-determining. Infinity as mere indefiniteness can be at most an impoverished starting point; it is not the fullness of the completion. The idea that there is fullness "before," at the origin, and not just at the end, is not to the fore in Hegel. It is also this thrust from the indefinite to the determinate and self-determining that makes Hegel's dialectic not the best way to bring to mindfullness what I have called the porosity of being—a porosity of relevance to the cathedral, for without this porosity it would be hard to make sense of the happening of *prayer*. Of course, it does seem odd to think of architecture in terms of the indefinite. The porosity is not Hegel's indefinite. And the Gothic cathedral suggests less the infinite as indefinite as a *whole world*, as Hegel himself grants. But crucially, in this instance, such a whole world yet points beyond—opens up an immanent porosity that points beyond the immanent whole. If Hegel grants the point about world, it is this ecstatic porosity and pointing beyond the immanent whole that shows up Hegel's hesitation. But such a "beyond," contra Hegel, might have nothing to do with dualistic opposition to a *Jenseits;* it might have everything to do with the very vector of transcendence towards transcendence as other that energizes human self-surpassing. Is this not perhaps one reason why Hegel himself become infected himself with the contagion of that energy when dealing with the Gothic?

Third, consider the *beyond within,* as one might call it, relative to the pervasiveness of the romantic in Hegel's time. Whether we speak of Christian or post-Christian art, nevertheless some sense of inner infinity seems absolute. Is this really a "beyond within"? Hegel understands this inner infinity as resolving

8. The ultimate is imaged in terms of a self-transcendence that looks like an erotic origin that becomes itself in and through its own other. There is no agapeic origination or creation of an other as irreducibly other. See my *Being and the Between,* chapters 6 and 7, on the difference of the erotic and agapeic origin; also *Hegel's God,* chapter 4.

itself into a process of dialectical self-determination that returns to itself; the true infinite returns to itself and hence is the circle that closes its end on its beginning. What if the transcending of the inner infinite is not the self-lacerating of the unhappy consciousness caught in dualism with the divine; nor yet the bad infinite of one damn thing after another; nor yet to be described entirely in terms of a circular return to self; suppose there is a different exodus from self that is not for a return to itself? If so, is there at work in us an infinite self-surpassing that is not surpassing self to self but surpassing self beyond self and towards transcendence as other?

This, I suggest, is truer to religious inwardness generally. As I will argue more fully in following chapters, especially chapter 8, hesitant, vacillating traces of some other such transcending are to be felt in a variety of post-Hegelian thinkers. Hegel did not look with great indulgence on what he saw as the indefinite indeterminacy of romantic innerness. Here again he resolves for self-determining being, that has tested itself beyond indefiniteness in an adventure into the determinate. If this is self-transcending, self will and must return to itself. This return may be in and through the other; but the other proves to be its own other, and hence the fuller circuit of the process of self-surpassing passes through the other and returns to itself. But again suppose there is an inner or inward otherness that, even were we to return to ourselves, could not be described as a recovered self in dialectical self-mediation? In the deepest and richest self-mediation something exceeds self-mediation. In the self-determination of the inner otherness something more than, something beyond self-determination is at work. In the inner otherness the "beyond" is at work incognito, so to speak: the transcendence as other is also as immanent, lifting us beyond ourselves as gathered to ourselves, as a cathedral gathers but also exalts. The surpassing to the "beyond" is as much immanent as transcendent. But such transcendence as other is not conformable to either a logic of dialectical self-determination in and through an other, or dualistic opposition relative to a *Jenseits*. Suppose the *peace* of the Gothic communicates this? The slight shrillness sometimes hinted in Hegel's criticism of the Romantics makes us wonder about an anxiety concerning proximity to what he came to despise. Is there a certain fragility in the self-certainty of Hegel's edifice, the foundations perhaps asking for more of the vertical stabilizing of some flying buttresses?

Fourth, consider the issue of what I called the post-Romantic symbol. Hegel does notice a recurrence to the symbol with romantic art. But suppose some such post-Romantic symbol does not necessarily imply a return to empty indefiniteness, but the resurgence of some intimation of the infinity of transcendence as other. True, one may well find in not a few post-Romantic figures a certain anxiety concerning determinacy, and this may be eviscerating to any great enterprise of creation. We find that fear of determinacy not only in Hegel time, as with the beautiful souls, but in postmodern culture with its never quite committed playing with possibility—or its lack of deep commitment to an articulate sense of what is ultimate, such as religions in the past tried to express symbolically.[9] Can one see in the Gothic cathedral some figuring forth or prefiguration of a kind of post-Romantic symbol, at least in this regard: it is the gathering place of inner and superior, our inner infinity and the superior infinitude of the divine: it materializes the house of a religious *metaxu* that symbolizes the between as the happening of passage between the human and the divine, the passing in communication between our self-transcending and transcendence as other; and all this without reduction to our self-determining power, or to our being merely externally determined by a crushing *Jenseits?* Could such a religious *metaxu,* just so far as it enacts the communication of transcendence as other, be fully describable in terms of self-mediating *Geist,* ultimately at home with itself through its own self-becoming in and through its own other?

Finally, consider monstrousness again. The monstrous is always a religious reality, but its business is devoted to the parody of the sacred. Monstrousness is a *parodia sacra* of divine greatness; it refashions the symbol into an impressive idol that mimics transcendence as other. The builders of Gothic cathedrals certainly did not forget the monstrous: think of the gargoyles that, on the outside, watch and mock and leer, high up. Was Hegel prescient enough of the incubation of the power of monstrousness in modern reason itself? Call this the incubus suckled by *Verstand.* Hegel knew how *Verstand* could effect a flattening of our sense of being to the pedestrian prose of the world. Yet does not this incubus of *Verstand* prove to hide a will to power that, in some ways, is shattering to the harmony sought by Hegelian *Vernunft?* We noted the massiveness of the Gothic cathedral but, as I indicated, its intimacy guards us from the dehumanizing monstrousness that has been more known to us since Hegel. The monstrousness may be the materialization of an instrumental reason, yet this latter has something crucial in common with Hegelian *Vernuft:* it *mediates with itself,* and finally nothing but itself. It thinks *itself,* thinks of itself; it does not sing what is other, and finally without that song, it does not even think of what is other. It builds monuments to its own monstrous powers: towers to heaven of monstrous humanity. This is a form of the tyranny of self-determination of the man-God. Who then would offensively dare to sing so inoffensively: *Humanus heisst der Heilige?* There is no "beyond," no transcendence as other, but only monuments to humanity as the monstrous power of history. Architecture can become the art of the building of idols. They scrape the sky and hope to scrape off any trace of the divine as other that may linger in the formless clouds.

Would Hegel approve? Though philosophy is said to be its own time comprehended in thought, was he clairvoyant enough of the monstrous powers

---

9. On this anxiety about determinacy in postmodern thought, see my "Neither Deconstruction nor Reconstruction: Metaphysics and the Intimate Strangeness of Being."

already harbored by instrumental *Verstand?* I have my doubts. The laurels he bestows on reason are offered too unknowingly. The will to power of humanity's instrumental reason laid slyly in waiting. It had a ruse that the ruses of Hegelian reason did not quite anticipate: soaring self-transcendence as monstrous will to power against which no otherness or transcendence will be allowed to stand as other, or be respected as transcendent. Is the dark double of reason itself just its own potential for a monstrous self-justification? And is not Hegelian reason a kind of blood brother of the *Verstand* it claims to transcend? For both play a game of self-determination in which transcendence as other must be shortchanged or refashioned in a form made to serve the further self-expression of self-determining reason or power. Both take form in a space between autonomy and transcendence. Should a tension, indeed antinomy, between autonomy and transcendence emerge, it is the latter that for Hegel must be sacrificed.[10] This is *not* the sacrifice enacted in the Gothic cathedral; it is a different sacrifice of transcendence as other. And finally, it is the sacramental reverence of transcendence as other, here now communicated in the *metaxu,* that is just the service of the Gothic.

---

10. This antinomy is unavoidable; see chapter 8 below. I do not find Hegel to be mindful enough of it. See also "*Autonomia Turannos:* On Some Dialectical Equivocations in Self-determination," in *Ethical Perspectives,* vol. 5, no. 4 (1998): 233–52. In this piece, I argue more fully that, relative to a certain apotheosis of self-determining being, there is a family relation of Kantian autonomy, Hegelian social self-determination of the will that will itself, Marxist social totality, and the Nietzschean will to power that will itself; and this, even though Nietzsche is a kind of mutant or black sheep in that family. On this more fully, see *Ethics and the Between,* chapter 4.

5

Art's Release and the Sabbath of the Will

Schopenhauer and the *Eros Turannos* of Origin

UNDER THE UNDERGROUND: ART AND THE SHADOWS OF AN OTHER ORIGIN

Schopenhauer is one of the most interesting of post-Kantian philosophers who highlights the central metaphysical significance of art. This is by no means peculiar to him, yet he does it with a systematic verve and sensitivity so as to touch a sympathetic cord in the nineteenth century and beyond. The list of artists he influenced would be long, including major names such as Wagner, Tolstoy, Thomas Hardy, George Bernard Shaw, Thomas Mann, and Samuel Beckett. My concern is Schopenhauer's response to art's otherness. There is its otherness to what he deemed the grim economy of everyday desire. There is the recalcitrance of the ultimate origin to complete rational comprehension. Metaphysical issues arise here concerning the *other* to the thought thinking itself that shines on the metaphysical high noon of idealism. Schopenhauer returns us to Plato's Cave, yes, but further still, to what seems *subterranean even in that underground.* His vision of things is dark, so dark we are perplexed as to what we can *see at all.* In that dark vision, or vision of darkness, art, it seems, will save us. What kind of "saving" can that be? Or is this where the sweats begin all over again, here in this second underground?

What can it mean to say there is an underground to the underground Cave? Think of it this way. Schopenhauer's major work is entitled *The World as Will and Representation.* Will is the thing itself, the original, while representation is its image. If we were to liken the world as representation to Plato's Cave, could we liken Schopenhauer's will to Plato's Good? Quite the reverse. Will is no sun, but a dark original, darker even than the shadow land of representation.

As first, it is a more like a second underground, *beneath* the first underground as its origin, not above it as the Good. One wonder is we can even meaningfully speak any more of what is *above?* Is Plato, despite Schopenhauer's stated debt to him, and long before Nietzsche, already being reversed here?

For if the representations are shadow images of the will, then they are not shadows of light, not even shadows of shadows, but shadows of this original darkness. What kind of strange shadow is this shadow of darkness? What kind of strange original is this, if its darkness casts shadows only apparently more lightsome than the original itself? To know this thing itself would be to know an original that, in a way, is no original, that casts less images than vanishing shadows of "itself." Do not these shadows then compound the darkness, not dispel it? What could art do to dispel the shadows of this impenetrably dark ground under the first underground?

Schopenhauer's vision of art's metaphysical importance places him in the broad stream of post-Kantian thought. Not that before him this importance was denied, certainly not by Schelling, or by Hegel, Schopenhauer's *bête noire*. The list of his significant predecessors and contemporaries might include Goethe, Schiller, the Schlegels. These share with his successors, like Nietzsche and Heidegger, a feel for the significance of art as other. For there is an important sense in which post-Kantian culture is an "aesthetic culture." I mean a culture which privileges the aesthetic in a manner analogous to the traditional privileging of religion and philosophy as articulating the ultimate dimensions of our metaphysical place within the happening of being.[1] Of course, much of modernity might be characterized as "scientistic," particularly in the wake of the Enlightenment, yet with the advent of Romanticism, "aesthetic culture" and "scientism" have coexisted side by side, always in tension, sometimes in open hostility. Now, I think, they are more and more in *collusion,* the one advancing our "objective" projects, the other ministering to our "subjective" comfort levels. In the past, the "scientistic" side arrogated for itself the exclusive claim for truth, while the "aestheticist" side has relinquished truth to science, happy to find itself rapt by beauty, or given over to "expressiveness," or "originality," or "creativity." Schopenhauer is one of a number of thinkers who attempt to reclaim some truth for the aesthetic—metaphysical truth not scientistic truth. He is not alone, however, in being caught in some of the tensions generated by the relation of truth and art.

---

1. On "aesthetic culture" in the Continental tradition one might consult the work of Gadamer *(Truth and Method);* in Anglo-American thought MacIntyre draws attention in *After Virtue: A Study in Moral Theory* (Notre Dame, Ind.: University of Notre Dame Press, 1981) to the emergence of the figure of the aesthete as one response to Enlightenment, while in a very different manner, Richard Rorty has recommended the "strong poet" and the "utopian revolutionary" as paradigmatic of human possibility (*Contingency, Irony, and Solidarity* [Cambridge and New York: Cambridge University Press, 1989]).

Much light can be thrown on that aesthetic culture by looking at the darkness of Schopenhauer's origin. For him there is an (ab)surd or primal nonrationality about the ultimate origin. But how can light come from looking at darkness? And how does this darkness surface in his thought, to be faced via art? And does not the ghost of Plato haunt Schopenhauer, not only relative to the underground but to the Ideas? We may pride ourselves on being "post-metaphysical," but something like a Schopenhauerian sense of the dark origin underlies many strands of contemporary aesthetic culture. And then we are also haunted by the question of art's release of humans into truth, release into an other truth than scientific truth, perhaps a "truer truth." What if this "truer truth" also releases us to vision of a primal darkness? Can such a release be called true? Can humans live with such a release? Does art release us to vision of this truth? Or save us from this vision? Or perhaps contemplate *abandoning us to that primal darkness?* How can it be *both* a release to the truth of this darkness and a saving of us from it?

Schopenhauer in Nietzsche's Shadow

We will come again to these hard questions, but we must first catch sight of Schopenhauer. A difficulty we have here is one effected by time and its forgettings. I mean that one of his sons stepped out of his father's shadow and cast a dazzling light which has tended to obscure father Schopenhauer, and make us forget the immense influence he had on aesthetic culture, and major artists, in the nineteenth and well into the twentieth century. I refer, of course, to the prodigal Nietzsche. But perhaps some readers may share an experience similar to mine. I had read Nietzsche extensively before I had studied Schopenhauer intensively. I had more or less been indoctrinated by Nietzsche's self-stylization, repeated again and again by many of his admirers: when I was young I fell under the spell of Schopenhauer; but when I came into my own, I put off these youthful ways, and struck out on my own path; and now I am Nietzsche, the antipodes of Schopenhauer; he the philosopher of pessimism, I the announcer of the great Yes! And now *my* experience on reading Schopenhauer intensively: How astonishing to read an author who seemed to have studied Nietzsche so closely! He echoed so many of Nietzsche's themes, even expressions! Schopenhauer too was surely a gruff fellow traveler along Nietzschean ways who had fallen under the spell of the *Maestro!*

After I rubbed my eyes before this magic effect, I realized, of course, I was looking at things upside down or back to front—one of Nietzsche's many tricks on his beguiled readers. I woke up with a start and saw how so much of Schopenhauer was at the back of Nietzsche, despite, too, Nietzsche's many later fronts. I sensed that these many fronts masked the extent to which fundamentally Schopenhauerian blood still circulated in Nietzsche's system. Strong or sick, Nietzsche remained Schopenhauer's blood brother to the end.

My diffidence about Schopenhauer, the so-called pessimistic nihilist, decreased, as my respect for Schopenhauer in his own voice grew, as did my questions about Nietzsche's own form of megaphone public relations, boomed out on his own behalf as an unprecedented original.

How many there are today who embody a variety of different Nietzscheanisms; how fewer there are who have studied Schopenhauer with the care and respect he deserves, and studied him as much more than a superseded forerunner of the dazzling Nietzsche. Schopenhauer offers a lucidity that does not let us blink away hard issues. And suppose Christopher Janaway is right in the main when he said: "Schopenhauer . . . is the system behind Nietzsche's anti-system"?[2] Why then, this might be a point for considering if it is really *Schopenhauer* who is more *radical* than Nietzsche: more honest about the nihilism that falls when we proclaim the "purposelessness" or overall "valuelessness" of the whole.

In the light of this darkness, is there finally such a great difference between what one might call the Schopenhauerian *renunciation of eros turannos* and the Nietzschean *intensification of Dionysian eros?* The "no" of one and the "yes" of the other seem equally as dark as the origin out of which they ultimately come, and as meaningless, finally. Does this mean that both the "no" and the "yes" are related forms of metaphysical whistling in the dark? Nietzsche's "yes" is undoubtedly a hyperbolic affirmation, but it seems to have no final basis, given the view of the valuelessness of the whole he inherits from Schopenhauer, and the intimation that at bottom being is darkness. Nietzsche wanted his hyperbolic "yes," but is he metaphysically entitled to it? One might grant him his desire to say "yes," but philosophically it seems very hard, if not impossible to make intelligible sense of it on his terms. His whistling in the dark is only another form of the darkness.[3]

Schopenhauer's "no" seems at least more philosophically coherent, given his views; which is not to say that either view is true to the worthiness of being to be affirmed. In rebellion against Schopenhauer, Nietzsche's instinct is more true to this worthiness, but philosophically he sits finally in the same darkness as Schopenhauer. Our advance from Schopenhauer to Nietzsche is on the surface only, and a matter of "say-so." A lot of Nietzsche finally does come down to: I say so. The move beyond Schopenhauer is, to borrow a trick from postmodern discourse, a *quasi*-move. Perhaps if Nietzsche had a bit more of Schopenhauer's talent as a systematic thinker, it might also have become evident that something may been evaded by means of "non-system." One might

2. Christopher Janaway, ed., *Willing and Nothingness: Schopenhauer as Nietzsche's Educator* (Oxford: Clarendon Press, 1998), 2. This excellent collection of essays does much to give us a better picture of Nietzsche's relation to Schopenhauer. See my review in *Tijdschrift voor Filosofie,* 61 (1999), 802–05.

3. In his contribution to *Willing and Nothingness,* David Cooper suggests something similar, though not in quite the way I do, namely, that finally global affirmation and global resignation might not be that much different.

even wonder, turning *Maestro* Nietzsche back to front: does the will to non-system show its own lack of integrity?

Mea culpa: I confess this is heresy to the doctrinal canons of postmodern "readings" of the Antichrist. Can I make scholarly restitution? I will perform dutifully the following penances (in any case, I have moved ahead too quickly). First, I look at Kant's legacy to idealism, in the general, as well as with more specific reference to the aesthetic. Second, I contrast Hegel and Schopenhauer, each as different claimants to that legacy. Despite Schopenhauer's vitriolic contempt for Hegel, their aesthetic views are by no means antithetical. Third, I look at the relation of will and Idea, and both with reference to eros. Fourth, I turn to perhaps the kern of the matter: art's metaphysical significance in light of what I call Schopenhauer's *erotic origin.* I will only now say that Schopenhauer's ultimate origin, the will, is described in vivid erotic metaphors, which turn on the *will willing itself.* The dark erotic other to thought thinking itself is this primal will willing itself. But this will willing itself turns out to be an insatiable *eros turannos* that holds humans in its vise. The central issue will turn on the claim that art releases us from this vise. How is this release possible at all, if this will is ultimate, and if ultimately all is will? Perhaps Schopenhauer is right to *name* a release. But is he able to guard the name, if the origin is the absolute eros turannos it seems to be? Do we need another sense of eros, and perhaps even an agapeic sense of origin, to be true to the release? At the end, I come back to the aesthetic character of post-Kantian culture, given the transmutation of Schopenhauer's doctrines by Nietzsche and his successors. I focus on Schopenhauer but try also to survey an arc from Kant to more recent times. My aim is not historical overview but to underscore the metaphysical appeal to art of post-Romantic modernity. Understanding Schopenhauer helps us highlight both the seduction and the shortfall of this appeal.

Idealism and Its Shadow

Schopenhauer, as is well known, explicitly acknowledged his profound debt to Kant (and Plato, also), though not without some correction and criticism. His claim is to bring together the Platonic Idea and Kantian freedom, and we will return to the complex tension of these two. But Schopenhauer's acknowledged debt predominantly centers on Kant's coupling of transcendental ideality and empirical reality, that is, on Kant's view of knowledge and being. Yet certain emphases of Kant's *aesthetics* recur with a transformed significance, especially art's disinterestedness and genius. But first some words about Schopenhauer as inheritor of idealism in a more general sense.

Schopenhauer is a *subjective idealist* for whom there is no object without a subject. There is a certain naïveté about his idealism, but this is undermined as the matter is understood. Consider a sort of physiological naïveté in his somewhat unthinking identification of mind with the brain. We find a naïve opposition of the mind "in here" in the brain and the object "out there" in the world. These are forms of naïveté that Husserl, for instance, sees as characteristic of "the natural attitude." Simple dualisms condition the terms of the philosophical discussion. Yet Schopenhauer moves into conceptual territory where he breaks free of these conditions. This physiological naïveté sits uneasily with his claim to be Kant's heir: anyone claiming the mantle of transcendental philosophy cannot be a true pretender to the throne unless he dethrone or at least critique such presuppositions. That Schopenhauer sometimes expresses them so unreflectively indicates that he was not always aware of potential tensions between such naïve "naturalisms" (in Husserl's sense) and the standpoint of transcendental philosophy. Nietzsche will see the tensions, but take the side of "nature," and subject some of the human-all-too-human presuppositions of the transcendental ego to a reductive critique; though he too, in a naturalistic setting, will retain the active, constituting, "creative" self.

At the outset Schopenhauer shows immense *confidence* in a strongly subjective idealism. "The world is my representation": his *magnum opus* opens with this imperious announcement, said to be a proposition that all will recognize as true, once understood; it is like one of the axioms of Euclid. Descartes' *cogito* is praised and so too is Berkeley's more developed idealism: no object without a subject, for in order for there to be an object there has to be a subject for whom the object is or appears. The defect of realism is its assertion of an absolutely identical object totally irrespective of a subject to which it is appearing. A moment's reflection shows the difficulty of this: the realistic claim concerning the totally other object is made by and for the knowing subject; thus the totally other object shows itself as not totally other but *for* the knowing subject asserting its total otherness.

This is very like Hegel, but Schopenhauer's idealism follows more the "way of ideas" and the theory of representational mind which has caused so much epistemological heartache since Descartes. We find immediate self-certainty on the part of the subject, and despite the correlativity of subject and object, an awareness that anything *genuinely other* inevitably lacks that same certitude. Immediate certitude on one side produces skepticism on the other, and most especially with regard to any irreducible otherness. But if consciousness is the only original reality we can know with immediate certitude, should we not expect a triumphant subjectivism in which the self-transparency of self-consciousness trumpets its ontological superiority to all of being? Should we not expect an apotheosis of self-knowing transcendental subjectivity, or something like Hegelian absolute knowledge? Why do we not get this?

One reason is this: Schopenhauer's modern idealism is joined with a more Platonic idealism, where philosophy "has to go back to what is first and original." This "going back" will bring us to more than "subjectivity," back to something like Platonic Ideas, but more importantly to *will as absolutely orig-*

inal. With this we come back, and in the intimacy of "subjectivity," to an otherness that shatters the pretensions to immediate self-certainty of subjectivity, and certainly blocks the way to anything like the triumph of Hegel's absolute subjectivity. Like Schelling, Schopenhauer explodes idealism from within, though he might not put it so himself, nor understood quite so the implications involved. Triumphant subjectivity meets its defeat in its very triumph.

One recalls Wittgenstein's remark that solipsism coincides with realism (*Tractatus,* 5.64). Think too of those controversies of Kant's *Ding an sich* between ontological and epistemological interpretations. We have to wonder if the difference finally matters. Thus Schopenhauer: starting with subjective idealism (the basis of the epistemological view), his exploration leads to will as thing in itself, but this leads to an ontological claim: the nature of original being as will is read off from the self. If this offers an ontology of subjectivity, it is also an ontology of what I called the inward otherness which directs us further to the ontological power of original being. There follows an explosion from *within* of subjective idealism: the unruly otherness is within the sovereign idealistic subject. In a way, that subject is no longer within itself; it too is the effect of the original ground as other to it: given to be, before it gives itself to be, or relates to being other than itself. Schopenhauer does not quite put it like that, I know, nor perhaps fully understand the direction pointed.

When Schopenhauer, contra Kant, says we can know the *thing in itself,* he would seem to agree with Hegel, who also says, even more loudly, that the thing in itself is the most easily known of all things. But for Schopenhauer, in knowing the thing in itself, we know the will which we cannot know, in the sense of entirely encapsulating it in a system of abstract concepts. The knowing is first in the intimacy of our own sense of will; then the intimacy of will is known as the energy of a source of being that, as more original than the intellect, can never be mastered by the latter. Something remains beyond even while acknowledged. The intellect is derivative from this more fundamental power which as original is always other. The knowing of the will, in a way, is a kind of *docta ignorantia,* mirrored perhaps in the way the art work resists being pinned down to any univocal determinate knowing (think of Kant's aesthetic ideas). The art work is inexhaustible, and this is its ever renewed freshness; the abstract concept kills this freshness and so betrays the intimate knowing of the will itself.

By contrast, when Hegel says we know the thing in itself, he asserts the superiority of thought over any resistant otherness: no thing in itself as other can remain other; for if we think the other we already begin the process of appropriating it to thought; and finally he claims that the other can be entirely overreached by thought. Thought, for Hegel, is just that power that overreaches both itself and its other; hence its return to self includes the other within itself; and hence we have the more complex dialectical self-mediation of thought thinking itself in its other. But the presupposition is that the other is of the nature of thought; thought can overreach the other because the other itself is but thought; the two are the same. But this is just what is denied by Schopenhauer in his doctrine of will. The will as the other of thought *is* the *other* of thought. Instead of Hegelian overreaching of the other of thought, it is the other way; it is the dark origin that overreaches thought, for thought is a derivative of this origin, an emergence from a ground beyond thought.

Thought is a moment within an original otherness, not as Hegel would have it, the speculative whole within which original otherness becomes a mere moment. Thought thinking itself in Hegel's fashion claims the whole contains the darkness of negativity within itself; thought thinking its other in the fashion implied by Schopenhauer suggests it is the darkness of the whole that embraces the frail light of thought within itself; and no matter how expansively this light extend, no matter how comprehensively it sheds its beam, it will never overreach the darkness, for it is the latter which will always be the more fundamental ground of the former. Of course, we can still question if our choice is just between Hegelian light and Schopenhauerian darkness, whether the darkness is mysterious without being absurd, and the light more enigmatic than Hegel can comprehend.

Shadowing Kantian Gifts: Disinterestedness and Genius

We turn more particularly to Schopenhauer's debt to Kant's *aesthetics*. One of the more influential messages of Kant's *Critique of Judgment* concerned the *sui generis* nature of the aesthetic judgment. By extension, the aesthetic seemed to show an important self-sufficiency. On the one hand, we cannot reduce it to scientific cognition; on the other hand, we must distinguish it from both sensuous gratification and moral duty. It enjoys a freedom within its unique realm. Kant speaks of its disinterested nature. There is the fact too that it is not definable with respect to explicit concepts. We are not dealing with scientific knowledge concerned with existing objects, as mediated though the categories of the understanding. And yet the aesthetic is not just sensuous immediacy. It frees us from desire's impulsiveness, riveted on objects as the means of its own enjoyment, as say hunger is on food in eating.

Consider "disinterestedness" and desire of the body: my body in desire, your body as desirable, or beautiful, or both. I look on your body as beautiful, but when I look aesthetically my eros is not interested, that is, interested in the enjoyment I can take from you. Beyond eros aroused, the aesthetic eye looks calmly, contemplatively. Not what you are for me, but what you are as beautiful for yourself: I am freed towards that, in the comportment of aesthetic contemplation. I behold flesh not as a means to the end of my gratified desire, but as eliciting a response that is its own end: the granting of the body's beauty as a value for itself. The artist looks at the body beautiful and beyond eros paints this nude. The nude offers a contemplative celebration of the flesh, and without the urge to consumption. What has just been said metaphorically encapsulates much of Schopenhauer's metaphysics of beauty, what it reveals, what it conceals.

In Kant the self-sufficiency of the aesthetic must be distinguished also from moral interest. While not reducible to theoretical cognition or sensuous immediacy, Kant's moral reason is interested, albeit in a good binding on all rational agents. Beauty may a symbol of the moral, but there is an aesthetic freedom to explore possibilities not directly good in a moral sense. (The ugly in Kant is admittedly ambiguous.) In sum, disinterestedness marks an aesthetic freedom, distinctive in not being reducible to scientific cognition, hedonistic satisfaction and strictly moral concerns.

Schopenhauer stresses this disinterested freedom in a manner which both simplifies and deepens Kant's insight. He simplifies: the aesthetic is not just a third term to mediate the various dualisms bequeathed by the *Critique of Pure Reason* and the *Critique of Practical Reason*. It is more overtly understood relative to a sense of the *whole*. Relative to this, will is said to be the primordial metaphysical principle; all being manifests will; will is the original source of being to which we have the most direct access through ourselves as will. Schopenhauer accepts but revises the so-called Copernican revolution of the transcendental turn. Will as origin must be dark relative to more determinate forms of cognition: it is beyond the subject/object split; it is the primordial source out of which plurality and differentiation are subsequently derived. It cannot be articulated in the more normal terms of a determinate rational structure. The darkness of this primordial dynamism is clearly evident in his description of this dynamism as a blind, goalless striving.[4] If will is called the thing itself, it does not "see." And if it appears to function analogously to the transcendental unity of apperception, we must add the qualification that it is the fundamental condition of the possibility of *being*, as well as knowing.

Schopenhauer's simplification is evident in this fact: his writing is less jargon filled, is more elegantly expressed, and generally free of an excess of technical terminology marking Kant's obsession with what look like

4. Passages in Schopenhauer where this is stated are numerous. See, for instance, *SW*, vol. 2, 771 ff., where in *WWV* he takes issue with the optimism he associates with giving priority or ultimacy to knowing rather than to blind will. Rationally speaking the existence of the world is groundless: *Daher wenn einer wagt, die Frage aufzuwerfen, warum nicht lieber gar nichts sei als diese Welt; so lasst die Welt sich nicht aus sich selbst rechfertigen, kein Grund, kein Endursache ihres Daseins in ihr selbst finden, nichts nachweisen, dass sie ihrer selbst wegen, d.h. zu ihrem eigenen Vorteil dasei.—Dies ist meiner Lehre zufolge freilich daraus erklarlich, dass das Prinzip ihres Daseins ausdrucklich ein grundloses ist, nàmlich blinder Will zum Leben, welcher als Ding an sich dem Satz vom Grunde, der bloss die Form der Erscheinungen ist und durch den allein jedes Warum berechigt ist, nicht unterworfen sein kann* (*SW*, v. 2, 741–42; see *WWR*, v. 2, 579 ff.). My citations take the following form: *SW* is *Sàmtliche Werke*, hrsg. Wolfgang Frhr. von Lohneysen (Stuttgart: Cotta/Insel, 1960–1965; Darmstadt: Wissenschaftliche Buchgesellschaft, 1968); *WWV* is *Die Welt als Wille und Vorstellung; WWR* is *The World as Will and Representation*, 2 volumes, trans. E. F. J. Payne, (New York: Dover, 1966).

scholastic distinctions. Not surprisingly, his basic view of art is more boldly set forth: art offers us pure will-less knowing. If we begin with will as a dark origin, art emerges at the end of a process, where becoming and its restless striving is stilled. By means of what many have seen as an astonishing turnabout, a will-less form of knowing supervenes.[5] Far from mediating (scientific) cognition and morality as already delimited territories, art witnesses to an emergence from will, an emergence charged with a significance beyond will. I will come back to how such an emergence of will-less knowing can *turn against* the condition of its own emergence, namely, will itself.

While Kant and Schopenhauer both show a measure of fidelity to aesthetic happening, Schopenhauer strikes one as the less artificial and abstract. So too he *deepens* Kant's aesthetics relative to its metaphysical import. While taking a stand against the Kantian formalism, he retains the emphasis on form through his version of the Platonic Idea. This Idea is not a merely subjective universal in the Kantian sense: it is revelatory of being. Just as we do have access (contra Kant) to the thing itself in our own will, so there can be privileged manifestations of will, not just in relation to ourselves, but with a metaphysical import beyond ourselves. In attributing to aesthetic form an essential ontological weight, Schopenhauer moves beyond the merely subjective universality of form as imputed by Kant to the aesthetic. Interestingly, this joins him with Hegel, himself a critic of Kantian formalism, and not only in aesthetics. We sense that for Schopenhauer aesthetic disinterestedness has some overtones of ancient *theōria:* a noninterfering contemplation, a nonviolating seeing of universality more than our finite selves and to which we are abandoned, or set free. This implies not only a liberation of subjectivity from exclusive particularity but also its release into its own possible universality, towards what is universal in being itself. This mingling in Schopenhauer, not without tension, of Platonic and Kantian strains, raises problems, as we shall see.

What of *genius?* Obviously, the cultural *Zeitgeist* of Schopenhauer's era luxuriated in this idea, especially in its Romantic form. Kant, we saw, speaks of genius as that favored one through whom nature supplies the rule to art; genius is the figure exemplary with respect to aesthetic ideas, those representations of imagination which occasion much thought without, however, any definite thought being entirely adequate to them. Genius stands at the edge of rational articulation in its more rule-bound, "logocentric" form, but genius is an original whose powers of articulation dip into the dark inarticulate ground of nature, and through whom speaks this otherwise silent origin. Kant is very cautious, we also saw: the dark origin may not always shine with reasonable light; like nature in its unmastered moods, it may erupt into the

5. See, for instance, D.W. Hamlyn, *Schopenhauer* (London: Routledge & Kegan Paul, 1980), 109 ff.

unruly. Kant has a double attitude: genius is needed but it is also necessary to subject it to rules of decorum and civilized taste. In Nietzschean terms, Dionysian turbulence must be checked by, subordinated to, Apollonian form.

Schopenhauer casts off Kant's caution, a casting off others will enact with even more unrestraint, even to taking leave of their senses. Genius and madness refill each other's intoxicating cups. Schopenhauer's adulation of the genius grants especially his or her *excessive* nature (see *SW,* v. 2, 484 ff.; *WWR,* v. 2, 376 ff.) A person set apart or above the common run, he is perhaps the fullest human instantiation of the more general specialness of the aesthetic. The genius is a kind of high priest of the "hidden god" of art. As in relation to art generally, we find a reverential air, bordering on religious awe or piety, surrounding the figure of the genius. (We are reminded of Schelling here.) Moreover, the indispensable "truths" revealed in art are manifested in and through this person. Genius erupts against a dark background of the chaotic and irrational: this excessive upsurgence testifies to the energy of the dark origin, the will itself, prior to its splitting into subject-object. Genius, it seems, is more *intimate* with the thing itself, will. The normal mortal is more bound to phenomenal reality, a mere empirical subject manipulating objects in a finite world determined by the principle of sufficient reason, be it in theoretical or practical concerns.

How can this upsurge of darkness bring light, how can such blind energy occasion sight? Schopenhauer suggests that the excess of genius is more than a mere excrescence of unruly will but bears a *surplus* of intellect and of disinterested contemplativeness. How can such an intimately murky blindness turn into such a lucid visionary power? It is not clear if Schopenhauer can satisfactorily explain this. What can be granted is that there is some fidelity to the happening, however we then explain it. This is his gloss.

Through this surplus of contemplative intellect, the genius *sees* the will in the form of its *universality,* prior to the subject-object split and the dispersion of will into the multiplicity of phenomena. The "ordinary" man is pragmatically busy with his small particular share of will but only in so far as this is manifested phenomenally. The genius rises above this (perhaps we should say: digs below this) to a freer, more composed, more universal comportment. In this he is the aesthetic prefigurement of the universal sympathy of the saint. The will drives itself upwards insatiably in genius, but in its excessive manifestation (excessive with respect to ordinary science and everyday pragmatic concerns) it paradoxically begins to be *liberated from itself.* It begins to wake up to itself, to its own pervasive universality, and indeed to its own final futility. A peculiar reversal of will comes to be effected here: will working against will to become will-less. Will, as the dark origin, becomes *self-conscious* in the genius, and so no longer is simply dark to itself. In fact, this self-recognition can produce in us the will to self-annihilation, that is, a will to do away with will. We witness here, I believe, a striking dualism in Schopenhauer between darkness and enlightenment which the excessive intellect of the genius is thought to both bridge and invert. Will drives forward, darkly, blindly; but in the excessive intellect of the genius, it produces an enigmatic reversal of itself into will-less knowing.

Schopenhauer Shadowing Hegel

What further of the universality in art which Schopenhauer identifies with the Platonic Idea? We find again something of the tension of a dualism, and its reversal. An interesting comparison here would be of Hegel and Schopenhauer on art and the philosophical concept. Of course, Schopenhauer is notoriously given to intemperate outbursts at the mere mention of Hegel. He brands Hegel, not without a grain of grim humor, as "that intellectual *(geistigen)* Caliban" (*SW*, v. 1, 18; *WWR*, v. 1, xxi). One has to laugh: Caliban, neither animal nor man; neither earth nor air; a monster aping a higher being; one whose access to the word merely conferred on him the power to curse. Schopenhauer denounces the sophistry, charlatanry and "humbug" foisted on German philosophy by Fichte, Schelling, and Hegel. These he sees as Kant's bastard children, while he alone is the legitimate heir. Many are familiar with Schopenhauer's vanity in rivaling Hegel, then in the ascendancy in Berlin, by insisting on scheduling his lectures at the same time. The challenge, as is also well known, was a dismal failure. There was a brief encounter between Hegel and Schopenhauer in the latter's doctoral defense,[6] though otherwise Hegel seems blissfully unaware of Schopenhauer in his own writings. Schopenhauer thought he had the better of Hegel, but his denunciations have a certain obsessional quality. Granted too his obsession was not quietened by his rejection for the prize in an essay contest, it seems, in part anyway, because of the violence of his polemic against Hegel and other respected contemporaries.[7]

Whatever psychological factors might throw light on the overkill in some of Schopenhauer's polemics—and they do risk diminishing his dignity as a philosopher—one must say, in mitigation, that one can understand his impatience with how mindlessly Hegelian language is glibly used to "reconcile" the finite and the infinite, the relative and the absolute, man and God. How easy it all is then! Given the darker vision, it is enough to drive one on to further rage against this light. No wonder that later, when Schopenhauer became well known, even *Kierkegaard* had not a little regard for him! This is this related factor too: what Schopenhauer's aesthetics signifies is an important cultural

---

6. See Terry Pinkard, *Hegel: A Biography* (New York and Cambridge: Cambridge University Press, 2000), 464–65.

7. See Arthur Hübscher, "Hegel and Schopenhauer: Aftermath and Present," in *Schopenhauer: His Philosophical Achievement,* ed. Michael Fox (Totowa, N.J.: Barnes and Noble, 1980), 197–214; also I. Knox, *The Aesthetic Theories of Kant, Hegel, and Schopenhauer* (New York: Columbia University Press, 1936).

strand responding to the decomposition of the Hegelian system after Hegel's death.[8] And this, of course, links him more intimately to more contemporary aesthetic thought that eschews the velvets of Hegelian "reconciliation" for the rougher cuts.

But still, I note some affinities on aesthetic matters. First, remember that Schopenhauer should be situated more clearly as a younger member of Hegel's own generation, hence as someone sharing its perplexities. We are misled too often by thinking of Schopenhauer as simply a post-Hegelian. Of course, there are persuasive philosophical reasons for this, but it is important to keep in mind that *The World as Will and Representation* was published around the same time as Hegel's *Science of Logic,* a time too not far removed from when Hegel was working on his lectures on aesthetics. What can mislead us here is viewing Schopenhauer retrospectively through Nietzsche's eyes, instead of seeing that his thought, and his *magnum opus,* arise in the same cultural milieu as Hegel. Not only does Kant's shadow hover over both, but both have a relation with Goethe and a bond to Weimar culture, Hegel while at Jena and later again, Schopenhauer through the salon of his mother. It is fascinating to observe *both* as loyal defenders of Goethe's theory of color. Both are high in their praise of Winckelmann in relation to the cultural recovery of the art of antiquity. Musically both shared a strong admiration for Rossini. Also Schopenhauer's sympathetic remarks on Dutch painting remind us not a little of Hegel's deep respect for the same. They shared the same cultural context as did the whole Romantic generation. Through Schelling, Hegel was in contact with the Schlegels and Tieck while at Jena. Schopenhauer's aesthetic views were developed in the same milieu and with personal contact with some of the same individuals. Note also how both Schopenhauer and Hegel admired the humor of Jean Paul.

Are there any substantive *philosophical* convergences? There is some affinity between Schopenhauer's pessimism and Hegel's admiration for the "nobility" of ancient skepticism and its acknowledgement of the nothingness of finitude. Hegel accords art a certain absoluteness, along with religion and philosophy. When Schopenhauer ascribes a *redemptive* significance to art in saving the will *from itself,* he is less far off from Hegel than one might think. Both see art as one of the richest modes of meaning where for us the sense of metaphysical ultimacy comes to appearance and expression. For Schopenhauer ethical and religious renunciation serve a similar saving role. Of course, in Schopenhauer there is nothing like Hegel's dialectical development of *Geist* from art to religion to philosophy. Yet there is the possibility of a provocative interplay between them, and especially for the great philosopher who tries to

---

8. See G. Lukacs, *The Destruction of Reason,* trans. Peter Palmer (Atlantic Highlands, N.J.: Humanities Press, 1981), 192–243; and H. Schnädelbach, *Philosophy in Germany, 1831–1933,* trans. Eric Matthews (Cambridge: Cambridge University Press, 1984), 143 ff.

see things whole. Schopenhauer thinks there can be a form of mind, philosophy, which has a more fundamental universality than even art: what art does implicitly, philosophy does explicitly. Nor could philosophical mind be confined to the principle of sufficient reason. How could it be, if Schopenhauer himself qua philosopher talks about will which transcends the principle of sufficient reason.

How does this square with Schopenhauer's great argument with what he took to be Hegel's trivializing of philosophy by an excessive *historicism* which reduces the essential perplexities of being to the relativities to the inconstant *Zeitgeist?*[9] Schopenhauer's argument here is, to a degree, more with certain Hegelians than with Hegel himself. In fact, he does not show much evidence of careful reading of Hegel himself. Given the swarm of epigones of Hegel, one can see Schopenhauer's polemic, even in its shrillness, as testament to his independence as a thinker.[10] Hegel and Schopenhauer (and indeed Nietzsche) are diverse philosophical offspring of Aristotle when he says in the *Poetics* (1451b), "poetry is more philosophical than history." Schopenhauer devotes an entire chapter (chapter 38) in the second volume of *The World as Will and Representation* to just this issue. Poetry (and by implication art generally) and philosophy belong together, because their care is for the essential and universal, not considered as disembodied abstractions but as concretized and individualized in actuality.

This issue of the *concreteness of the universal* testifies to crucial convergences and divergences between Hegel and Schopenhauer. As previously indicated, Schopenhauer appeals to the Platonic Idea when trying to make intelligible the metaphysical stature of the art work. Some commentators have been puzzled by this, and have suspected incoherence. The following considerations are relevant. For Schopenhauer will in itself is not a static substance but a dynamic power that objectifies itself at different grades. These different grades of objectivity of the will, he tells us, correspond to different Platonic Ideas. The art work, he claims, serves to lift the mind to the contemplation of the Platonic Ideas. I think that the *metaphor of the artist* is working at a number of different levels in Schopenhauer's thought. Suppose we ask: How are

---

9. There is a passage in *Beyond Good and Evil* (§252, *Werke: Kritische Gesamtausgabe,* herausgegeben von G. Colli und M. Montinari [Berlin: de Gruyter, 1967–], VI, 2, 203, hereafter *W* in the text) where Nietzsche speaks of Hegel and Schopenhauer as "hostile brother geniuses"; with Goethe, they were of one mind in "their struggle against the English-mechanistic world-idiotizing." There too he speaks of Schopenhauer's "unintelligent rage against Hegel." See §204 (*W,* VI, 2, 133 ff.) on the historical sense as one of German's finest achievements, and its dangers for young philosophers. This is, of course, the theme also of *On the Advantages and Disadvantages of History.*

10. I argued in *Art and the Absolute* that no trivializing historicism can be charged against Hegel in connection with art, in so far as the latter is credited with an absolute dimension. This does not mean that there are not serious problems attendant on Hegel's self-determination of the absolute as immanent in time, as I argue, for instance, in *Beyond Hegel and Dialectic* (see chapter 1).

we to understand the objectification of the will at all? An answer that suggests itself (and not only to those schooled in Hegel's thought, as we see with the younger Nietzsche) is that the world as will can itself be likened to an artistic creator seeking to externalize itself and in the process of self-externalization come to some self-recognition or self-knowledge. Hegel's Idea must externalize itself in nature, undertake a long trek through nature and spirit, before it enters in the spiritual daylight of its own self-comprehension. In a certain sense, the origin is as dark in Hegel as in Schopenhauer. In the beginning it does not know itself; the dynamism of its becoming is just the process of its self-articulation by which it both realizes its own power and comes to contemplate itself for what it is. The cosmic artist is a metaphysical metaphor, differently applicable to both views.

Schopenhauer was bitter in his rejection of what he took as the excessive anthropomorphizing of cosmic *Geist* by the Hegelians. This view suggested that the whole of nature and history simply served the narrow ends of European man at the beginning of the nineteenth century. European ethnocentrism aside, the fact is Schopenhauer understands the whole as will on the model of himself as will, of the human self as most certainly and immediately known as will. He is quite explicit about this: we understand the external world on the image of the self. We should not say that man is a microcosmos and the world a macrocosmos. Rather, understood on the human model, we should say that the world itself is an *macranthropos:* the world is, so to speak, man writ large, not man the world writ small.[11] Here is another afterlife of Kant's *subreption* that points towards distinctly non-Kantian ends.

Does the doctrine of *genius* not make itself here felt: genius as the richest exemplification of our deepest powers which are the intimate powers of the process of being itself? The metaphysical metaphor of the creative artist aestheticizes Kant's transcendental imagination. Schelling was one of the first to exploit this possibility in its aesthetic and metaphysical implications. Nietzsche was to credit himself with too much originality when in the *Will to Power* he was the echo of his heritage in naming the world as a work of art giving birth to itself.[12] In all cases, an exploitation of the immanent otherness and originality of the human self is crucial for an interpretation of the process of being as a whole.

In both Hegel and Schopenhauer, despite the darkness of its own ontological origins, the self needs to *know.* A question mark will be thrown over this need by Nietzsche when he wonders if the need for truth is a necessary illusion. Will in Schopenhauer, whether thought cosmically or individually,

---

11. *SW,* v. 2, 824–25; *WWR,* v. 2, 642; *"Ich habe den Satz umgekert und die Welt als Makranthropos nachgewiesen; sofern Wille under Vorstellung ihr wie sein Wesen erschöpft. Offenbar aber ist es richtiger, die Welt aus dem Menschen verstehn zu lehren als den Menschen aus der Welt . . ."*

12. *The Will to Power,* trans. W. Kaufmann and R.J. Hollingdale (New York: Vintage Books, 1969), 419 (§796); *Der Wille zur Macht* (Leipzig: Kröner Verlag, 1930), 533.

objectifies itself in order to know itself. Despite the fact that Schopenhauer might be seen as one of the first post-Kantian "irrationalists," there is something essentially traditional in his proposing the Platonic Idea as the objective of the desire to know. Less traditionalist, Nietzsche's will to power will swallow this role of the Platonic Idea, and there will be no Platonic Idea. But this is to anticipate.

When Schopenhauer claims the art work lifts us to contemplate the Platonic Idea, he seems to be contradicted by many aestheticians who emphasize the *particularity* of the art work, the inescapable individualizing concern of art. Schopenhauer, however, does not neglect this. Rather he sees in the individual art work an epitomization, concretization of the Platonic Idea. As he repeatedly insists, art rescues us from the barrenness of the merely abstract concept. The concept is barren (and not only in art) because, in contradistinction to the Platonic Idea, it does not spring directly, immediately, from the will itself. It is an abstraction we construct after the fact of experience by a certain withdrawal from the promiscuous richness of the sensuous flux. As Schopenhauer makes clear in his discussion of *allegory,* the relation of artist to Idea cannot be merely external. A bond more intimate is needed than that supplied by the abstract concept. The abstract concept, as allegory reveals, can be set forth or illustrated in a number of different ways, each marked by some degree of arbitrariness. But the true art work reveals the Platonic Idea in individual concreteness. Thus the art work remains fresh in itself, even beyond the time of its production, because of its epitomization of the essential, and its intimacy with the will, albeit mediated by the will's objectification in the universal (see *SW,* v. 1, 261 ff.; *WWR,* v. 1, §35).

Is there some similarity here with Hegel's concrete universal? Perhaps. Is there something superior about the latter? It does claim to free us from oscillation within the dualisms of "Platonism" between instance and universal, sensuous and supersensuous, individual and Idea. But for Schopenhauer it is not the Idea that mediates that difference but will. Idea mediates between will and instance. The most original "mediation" is directly will-ful and only indirectly the work of Idea. The fuller significance of this will appear with music. For Hegel the great art work is a concrete universal, and like Schopenhauer, he is critical of the abstract concept. This is but a subjectivistic construction of *Verstand,* or the analytical intellect. Hegel's *Begriff,* his true concept, is referred to *Vernunft,* or synthetic reason. Here the universality of Hegel's Idea finds its home. Not surprisingly he criticizes the Platonic Idea as indeterminate and empty, and explicitly so in an aesthetic context. He reenacts an Aristotelian concretization of it, in the context of post-Kantian transcendental thought. But this does not obviate the necessity of universality: this is absolutely essential for any proper philosophy of art.

We need only recall Hegel's treatment of beauty as the Ideal, that is, as the shining *(Schein)* of the Idea. It is not difficult to hear Platonic tones, but his attention to Aristotelian concreteness perhaps displays more nuance than Schopenhauer. We find him more attentive to the problems of dualism that accompany any bifurcation of Idea and concretization. Schopenhauer tends repeatedly to set up the issue in traditional dualistic terms, only then to strain against these terms, not least with regard to the great work of art. Schopenhauer is right to look beyond dualism here, because the richness of art does drive us beyond. But there lingers the suspicion that the movement beyond is not quite legitimate. The bad conscience of Kantianism sweats again, if we transgress dualism set fast as unimpeachably unsurpassable. This is no sweat to Hegel, because his *starting point* is a relativization, even a repudiation of problems posed by a variety of dualisms. But where Kantians maybe sweat too much, maybe Hegelians should sweat a lot more.

Hegelian reason claims not to be dualistically opposed to the aesthetic but plurally concretized in art, religion and philosophy. The art work is a sensuous concretization of *Geist;* and though it may be antithetical to analytical abstraction, it need not be so to concrete reason. So Hegel claims. We need not find ourselves forced into a false dualism. Is the art work then as kind of *sensuous reason?* Hegel calls it: the spiritualization of the sensuous, or the making sensuous of spirit. It imaginatively articulates *Geist*. But what *Geist* is for Hegel, will is for Schopenhauer—and with results that reverberate from beginning to end of their respective systems. Will as a dark origin in Schopenhauer tends to be *opposed* by the brightness of aesthetic enlightenment that the artistic vision of the Platonic Idea yields. *Geist* in Hegel may be initially dark to itself, but the sensuous self-knowledge of art is not the antithesis of *Geist* as origin but the aesthetic unfolding and fulfillment of the light already implicit in that beginning.

One final point on this. Hegel claims there is a synthetic reason, *Vernunft:* reason is not merely analytical nor instrumental. Whatever else we may say of Hegel, he is committed to a form of rational thought that seeks not to falsify being through the poverty of instrumentalized abstractions. If he is guilty of some totalism of the speculative concept, this is not quite a "totalization" of the instrumental concept. The case is more complex (as I suggested at the conclusion of chapter 4), given the *sameness* of *Verstand* and *Vernunft* with regard to each being finally, for Hegel, *self*-mediating thought. Hegel was too naïve about the monstrous possibilities latent in *reason as self-mediating through the other*. And this also applies to *Vernunft*.

Still I doubt that Schopenhauer understood the meaning of *Vernunft* in Hegel. Given his insistence on reason as instrumental, this would be hard. Reason is in the services of the more primordial will which is not rational. How then avoid some form of *antithesis* between will and intellect? Intellect will and always will be subordinated to will. Nor is it clear if we can say that will has any claims to rational intelligibility. But if this is true, then all we seem to be doing is escaping the tyranny of a totalism of abstract reason to fall foul of the tyranny of a totalism of blind will.

And so we come to this striking tension in Schopenhauer. Will in itself is irrational. Reason is derivative of this dark origin, parasitical and subservient.

Yet there is a will-less *knowing* which releases us from and lifts us above the will. In the aesthetic knowing of the Platonic Idea, Schopenhauer claims we are given some ultimate meaning or consolation for human existence. Yet this "salvation" must both work against will (will-less knowing), reveal will in its universal objectification (Platonic Idea), and yet not do this in terms of any abstract concept (which is the product of intellect working within the phenomenal realm bound by the principle of sufficient reason). The art work gives us metaphysical knowing, yet this knowing ambiguously strains against the very metaphysical conditions of its own possibility, namely the will itself, and indeed precipitates a metaphysical *turning against* this will. In a word, it reveals a metaphysical truth *at war with itself in the very peace it claims to offer*. It reveals a metaphysical truth that, from the opposite angle of the same perspective, seems to be indistinguishable from metaphysical absurdity. From this latter perspective the final truth is the futility of being. The basis of intelligibility is itself unintelligible. Does it not seem, then, that the metaphysical knowing Schopenhauer recommends to us in art is, at one and the same time, both the most intelligible and the least intelligible?

Plato Shadowing Schopenhauer: On Art, Will, Idea

These paradoxes requires us to look further at the relation of will and Idea and how the artist mediates between them. Certain Platonic themes reemerge, and not least in Schopenhauer's tendency to couch the issue in terms of classical binary oppositions. Schopenhauer is not always self-conscious of a hidden *dialectic* operating in such dualisms. He sometimes oscillates from one side of the opposition to the other, even as he also struggles to be free from stark, unmediated dualism. I suppose these ambiguous Platonic strains in Schopenhauer link his thought to what Heideggerians and post-Heideggerians name as the "metaphysics of presence." I would say that unresolved tensions between Platonic and Kantian emphases rather prepare the way for Nietzsche's and the post-Nietzschean's efforts to "deconstruct" traditional metaphysics.[13] One gets the impression that in Schopenhauer many traditional dualisms are set forth in more streamlined form than one finds in some of the key figures of the tradition, most notably Plato himself. This makes one wonder whether post-Nietzschean deconstructionists have inherited from Nietzsche (hence indirectly from Schopenhauer), and with not enough historical self-consciousness, a caricatured picture of the "binary oppositions" said to vitiate traditional metaphysics.

---

13. On the affinities and divergences of dialectic and deconstruction and what I call the "open wholeness" of the art work, see *AA*, chapter 5, also BHD, chapter 5.

The relation of will and Idea is intimately bound up with the central contrast for Schopenhauer between the genius and the "ordinary" person. The latter is defined by the everyday phenomenal attitude wherein we are both the products and victims of the will. Products: as embodied beings, we are driven by an insatiable desire which can only be temporarily allayed, only then to sweep onward ever in further dissatisfaction. Victims: because desire erupts in us unbidden, spontaneously, crystallizing us into an ever-renewed dissatisfaction. We are metaphysically doomed to lack and unhappiness. In Schopenhauer's graphic image, we are the beggars who are thrown crumbs for today, only for tomorrow to be hungry again. We are victims in this further sense: in the phenomenal world desire is driven deterministically, and (the voice of Spinoza breaks through) free will is illusory. By contrast, the artist as genius, as excessive contemplative intellect, somehow escapes this fate: he alone is free, if only for some few privileged moments (the saint sustains this freedom more fully). He is lifted above the incessant becoming of will, its ever renewed lack and restlessness. His intuition of the Idea attains a contemplative composure that yields metaphysical insight into the deepest nature of being, namely the will itself. Ideas for Schopenhauer, as was said before, are objectifications of will itself; hence art as will-less knowledge of Ideas, is only indirectly knowledge of will itself. Music alone among the individual arts is not knowledge of Idea, but directly of will itself. Hence its privileged position in Schopenhauer's aesthetic. "Unlike the other arts, then, music is in no way the image of Ideas; but rather the *image of the will itself (Abbild des Willens selbst),* whose objective form the Ideas are also: it is for this very reason that the effect of music is so much more powerful and penetrating than that of the other arts: since the latter only speak of the shadow *(Schatten),* while music speaks of the substance *(Wesen)*" (*SW,* v. 1, 359; *WWR,* v. 1, 257). But do not forget my opening remarks about the original, the *Wesen* being itself even darker than all the shadows!

I remark. There are passages where Schopenhauer shows himself finely attuned to the power of music to open up what I call the porosity of being. He knows along the pulses that music speaks to what is profoundly *intimate* to the human being, something implied when he speaks of melody, for instance, as the "secret history of the intellectually enlightened will" (*WWR,* I, 259). Yet more often than not, Schopenhauer's sense of the will corresponds dominantly to the *conatus essendi* rather than the *passio essendi.* Sometimes perhaps he mingles these two together but, I would suggest, that it is to the *passio essendi* that music first addresses itself. This means that the language of the will has to be revised, and we would have to acknowledge, as it were, a different *willingness before will.* The *passio essendi* has to do with our being given to be, prior to our giving ourselves to be, determining ourselves this way or that. This is why there is something on the *other side* of will, something *involuntary,* about the intimate appeal of music. The appeal has to do with gift. It has to do with what is secret to the idiot self. This is why also we should speak of the extraordinary power of music to open up again the porosity of being, as music often communicates its intimate appeal beyond the fixation of this or that determinate formation of our selving. If this remark is understood, and music has this significance for the intimacy of being, and its porosity, it must mean that its ultimate origin cannot be as Schopenhauer describes the will. Schopenhauer's self-insistent will cannot account for the opening up of the porosity of being in which the powers of communicability and communication come to form, and within which the expressions of music, and all art, show themselves intimate with the *passio essendi* prior to our *conatus essendi*. The original giving of the porosity is agapeic.

To return more directly to why Plato and Kant are the only predecessors to whom Schopenhauer confesses a deep debt. Does not the will's restless striving indicate this significant overlap with Plato, one not explicitly or fully exploited by Schopenhauer himself? I refer to the overlap between will and *eros*. Platonic eros, as Diotima tells in the *Symposium*, has one its sources in lack *(penia)*. It is lack or deficiency that is the driving source of desire and will in Schopenhauer. Lack dynamizes the human self into restless search for some satisfying fulfillment or peace. In Plato it is beauty itself *(auto to kalon)* which confers peace and completion on eros. Likewise the *eidos* provide an ontological telos to eros to stabilize its otherwise wavering motion and to guide the psyche to its fitting ends. The restless eros of the human psyche is grounded and fulfilled in a more ultimate condition of being than the human condition alone.

The differences of will and Plato's eros are equally important, perhaps more important. Schopenhauer has philosophical eyes only for lack; and if there is *poros* (resource), it is merely instrumental to negotiating provisionally with the infinite hydra of lack. Will has lost its memory of the archaic trace of divine festivity that slumbers in the sources of Platonic eros. It must topple always into emptiness. Indeed, instead of festive celebration of the good of the "to be" that eros can be, Schopenhauer's will brings home to us again and again the horror of being at all, a disgust at the "to be." At the origins of the coming to be of finite happening there is nothing of the agapeic origination of the "to be" as good. It is better not to be, as Schopenhauer, echoing the so-called tragic wisdom of the Silenus, reiterates. Art compensates for this horror. His moral doctrine of compassion looks like agapeic regard for the other as other. In fact, it is more like its counterfeit double, in that Schopenhauer's compassion evinces its own self-regard via the suffering of the other, and again the archaic trace of the good of the "to be" is nowhere at work in it. Schopenhauer's "heart" might seem to be in the right place, but his resources for understanding compassion could easily turn it into a nihilistic mimicry of agapeic love of the other as other.

Schopenhauer's will is a form of *eros turannos*, and there is no hint of something corresponding to *eros uranos*. And so his articulation of the possibilities here, when followed through in certain directions, will spell the death of Platonism. These differences are not just reducible to the fact that will for Schopenhauer has greater overtones of Romantic, post-Christian inwardness than Plato's eros could possess, though this is an important difference. Plato also recognized the problem of unanchored and limitless desire in the figure of the tyrant. Plato's depiction of the ultimate misery of the tyrant finds significant echoes in Schopenhauer's description of the will as finally the source of man's ineradicable misery and wretchedness. The tyrant and his will to power were a deformation of desire for Plato, not an echo of the underlying nature of Schopenhauer's bleakly dark origin.

This too is an important difference: beauty for Plato is the *natural* culmination of properly unfolding desire: it offers desire's fulfillment, not its extirpation. Beauty crowns the full unfolding of human desire. On this score we again find in Schopenhauer unresolved tensions between will and Idea. The Idea, on the one hand, is an objectification of will; yet aesthetic knowing of the Idea is said to be will-less; but how so, if aesthetic knowing must also be an expression of will (as the fundamental metaphysical principle of the whole), if indeed also the "object" of this knowing is also inescapably will too? The sense of will as dark origin is counterposed to the peace "beyond" will that is conferred by the contemplation of the Idea. But what is this "beyond"? There seems no "beyond." Is it any surprise then that the attainment of the Idea is not said to crown the unfolding of eros as to offer temporary alleviation of the misery that will inevitably engenders? There is no ontological basis for peace, if will is as Schopenhauer describes it, namely, a kind of eros turannos.

In Schopenhauer's "Romantic" rendition of desire, we sense the Germanic brooding on the problematics of infinite inwardness and the prevalent theme in the culture of his time of *das Streben nach dem Unendlichen*. Not unlike the Faustian inability to come to rest in a determinate finite satisfaction, we find the music of eros unfulfilled and the plaint of its metaphysical melancholy. Given Schopenhauer's aesthetic and metaphysical concerns, or rather his concern with the metaphysics of art, it is not perhaps surprising that we find traces of Kierkegaard's Don Juan in his description of the destiny of desire: desire hurrying from particular conquest to conquest, each taken as absolute in turn, only to breed disillusion at every turn, and forcing desire to set out in search again, forever. We see a variation on Hegel's "bad infinity" in aesthetic dress: desire without end becoming a vanishing infinity because eventually an objectless restlessness. Nothing can satisfy it, no finite thing will ever satisfy it, hence its anguish.

And look there, is that not also a silhouette of Nietzsche coming to form out of this anguish? Of course, "Nietzschean" desire is multiform, even hydra-like in its own way. Yet in its many forms, a bleak sap comes up from hidden roots in the darker chaos of the origin. Nietzschean desire too will face the metaphysical horror of this origin, though unlike Schopenhauerian desire, it will seek a defiant, not melancholy rejoinder to the darkness. Not grim defiance, not ineradicably anguished, at least on the surface, but more a cheerful nihilism. Indeed, it will be almost impossible to separate defiance and celebration in this Nietzschean rejoinder. If one was tempted again to call it "whistling in the dark," one would have to remember there are different songs that can be whistled, and there are darks and darks, and not all of them are voids of outright horror.

Plato, Hegel, Schopenhauer and Nietzsche differently address an elemental theme: How find fulfillment in face of desire's equivocity, and its potentially infinite restlessness. Yet one must acknowledge that something about Schopenhauer's bleak vision does have an *attraction*. I think the attraction lies partly in his *phenomenological appreciation* of the labyrinth of desire. He knows we can express an insatiable hunger for wholeness, yet equally we are intimates of bitter frustration and repeated disappointment. Here we find Schopenhauer's openness to some of the originating sources of religions, both of the East and West: their common concern with desire and suffering, with salvation from suffering, through untying the tangle of desire. Schopenhauer realizes we desire salvation but thinks desire as such blocks salvation. Hence the likeness of Schopenhauer's description of will to Hegel's "bad infinite": both are marked by the endless succession of the *progressus ad indefinitum*. As manifested in desire, this becomes endless renewal of craving and dissatisfaction. Hegel criticizes this "bad infinity" especially in relation to the Kantian "ought." In Schopenhauer's terms, desire thinks that it "ought" to be happy or capable of being happy, but it really is self-contradictory. Why? Its very craving of happiness is what guarantees its inevitable unhappiness.

What of Hegelian healing? Hegel held that we can attain some completion, some attainment of the "true infinity." His ascription of absoluteness to art is witness to his belief that there is an aesthetic overcoming of the "bad infinite." Desire can overcome its aimless craving because it can become dialectically self-mediating in and through otherness. I would ask: can this be the healing, if there is an inward otherness to desire that transcends self-mediation? If there is a healing to its craving, it must be beyond both Hegel's "bad infinite" *and* his so-called "true infinite." There is more than the Hegelian self-mediating whole. Schopenhauer would not entirely disagree. He would agree that aesthetic contemplation does rescue us from the "bad infinite," that is, will as limitless dissatisfaction and as lacking desire. It gives us some access to a kind of wholeness, some privileged, if only momentary, presence of perfection. This is not a mere "ought." It occurs. But unlike Hegel, this momentary wholeness is not incorporated into any Absolute Spirit, which finally for Hegel is the Whole. As with Schelling, artistic perfection is episodic. Yet it is still significant enough to sustain a kind of "salvation" from the despair felt at desire's useless passion. But then Schopenhauer seems *again* to doom us to despair, given his description of what lies beyond the rational self-mediation of Hegel's whole, namely will as eros turannos. What true healing or saving of this can there be? None finally, since it is that from which he believes we must be saved.

For Plato philosophical reason is the fullest *expression* of eros, just as the deepest promise of desire may be the noblest expression of reason. If for Schopenhauer, by contrast, reason is parasitical on an otherwise irrational origin, philosophy must be seen as essentially *unnatural:* logos is at odds with the dark origin. We see this reflected in Schopenhauer's preference for *music* and its metaphysical consolation. The fact that Kant and Hegel opt for poetry as "higher" than music reflects a difference in philosophical response to the question of the origin. The darkness of the origin resounds in, so to say, the logical silence of music, in this sense, that the happening of music is not amenable to articulation in words, with their inevitable drift towards determinate concepts and "logocentrism." Music can be more powerful on this score than Kant's "aesthetic ideas"—namely, as occasioning much thought without any definite thought being adequate to it. Nietzsche will concur in privileging the "musical," to the chagrin of the "logocentric." Music lets us sing the will, or hear it, beyond logic. And one might well ask of Kant and Hegel: does their opting for poetry, even on its own terms, do justice to what remains resistant to determinability in poetry itself? Do they do justice to *poetry as music* in this sense: not the prose of the origin, but its singing speaking?

If Ideas refer us to determinability, eros and will refer us to what exceeds determinability, since they express passages of determining power. True, when the Schopenhauerian genius "sees" the Ideas, there is something very "Platonic" about the "seeing": the Ideas are not subjectivistic constructions; we do not determine them, but their form gives form to our otherwise formless striving. The balance of Idea and will is all important. If I am not mistaken, the *creative power* of the Schopenhauerian artist exist in uneasy equilibrium with the ontological weight of the Idea. Schopenhauer's successors will tilt the balance more towards the genius's creative powers; meanwhile the "Ideas" themselves will be more identified with *projections* of the power of the genius, indeed, eruptions ("subreptions"?) out the dark origin itself. Out of this comes the Nietzschean turning of the screw of Kantian transcendental imagination in an uncompromising aesthetic direction.

Schopenhauer is still a Platonist, since the artistic genius *sees* the Ideas, he does not construct them. In Nietzsche the "Idea," if there can be said to be any at all, is a creation of "genius"; "genius" makes the "Idea," he does not find it. There is nothing "eternal," "metaphysical" about "Ideas"; these are nothing but idealizations of a secret self, which can equally be unmasked and deconstructed. The Nietzschean "genius" is the creator of "Ideas" from himself in the face of the (ab)surd of fluxed becoming. The ontological status of Ideas is expropriated by the Nietzschean self. Of course, there is the complication that this "self" is also an upsurge or project or "subreption" of will to power, and so in turn is enveloped in the flux of Dionysian becoming. Does not the dark origin then engulf all in an ultimately inarticulate night? Not inappositely, one of the most lyrical passages of *Also Sprach Zarathustra* is Zarathustra's Night Song. One also thinks of the more somber refrain of Heideggerian *Dasein,* thrown into finitude, doomed to be an ecstatic project, solitary before the empty horizon of *Das Nichts,* hurled again towards the nothingness out of which it first was thrust.

In a way, Schopenhauer is more profound than his successors, in already understanding (at least implicitly) the need to balance properly the creative self (here, genius) with the ontological context of creation (here, will and Idea). If human creativity is unloosed from its ontological moorings, it risks exploding into a destructive nihilism. The later Heidegger in his meditations on technology and his appeals to the "saving" power of art was attentive to such a possibility. This possibility might equally be called an aesthetic version of the dialectic of absolute freedom and terror that Hegel examines in the *Phenomenology*. The aftermath of the French Revolution helped him see that abstract freedom, that is, absolute, unsituated freedom, degenerates into the terror-filled night of undifferentiated, weaponed shadows, the night in which the "creative" self is reduced to maintaining by murder its own bare being against the always suspect other.

Schopenhauer *does* offer encouragement to something like the above unanchoring, given his account of the self's "ground," or ontological context, in terms of will. Will as dark origin is more primordial than Idea, and so inevitably the latter must be subordinated. It is unclear how one gets from will to Idea, or why will as a dark origin might *necessitate* the Idea. The Apollonian lucidity of the Idea must be understood, in fact, as merely the bright mirror of a deeper, ultimate principle, will, that is ineradicably dark. It is difficult to understand how the Idea can be anything but a consoling gloss on this deep-down darkness. The thinker who is genuinely convinced of this senseless darkness of the origin cannot be fooled into taking this consolation with ultimate seriousness. Such consolation can only be a high-minded escape, but just because of this, it cannot be finally other than a confession of failure. Generally Schopenhauer is admirable in refusing to dress up failure in the swaddling rhetoric of success. But if his version of aesthetic consolation is thought through fully in terms of will as an ineradicably dark origin, *any* possibility of success, aesthetic or otherwise, is hard to maintain. Let Nietzsche revolt against this, nevertheless his revolt continues that against which he revolts. He will dispense entirely with the Platonic Idea, lift "logocentric" restraints on Schopenhauer's erotic origin, and loose an intoxicated outpouring of its Dionysian darkness. But is this not the same darkness again, and can one *love* that?

Overall, then, with respect to the constitutive power of the transcendental imagination, Schopenhauer is both an heir of Kant and also a significant *middle ground* between Kant and Nietzsche. With respect to the Idea, Schopenhauer is a *return* to Plato (something very non-Nietzschean). But because this return is complicated (some might say infected) with ill-digested Kantians notions, Schopenhauer unwittingly prepares the way for the more thoroughgoing Nietzschean dissolution of Platonism. We may summarize this way: For Plato the Idea allows eros to be made whole; for Schopenhauer the Idea is our savior or escape from eros; for Nietzsche the Idea is eros falsified and hence the Idea must be metaphysically unmasked. My suspicion is that Schopenhauer himself (given his often "classical" aesthetic preferences) would have abhorred some of the more extreme consequences of the Nietzschean effort to subvert Platonism. And so in many ways Schopenhauer is more akin to Hegel and Plato than to his successors, those who claim *his* inheritance, and not always with the gratitude of heirs.

Art's Release: Shadows on the Sabbath of the Will

Schopenhauer's will is blind, and in itself beyond the principle of sufficient reason. The art work is a deliverance from this, an escape from the eros turannos of the origin. In describing the resting place outside will's craving, Schopenhauer uses very revealing language: art offers us a Sabbath from the penal servitude of the will (*SW,* v. 1, 280; *WWR,* v. 1, §38). My question is this: Can there be *any* Sabbath here: the seventh day on which the Creator rested and saw that "It was good, very good"? Can we take Schopenhauer at his word? Is it possible *at all* to say, in his words, "It is good"? I said early on that the kern of the matter relates to Schopenhauer's understanding of the *erotic origin.* His dark erotic other to thought thinking itself is the primal will as willing itself. Does this will willing itself hold humans in the vise of its eros turannos? Can art release us from this vise, as is claimed? Do we need another sense of eros, even an agapeic sense of origin, to be true to the release? In a word: Can there be here any *Sabbath* of the will?

Remember we are dealing with a *family* of philosophical possibilities with respect to will as ultimate, and Kant stands at the head. Kant invests the good will, the moral will with *unconditional* worth. Hegel speaks (in *Philosophy of Right,* §27) of freedom as the "free will that wills the free will." Both think that this ultimate freedom is *rational.* Schelling will say: Will is absolute being; but now the comforts of Kantian and Hegelian reason will come to seem too weak. There is even less comfort in Schopenhauer's will. Interestingly, it will be Nietzsche who comes as the comforter: his will to power finds joy, its ultimate "yes," in its "yes" to itself; but this has now nothing to do with reason, or morality.

Differently put: the transcendental ego, by and by, has let its hair down and now dances as groundless will or creativity. It defies Kant's rational or good will, and courts the night, at times seeming more in love with evil than good. Schelling's will as absolute is the dark other of self-mediating thought, as well as drawing us to the recalcitrant otherness of existence to idealistic thought. Schopenhauer baptizes the dark other as his will, and turns to the otherness of existence, with a gusto sometimes coarse, sometimes remarkably perspicacious. For there is a gusto in his insights and oversights. It is as if idealistic thought thinking itself had brought about an existential and ontological malnourishment, and we recoil from an emptiness crowing about itself as the apex. And then we turn back to the "too muchness" of existence, turn back with a hungry desire that seems now unable to slake itself. But there can be a hunger gone so far in ontological lack, that the "too muchness" of being in its splendor always exceeds it. It gluts itself on darker fruits, fruits whose skins only have been whitened by idealistic thought. But what nourishment is there beyond the whitened skins? After a long fast one can feed one's rightly irrepressible desire wrongly, and the result of the glut of desire may also be death. Not renewal of the love of being, but a disgust with being that in an "irrational" register mirrors the idealistic turn away from the splendor of being into "reason." Perhaps in life Schopenhauer was saved here, not by his philosophy, but by his common sense. Or was there something of Caliban in him too?

And so in Schopenhauer's will willing itself, we find an unstable mixture of lack and power. Lack: for all striving and desire arises from deficiency, he says. Power: here in the imperious form of insistence on itself. What is the mix of the lack and this self-insisting power? You might say that the self-insisting is necessary to overcome the lack that it also deeply intimate to it. But if the lack is *so intimate,* how can it will itself affirmatively, that is, *be* self-affirming power? For self-affirming will also be *affirming lack,* itself as lack. The contradiction seems to be inherent in it as such. And while you might then go on to say: this inherent contradiction is just why it must affirm itself, else it were nothing; the fact remains, that its affirmation of itself thus must also be infected by that same *nothing* its affirmation seems, on the surface, to overcome. Will willing itself then is also will willing *nothing*—or indeed, is will willing itself as a nothing. But does this do justice to the *positive power of the self-affirming will,* without which this whole process would not *be at all,* much less be in any form of which we could even speak, and make some sense?

This claim of inherent contradiction in the origin is something we find in Schelling, and in Hegel also (the negative, and hence evil is immanent in the absolute, for there is nothing transcendent). It is also to the fore in the younger Nietzsche—he will acknowledge this in *Zarathustra,* though claiming that he somehow transcended it (I will contest this in the next chapter). We have here a variation on the double parentage of eros in penia and poros, as mythically spoken by Diotima. Notice with Schopenhauer: while the penia, or lacking, is foregrounded well enough, the poros has been contracted to the more cunning ruse of self-seeking interest. It is poros for which what is other will serve to close the circle of lack within itself. It will simply be ontologically incapable of that release of generosity that gives itself over to an other, an "outside" itself. This will is playing with the others but really only playing with itself. That is, the divine festivity, the intoxication of poros at the *feast of the gods* is not remembered, and hence also the sleeping agapeic powers of eros itself: its being beyond itself in a release that is not simply for itself alone.

This oblivion of the promise of agapeic release changes the whole countenance of eros. Its promise of the heavenly eros, the eros uranos, is kept asleep, perhaps smothered or murdered, so that it will never awake from the divine intoxication. But keep that promise asleep, and the energies of eros awake will give birth to a new monster—an eros turannos untramelled in its self-insistence. Universal creation must become universal destruction. And even if creation *seems* the first act, it is counterfeit creation, for the point of the whole is just that there is no point. Since it is all pointless, creation is only the beguiling side of the mask of universal destruction. The "yes" to life, the "yes" of life to itself, only covers over the grinning, triumphant skull of death, the face of facelessness, the "face" of the absolute "no." There is, and can be, no Sabbath.

And so honesty dictates that, if the above is true, there is no "It is good." (I forbear to pursue the question: how could *honesty* dictate anything, if there is no "It is good." For honesty is fidelity to the "It is good" of being true; and ultimately there is no good in being true.) But you reply: There *is to be* (in the sense: there "ought to be") an "It is good," and *we* must utter it in the face of the comfortless fact about being that "It is not good." But then, I reply, what this "It is to be good" really means now is: "It is no good." No wonder that we flip from the "to be" as good into a cry of: "Better not to be at all." Little wonder that Nietzsche threw up his hands and shouted "no!" to this "no." But did Nietzsche have to shout his "no" to this "no," only because he felt too deeply its seduction? Did he feel he must lash himself to a mast of "yes" to resist this Siren "no"? And how could such a lashed "yes" be the released "yes"?

Here and there Hegel refers to the notion of God as "love disporting with itself," and while agreeing with this, he claims it becomes "insipid" if we omit the negative. Perhaps we avoid the "insipid" (a favorite term of disfavor for Hegel), but can we avoid horror? Horror, if the *horror of the negative* is inherent in this "love disporting with itself"? We escape the slight to our philosophical self-esteem by sentimental insipidity but in the process we blithely run the risk of sanctifying evil. Think of how Schopenhauerian eros is also "love disporting with itself," but it seems to be so gluttonously contracted on its own self-seeking and satisfaction, it is finally alone with itself and nothing but itself. Of course, Hegel's God disports with itself by playing with the whole world, nature and history; and it too seeks to be at one with itself, reconciled with itself. I wonder if there is more honesty in Schopenhauer about this "God" that disports with itself? Honesty in seeing that it now flips into its opposite and shows a face more like the *evil genius* disporting with itself? And with us?

"As flies to wanton boys are we to th' gods, they kill us for their sport." Thus the blinded, comfortless Gloucester in *King Lear* (IV, 1, 36–37). But Gloucester *sees* in his blindness. Schopenhauer's evil genius is a wanton god whose disporting with himself is staged in nature's horrors, and history's. Hegel talks of nature and history as God's two *temples*. Nature and history might "objectify" Schopenhauer's will, but these "objectifications" are not temples but slaughterhouses and torture chambers. Hegel's absolute is an erotic origin also, but it is as if now the dark evil immanent in that absolute reveals more fully the nothing, the destruction in all its creation. The logic of the eros turannos that has evil immanent in it is simply more forthrightly shoved in our faces by Schopenhauer.

Must we then conclude the following about Schopenhauer's will willing itself: as erotic it cannot be released to the "It is good"? But what of the *art* of this will? What of creation? Then there is no releasing of its "creation." This is all the sport of the wanton god. Think of it in human terms. The will, our willing, is blithely intent on building crystal palaces, only then to find itself miserable in them, and then again it proceeds to destroy them, again once more to repeat its own futile building. And so this will *comes to itself* in its creation as finally *nothing*. The active lack that drives it to being, that drives its "to be," is everything and nothing. There is no plenitude of glorious being in itself; no glory of existence communicated to the other in the release of the creation. The drive from will to something is only a *quasi-move* to something. For overall it is a drive from lack to nothing, with "what is" in-between as the vanishing medium of its own insatiable self-deluding willing of itself. Schopenhauer's will as an erotic origin is the dark mirror image of the *self-satisfied, self-certain, self-mediating* reason of Hegel's absolute. Its willful "mediation" is from nothing to nothing. What Hegel glorifies as "determinate negation" is only a mere provisional satisfaction deluded about itself. Hegel absolutizes this self-delusion, and calls it the absolute. This absolutization of reason is absolutely irrational. This absolute knowing is absolute self-delusion, for when "full" self-knowledge hits us we are hit with absolute "emptiness" and we must sweat hard to stifle the cry of horror.

Again one is brought to ask: Is this to be more honest than Hegel? See the death that is the counterfeit life of the absolute. See the life that counterfeits the death that is absolute. No wonder, reversing Leibniz, this world seems the "worst possible" for Schopenhauer. No wonder the evil genius seems to hold sway rather than the good God. No wonder it is "better not to be." And art? But it too seems impotent to release us to an "It is good." Can the holy? The honest answer must be No. The only release is an escape from the "It is"—the "It is" as evil. How far we are from Parmenides' *"esti"!* Any "It is" means "It is not." Any "It is good" counterfeits "It is evil." There is no Sabbath, only its counterfeit. If this is the ultimate "truth," (I say "truth" since this too may counterfeit "untruth"—with a bow to Nietzsche), the release of art and the holy cannot bring us to life or towards life as worthy. They can only turn us away from it as unworthy. Beauty gilds the more basic ugliness, as the holy hides us from, hides from us, the "unholiest of unholies."

Schopenhauer Shadowing Us

You might expostulate: Why get worked up about all this? Humbug—Schopenhauer is *merely* of historical interest! But this is not at all the case. We have as much difficulty now, as then, in saying "It is good." In fact, we seem more comprehensively deprived of a Sabbath than ever, in a world defined by the dominion of serviceable disposability (see *EB,* chapter 14). There everything is a means, and nothing an end, and art seems to place itself in servitude to that dominion, servitude less penal now, as too well paid. And we do live culturally and philosophically with something like Schopenhauer's legacy, its continuing influence, especially as transmitted through Nietzsche. That original has casts this darkness over Nietzsche on us. You say that Nietzsche repudiated what he took to be the nihilistic implications of Schopenhauer's pessimism. Nevertheless, key Schopenhauerian themes resurface with a new modulation, especially in regard to art and the "beyond" of reason, or the other to thought thinking itself. Schopenhauer's suspicious anti-Hegelianism makes him our contemporary. Since Nietzsche's search through art for a pagan "Sabbath" will occupy us next, I close for now with some remarks bearing on this anti-Hegelianism.

This anti-Hegelianism follows from ultimate will as driven by an irrational, insatiable striving. Where Hegel sees the concordance of beauty and truth, and where Schopenhauer sees beauty as an escape from the pain of willing, Nietzsche more radically turns from concordance towards the discordance of art and truth, as Heidegger reminds us. Schopenhauer, despite his concordance, begins to *break down* our defenses against this other discordance. Look at the darkening shadow of Schopenhauer in Nietzsche's *The Birth of Tragedy:* if we grasp the truth of being, it leads to *horror* in the face the darkness of the origin; art alone will provide us with a proper redemption of this horror. But art's consolation amounts to a *necessary illusion:* necessary, if we are to continue to live, once having gazed upon that metaphysical horror; illusion, because beneath the bright aesthetic surface lurks the still more ultimate irrationality. In a later preface Nietzsche was to voice self-criticism about the work, but we must take this with a grain of salt. Nietzsche never reneged on the potentially transfiguring power of great art; but neither does he deny the dark horror of the origin. "The world is to all eternity chaos." In fact, the transfiguring power of art is *secondary, not original,* since it is just what is needed both to name honestly the horror and the live beyond this honesty. Without art's saving power we would be destroyed by the darkness we "see." But the darkness we "see," is the thing itself.

I know we today easily caricature Hegel as a rampant rationalist. We should be fair: he too was not incognizant of the dark underside of Dionysian possibility. But for him beauty and the truth of art are inseparable from an essential Apollonian formation. The originative act forms itself into beautiful Apollonian presence, and this is the *fuller truth* of the origin itself. Though Schopenhauer holds to darkness at the origin, he holds also to a *rupture* between this darkness and beauty, and then, as with Hegel, Apollo holds sway. The Platonic Idea, like a statue of a Greek god, offers repose, lifted above finite transience and the turbulence of desire. Hegel and Schopenhauer, at least in this, are closer in their predilection for classical harmony over formless Romantic ferment. Yet Schopenhauer is a halfway house to Nietzsche. Formless Romantic ferment is philosophically reflected in will as the primordial metaphysical principle.

What Schopenhauer names as will and Idea, Nietzsche renames as Dionysus and Apollo. And while Nietzsche always implied the copresence of the two, especially in his earlier writings, progressively Dionysus is distributed over the whole and tends to absorb Apollo as a subordinate principle. I know Nietzsche despised certain forms of Romanticism as decadent, but in another regard, he does more hyperbolically unloose that restless ferment. He raises the stakes with respect to the primordial darkness of the origin, and courts more extremely all the hazards of nihilism. He risks the disequilibrium of an intoxicated eros that has depreciated what it most needs in its self-surpassing, namely, the balancing temperance. This is to jeopardize lucid mindfulness, and risk collapsing divine madness into, well, mad madness. Salvador Dalí used to say repeatedly: "The only difference between me and a madman is that I am not mad!" There you have it: the inspired say-so of artistic sanity. Or madness. Why do I will it? Say-so: I will it because *I* will it.

Given the free equivocity of desire, these possibilities above can assume actuality in human life. Though not all need be endorsed, all must be understood. We need a philosophy generous enough in that understanding. To understand madness one must not be mad, though one might well need a touch of divine madness. Schopenhauer was concerned with the significant proximity of madness and genius (see *SW,* v. 1, 272 ff., *WWR,* v. 1, §36; *SW,* vol. 2, 514 ff.; *WWR,* v. 2, 399 ff.), but he retained a sobriety, mostly (the mere thought of Hegel made him lose it). Again his tastes strike one as more soberly classical than Nietzsche's, closer to Hegel's.

While Nietzsche too seeks a transfiguration of the dark origin, while he wants to say "yes," he cannot just say "yes" to that. The Dionysian will to power must be freed into an excess of affirmative energy, when the lion of self-assertive will becomes the child of rejoicing play. But the sacred "yes" of this child is a self-propelling wheel, is also a "yes" to itself.[14] The *Übermensch* replaces Romantic genius as the exemplar of human transcendence or creative excess. But as in Schopenhauer, this excess must produce a *reversal.* The energy of the will to power, emergent from the (ab)surd origin must reverse this surd: out of itself and its overflow, it must *create* significance and worth for life. The extreme urgency of Nietzsche's call for transfiguration is evident in his hyperbolic demand: transvaluation of all values. Behold I make all things new? Not quite, but quite close.

Can we, must we, chose between the Schopenhauerian and Nietzschean reversals? The first tends towards resignation, awaiting a change of being reminiscent of a gift of grace; the second commands an intensification, not abne-

---

14. On different senses of will to power, see my "Caesar with the Soul of Christ: Nietzsche's Highest Impossibility," *Tijdschrift voor Filosofie,* 61 (1999): 27–61. There I also speak of the difference of erotic sovereignty and agapeic service; on these, power, and being religious, see *EB,* especially chapters 15 and 16.

gation, of self-affirming will, of the will willing itself. But the darkness of the original will remains ultimately *dark for both,* regardless of whether the transfiguration is renunciation of eros or intensification. In the light, or darkness, it is the *similarity* of renunciation and intensification that strikes one. Whether one says "yes," or "no," this dark origin remains thus dark.

Aristotle spoke of tragedy evoking terror and pity, or horror and compassion. Schopenhauer and Nietzsche are strong on horror, but equivocal on compassion. Schopenhauer's saving release in face of the horror of will might be called an "aesthetic compassion," even though the origin cannot source an "It is good." Is Nietzsche more tempted by pity, not only for us, but for the dark god of tragedy? That god too cannot say "It is good," but Nietzsche in his pity will say "It is good," for him. Nietzsche is the redeeming herald of the tragic god. I find it strange: Schopenhauer shows us horror, and enjoins pity, yet he is often pitiless; Nietzsche shows us horror, and warns against pity, yet he shows more "pity" (or its surrogate) in the comforting benediction of his "yes." But Nietzsche can only half reverse Schopenhauer's inversion of the "It is good to be" into the "It is not good to be," since as Schopenhauer's son he inherits a mutilated form of agapeic willing beyond self, in his erotic self-affirming will to power. And the half reversal will revert again to the original inversion.

It seems to me that shadows of something like Schopenhauer's dark origin, transmitted from the Romantic era to us, not least through Nietzsche, have had afterlives till this day. Recall the "vertiginous inner descent" and the "ceaseless promenade in full forbidden zone" of the surrealists (Breton). Existentialism and the literature of the absurd are only two examples from the recent past. The metaphysical presuppositions of much psychoanalytically oriented thought strike one as very Schopenhauerian, not only with regard to the tyranny of the original eros, but also the ceaseless seeking and dissatisfaction of the libido, meaninglessly death-bound. You say that is all old hat? But then one wonders about some of the implicit assumptions of postmodernist thought. Perhaps now the elusiveness of meaning has debilitated the defiant will to overcome absurdity of Nietzsche and his existentialist heirs. But we do find a hyperbolic skepticism that strikes one as an *ironical* version of Schopenhauerian pessimism. A parody of that pessimism, it holds itself superior because it is *unsurpassably self-conscious of its own final futility.* Elsewhere I coupled some skeptical currents in contemporary aesthetics with the romantic irony that was widespread in the cultural ethos of Schopenhauer and Hegel (see *AA,* especially chapter 6). By contrast with the coy academic game of tease and guess that passes itself off as state of the art irony, there is a certain bracing *joy* in Schopenhauer's pessimism. Schopenhauer more robustly fits Nietzsche's desideratum of a strong nihilism, than the camp followers of deconstruction that have declaimed, in Nietzsche's name, their cheerful nihilism.

Oddly enough, Schopenhauer's dark origin comes to mind when I think about even the ethical Levinas, and his postmodern admirers who are now doing ethical penance for their previous Nietzschean aestheticisms. (A perplexed parenthesis: Are there surprising reversal going on here? How do Nietzschean aestheticists become Levinasian ethicists, as seems to have happened with some recent continental thinkers? Does the leopard then change its spots? But is this not a *metabasis eis allo genos?* Is this not, with a low bow to Schopenhauer, a reversal beyond the principle of sufficient reason? Is it not, dare one say it, a miracle? And further, what if this leopard or ethical penitant starts to speak about religion? Another miracle, another *metanoia* beyond reason? The aesthetic, the ethical, the religious—was Kierkegaard a genius or a prophet? A different scenario of reversal: A thinker becomes famous, a veritable celebrity, by speaking the language of transgression. It happened in the time of Romanticism and idealism, it has happened in our time. The celebrated thinker later begins to dip in the baptising waters of "religion." His followers feel as if a *nihil obstat* has been pronounced and rush to write of "God." Would the celebrity ever have become famous and found followers if he *began,* not transgressively, but speaking solemnly of the ethical Good and of "God"? Would the fashionable crowd not have yawned and said: How boring!? Or are the spots, dare one say it, palimpsestic? The aesthetic spot first shines, but then the glow fades, and the ethical spot comes to the fore, but then, time and age and a little suffering later, the religious spot glimmers darkly.)

Why does Levinas comes to mind when think of Schoperhauer's dark origin? Because Levinas seems to reiterate again and again, not only the horror of the *il y a,* but the *evil of being* in the relentless self-insistence of the *conatus essendi.* Is this his version of the "It is evil to be," and the evil of the will willing itself? His *version* of Plato's Good beyond being dictates a saving trauma and reversal from myself to the other. But is there not *an evil in that ethical good that sees being as evil?* I know Levinas speaks also of enjoyment, but can we eat our bread in joy (we—not I alone—the other too), having tasted of this evil of being (*la mal de l'être,* as he puts it in *Existence and Existents*[15])? This ethical rupture to Nietzsche's half-reversal brings us back uncomfortably close to the inverse original, or the original inversion, of Schopenhauer's "It is evil to be." We have not been quite released to the agapeic "It is good."

Let this evil eye of ethics for the "evil of being" take itself too seriously, and we are almost ready to welcome back the laughing Nietzsche. But before we can laugh more freely, we must reconsider the modernist faith, recently the target of irreverent debunking, in an aesthetic culture and in art as affording "post-religious" man some possibility of salvation from nihilism. In this faith, and its postmodern heresies, we stand in the forgotten shadow of Schopenhauer, hiding many metaphysical assumptions (no amount of talk about a "post-metaphysical" age can mask the inescapability of some such assumptions). At vari-

---

15. See E. Levinas, *De l'existence à l'existant* (Paris: Fontaine, 1947), 19; *Existence and Existents,* trans. A. Lingis (The Hague: Nijhof, 1978), 19.

ance with the longer philosophical tradition, the basic metaphysical biases of contemporary aesthetic culture continue to be more Schopenhauerian than Platonic or Hegelian. We are less candid than Schopenhauer in confessing the ruses by which we protect ourselves from the darkness of the origin. We lack Nietzsche's intoxication, and his philosophical eros has been enfeebled, often by his most fanatical followers. Art itself has become so "aestheticized" that it is a genuine question as to how seriously we can take it anymore.

And even were one to accept consciously the Schopenhauerian assumption, one still is left with having to swallow the unintelligible rupture between the dark origin and the saving reversal that art (and indeed ethics too)[16] is said to effect. If this dark origin is the principle of the whole, then the reversal, while seeming to free us from that origin's tyranny, takes place within its embrace, and will inevitably be pinioned to the absurdity that supports and surrounds it. If this is the truth of being, then art as a meaningful consolation is nothing more than metaphysical whistling in the dark, no matter how elegant, plaintive or intense its song. We need to ask again, with fresh seriousness, and with audacity enough to listen even to untimely thinkers like unfashionable Plato: Is the origin *thus* dark?

---

16. On the religious reversal, or "dying to self," see *SW*, v. 2, 772 ff.; *WWR*, v. 2, 603 ff. Why does the enigmatic reversal and will-less knowing remind me of Heidegger's *Kehre* and *Gelassenheit*—as well as his advocation of the great work of art as revelatory?

6

Eros Frenzied and the Redemption of Art

Nietzsche and the Dionysian Origin

NIETZSCHE'S ORIGIN AND THE OTHERS

If the origin is dark, how dark? As dark as eros turannos is dark? Or perhaps dark with a more mysterious eros? Or perhaps with a love yet other again? The question returns with Nietzsche, whose response is not Platonic, or Kantian, or Hegelian, or Schopenhauerian, though in all these, with the exception of Kant, the draw of the erotic origin is felt. Schopenhauer's influence remained immense: his erotic origin, prior to reason, other to reason itself, beyond complete determination by the principle of sufficient reason, since it determines this principle, is rendered even more intense in Nietzsche's *Dionysian origin*. This Dionysian origin mixes eros and mania in a frenzied creativity, an "heroic furor," to echo Bruno. And here too are made more extreme claims for an intenser form of art's redemptive power.

Of course, Schopenhauer's view of reason suggests many variations not quite Schopenhauerian. One thinks of Hume famously saying: reason is and always will be the slave of the passions. Hume's "fall back" position seems to be an ungrounded, because not ultimately justifiable, respect for common sense. Is this a form of "say-so": custom—it just happens to be so, and further reason we must not ask? Hume's "fall back" turns away from a kind of abyss that gapes at that point of maximum skepticism. He fortifies himself against horror with a glass of claret and a game of backgammon. The sweats subside as the accustomed conviviality of company lulls to sleep the dread. Hume has no further relevance here, except that what he puts to sleep reawakens differently in other thinkers. Kant's transcendental strategy, his discipline of taste for the terror of genius, or his moral therapy for the rupture of the sublime, show strategies that shield us from this abyss. They do not quite lay to rest disquieting hauntings of otherness beyond the self-determination of reason, hauntings taking darker forms in Schelling, Schopenhauer, and now Nietzsche.

Nor does Hegel's dialectical origin give quiet. Plato and Hegel do differently deny reason's instrumentalization: there is a reason ontologically intimate with the deepest nature of being. Of course, we must make qualifications. A Platonic advocacy of reason knows the limit of human reason, hence is open to an appeal to a "beyond," the sense of whose otherness might necessarily have to be expressed in *muthos* rather than *logos*. By contrast, Hegelian reason, far from acknowledging a limit, claims to incorporate all limiting others within its own progressive self-justification. The Platonic origin is other and excessive, not because it is antithetical to reason but because it is too much for human reason: excess of light dark to us, but not dark. Dialectical paradoxes arise: excessive illumination stuns the beholder into a dazzled blindness. The ultimate light blinds us because we are not gods. This blinding is not the rebuff of the jealous god. It is the gift of the Good.

Hegel's god is not jealous, to be sure, but not because its gifts are agapeic, but because in everything it is concerned with itself. Hegel's dialectical origin, as self-mediating in otherness, is such that there is no surd of otherness, or mystery of transcendence: otherness as rationalized is simply reason's own otherness, hence no irreducible otherness; reason masters mystery in the circle of its own self-determination. Hegel forfeits the Platonic finesse for the inspiring disjunction between humans and gods, and remakes the between, as the milieu of their communication through eros and mania, into the medium of reason's own comprehensive self-communication.

Nietzsche is closer to Plato, in being closer to Schopenhauer's sense of the excess of the origin to idealistic self-determination. In an intriguing juxtaposition of opposites Nietzsche refers to himself in *Daybreak* (preface) as one of those underground *(unterirdisch)* "who tunnels and mines and undermines." How remain true to the earth under the earth? Where does the light of day break? Under the ground or above it? At the end of what tunnel is there light to see? In what caves of night are we?

There is in Nietzsche also a mingling of darkness and *festivity* which has a quasi-Platonic flavor: at the limit of our reason, we may *celebrate* an otherness that resists any simple logicizing, in the release of the disruptive powers of eros and mania. Socrates delivers, indeed sings, his second inspired speech about eros in the *Phaedrus* at shadowless noon when the sun is at its height. Nietzsche, like Schopenhauer, even more than Schopenhauer, wanted to sing at the great noontide, yet for both there is a shadow at this time of no shadows, as the noonday demon of nihilism haunts their songs. The contrast with Plato is obviously crucial for Nietzsche's own self-understanding, and I will come again to this. How far is one to push the contrast of "Plato versus Homer," especially if eros and mania are to be taken in a more metaxological manner? Into their polemos something of a deeper *agonistic affiliation* may have seeped. The contrast of a logical versus aesthetic rejoinder to the darkness of the origin might not go far enough.

Nietzsche shares with Schelling a willingness to brood on the unconscious as other to transparent subjectivity and speak its knotted, alarming truth with a new honesty. There is no Hegelian *Aufhebung* of an opposition of reason and non-reason, yet in "reversed Platonism" a transcending of such an opposition is sought, a transfiguring reversal, one might call it, though artistic rather than logical. Nietzsche does not rule out some aesthetical reconciliation of the warring powers of the human being in a new, transfigured wholeness. Some such artistic transfiguration represents Nietzsche's most endorsed rejoinder to the darkness of the origin. Tragic art-life embodies the most creative response to the otherness of primal being: tragic suffering of the otherness of being releases our originative power in celebration of the original otherness of being, and this despite the suffering.

Nietzsche offers us the "absoluteness" of art without Hegel's absolute. He furthers the aesthetic "salvation" of Schopenhauer in a will-affirming rather than will-less way. He continues, in a qualified way to be explained below, the Platonic salutation of the otherness of original being. He shares with Kant an emphasis on the active self; and though he deconstructs its transcendental form, he is the heir of Kant's sense of the unruly genius though, lacking Kant's caution (Nietzsche would call it cowardice), he transforms its Dionysian self-expression into the *Übermensch*. It is important to grant here how much the genes of Nietzsche are Kantian: without the transcendental turn to self, and self-activity, no Nietzsche. He is a disturbing mutant in the family Kant, a recessive gene that flowers into strange and exotic fruit, two generations later, having passed through the early mutations of the first generation of post-Kantians, who in their own way bred a stronger seed of self-affirming will from the recessive genes in the Kantian seed bed: from rational self-legislating will, through will as absolute being, through the will become the eros turannos of the dark origin, to the self-affirming will, self-transcending will, that is not either rational or good as Kant would have it. We come from the stern self-legislating will willing to submit itself to the moral law, to the extreme claim to autonomous self-legislation, for which there is no superior principle other than itself: eros intensified in seeking its own self absolutely, as the highest. "No God above me, and no man either." Not a "just Prometheus under Jove," but a higher Prometheus *above Jove;* and above, because *ascending to its own heights,* and from the deepest origin below underground in the darkest chambers of Dionysian eros. Who was this strange amalgam, Nietzsche, not an amalgam at all, but an astonishingly singular outcry?

TRAGEDY, THOUGHT, AND PLATONIC ART

One of Nietzsche's masks that has dominated so much of discussion is this persona: enemy of philosophical enemy number one, Plato. To those who see

Nietzsche as "Plato inverted," the *proximity* of the two will seem odd. There is something to that, if Plato is reduced to the "Platonism" of the dualistic beyond of univocal Ideas. There is less to it, if Plato is a thinker of eros, mania, mimesis in the metaxu. Reflection on tragedy, thought, and philosophical art will shed some light on this. Some of these themes Nietzsche importantly brings to our attention.

Schopenhauer said that every great work of art answers the question of life's meaning. Tragedy addresses the question in light of suffering and evil. Tragedy tries to redeem suffering by naming its horror as sacred. Nietzsche's name for the god of sacred suffering is Dionysus, the god also of divine intoxication. Dionysus is a mythic name for a happening of the origin: individuals issue from the origin but grief of being follows individuation, and this must be faced in a way that brings the individual to intoxicated communication with the origin again. Think of Anaximander: the *guilt of being at all* follows when the individual is torn free from the embrace of *to apeiron*. Schopenhauer interprets this guilt as the evil of being. Nietzsche believes we face and assuage it in tragedy. This is his Dionysian reformulation of Aristotle's *deinos* and *eleos*, horror and pity. Horror in facing the dark origin; and if pity at all, not Christian pity, not Schopenhauerian, but pitiless pity—the pitiless "yes" to being, even in its horror, that yet, as a "yes," is perhaps—"pity."

Philosophy too deals with the meaning of life and hence, despite its mask of disinterested contemplation, it is a dealing with the suffering of being. It is not intoxicated but reflective and hence distances itself from the horrors of lived engagements. Nevertheless, in the suffering of being an otherness strikes at us beyond our control, and this may bring home to us an awareness of metaphysical limit. Philosophers are tempted to turn from that suffering and otherness, though the turn will mask its flight as reasoning. We run from horror by rationalizing it. So running, the terrible may seem to become logically justified, even moralized (think of Kant and the sublime). And then henceforth all suffering, all otherness that breaks us has a reason, will have a reason, and even though we know not the reason, we will not surrender the conviction there must be a hidden reason. We become the conceptual brothers of Job's comforters. (Intriguingly, God esteemed them less than the Job he conspired to torment.) What has happened? Philosophical thought has thought the otherness and made its suffering submit, if only in principle, to thought itself, and its enlightenment. Thought thinks *itself* again in its own conceptual self-assurance. It does not think the suffering of the breaking otherness.

What Nietzsche names as "Socratism" or the "theoretical man" suggests an abbreviation for this: thought dreams its empire of the whole such that even its most destructive moments are domesticated as not yet properly interpreted signs of inherent reason; for everything has a reason. The principle of sufficient reason rises again out of the suffering. And who can doubt there is a comfort in this. It allows one to endure, for now the suffering is meaningful suffering, even though one cannot actually state the specific meaning. Philosophy flies from suffering into thought, and the more complete the flight the more complete the reinterpretation of the otherness of suffering as our mortal transition to the hidden reason.

Is Plato also one of Job's comforters? Plato, the philosophical exorcist of the dark god of tragedy whose infliction of affliction defies the sobrieties of reason? There is undoubtedly something in the view that Plato did want to relativize the dark god of tragedy: God is not jealous. For Nietzsche tragedy is superior in that the suffering is named as suffering. The deflection of its otherness, such as it is, is not a denial of its otherness. Suffering is not turned into the dark cloud of unknowing of which deeper reason is the silver lining. Tragedy stands in the sundering of being, the suffering of its otherness, but its affirmation is in the sundering. The sundering and the suffering are the gifts of Dionysus. Quite clearly Nietzsche also communicated to us that without his own suffering, he would not have seen what he had seen, been blessed as he was blessed. And perhaps cursed.

"What does not destroy me makes me strong." It is not true. One can be wounded and weakened and not destroyed. One may limp afterwards, but if I have wrestled with an angel it is not I now who is stronger: there is something greater than I. Nietzsche, I think, *willed himself* to be superior to the wounding: he willed his health, as if he wrestled with himself. Whether this willing is enough remains to be seen. For now I say: tragedy asks a willing that one cannot just will. One might say tragedy speaks in the middle of the darkness itself, it sings the darkness. It not only means that thought must think its other, it means that thought must sing its other. It is by no means incidental that in a later preface to *The Birth of Tragedy,* Nietzsche rightly said that the writer of the book should not have spoken but *sung*.

What is at stake here is less "irrationalism" as a changed understanding of the vocation of the thinker. When Nietzsche formulates the ancient quarrel of poetry and philosophy as "Plato versus Homer," his sympathy is with the honesty of the tragic artist. But he asks for a new *thinking* in which artist and philosopher are not opposites, but different voices within a mindfulness at once more tensed and finessed. His pursuit of this vocation is conditioned by Schopenhauer's dark origin but, if one could say it, the darkness shines differently for him. Least of all should we forget the laughter in Nietzsche, laughter itself often inseparable from the suffering it may contain. Nor should we forget that Plato too has his laugh.[1] Of all philosophers, with the exception of Plato, Nietzsche is the most brilliant as artist, as poet. Thought and art undergo transformation at his hands. Just as in Plato we have the deep riddle

---

1. See *Beyond Good and Evil* with regard to Aristophanes; *Werke: Kritische Gesamtausgabe,* herausgegeben von G. Colli und M. Montinari (Berlin: de Gruyter, 1967–), hereafter *W* in the text; where possible I will refer to translation of Nietzsche in *The Portable Nietzsche* (abbreviated to *PN*), ed. and trans. Walter Kaufmann (New York: Viking Penguin, 1976). On philosophy laughing at itself, see *BHD,* chapter 6.

of one who in attacking poetry epitomizes its power, and thus undermines in act the dualism he proposes in theory, so differently Nietzsche redefines the traditional opposition of poetry and philosophy. Nietzsche reverses the Platonic paradox. In attacking traditional philosophy from the standpoint of the tragic, he gives to philosophy itself a new imagistic concreteness, and most importantly commands a new honesty about the task of thought—in its human-all-too-human achievements and evasions.

Plato, you might say, is more extreme than Hegel who, after all, does not outrightly reject art for philosophy's sake but claims to sublate it dialectically. Plato seems to subordinate art, and in a way devoid of dialectical nuance. We hesitate, however, when we remember eros and mania in the metaxu. If we interpret Plato's *practice* as itself showing the art of plurivocal philosophizing, we see more at play than the search for the definition of an *eidos*.[2] Platonism is Nietzsche's stated enemy: the dualistic Platonism that subordinates the sensuous to the supersensuous, the aesthetic to the noetic, this world to the other; Platonism under the dominion of the univocal concept. But that there is more to Plato than Platonism, Nietzsche knew too well. "My Plato a caricature"—thus Nietzsche himself in the *Will to Power*. In *Beyond Good and Evil* Plato is named as the philosopher with the greatest power and amplitude of resources in the tradition; no philosopher comes close. This is the Plato who is Aristophanes' soul mate; the Plato who dims himself down to make himself compatible with his mentor "Socrates." If you have to "dim" yourself thus, the dimming shows you paradoxically "beyond" "Socratism," here understood as the merely theoretical life.[3] This is the masked Plato, who never appears in first person in his dialogues; who can never be unambiguously identified with any of the dramatic personae that appear in the dialogue, not even with Socrates. Cusanus accuses Plato of timidity on this score; he will not come out straight and assert for himself the bold speculative truths he holds. I think it is less timidity as a kind of philosophical finesse.

For Nietzsche, by contrast, the masked nature of Plato's thought is a sign of his superiority. Like Zarathustra, the result can be a communication that is *"für Alle und Keinen,"* for everyone and for no one (as the subtitle of *Thus Spoke*

---

2. See "Plato's Philosophical Art and the Identification of the Sophist," *Filosofia Oggi*, 11, no. 4 (1979): 393–403; also remarks in *BB*, 374–75.

3. There are admiring remarks on Plato in *Joyful Wisdom:* Plato is one of the strong, overflowing natures of ancient culture, one of the strongest ever; his idealism is partly a mask and defense against his powerful sensualism; his philosophizing does not originate simply in weakness. Nietzsche also recognizes the spiritual kinship with Aristophanes, another strong Athenian. His attack on "Platonism" reminds one of his attack on Alexandrine culture, and the ideal of the scholar in *The Birth of Tragedy*. This last is a frightening thought, if this is the only ideal; luckily Kant and Schopenhauer prove victorious over the optimism of logic. "The Alexandrian man is at bottom a librarian and scholiast, blinding himself miserably over dusty books and typographical errors" (*BT,* §18; *W,* III, 1, 114). I think you would be mean-minded to think this applies to the scholars of today, especially Nietzsche scholars.

Zarathustra has it). The aesthetics of Platonic thinking, the art of the philosophical question, is significant. If thought is masked, there is always a significant silence in the very articulation itself. I say significant silence, because if we are too bewitched by a Hegelian sense of articulation, silence quickly becomes *merely silence,* hence a testimony to the failure of the thought. Silence would then be an abortion of the concept that even Socrates fails to midwife. What if there is a silence that is a sign not of our failure but of the otherness of the origin? Silence might mark a respect for its inexhaustibility or reserve. One of the places we find such successful silence is in the speaking of a great work of art: it says nothing, yet says everything; and if it is a dialectical togetherness of silence and saying, neither the silence nor the saying can be *aufgehoben* into a Hegelian dialectic. That dialectic, by contrast, might well strike one as conceptual chatter, shamelessly loquacious when reverent attendance is the more fitting.

Does not the art of the Platonic dialogue show such a dialectical togetherness of saying and silence? For the dialectic of question and answer is only possible on the basis of *multiple silences.* In the interplay of saying and silence we witness a dramatics of the origination of thought. The embodied becoming of philosophical questioning and its maturing transforms the metaxu between I and an other. The metaxu is a porous space of communicability and communication. A question is addressed by you to me. Your speaking asks my silence, as it breaks yours. I respond, and my speaking asks your silence, even as I break mine. Address and reply are framed by silence, even as the space of communication between us is. Without multiple silences there would be no speaking and certainly no communication. The speaker and listener must both be willing to fall silent to allow the middle space to be charged with what the other says, and with what the dialectic of the question presents and insinuates. And neither you nor I are exhausted by the communication that does eventuate, since that event of conversation points to more than what it determinately articulates—my silence and yours that is not now here relevantly engaged by the conversation. These silences are other again.

Moreover, the effort in the Platonic dialogue to speak a satisfying response, an answer, seems to bring us to another significant silence. I do not just mean the act of noetic intuition by which it is said the form is grasped, though there is a significant silence to this. I mean the repeated dramatization in the dialogues of not being able now to "go further." I mean the fact that when logos reaches its own limit in a limiting silence, saying is not exhausted but rather taken up by a different saying, a poetic saying of myth, which is itself the bearer of a silence that, though exceeding univocal conceptualization, yet is addressed to philosophical thought. Plurivocal saying is twinned with plural silence: the otherness of the silence of encompassing context that grounds the dialogue; the otherness of the singular souls of the speakers; the silence of the between that becomes the charged space for the elicitation, solicitation of response in the dialogue of one and the other; the silence at the edge of the articulate concept that is carried into further articulation by mythopoeic speech, that in turn is the bearer of a silence that points again beyond the dialogue to an encompassing silence, a porosity to the communication of the divine. Is there a Hegelian concept that embraces in itself all of *that* dialectic?

Plato's philosophical practice suggests "no" is the answer. Nietzsche's rhetoric points in similar directions. Nietzsche is not a univocal thinker; he is plurivocal. The many voices might be dismissed as a failure, if one's sense of philosophical speech were dominated by the ideal of univocal clarity, undoubtedly a major strand in the whole tradition of philosophy. Nietzsche is not a systematic thinker, and we might charge him with inability to reduce the multiplicity of his thought to a set of basic concepts. Both these charges are too simplistic. The plurivocal character of his thought is not a mere matter of form; it reflects the "content" that is being spoken; the separation of form and content has to be discarded when reading him, and not just as a concession to an exuberant rhetoric. The excess of the "content" takes Dionysian form, and this forming can never be reduced to univocal form. Sometimes the flushed excess of his mind expressed itself in a certain chaos of arrangement.

This is true of all thought in the process of its emergence. Even if it comes slowly, it still comes in a kind of rush. The nonsystematic voice is essential, though this does not mean the systematic voice is necessarily lacking its integrity. The Nietzschean rush might have benefitted from listening to that other voice. Being truthful asks an attendance of mindfulness that tries to stay as close as possible to the energy of emerging articulation. The energy of being and mind do not originally shape themselves as philosophical systems. Even were one to wrestle with the energy and somehow form it in the shape of system, the same energies that nourish the system, now show themselves as exceeding that form. It is the necessary drift to excess in all serious thought that is communicated in the nonsystematic character of the thought. Nietzsche suggested that the will to system is a fundamental dishonesty. This is true if it means we blind ourselves to the "too muchness" of being as happening, or blunt our awareness that the mind holds too much to be contained within a system. Excessive mindfulness has to find a different form to be true to the "too muchness" of the happening of being. Plurivocity invites the nonsystematic voice also needed by philosophy to speak what is in excess of system.

Some will still say that failure to conceptualize is a miscarriage of philosophy. But this may well be to miss the point when questions of art, origins, otherness are at stake. Failure itself may be what is most significant, not for another attempt along the same lines, but for a venture into different articulation, and indeed venture into another silence. There is a sense of philosophical failure here that is in fact a very important philosophical success. Jaspers understood something of this in speaking of foundering, as did Heidegger in relation to the "failure" of Schelling.[4] I think it is implied by Nietzsche's description of himself as the *first tragic philosopher*. Not a philosopher of tragedy, but a tragic philosopher. We must not dishonor the sacredness of suffering. We break on the otherness. Thought sings the otherness in its own destruction. Perhaps few have had a glimmer of what this might mean.

One wonders how well Nietzsche himself understood this. There seems to be a hint of the plurivocal task of philosophical thinking in Nietzsche's discussion of the philosopher in *Beyond Good and Evil* (§211; cf. §212; also *W,* VI, 2, 149). One closer inspection I am not so sure. Here (§211) the others—the scientific laborer, the critic, skeptic, dogmatist, historian, poet, collector, traveler, and so on—"are merely preconditions of his [the philosopher's] task: this task itself demands something different—it demands that he *create values. . . . Genuine philosophers, however, are commanders and legislators:* they say, "*thus* it *shall* be!" They first determine the Whither and For What of man, and in so doing have at their disposal the preliminary labor of all philosophical laborers, all who have overcome the past. With a creative hand they reach for the future, and all that is and has been becomes a means for them, an instrument, a hammer. Their "knowing" is *creating,* their creating is a legislation, their will to truth is—*will to power.*" Considering this, it is hard not to think of a hyperbolic ambition that exceeds even Hegel's claims to comprehensiveness. Everything is a means ("merely preconditions") to that one dictating voice of the future philosopher. Self-exalting say-so: that is not what is at stake in what I mean by plurivocal philosophizing.[5]

Hegel described the art work as a thousand-eyed Argos. Plurivocal philosophizing requires a tolerance of otherness something like that. One would have to twist and turn to detect something like this tolerance in Nietzsche's above description and the instrumentalization of the others it seems to exalt. And yet, what is best in Nietzsche is precisely what betrays the tyranny implied in his own description, a betrayal shown when generosity overtakes "overcoming." "Overcoming" is still a god too jealous by far.

Philology, Origins, the Otherness of Words

Nietzsche was concerned with "origins" in many ways, and we need to note some of these. He is heir to the nineteenth century historical consciousness with its stress on understanding a phenomenon as the outcome of a prior development whose process may not be evident on the surface of the result of

4. See also *PO,* 242–58 on being mindful and failure; also "Being at a Loss: Reflections on Philosophy and the Tragic," in my *Perplexity and Ultimacy* (Albany: State University of New York Press, 1995), chapter 2.

5. See *PO,* chapter 1, on the many others of the philosopher.

the development. He is a son of "Hegelianism" in one respect, though he early saw the dangers implicit in unbound historical consciousness. Critical and antiquarian uses of history can drain away the sources of creative work in humans, though monumental history may offer outstanding exemplars to inspire new creativity. He is certainly at odds with the Hegelian way of trying to secure a presuppositionless beginning for philosophy itself. Thus he attacks (in *Twilight,* 'Reason' in Philosophy, §§1–4) what he sees as the philosophical prejudice against origins. Why? Because here "origins" always implicates the notion of becoming, and this the philosopher shuns in favor of what does not change. The philosopher wants everything to be *causa sui* and most especially himself and his own system. Clearly Hegel does not shun becoming, but his desire for presuppositionless science does feed on a view of thought as self-determining, and in that sense as *causa sui.*[6] I spoke of this in terms of dialectical self-mediation through otherness in which the implicit origin brings itself to explicit articulation, returns to itself by incorporating otherness, hence closing the circle. Does Nietzsche himself escape the spell of *causa sui?* As we shall see, he transposes it into the more aesthetic register of *self-affirming* will to power.

That said, "origin" in the Nietzschean sense implies a relatedness to *otherness* that cannot be subsumed in a closed dialectical circle. What is original is significantly other, though implicated in an unfolding of relations which constitute an equivocal process whereby we arrive at our provisional present. The present is transition, outcome of the equivocal mediations of submerged or hidden powers in what presents itself. While this is not a non-Hegelian thought, the otherness of the origin as will to power precludes complete dialectical self-mediation; it may make possible all mediations as provisional, but it itself eludes exhaustive mediation. This is evident in Nietzsche's philological bent. His *philia* of *logos* shows logos itself to be a historical process and product. The word carries and covers over its history and origin. At times Nietzsche shows the solid, even pedantic respectabilities of the scholar: recall his advocacy in *Genealogy* (note to Essay 1) of a prize essay contest on etymology and moral value. A hidden history is ingrained in words. Nietzsche has the feeling for concepts themselves as palimpsests of histories of conceiving (even the very word concept itself carries direct reference to generation!). The significance that surfaces may be a revelation but it also a hiding: clear concepts conceal.

Contra any Cartesian clarity and distinctness of ideas, or Hegelian self-determination of concepts, the self-transparency of thought becomes a problem to itself in the very happening of putative transparency. An inward other-

---

6. See Hegel's discussion of "cause" in his *Logic* (the chapter on "The Absolute Relation," Miller trans. 554–71): the defects of all other notions of cause lead for him to the notion of reciprocal causality, itself pointing beyond substance to the self-determining of subjectivity.

ness arises in the very instruments, the "words," we use to express our mastery in thought. Words that are true are also dissimulations of something other, and hence they are also lies. Delve into the word's inward otherness, and we discover less an instrumental tag, as the bearer of a potential world, with all its equivocity. Words are not useful sensuous vehicles for the outer expression of univocal concepts mastered in the mind. They are the traces of the struggles of people and peoples, of a people with itself. The highest words are the words of value, the legislative words which stamp a people's table of laws and customs. This stamp is the seal of a people: seal as the sign of authority of the dominant will to power; seal in the sense in which something is sealed, wrapped up, hidden, kept in its totality from clear view. The apparent stability of given univocities becomes questionable, if we have an honest philological respect for linguistic origins. Clear words are the shiny surfaces of a sea that, for all we know, may be bottomless. Let words be the means of our Hegelian self-mediation, and the otherness be there, right there in the self-mediation, but the otherness is there in a *non-Hegelian* way, because resistant to complete dialectical transformation into Apollonian light. Brightness is the outcome of a darkness forgotten, and what carries memory, the word, is itself cause of our amnesia.

Post-Cartesian philosophy skirts the problem and flirts with it. Think of Leibniz: there are perceptions below the threshold of explicit self-consciousness, apperception in Leibniz's terms. Here we are alerted to internal intricacy within the Cartesian subjectification of being. Leibniz is not a Cartesian, but an heir to Cartesian problematics. His notion of the monad as radically individual does continue the Cartesian turn to the self; the stress on the monad as self-enclosed anticipates the stress on self-relation, self-mediation that we find carried to its extreme conclusion by German idealism, especially Hegel. But the *petit perceptiones* that are active, energetic in the sense of at work *(energon),* regardless of explicit recognition by self-consciousness, these introduce a troubling nuance of recalcitrant otherness within the inwardness of the monad. We do not usually couple Leibniz and Nietzsche. Leibniz: the bland faith of theodicy, not troubling inward otherness, another comforter of Job. Nietzsche: explorer of this turbulence who thunders imprecations at all such theological blandness. Yet Nietzsche praises Leibniz (in of all places, *Joyful Wisdom,* §357): Leibniz realized that consciousness is only a very late development, hence derivative; derivative of what mostly goes on unconsciously. Nietzsche's warmth towards Leibniz is quite striking: the profundity of his insight has not yet been exhausted.

Everything bright is doubled by its own darkness, and perhaps it is the darkness that *doubles itself* as brightness. What is unconscious remains as an inward otherness that resists transformation into complete conscious transparency. On this score, Schelling, Schopenhauer and Nietzsche each are different trouble makers for idealism. Schelling troubles idealism by reminding us of the other of logic, the unconscious, right within the horizon of idealistic logos and its stress on encompassing identity. An unconscious ground makes self-consciousness possible but can never be completely elevated to self-consciousness; were it to be so elevated, self-consciousness would be undermined, for its own necessary prior ground of otherness would have been transformed into a non-other. Self-consciousness is only possible because of what is other to self-consciousness. For reason to think its other, reason requires its other, requires that the other remain as other.

Philology gives us an instructive lesson concerning the other in logos itself. It too troubles any totalizing of the principle of sufficient reason. Words are overdetermined; they mean more than they say explicitly, carry around within themselves unacknowledged origins. Words are excess: they express reserves of meaning but also reserve recesses. The treasure they bury may also have horror, in a depth that is no depth, for it is the otherness of the human in its protracted historical inwardizing. Nietzsche did see historical process as producing inwardness, just like Hegel; but far from being the dialectic of the logos concretizing itself historically in the human spirit, *a là* Hegel, this inwardizing is produced by man's violence on his own animality. Violence on self generates a memory; inwardness is cruelty to self, a wound in being necessary to keep reminding us of ourselves, bringing us to ourselves in suffering, keeping alive the painful split of difference that cuts us off from immediate immersion in animal being. Man may be the sick animal but sickness opens inwardness. This, in its immanent otherness, is never rational self-possession. (Incidentally, philology hath charms that can bring the philosophical etymologist to the verge of a sacred mania. For some reason I have been sometimes struck by the analogy between some admirers of Tolkien and devotees of Heidegger when they speak the mother tongue. Tolkien, I believe, held he had rediscovered the old original language of the elves. I have seen his followers chanting this archaic "Elfish." It was charming and harmless. Though it would have been less charming if the friends of Tolkien claimed primordial ontological significance for their incantations. The charm would be broken.)

The philological finesse for words as exceeding us can give rise to a spirit of suspicion towards the pretensions of surface meaning, and the will to univocal concepts that we find in positivistic science and in logic. Was it not Peter Damian who said that the first grammarian was the devil? Increase in the spirit of suspicion is perhaps the most evident effect of Nietzsche's influence, and with this an increased wariness towards tradition. But one could also argue for something of the opposite. Without tradition, creation from nothing becomes creation of nothing. And so philological finesse can also produce a belief that "creativity" necessitates a long temporal build-up of a deposit of significance that is mostly unconscious, instinctual in Nietzsche's sense, the effortless functioning of an ingrained cultural formation, not in any biologistic sense. "Instinct" is a mediated result which condenses a web of relatedness to otherness impossible fully to lay out. As such a result, "instinct" is a beginning, a reserve for new origination. Creativity in a genuine sense is only possible when the originative urge of the inward otherness has become (as we say) "second nature." The master is instinct: all but thoughtless eye, or ear, or hand, or even mind (the thinker does not think) for the essential matter of his craft.

The voice that speaks or sings is the break or breach of consciousness on the surface of a depth that in itself is unknown but that harbors "more" or excess. The excess of origins is hence the necessary unknown ground for genuine creativity. Hence creativity comes to those who are *heirs* of millennia. The creators are the latecomers, harvesters and harvest in one, the prodigal squanderers of the spirit that has conserved itself over many generations. The bearing of origins through time (normally called a tradition) is essential to what we think of as individual origination. The latter is only a last result, not the true origin. It is the final moment in which the root, now grown, bursts into the song of its flower. It is the swan song. The useless ornament may broadcast fertile seed for another sowing whose harvest may be epochs away.

Lyrical outpouring? But Nietzsche did conceive of himself as such a flower and seedcaster. He claimed to be the heir of millennia and also the philosopher of the future who has to go under to be fertilizing ground. He explicitly calls himself both a decadent (literally what falls down, or away: recall too Zarathustra's *Untergang*) and a new beginning. This relatedness to heritage is important for the theme of overcoming the individualistic subjectivity of modernity. Individuals are results who can become new beginnings only because of what they have inherited. What breaks through in the "original" individual is both the wisdom and error, the ugliness and the beauty of millennia. Origin is not back there; origin is hidden in the inward otherness, especially of words. Nietzsche's fussing (in *Ecce Homo;* see *W,* VI, 3, 262 ff.) about his own ancestry may strike some as silly, but he was quite convinced that he was just his father and mother, and forefathers. Creation is not simply "mine," and it can be act of gratitude for the forerunner. It is their act too, a history of significant acts, finally fructifying. My act can be gratitude consummated in a new act of origination. Gratitude in origination produces the decentering of solipsistic selfhood. To the contrary, the self is a gathering of all the generations of the others. At its richest it is a present community of past others, including its own prior selves, now assimilated as the intimate others of the present self. The self is a history, a gathering and heritage of otherness.

Nietzsche does not quite put it this way, nor, I think, does he live up to the promise of gratitude. He was waylaid by his own hypermodernity, and the excess of its individualism. We must say that art's creative saying is the voicing of all those others. Nietzsche himself suggests: the creative ones who know themselves, know themselves least. Why? I would say: the self is idiot—there is something other in it, more intimate to it than it knows with complete determinacy. It is the intimate otherness of the self that speaks in such a self. It is its own voice and the voices of others. Such a self is sometimes a babel of these voices of others, sometimes a symphony; and if he conducts himself as his own multitudinous orchestra, the music played is never simply his "own."

One cannot absolutely fix a distinction between self and other, for the music envelops both. It has no name, like the music heard on the bridge in Venice, and it has all the names in history, as Nietzsche said about himself (letter to Burkhardt, 6 January 1889).

I do not want to understate how Nietzsche's aristocratic "individualism" complicates matters for acknowledgment of the other as other. This is connected to will to power as *willing itself,* and I will return to this. I will also return to the related problem, namely that this individualism more often makes Nietzsche the *denouncer* of the errors of the tradition, rather than the grateful celebrant of its enabling power. Most especially in relation to Christianity, the blessing he bestows is a curse.[7]

MORALITY, ORIGINS, OTHERS

Of course, Nietzsche's concern with origins has its ethical expression. That he calls himself the first immoralist and claims to be beyond good and evil in no way contradicts, in fact, is entirely consistent with, his concern to uncover the origins of the ethical. *The Genealogy of Morals* instantiates the presuppositions mentioned above. The high ideal is only an indirect interpretation of a chaos of impulses, an indirection as much falsifying as revealing: its truth "plays false" by implying that the "high" ideal floats in the ether of the moral order without relation to the "low," when it is the development, because the sublimation, that is, the "higher" mediation, of the "low." The genealogist traces the present to its equivocal antecedents which cast doubt on the univocal stability of the ethical ideal, and the rosy self-assurance it seems to arrogates to itself. Once again, concern with origins becomes a suspicion of presentness. The point is now well rehearsed by many admirers, and kindred masters of modern suspicion. I will only say that genealogical ethics is bound up with an *archeology of the aesthetic.* The inseparability of the aesthetic and the ethical, indeed of the religious, is evident from *Birth of Tragedy:* we are not dealing with "works of art" in a standard post-Kantian "aesthetic" sense; when Nietzsche claims the world can only be justified aesthetically, he is at odds with any mere "aestheticism." It all bears on "religion." I will come again to this.

Suspicion of presentness makes Nietzsche's genealogical strategy into a process of rupturing and reversal. The univocal is shown to be equivocal, hence ruptured; but the rupture reverses, in that the univocal *is* the equivocal;

7. There was originally a subtitle to *The Anti-Christ,* written in the spiky hand that portended his "breakdown"—A Curse on Christianity. Despite the fact that this was crossed out, its appropriateness is evident. At the end of that book, he calls Christianity the one great curse humanity has had to endure (*Ich heisse das Christenthum den einen grossen Fluch* . . . [*SW,* VI, 3, 251]); his "no" takes on the implication of his curse on it. See my "Caesar with the Soul of Christ: Nietzsche's Highest Impossibility," in *Tijdschrift voor Filosofie,* 61 (1999), 27–61.

the truth of univocity is equivocity. The familiar reversals are well-known: the intelligible into the unintelligible, the altruistic into the selfish, the noble into the ignoble, the Platonic original as form or *eidos* into the creative chaos of will to power. If there is a dialectic between univocity and equivocity here, it is itself an *equivocal dialectic*. Certainly it would so appear to Hegel, to whom it would be a negative dialectic that truncates the reconstituting *Aufhebung* beyond antithesis. While this Hegelian point is not untrue, is not true enough to the whole of what is at stake with Nietzsche. The passion for reversal without regrounding in a reconstituted harmony becomes more and more accentuated in the later Nietzsche. The explosive power of equivocity, immanent in dialectic, is unanchored from the ontological grounding or reason in which Hegel claimed to root it.

One might well ask, in analogy with Hegelian dialectics: if with Hegel, dialectic as negative yields to speculative reason as affirmative, as reconstituting a whole which contains the opposition, is there such a thing as a *genealogical apotheosis,* or affirmation, to surpass the genealogical suspicion and its equivocal debunking of univocal identities? Can one get such a "yes," from such a "no"? Or is there a "yes" more primal than every such "no"? If so, why are we so steeped in the corruptions of nihilistic negation? If there is such a more primal "yes," does Nietzsche stay true to it? Is one not necessitated to play false with it, if all is necessarily equivocal? Or is there a "yes" more true than the univocal identity of logic, the dialectical holism of speculative idealism, and the bacchanal of eroticized equivocity?

My remarks above about *gratitude* to the forerunner here find application. One side of Nietzsche wants to gratefully acknowledge this debt to heritage or patrimony. There is a section towards end of *Joyful Wisdom* where he thanks the honest integrity of his Christian forbears: their Christian honesty made possible his un-Christian honesty. One notes in *Ecce Homo* his piety towards his father, the Lutheran pastor. What Nietzsche (nicknamed as a boy: "the little pastor") claims not to want is humbug, pretense. Even the ugly origin can be, must be affirmed. The eternal return is the most radical statement of this. If we think of everything returning, then the dark origin out of which we try to struggle also comes around again. Hence everything at some point of the circle is both origin and end. I cannot avoid thinking of the resemblance to the dialectically self-mediating origin: in the Hegelian circle everything is always both beginning and end, though *we* do not understand this in the beginning but in *our end,* that is, when we have attained the standpoint of Hegelian philosophy or absolute knowing. In Nietzsche there is not this conceptual clarity at the end, for in Nietzsche we find, as it were, a radical promiscuity of beginning and termination, for everything and every episode is each and both. Against Hegelian self-comprehension, this is to affirm the *ineradicable equivocity* of all being.

Consider again *Joyful Wisdom* where he attacks positivism as the weakest, most stupid interpretation of being. In other words, what seems the most scientific, hence the most intelligent interpretation of being is the most meaningless. One reason is that positivist science will smother the ambiguity of being in favor of a logic of univocity: things will have one meaning, one only. This is not *the* truth, but the *will* to a certain truth, one which shears off as excess the troubling otherness of ineradicable ambiguity. Being is questionable, the human being is questionable; and both finally will always remain questionable. For Nietzsche, the strongest interpretation would affirm the ineradicable ambiguity of all being.

This marks again his proximity and hostility to the purely self-appropriating origin whose end entirely mediates the darkness of the beginning into conceptual clarity. It is as if every such appropriating end turns out to be inherently opaque, intrinsically *other to itself,* since it carries an infinity within itself and hence is the living refutation of any pretension to self-transparency. When we "absolutely" know ourselves, we know that we do not know ourselves at all. The circles turns again but not in a Hegelian way. It spins off into darkness; or rather its very light is simply its own spinning darkness. Nor can we stop the circle and get off; we cannot even "see" the darkness, we only get brief, blinding flashes of its black otherness.

Thus concern to uncover ethical origins shades into Nietzsche's concern with the origins of logic. This is a concern of *Joyful Wisdom,* appropriately so since philosophers traditionally have seen in logic the royal road to wisdom.[8] Where is the joy in logic? In the *Will to Power* the same concern with the origins of the logical recurs: this origin lies in the will to power, the will to regularize being by means of the constructed concept of "equality," "sameness," "unity." The origins of the logical reside in a turn from the ambiguous otherness of being as an incessant process of othering itself, that is, of becoming, of becoming other to any simple sameness, or self-related identity. Heraclitean logos is subordinated to Heraclitean flux; or rather the logos itself is *derivative* from the process of becoming, considered as the genuine original. This issue has many post-Nietzschean implications.[9]

The origin of the logical is especially relevant to *The Birth of Tragedy,* a book as much genealogical of the logical, as of the tragic vision. "Socratic man" is here presented as the exemplar of the "theoretical" approach to being, that is, the logicist will to power over the originary power of being in the process of becoming, originary power in its otherness to the efforts of the human mind to comprehend it completely in a system of concepts. Again the critique of logic is related to the sense of origins uncovered by philology,

8. Note how in *Joyful Wisdom* many sections have titles like: the origin of logic; the origin of the religious, and so on.

9. For instance, what I called above the suspicion of presentness might be linked to his post-Heideggerian heirs who speak of "the metaphysics of presence," itself linked with a Heideggerian interpretation of logic and metaphysics as onto-theo-logic—a fetishization of univocal identity as the category by which the meaning of being is to be thought.

though the critique entails a kind of "dialectical" reversal. The philologist is the friend (philos) of the logos, but in the course of carrying through his search for origins, friendship reverses itself into a suspicion of a certain logos: suspicion of philosophical logos as logic.

I would summarize by calling Nietzsche a kind of heir of *Vico,* perhaps the first great philologist-philosophy in the modern era to oppose the logicist pretensions of the Cartesian mathēsis of being. See Nietzsche as taking issue with what Vico calls the "conceit of scholars." This conceit consists in taking, mistaking, the developed phenomenon for the original reality. The conceit of scholars is amnesia, what one might call a *fugue state* with respect to origins. Logic without history (Descartes dismisses history in *Discourse on the Method*) yields a fugue state of mind, one not only memoryless about logic's own being, but ontologically fugitive from the sometimes violent, barbaric otherness close to beginnings. Would it be possible to map onto Nietzsche, Vico's archaic triad of gods, heros, mortals? If mortals are the last men, and the heros the *Übermenschen,* who or what are the gods? The thunderbolt of Jove is singular for Vico in transforming feral man first into humans, and there is a thunderbolt in Nietzsche, but what can it be, if there is to be no god *above* the *Übermensch?* But perhaps there is a god *below?*

I see Nietzsche as also very Vichian in recognizing that earlier peoples were quite different to us more "civilized" humans, more full of blood and lust and cruelty, and perhaps also full of gaiety. Nietzsche's remarks on the Titans in the *Birth of Tragedy* remind one of Vico's obsession with the Giants in *The New Science.* As one of the first philological philosophers, Vico saw in advance of Nietzsche that the word carries the heritage of past interpretation; hence it is implicitly a *world* of meaning—aesthetic, ethical, legal, religious, philosophic. Like a Leibnizian monad, the articulated word inarticulately reflects the whole world from a particular point of view. The task of thought in *The New Science* suggests a kind of *divination:* reading the traces, the signs, the omens. Thought asks interpretation, a new service of Hermes. Divinatory thinking also concerns the loss of the first origin when, according to Vico, the young world was awash with the divine. In the age of reflection we live in a world washed of the gods. Some cleansing agents make the world antiseptic. But then do they not also make it *septic for humans?* Being is made "neutral," made valueless, made a thereness finally hostile to our being at home on the earth. This is the world after the death of the gods. But can we live in a world that has no perfumes?

Nietzsche knew we lived in Vico's third age of mortals, but he desired a new heroism, beyond the death of the old gods, and to heal the plague of the last men. Did he divine well enough the omens before him in Vico's "barbarism of reflection" when men go mad and waste their substance? We may dream of the *Übermensch* surpassing the last men onto new heights. But in these dream, the Titans underground are as light as air, and float aloft to the Empyrean in these dreams of new heights. The old monsters come alive again in the new heavens. Do they make a new world? In the "barbarism of reflection," I doubt that Nietzsche was divinatory enough about the *evil harvest* of unbound will to power that was soon to darken the world.

THE AESTHETICS OF ORIGIN

True, Nietzsche often presented himself more as a *herald of futurity* than a philosopher of origins. Does he risk an empty apotheosis of futurity in which gratitude for those coming before us is less and less in evidence?[10] I think he does, and it is not unconnected with a certain view of origin. Nietzsche figures as an important influence shaping some of the caricatures we find here, for instance, the antimetaphysical superannuation of a divine origin as a grammatical mistake. But beyond the above noted moral concerns with origins, is there not also a "metaphysical" concern? The mere mention of "metaphysics" will stop some in their tracks and cause them to throw up their hands in exasperation: What! we all know that Nietzsche had nothing but contempt for metaphysics. How dare you insinuate a concern with the metaphysics of origin! I will not recant. I will go further. I would align him, not only with Schopenhauer, but with Hegel. Postmodernist of the strict observance will

---

10. I have benefitted much from what George Kline has written about futurity. Though Kline is well known as a commentator on Whitehead, Hegel, and Russian philosophy, he has written very insightfully on Nietzsche on this theme. I refer to his Presidential Address to the Hegel Society of America, entitled, "The Use and Abuse of Hegel by Nietzsche and Marx" in *Hegel and his Critics: Philosophy in the Afermath of Hegel,* ed. William Desmond (Albany: State University of New York Press, 1989), chapter 1. This offers penetrating understanding of the instrumentalizing of time in Nietzsche and Marx, in train of a seriously flawed apotheosis of the world-historical future. Moreover, his documentation of Nietzsche's fetishization, not to say idolatry of futurity, is impressive. Below I cite Zarathustra's lament that he walks among men as among fragments of the future. But Kline also draws our attention to Nietzsche's obsession with the "... man of tomorrow and the day after tomorrow *[Mensch des Morgen und Übermorgen],*" and with the philosophers of the future. He cites Nietzsche: "In order to create [we need] liberation from morality and relief by means of festivals. Anticipations of the future! To celebrate the *future* not the past! To compose *(dichten)* the *myth of the future*" (*Hegel and His Critics,* 17). He notes (*ibid*, 22) that Zarathustra speaks of "our great, far off empire of man *(Menschen-Reich),* the thousand year empire of Zarathustra *(das Zarathustra-Reich von tausend Jahren).*" Ultimately the rhetoric that glories the future in instrumentalizing past and present is empty—a paean to a "coming god," call it Dionysus or the *Übermensch,* it hardly matters, a paean that seems to be as empty as the nihilism from which that "god" was to save us. The disastrous results for the human spirit in instrumentalizing time and idolizing futurity are now hardly debatable with respect to totalitarian Marxism, but the Romantic aura of a Nietzschean faith and hope still persists for many, not least due to the equivocating faith of some French Nietzscheans. I think, for instance, of Bataille; or of Foucault's quest of Nietzschean excess in relation to sado-masochism and orgiastic revolutionary politics. Frenzied eros without the finesse of *phronēsis* is as disastrous as totalizing projects of instrumental reason. Kline helps us see that the ringing affirmation of a glorious transfigured future, somewhere over the rainbow, has about it the hollow ring of spiritual desperation.

quickly rush to exorcise, with the sign of Dionysus, that dread panlogical spectre. But Nietzsche, as much as Hegel and Schopenhauer, offers us a variation on a metaphysics of the erotic origin.

What here of two recent, influential interpretations of Nietzsche, the Heideggerian and the deconstructionist? The first sees Nietzsche as the last metaphysician, the second as having transcended "metaphysics" in a new artistic philosophizing. I will not adjudicate between them, except to say that Nietzsche was as much a metaphysician as Plato, and to that extent Heidegger was right. Yet this metaphysics is intimately tied with the privileged place of art, and there is an aestheticist Nietzsche whose voice cannot be reduced simply to the voice of the last metaphysician. I am not endorsing either Heidegger's or Nietzsche's view of the tradition of metaphysics. I contest it. But metaphysics is inescapable, even when one claims to overcome or overturn, or deconstruct it. Metaphysics is just what we need, honest thinking about the origin and the ultimate. There is no escape from metaphysics, and not because we risk some kind of dialectical illusion *a là* Kant, unfortunate but inevitable. Honest, perplexed thinking about origin and ultimacy constitute the commission, responsibility, indeed the destiny of human mindfulness.

Heidegger rightly sees many hidden continuities of Nietzsche with previous philosophers. But he is not entirely true to the *plurivocal* nature of Nietzsche's philosophizing: there is the suffering, laughing Nietzsche, he who in all naïveté would offer advice about the proper beverage to drink in the morning; there is the poetic Nietzsche, the playful Nietzsche, the buffoon. While the Derridean focus on Nietzsche's styles does address something of this other Nietzsche, we do not have to choose between the poet and the philosopher/metaphysician. Again like Plato, Nietzsche was a poet-philosopher, and the poetry is not devoid of philosophical significance. A mere "aestheticization" of Nietzsche is not enough, in the end trivializes him, as it would trivialize art.

In his first major work, *The Birth of Tragedy* Nietzsche returns to the age of gods and heros. Origin here is as much ontological, as aesthetic and religious and cultural. This is a strange work: not mere "aesthetics" nor history of Greek cultural life, though Greek tragedy incarnates the Dionysian origin. In a certain sense, *The Birth of Tragedy* is a work of *first philosophy*—unrecognizable to any Aristotelian, I know, but nevertheless it offers thought about the primal—primal in an other than more standard philosophical sense, that is, a rational principle. We must become free of the conceit of scholars, as well as the barbarism of reflection. One has to have a sense of the excess of the origin to rationalization to understand what is happening here. Something other to thought is to be thought.

Art has metaphysical significance, early and late in the philosophical tradition, and Nietzsche is no exception. This significance is pervasive in Nietzsche's thinking. This is evident in the metaphysical aesthetic of *The Birth of Tragedy*, where the origin is called the primordial one, *das Ureine*. Here we encounter ultimacy articulated under *the sign of unity*. The "metaphysical" may be dissimulated in the later writings of Nietzsche but it is still at work in the aesthetics. There we find ultimacy, as will to power, articulated under *the sign of difference*. Origin becomes the self-production of the many; the primordial One, under the sign of difference, is reformulated as the will to power as diversification.

The atheistic god, Schopenhauerian will, goes more deeply underground, as it were, but it is not denied. If there is a change, it is a deeper appreciation that descriptions of the underlying power in terms of unity, oneness, identity, sameness risk a misstep: the undergrounding source as a Dionysian will to power is a kind of centrifugal "unity," that is, an explosive "unity," a scattering source. *Difference as differentiation* rather than oneness as unity would better describe this explosive energy: the primal unity is simply the energy of absolute othering—always becoming other to itself. It is not hard to see the prefigurings of Heidegger's difference qua difference, and Derrida's *différance*. Nevertheless, this diffusive, self-scattering source is a Same, a deep down unity to things: hence the reiterated cry: everything, all things are *nothing but* will to power; everything is *at bottom* will to power. This undergrounding Same is *Das Ureine* of *The Birth of Tragedy*, but given the self-scattering of this One, it is not surprising that Nietzsche will also say: the world is to all eternity chaos. Chaos here is creative formlessness, prior to form, the indeterminate energy, dunamis that in itself is formless. Nietzsche recoiled more and more from the superimposition of the category of identity on this chaos.

Metaphysically the two sides, identity and difference, sameness and otherness are unavoidable, which is not to say that Nietzsche offers an adequate account of their relation, or of the one and the many.[11] Quite to the contrary,

---

11. I note the disagreement of W. Müller-Lauter (he stresses the plural: wills to power) with Heidegger (who emphasizes the one will to power). See his *Nietzsche: Seine Philosophie der Gegensätze und die Gegensätze seiner Philosophie* (Berlin: de Gruyter, 1971); translation, *Nietzsche,* trans. David J. Parent (Chicago: University of Illinois Press, 1999); also "Nietzsche's Teaching of Will to Power," trans. Drew E. Griffin, *Journal of Nietzsche Studies,* 4, no. 5 (1992–1993): 37–101. What I say makes clear that the occurence of one will to power and wills to power reflects the inseparability, perhaps sameness of the stress on same/one and difference as "differenting." While Nietzsche's pluralism is important for Müller-Lauter (also for Deleuze), the stress is on *derived* unity, unity derived from interplay of different crystalizations of will to power, not the *underived* "unity," earlier called by Nietzsche *das Ureine*. As I have indicated, I think this "unity" is transposed to the register of *difference* (differentiation) in the later work of Nietzsche. For there is a sense in which will to power is underived—because derived from nothing but itself, from nothing other than itself. In that sense, it is ultimate and irreducible, since all plural forms of will to power are derivations of it. The transcendental unity of a more classical form has passed through *das Ureine of The Birth of Tragedy* to become origin of its own differences, its self-multiplying forms. Will to power is *das Ureine* become equivocal difference. The pluralism emphasized by such as Müller-Lauter, and more recently by Paul van Tongeren in his fine book *Reinterpreting Modern Culture: An Introduction to Friedrich Nietzsche's Philosophy* (West Lafayette, Ind.: Purdue University Press, 2000) is not without its merits but in practice and in theory one must demur

he offers us an interpretation of difference which, qua interpretation, is *reactive* to an excessively univocalized sense of unity or identity. This interpretation tends to privilege an equivocal sense of difference. But if being is plurivocal this does not mean that being is just equivocal. I cannot detail here some of the fuller implications of these statements, beyond to say that the plurivocity of being does suggest some exoneration of the poet-philosophers. This point also applies to the exoneration of Plato as a plurivocal philosopher. As such, he is not the first metaphysician in either Nietzsche's or Heidegger's sense, nor can he be deconstructed in Derrida's sense. No plurivocal philosopher fetishizes an excessively fixated univocity, such as seems to be in question in relation to the so-called "metaphysics of presence."

Where Heidegger underscores the same, Derrida puts emphasis on difference. The equivocity of Nietzsche allows both. Indeed his equivocal philosophizing sometimes allows almost anything. This can be a virtue, though not always, and indeed not frequently. Recall his writings are for everyone and for no one, *für Alle und Keinen*. One might say that equivocal philosophizing allows everything and allows nothing.[12] Nor should we be fooled by Nietzsche's air of superior self-confidence. Quite simply, Nietzsche did not always know what he was talking about. He was *trying out* ideas, many of which he finally did not take seriously. Sometimes he is, as we say, just doing the fool. I am not insulting Nietzsche. He is quite happy to call himself a buffoon. He is often at his best when he is doing the fool. Then he is a laughing philosopher. But when he puffs himself up in praise of his own genius, then there is something laughable, and not in Nietzsche's better sense either. There is something ever more laughable about the hagiography of his contemporary followers and the academic industry they have fabricated from his texts. One laughs with Nietzsche himself against the Nietzscheans, as when he speaks of the scholars reading themselves to death, their heads smoking night and day.

A notable characteristic of Nietzsche is that he somersaults between opposites: now ironical, sarcastic, now deadly earnest; now clown, now vates. Did

---

about a primary stress on difference and derived unity. In theory, some sense of will to power as somehow the same in all the wills to power cannot be evaded. Nietzsche too faces the old problem of the one and the many. In practice, Nietzsche cannot help but talk of *the* will to power, and, at times, in strongly totalizing terms, as I will indicate later. The problem with Nietzsche is not that he is anti-metaphysical, or post-metaphysical, but that he is not always a good enough metaphysician, and not least because he might think he is beyond metaphysics.

12. The sometimes disastrous consequences of this equivocity are evident in the political legacy of Nietzschean thinking. Steven Aschheim in *The Nietzsche Legacy in Germany 1890–1990* (Berkeley: University of California Press, 1992) has very revealingly and dispassionately documented how Nietzsche could serve almost every shade of political and cultural opinion, including, of course, National Socialism. Nietzsche may say he writes for everyone and for none, but it seems that "everyone" has found some residence in his house of many mansions. Perhaps his house is for everyone and for no one because it is, we might say, hospitably empty.

the mocking Nietzsche fall for his own mimicry? Nietzsche has a penetrating remark in *Human, All Too Human* (§52) about the deceiver who gets taken in by his own act:

> In all great deceivers a remarkable process is at work to which they owe their power. In the very act of deception with all its preparations—the dreadful voice, the expression, the gestures, they are overcome by their *belief in themselves:* it is this belief which then speaks so persuasively, so miracle-like to the audience. Men believe in the truth of all that is seen to be strongly believed. [*W,* IV, 2, 70 f.]

Not only does he communicate that to the audience, but the audience returns it to him and strengthens his belief.

I fear that Nietzsche in some of his moods, and perhaps because in his solitude he had to be both the actor and *his own audience,* fell *under his own spell*—the actor who falls for his act, and forgets it is an act. He was half-lucid, half-blind about this in his later half-lucid, more than half megalomaniac years. I mean the years *before* his "official" madness.[13]

Returning to the community between philosophy and art, we must say there is also a community between both of these and religion. Relevant to our theme, mindfulness of origin is bound up with religion: mythic stories image the sense of the ultimate origin or origins. Why is this important? Because if one philosophically understands the religious image or mythic story as one of the richest forms of human articulation about the ultimate, the affiliation of metaphysics and religion may be seen to redound to the *credit* of metaphysics. This tells against the debunking of both metaphysics and religion as alleged forms of ontological cowardice. To "announce" that religion and metaphysics are in flight from the truth of being as a dark condition on the other side of reason is not to escape metaphysics, but to be metaphysical again, just in the indictment of metaphysics as falsifying the truth of being.

Does Nietzsche not give the game away when he proclaims that only as "aesthetic" is the world justified: the only theodicy must be an aesthetic theodicy? But "aesthetic" here has nothing to do with "aesthetics." And does not "theodicy" have to do with a *divine* justification, even if you say God is dead. In any event, metaphysics, myth, art intertwine.[14] This is something of which

---

13. By the way, Nietzsche's description above of the deceiver looks to me like a variation of the dynamic of erotic sovereignty as I describe it, say, in *EB,* chapter 15; though here the dynamic of self-mediating in and through the other is in and through *Nietzsche's own otherness.*

14. How can one avoid a certain affinity of Plato and Nietzsche when we think of the relation of art and metaphysics? "Plato versus Homer": how can this so-called fundamental antagonism be starkly stated, if we remember the Plato of the *Timaeus?* Below I will suggest a move from "self" to "art" to "world" on an aesthetic model; nor is the artistic metaphysics repudiated in Nietzsche's later suggestion that the world is a self-birthing artwork. What would an aesthetic theod-

Hegel will not altogether disapprove. Hegel will locate art, religion and philosophy at the level of absolute spirit. The role absolute spirit plays in Hegel is played by the aesthetic theodicy of will to power in Nietzsche. I need hardly add that there are glaring differences between them. Yet Nietzsche's clear concern with the metaphysics of origin in, say, *The Birth of Tragedy* focuses on religious art and ritual: in a word, tragedy is sacred art. The cult of Dionysus after all is *cult*. It is, in a word Hegel strategically uses, *Gottesdienst*.[15] Obviously too, the god served in Hegelian and Nietzschean *Gottesdienst* is different. But whether we bow before *Geist*, or celebrate Dionysus, the difference of the dialectical origin and the Dionysian falls within the same temple of the erotic origin. Neither god is sufficiently agapeic. What is this difference within sameness?

Hegel's dialectical origin is understood in terms of *Geist's* self-becoming, self-completion: first an indeterminate beginning; second a determinate self-production; third, a self-determining self-completion. If we invoke the religious language of "creation," clearly this creation is not the bringing into being of something *essentially other* to the origin: it is the *self-externalization of the origin* in the finite world. It is the origin's dialectical self-mediation, in that the other produced *is* the origin *itself* in its own otherness. In becoming *itself as other*, it is mediating with itself; it is becoming itself in its own *self-othering*. Hegel claims this self-origination is teleologically bound to self-completion. In the *end* the initial indefiniteness is overcome. The end is the complete self-determination of the origin and what was merely implicit in the beginning.

In the case of Dionysus, the origin in itself is dark. Certainly in the younger Nietzsche we find the suggestion that there is a pain and suffering in the origin, to assuage which the Dionysian origin has to create beyond itself. There is an echo here of Schelling's view of origin in which the conflict and contradiction of conscious and unconscious plays a significant role, leading to the aesthetic resolution of conflict in the great art work. The darkness of the Dionysian origin is indicated by Nietzsche's use of the image of the maternal womb in *The Birth of Tragedy*.[16] In the beginning is ontological pain. There is

---

icy be without a world artist? Let us not forget Plato's *Timaeus* as picturing the world artist at work in fashioning the cosmos as a visible work of art, the most beautiful possible, even granting the recalcitrance and vagaries of the Errant cause. Recall Plato's philosophical art and the eikonic nature of the cosmos: "It is everyway necessary that the cosmos be an eikon of something" (*"pasa ananke tonde ton cosmon eikona tinos einai," Timaeus*, 29b1–2). Plato gives us too a kind of aesthetic theodicy, but we are not "beyond good and evil" in Nietzsche's sense. The cosmos itself is called a sensible god, an aesthetic god that images the intelligible (*eikon tou noētou theos aisthētos, Timaeus*, 92c). But none of this could be without the beyond of the Good.

15. For fuller discussion, see "Speculation and Cult: On Hegel's Strange Saying: Philosophy is God-service" in *BHD*, chapter 2.

16. This image of the mother giving birth recurs throughout Nietzsche's writing, particularly in relation to Nietzsche's sense of the pain of the creator. We also find the maternal image scattered through the writings of Schelling, and especially after 1809. The metaphorics of "being born" arises again and again, with aesthetic and ontological significance.

the *sundering* of *das Ureine* into individuality. Again as with Anaximander's *to apeiron*, the primal guilt is the splitting of the individual from the primordial One (on Anaximander, Nietzsche and evil, see *BHD*, 199–202). Recall also Hegel's original *Ur-teil* of the One into subject and object. But if there is rupture here for Nietzsche, it does not point teleologically to Hegel's consummate self-mediation. There is implied some coming to "wholeness" and a certain "mediation" of self-becoming. Individuality and separation make us *other* to the Dionysian origin, but tragic vision comes to understand the truth of the origin, beyond every human rationalization and moralization of being. In celebrating tragic vision, the boundary that separates the individual from the primordial One is dissolved. The sin of separateness is purged, and there is exultation in the original energy of being in its indestructible surge of self-affirmation. It is very noticeable that there is a stress on self-dissolution, self-loss in a more ultimate original energy of being. The maternal womb takes back its separated issue. The Dionysian origin functions as what I have called an absorbing god (*DDO*, chapter 1), a principle of encompassing wholeness that in engulfing the individual assuages the pain and suffering of separateness, and most especially seems to overcome the sense of lack infecting the restlessness of human desire.

Dionysian and Dialectical Origins

I know some commentators will immediately object that this is the younger Nietzsche still in thrall to Schopenhauerian metaphysics. The maturer Nietzsche was different. I promise to touch on this point again, but I think the differences between the younger and older Nietzsche are undergirded by a continuity deeper than is normally granted. For that matter, I think Nietzsche remained far more in thrall to Schopenhauer than he was capable of publicly acknowledging. I recounted in the previous chapter my own experience in reading Schopenhauer: I had *already* read Nietzsche extensively before studying Schopenhauer intensively; I knew the official story that the mature Nietzsche had "transcended" Schopenhauer; imagine my surprise to discover how astonishingly *Nietzschean* I discovered Schopenhauer to be! Of course, this was all topsy turvy. A fresh reading of Schopenhauer rather reveals how Schopenhauerian Nietzsche always remained. When Nietzsche reminds us of the *masked philosopher*, this actually means we must always *beware* of what Nietzsche says about himself. We must beware of his self-presentation and self-interpretation.[17]

---

17. See again the essays in Christopher Janaway, ed., *Willing and Nothingness: Schopenhauer as Nietzsche's Educator*. Julian Young is also helpful here, *Nietzsche's Philosophy of Art* (Cambridge: Cambridge University Press, 1992).

I find that a certain metaphor of aesthetic "self" permeates the thinking of origin in both Hegel and Nietzsche. In Hegel's case the understanding of origination is mediated through an appropriation of Kant's transcendental self. The Idea or *Geist,* of course, is not simply subjectified self, since it calls attention to an ontological and indeed historical power, as much as to an epistemic or categorial power. Yet the language of "self"—and again understood in no Cartesian or subjectivistic sense—informs the discourse. The Idea after all externalizes *itself,* the world is the *self*-externalization of the Idea; while the process of *self*-becoming is teleologically oriented to a *self*-determination and *self*-mediation, all the way to the absolute *self*-determination of the whole. Indeed, in the dialectical interplay of self and other, it is self that is offered the privileged position, in that the other is the self in *its own* otherness. Hence the *return to self* through the other is the culmination of the fulfilled dialectic.

Recall the triadic unfolding of Hegel's dialectical origin: first the moment of immediate unity; second the sundering, self-sundering of the unity into difference and opposition; third the mediation of opposition, and the reconstitution of unity in a self-mediated whole. Translate this now into the metaphorical terms of the artistic creator as "self." First we have the artist in his inarticulate unity and immediacy. Then the artist gives expression to what is implicit in the immediate, thus bringing to articulation difference and opposition. But in this difference, the artist is, in fact, mediating with self, bringing the original inarticulacy to more explicit self-knowing. Then finally, the end is the constitution of the mediated whole, which now fulfills the destiny of the originator to self-knowing. For this "artist" we could also substitute Hegel's "God."

This might seem very different to the Dionysian origin, but the family resemblance is unmistakable. In *Joyful Wisdom* (§357) Nietzsche tells us that "we Germans are Hegelians even if there never had been any Hegel" because "we" attribute greater value and deeper meaning to becoming rather than being. Wagner whom Nietzsche so hopelessly loved—and despised—Wagner who so loved Schopenhauer, was Hegel's *heir* in music—music as "Idea" (*The Case of Wagner,* §10). As already suggested, Nietzsche owes an enormous amount to the Kantian "Copernican" turn to self, though he will not talk about the transcendental ego or idealistic *Geist.* Why? These dissimulate the dark origin that Nietzsche himself, following Schopenhauer, divines. Dionysus is a truer, mythic name for that. That the Kantian heritage lives on is evident in some of his coarser "idealistic" epistemological utterances: the knower imposes form on the formless; the strong philosopher dictates or legislates the truth of being; will to power affirms itself in legislating the truth of being which in itself has no truth at all. Nietzsche continues the line laid down by Kant's subreption, Hegel's self-mediation through the other, Schopenhauer's world as a *makranthropos.* Obviously, this can be given crude or more refined renditions. What is clear is that we cannot avoid ultimate *metaphysical metaphors* when we ask about the meaning of being. All being is interpretation for Nietzsche;

indeed all truth is "my" truth. What is this but a less dissimulating projection ("subreption") of "self" onto the supposed formless chaos—less dissimulating than the idealistic projection, which would elide "self" in the projection, but projection nonetheless? With Nietzsche, projective interpretation is affirmed even more virulently than in idealism. The metaphorical power of "self," of "creator," of "artist"—and one might interject, "god"—is accentuated to an unprecedented degree.

When Nietzsche proclaims the *Übermensch* as the meaning of the earth, he will not be *overt,* that is to say, entirely honest, like Schopenhauer, and say that the world is the *Übermensch* writ large. Nevertheless, he will suggest that apart from the extraordinary origination of the exceptional will to power the world is void of meaning, absurd, all but nothing. In *The Birth of Tragedy* there is no reticence about invoking the notion of the *world artist* as giving rise to the entire panorama of what is. This invocation of the artistic creator has ontological weight. Nietzsche may later become less explicit in his use of such a metaphysical metaphor, yet when he speaks of will to power, of all being as will to power, there will be ontological weight to this also. And the creativity of the *Übermensch* will not be at all divorced from this ontological weight, but rather will be the highest expression of the original power of being.

There is more to be said on this point, but for the moment we might say that the transcendental origin becomes orgiastic in Nietzsche where it is dialectical in Hegel. Its excess to rational mediation or dialectical appropriation is proclaimed. It is in excess at the beginning, before reason comes into play; it is excess at the end, after reason has done its work to rationalize the world. The case is different with Hegel: there is no final excess to reason, not in the beginning, not in the end. Hegel may anticipate Nietzsche when he says that truth is the bacchanalian revel wherein not a one is sober, and yet the revel is a state of transparent, unbroken calm.[18] But if Hegel's final emphasis falls on the calm sobriety of reason, Nietzsche's falls on the intoxicated rapture of eros. Philosophical sobriety is only one mask worn at the bacchanalian revel, and not necessarily the best one. Sobriety is a mask, a masking, of revel.

Notice, however, that the insinuation of the metaphor of "self," whether dialectical or Dionysian, is only *one side* of the story. In both thinkers we find a tendency also to *elide* the "self." This is an old philosophical proclivity: mortal selfhood is to be given over to a more ultimate power transcending self. We see this in Hegel's "selfless speculation." We must surrender or sacrifice self to the universal: for Hegel it is an oxymoron to say "my philosophy." Nietzsche seems entirely opposed to this, and in many respects he is. Every philosophy is ultimately a confession or betrayal of the philosopher, and truth is said to be "my" truth or truths, not the truth. And yet the highest moment of

---

18. *Phanomenologie des Geistes,* ed. J. Hoffmeister (Hamburg: Felix Meiner, 1952), 39; *Phenomenology of Spirit,* trans. A. V. Miller (Oxford: Clarendon Press, 1977), 27.

self-affirmation in Nietzsche seems also to be a moment of self-transcendence and self-dissolution. We come to Nietzsche's *amor fati*.

We are reminded of Schopenhauer's reversal from willful striving to will-less knowing, except that Nietzsche's *amor* is an accentuation of willing, not its extirpation. Nevertheless, there is a transcending release towards what seems beyond the will of self. There is a doubleness here that is full of tension. On the one hand, extreme self-affirmation; on the other hand, consent to the necessity of the course of being beyond the will of self. And does not the first block the second? Does not the second undermine the first? Can we have both together? Is there not something essentially equivocal, indeed disingenuous, about Nietzsche's position? Does he not end up, just like Hegel, singing hymns, now called Dionysian dithyrambs, to necessity, though Hegel called his hymns logic?

To what degree does Nietzsche's sense of origin mimic Diotima's myth of the double parentage of eros? *Poros* and *penia,* resource and lack: the first points to an already available power to be, the second points to a wanting to be, a striving to be. Nietzschean eros seems both full and empty: full of self-affirming power, and lacking in its own full self-being; hence always in search of itself, and always itself and nothing but itself; both absolutely determined to be what it is, and driven to be self-determining in an intoxicated self-regarding manner. And is this what his *amor fati* portends? And eternal recurrence? Is it a portent of the moment of coincidence of absolute fullness and absolute lack: the moment that is everything, since all moments are in it, past and to come; the moment that is absolutely nothing, since it is nothing but vanishing transition to what is to be, from what has been and is not now: the coincidence of the whole and the void? And do we not need an *other origin,* beyond both the void and the whole? Do we not need the metaphor, indeed the hyperbole of the *agapeic origin* to shed some light on the double parentage of eros? And Nietzsche's will to power, while hyperbolic, is not *that* hyperbole, and its "yes" is not the "yes" that issues from *that*.

At his best Nietzsche is a philosopher of the equivocal; but he is also an equivocal philosopher. He does not always think through the equivocities; instead he celebrates them. I do not think he ever gives a satisfactory account of the togetherness of the above two positions, nor had an inkling of an origin beyond both. On the one hand, he was infected by the modern apotheosis of self, aesthetically expressed in the cultural elevation of genius, of which the *Übermensch* gives a masked version. The metaphysics of will to power is continuous with that apotheosis. On the other hand, there is something essentially unmodern about Nietzsche's deepest vision, which hearkens back to preSocratic cosmologies and tragic vision. He vacillates between these two, though wanting sometimes incoherently to affirm the two together. In the end, I think, the first wins out, and we find Zarathustra saying: "What returns, what finally comes home to me, is my own self. . . ." And as if that were not enough, he exclaims: "For me—how could there by any 'outside-me'" *(Ausser-mir)?* "There is no outside!" *(Es giebt kein Ausser!)* (*W,* VI, I, 190, 268; *PN,* 264, 329). If there is no *Ausser-mir* what would be the *fatum* one would love? If we are consistent, one would have to answer: Nothing but oneself. And then, nothing really, since one is nothing but a vanishing transition in a never beginning, never ending circle of recurrence of will to power.

Of course, consistency may be the hobgoblin of small minds. But there is a big-minded consistency too, and this we love. And even then, in all fairness, Nietzsche could not escape his own passion for self-debunking. There is often much of self-mockery in the too much of his self-inflation. He will trumpet in *Ecce Homo:* Why I am a destiny. Is this a way of bringing the two, the "I" and fate, together? But one is not entirely sure if Nietzsche has his tongue in his cheek in proclaiming himself a destiny. He seems to be laughing at himself—lightly. But then there is no doubt but that the excess of a megalomania—laughable but no joke—is not far below the surface. It certainly breaks the surface in *Ecce Homo* when he informs humanity in full seriousness that *Zarathustra* is perhaps the greatest gift ever offered to it. Moreover, in *The Anti-Christ* he suggests—and I cannot find any trace of self-mockery, despite the self-consciousness of the bombast—that time is no longer to be measured from *anno domini,* and what he calls the *dies nefastus* that defines the beginning of Christianity. Now it should be measured from now, from the time of Nietzsche himself, he who has broken the back of history in two and inaugurated a new epoch of being, a truer, higher history. In a letter Nietzsche wrote to his sister in his last (officially) lucid months (mid-November, 1888): "You haven't the remotest conception of the fact that you are closely related to a man and a fate in whom and in which the question of the millennia *(die Frage von Jahrtausenden)* has been decided. I hold the future of humanity, quite literally, in my hands." For not a few today Nietzsche is *the* philosopher, but how can one read such passages and not be embarrassed? Embarrassed not by Nietzsche, but for Nietzsche.[19]

It is significant that when the "modern" Nietzsche predominates, *futurity* receives the main emphasis. Zarathustra puts the point in terms that indicate that without faith in a transfigured future, life would prove intolerable, unlivable. Thus Zarathustra laments that he walks among present human beings as among fragments of human beings:

> The now and the past upon the earth—alas, my friends, that is what I find most unendurable; and I should not know how to live if I were

19. George Kline (*Hegel and his Critics,* 19) draws our attention to this letter. I find something similarly embarrassing about the bogus prophesying of Heidegger at the end of his *Beiträge zur Philosophie (Vom Ereignis)* on the last god (GA, 65, 508 f.). I will mention this again. At least Nietzsche's great sense of *humor* allows one to be more forgiving of his forced prophesying.

> not also a seer of that which must come. A seer, a willer, a creator himself and a bridge to the future—and alas, as it were, a cripple at this bridge: all this is Zarathustra. . . . I walk among men as among the fragments of the future—that future which I envisage. And this is all my creating and striving, that I create and carry together into One what is fragment and riddle and dreadful accident. And how could I bear to be a man if man were not also a creator and guesser of riddles and redeemer of accidents?[20]

The *One* here is not the origin as *das Ureine,* but *the future One* that will be created through the saving help of Zarathustra's will to power. *Amor fati* ostensibly says its amen to all being, regardless of past, present or future, but in practice Nietzsche was unrelentingly disparaging of the past and present, as the mostly sorry tale of the miserable miscarriage of human creativity. That is why the "It was" is such a heavy burden to bear for Zarathustra: it is other to present willing and a potentially debilitating weight on the pure openness of future possibility. Only by saying "Thus I willed it" is the relation to the past transfigured. Say-so again?

How transfigured? That is the question. There is rhetoric here which masks nonsense, and indeed a kind of cowardice before time's own recalcitrant otherness to our will to be future creators or creators of the future. The notion that the future will be, must be, the glorious realization of human creativity is the bombast of a *groundless faith* in future humanity. Nietzsche does not remain true to the earth. Instead of the eternal other-world, he flies, as in a fugue, towards a future other-world. *Amor fati* is entirely incompatible with this glorification of a possible future about which nothing can be said, except that yes one knows, oh yes one surely knows, that it will be immeasurably great, yea my brothers verily it must be so. Well, it ain't necessarily so. Indeed, just the self-apotheosis of the human being may be an ontological *degrading* rather than elevation.

Do not accuse me of mocking Nietzsche. I am mocking Nietzsche. I also say: When he wants to offer us his Zarathustrian redemption—yes it is "redemption" that is on offer—*that* is how he preaches to us. No my brothers, do not stone me. Verily I say to you, out of their own mouths they stand convicted!

But perhaps I am too harsh on Nietzsche. Perhaps. But perhaps I am goaded to ire by the hurdy gurdy song, tunelessly ground out by the host of his contemporary acolytes. Perhaps.

---

20. *Zarathustra,* "On Redemption," *PN,* 250–51. See Kline, *art. cit.,* 8. Stanley Cavell points out the voice of Emerson resounding in Nietzsche use of metaphors of fragments of humans, no whole human.

Flying Up, Falling Down: Self-elevation and Self-dissolution

Be that so or no, suppose we consider further if Nietzschean self-elevation leads to self-dissolution, or if flying up leads only to a different downfall? I mean now with respect to human origination and its ontological grounding. Recall my claim that Plato's approach to originals seeks in the metaxu an ontological balance between mimesis, eros and mania, and with respect to *eidos,* and the Good. Kant is sensitive to the problem in relation to taste, genius and morality. Hegel thinks individual originality wastes its substance if not related to the absolute spirit that offers the holistic context of all origination and self-becoming. Schopenhauer tries to balance the two with reference to will and the Platonic Idea. And Nietzsche? He rejects any Idea, Platonic, Kantian, Hegelian, Schopenhauerian, as serving an ontological "anchoring" in the otherness of being, as serving to rescue the process of artistic origination from its own invidious subjectification.

This rejection is by no means straightforward. Consider. Any reference to the Idea as *other,* solicits the self to transcend its own particularity and rise to the level of the universal in its otherness. The self must other itself, become to some extent a universal self; hence "creativity" would extend the self beyond itself; there is a directionality in that "creativity" that orients both itself and the creative self to the universal. Now when Nietzsche claims to deconstruct the Idea as a universal that is ontologically other, he proceeds *in the reverse direction* but the point comes to something similar. He wants to bring us into greater intimacy with sources of creativity in self; he sees any *otherness* as initially a curb on the self-assertion of human creativity in its freedom; that otherness must be dismantled; an immanent otherness will take its place. This is nowhere more evident in his rejection of Christianity as Platonism for the masses (*BGE,* preface; *W,* VI, 2, 4). Christianity is a religion of otherness, a *dishonest otherness* that bounds free creativity, even as it is a subterranean exploitation of that same creativity in self-emasculating form: power as powerlessness, and the betrayal of its own power to an otherness beyond. The origin is subrepted onto an other, producing a divided self, neither here not there, not one thing or another, not fish or fowl, a miscarriage of humanity (see Hegel's unhappy consciousness). The origin must be de-subrepted, restored to its immanent intimacy with the self. This intimacy becomes an identity in crucial cases.

Certainly here, Nietzsche is an exemplary representative of a sense of freedom that has been the hallmark of modernity, despite his claim to be a critic of modernity. Otherness is a restraint on free selfhood that in the long run can debilitate the inner source of creativity. Such otherness must be dethroned for that source to reclaim its own. This is Feuerbach as lyrical existentialist. Nietzsche has genes from the Feuerbach family, try as he might not forthrightly to acknowledge that line of inheritance. If God or gods exist, how could I tolerate it not myself to be a god? If we have murdered God, we must live up to the deed and be ourselves as god. The postulatory theism of Kant's *als ob* God becomes the postulatory atheism of Nietzsche *als ob* Overman. The absolute otherness of God must be destroyed as a destruction of my creative freedom, and that same absoluteness now invested in my inward otherness as the enigmatic source of the creation of values. The abyss is not transcendent but immanent. And so the Schopenhauerian inheritance is put to work differently: the will is the intimate otherness of the self, but this inward otherness is participant in what resists all systematization, all mastery: the radical inward otherness we can hardly bear to acknowledge Nietzsche re-christens as will to power: I am not will to power; all being is will to power; I am the creative celebration of that will in its otherness and intimacy.

The result is something like eros without Ideas, or inspiration and mania in a world of becoming as creative chaos. It is Heraclitean becoming without the logos that runs through all things. Eros and mania, without *eidē* and without guiding logos, must forge their own lamps. Every light and logos is a means to an end: the intensification of eros, the opening to inspiration. Is this the lightning flash—Platonism without mimesis? Or Platonism reversed—and without originals? But is it true that we have no originals? Is not will to power now the absolute original? Far from being without original, we have a different way of thinking the origin: one that debunks the Platonic otherness and its power of metaphysical anchoring; one that affirms the "self unanchored," the creative self at sea, on the open sea (Nietzsche's images); one that takes up the modern turn to the self, though there is no Cartesian self-transparency, only unsystematic otherness, resistant to conceptual mastery. This dark immanent originality is best expressed by genius—the hero, the *Übermensch*—whose immanent otherness is the exemplar of the otherness of the creative power of the ultimate will. A (trans)human self as exemplary replaces the Idea exemplar, but both have ontological significance. The Overman, the genius, is the going across, the bridging of the gap between the sensuous (the animal) and the supersensuous (the god).[21] The genius is the midpoint of being in its creative promise: between lower and higher; though the higher is to be created out of the lower, not discovered as an always already there fundament of being.

It is important to note that a *doubleness* is reproduced in Nietzsche's view: a doubleness in *immanence,* not *between* immanence and transcendence. Thus the intimate otherness of creative power in the genius/*Übermensch* is falsified if one merely says this is "mine"; rather all "mine" is a falsification; "my" power

---

21. When one thinks of the image in *Zarathustra* of man as self-surpassing, a tightrope walker across an abyss between the beast and the *Übermensch,* one cannot but recall Platonic mimesis, eros and mania as three different ways of bridging the gap, as crossing the metaxu between the animal and the god.

is the upsurgence of the otherness of the power of the will; it is not mine; it is Dionysus. The Dionysian origin is the most intimate other: never mastered but always there drowsing in our daily domestications; destructive of those domestications, creative of new forms which in turn become new domestications; the rhythm of creation and destruction is what we as humans know of the Dionysian origin. This is why I think some of Nietzsche's deepest insights have to do with *suffering*. Thus also the absolute centrality of the tragic vision. But relative to this doubleness, I think Nietzsche is forced to perform an astonishing somersault vis-à-vis the presuppositions of modernity: the modern self is de-selved. The tightrope walker is tumbled into the abyss, for there is no rope, and there is no walker.

This is not like Kant apprehensive of breaking into a sweat on his afternoon walk. There is no sun to bring on that sweat, though because there is no sun, there breaks out instead an icy sweat of night, and the tightrope walker must *sing* to keep himself steady and warm, but if he looks down he is undone, for he will see there is no rope on which to walk—there is only chaos, and what rope is there is one that he has *made to be there instead of the chaos*. The problem is: if he is honest about this, *the rope will vanish,* and he will be in the chaos; he may vanish, perhaps should vanish *himself*. But mysteriously still *there,* he must be honest, for after all, has he not just now denounced those religious magicians who have conjured up *other ropes* to the beyond? He must be honest, he cannot be fully honest, for were he so, it would be the chaos of destruction, not the chaos of creation, that would show itself the older, deadlier brother of these fated twins. If that is "honesty," it will destroy not only "Plato," but Nietzsche too.

Otherwise put, I wonder if Nietzsche ever became adequately self-consciousness of the extent of his entanglement in the presuppositions of the modern activist self. If we take seriously the revelation of the origin in tragic suffering, it is impossible to continue to adhere to this concept of self. Nietzsche did see the point, but did he see it through? Can we see it through in his terms without the destructive consequences of creation just noted? One might say: a certain self-assertion of the creative will must be sacrificed; and while Nietzsche knew this, did he, can he, resurface on the *other side* of this sacrifice? Sacrifice is literally a "making sacred"; but if the deification sought is an asserted apotheosis, then this will, if willful, would distort the whole basis for true transfiguration. *We cannot just will it, though we have to be willing*. If willing is, so to say, to resurface on the other side of willfulness, the happening of being would have to be seen in terms different to will to power, and the opposition of self and other more radically transcended than Nietzschean terms can allow.

Self-glorification and Fate

Let me try another approach to the tension between extreme self-affirmation and *amor fati*. Suppose we accentuate self-affirmation; and suppose that at an extremity of this affirmation, what breaks forth cannot be called "self" in any straightforward sense; what breaks forth is will to power affirming itself; it breaks forth in inspiration. And Nietzsche himself—without a blush—tells us that he has had experience of inspiration such as has not been had for millennia, perhaps never had. In other words, one brings together the two sides by proclaiming that the creative, original self *is* the origin, is the breaking forth of the origin in its radical self-affirmation. One is reminded of the dialectical identity of the human and the divine in Hegel. The full self-affirmation of the human becomes identical with the creative self-affirmation of the absolute or will to power. It is hard not to think that something like this is equivocally at play in Nietzsche. In affirming self, Nietzsche affirms Dionysus, because he is Dionysus: Dionysus is being affirmed in and through him. That is why he is a destiny.

Here we meet disturbing equivocity again: Nietzsche imposes thought on otherness; Nietzsche lets otherness be. Nietzsche is both imposing and allowing, but how be both? The excess of the origin as Dionysian tends to foster a heroic self-assertion; the inward otherness breaks down the domestications of being that the common self and society stabilize; yet the inward otherness in moments of inspiration is not just mine; one is under necessity; one has no free will; it is the radical otherness of the origin that is communicating in the inward otherness; and though the latter seems extremely selfish, in fact it is a "higher" selfishness that in another sense is quite selfless. We seem to have not only the union of freedom and necessity in inspiration; we have the contradictory unity of selfishness and selflessness; we have the dissolution of the self in a more ultimate originary power and the most extreme self-assertion of the human creator's power. At the moment of absolute self-assertion, the self asserting itself dissolves in the absolute of which it is a moment: the I and the Dionysian origin are one. Absolute self-assertion produces mystical intoxication in which there is no self. Is this the divine madness of Plato again? Is this the excess of meaning, or meaninglessness, in the deepest knowing that we do not, cannot "know"? Does the artist "understand" this paradox more often than the philosopher? But is this "art"? Is it not "religion"?

Consider also Nietzsche's claim in relation to inspiration that there is a creating out of *abundance*. Does his description of will to power testify to what we might call a generous overflow of bestowing energy? I find the case again to be very equivocal.[22] One might argue, as I have tried to do, that creation is inseparable from the generosity of being. Origination entails a giving of the other its otherness, and not simply for the self, or for the return to the self. Nietzsche has some equivocal intimations that there is a radical self-transcendence that gives beyond itself, that does not originate for a return to self at all.

---

22. On the difference of Zarathustra's "gift-giving virtue" *(die schenkende Tugend)* and agapeic giving, see again my "Caesar with the Soul of Christ."

This too is a kind of selfless origination, even though the "self" is never more truly itself than when it gives out of its bounty to the other and for the other. It does not think of itself, or reckon on a return. Its originative being is its simple being for the other in radical self-transcendence. But while there is a creating from abundance in Nietzsche, it takes the form of self-affirming will to power that simply exceeds itself, not for any release of the other as other, or release towards the other as other, but simply because his excessive overflow is simply to be *self-affirming will.* This exceeding of self, as beyond itself, remains entirely within the circuit of its own self-affirming will to power.

To do justice to creation as a release of, and release towards the other as other, we need to think in terms other than erotic origination. Nietzsche, and indeed Hegel, are here caught in equivocations neither escaped. Perhaps both might have wanted to think the meaning of original self-transcendence, but they could not properly do so, while still captive to the metaphysical metaphor of erotic self-origination. We need to think of an origination from excess as abundance of creative being that gives other-being its being as other and for itself, and not for a return to the origin. We need to think of the origin as agapeic rather than erotic.

Without a proper sense of the plenitude of being as gift, we are tempted to define creative self-transcendence as an incessant vector to futurity. We are tempted by an instrumentalization of time and an empty apotheosis of futurity. Something of this is reflected in Nietzsche's concept of genius (*W,* VI, 3, 139 f.; *PN,* 547–48): the explosion of a force that has been stored up over many generations. "The great human being is a finale" who squanders himself recklessly. Superficially this might look like "self-sacrifice" but really it is just the involuntary fatality of the outflow of stored forces. Nietzsche uses the image of the explosive. Remember Nietzsche's ejaculation, borrowed from a reviewer more shocked by Nietzsche than celebrating: I am not a man I am dynamite. He also uses the image of the river that floods the land. Genius is like all beauty—"the end result of the accumulated work of generations. . . . All that is good is inherited: whatever is not inherited is imperfect, is a mere beginning" (*W,* VI, 142 f.; *PN,* 551–52). Superficially again this seems like a hymn to the past that is inherited, and also gratitude for what one has been given. And one recalls an earlier point made about philological finesse nurturing respect for tradition. But when one remembers that Zarathustra walks among present and past humanity as among misbegotten fragments, and that futurity alone will redeem time, we quickly understand that past and present are to be instrumentalized to produce the cultural resources, themselves the necessary means for the end of unparalleled future creation.

In *Twilight of the Idols* (*W,* VI, 3, 152 ff.; *PN,* 560–62) he recurs to the Greeks and his early view of Dionysus: Dionysus "is explicable only in terms of an *excess* of force." Incidentally his discussion here gives the lie to the view that there is a significant departure in the later Nietzsche from the central notions of *The Birth of Tragedy.* He reiterates the orgiastic nature of the

Dionysian and its relation to the tragic affirmation of life even in its pain and destruction. The image of the mother giving birth, the pain of birth pangs, also to be found in *Birth of Tragedy,* now named as his first effort at the revaluation of values, is repeated, indeed it is pronounced *holy*. The futurity of life, identified with its eternity, is experienced religiously in affirming procreation: procreation is the *holy* way to life. The Christian view is denounced for making sex unclean and casting "*filth* on the origin."

Does Nietzsche have a notion of agapeic creation? I think not. His expression of the overflow of fullness ultimately has an erotic modulation: it is an expression of "self" for "self." As I have pointed out, even when Nietzsche speaks of affirmative will to power, such will to power affirms *itself*, it does not affirm what is irreducibly other to itself. Consider his "psychology of the artist" in *Twilight of the Idols* (*W,* VI, 3, 110 f.; *PN,* 518 ff.). First frenzy is a necessary condition, sexual frenzy, frenzy in destruction, in cruelty, in daring, a frenzy that finally is "the frenzy of an overcharged and swollen will." Out of the feeling of increased strength and fullness, essential to this frenzy, "one lends to things, one *forces* them to accept from us, one violates them—this process is called *idealizing*." Consider further (*W,* VI, 3, 110 f.; *PN,* 518–19):

> In this state one enriches everything out of one's own fullness: whatever one sees, whatever one wills, is seen swelled, taut, strong, overloaded with strength. A man in this state transforms things until they mirror his power—until they are reflections of his perfection. This *having to* transform into perfection is—art. Even everything he is not yet, becomes for him an occasion of joy in himself; in art man enjoys himself as perfection.

And this forcing, violating, glory in self is identified, believe it or not, with the "yes" of Raphael!

This one might think is eros frenzied, but is there not also something adolescent about this phallic psychology of self? The imposition of self is revealed in the passage from *Zarathustra,* reiterated to conclude *Twilight of the Idols:* The Hammer Speaks. What this says is "Be hard!" What is this? If one wants to be a destiny one must cut and cut like a diamond: "For all creators are hard. And it must seem blessedness for you to impress your hand on millennia as on wax, blessedness to write on the will of millennia as on bronze . . ." (*W,* VI, 3, 157) Creative destiny is *self-glorification*. Indeed, for Nietzsche the whole point of the Greek festivals and arts was "nothing other than to feel *on top,* to *show* themselves on top. These are means of glorifying oneself, and in certain cases, of inspiring fear of oneself" (*W,* VI, 3, 151; *PN,* 559). This corresponds in some ways to what I call erotic sovereignty (see, *EB,* chapters 10 and 15) but it is too asleep to the temptations of tyranny. I fear we have here no twilight of the idols but the manufacture of a new idol, whose name might be "Nietzsche" himself. *"Nietzsche" turannos*—and not asleep either.

Erotic Origins Again

The metaphysical metaphor of an erotic origin suggests something like this. An erotic origin is an origin that *is its own self-becoming*. Eros is a dynamic movement of desire, a striving of self-energy that reaches out of itself to fulfill itself in appropriating to itself what is other to itself. Eros, out of its own original lack or incompletion, transcends itself towards the other. It thus transcends its own lack, but it relates to what is other by taking it to itself. In this taking to itself, it fulfills itself. The fullness, the fulfillment, properly speaking, comes in the end. Hegel's dialectical origin certainly fits this description. But does not Nietzsche's *Ureine* also fit? For the beginning is contradictory and incomplete; it is only in the end that the initial darkness is somehow redeemed, and the One reconciled with itself, even in its self-contradiction and suffering. One might say that the precipitation of individuals out of the primordial One generates time and history. It seems that the primordial One *must* generate time, in order to overcome its own suffering and self-contradiction. Nietzsche speaks of the lust for life, the insatiable hunger for existence of the primal being. Time is needed to overcome the torment of the origin. The tragic god (like Hegel's god) must redeem *itself*.[23] Creation beyond self issues from such torment. I think that Nietzsche's glorification of "redeeming" futurity cannot be uncoupled from this tortured sense of the beginning. Thus in *Zarathustra* the past invariably is seen in the light of a necessity to be *redeemed*. Moreover, redemption is only thinkable in terms of a future transfiguration. Nausea at mankind's past and present can only be overcome by *willing backwards*, but not because there is an inherent good to be affirmed in past, and present, but in order to release will from what seems beyond will and release it for what Nietzsche supposes is within will, namely the "redemptive" future.

But you will rightly raise the question: Did not Nietzsche in *Zarathustra* also say that he once did think, but no longer does, in terms of a god who suffered, and who because of suffering had to create beyond himself? Now that he has put away such ways of thinking, and to amplify a point already hinted, his song is a kind of lyrical Feuerbachianism: God and gods are projections of man's will to power out of a condition of weakness, projections that have to be reclaimed for man himself. Marx, Nietzsche, Freud are all Feuerbach's children here, and Feuerbach is only a deformed dialectical son of the father of modern dialectics, Hegel. Marx is a social Feuerbachian, Freud a psychoanalytical, Nietzsche a poetic Feuerbachian. But even when God is reduced to a projection of human power, a logic of erotic origination operates: out of initial lack, weakness, emptiness, desiring man projects beyond himself, he transcends himself ("externalizes himself") in religion towards an other that is not finally an other at all; the other is the self again; and the major trouble with previous

---

23. I criticize the incoherence of Hegel's version of this in *Hegel's God: A Counterfeit Double?*

religions is that they broke the circuit of self-appropriation on an unappropriated otherness, did not allow the *return* of the human being to itself. What do the sons of Feuerbach want? They want to close the circuit again, and allow the otherness of the human to return to itself. The truth of "God" is, or will be, man. The truth of creation is, or will be, human self-creation.

Of course, this circuit of self-creation is understood differently by each. And they may *want* some human self-appropriation, but they do not always get what they want, or even realize that what humans want thus is impossible. In Nietzsche's case there is an intimation that "self" is an abyss, and in truth beyond complete self-mastering. If so, how could we ever get, or create, the "self" we "want"? And because this sense of the "beyond" is inherently equivocal in Nietzsche, there emerges something significantly at odds with Zarathustra's claim, previously noted, that "what finally returns, comes home to me, is my own self." *Can anything return?* And least of all can "my own self" return? What emerges also throws light on the *continuity* as well as discontinuity between the earlier and later Nietzsche. What I mean is this.

Nietzsche's atheism cannot be assimilated to any normal species of humanism, precisely because there is a sense of excess to the human being that resists complete self-mediation. This excess opens up the human being to something other than the human. Hence the opening of radical self-apotheosis to what passes beyond self and *amor fati*. There is still a concern with origin as other to the human but this is the shift. The *Ureine* conceived the origin under the sign of unity and identity; but the sign will be changed from unity to multiplicity, from identity to difference. Still named Dionysus, but more as will to power rather than *das Ureine*, the primordial One becomes what one might call the "self-broadcaster," under the sign of multiplicity and difference. There is a reversal from identity to difference, and yet the will to power is still a self-broadcasting, in the sense of a self-scattering, a self-othering, and self-dissemination. Nietzsche praises himself for his acquired power in "the reversal of perspectives" (*Ecce Homo*, chapter 1, section 1; *W*, VI, 3, 264; *PN*, 659). One might say that the "One" has now become "Self-Othering." But even in this "self-othering" under the sign of difference, Nietzsche will still continue to say again and again: will to power affirms *itself*—itself and nothing but itself.

The devotees of Nietzsche will forgive me for harping on the affinity with Hegel, a fast-handed dialectician who could claim to reverse into its opposite any perspective you could care to conceive. Hegel's speculative thinking of the One implies that the One is not truly absolute until it becomes self-othering: the One others itself into multiplicity and difference, and this is indeed its inherent nature. Why Nietzsche and Hegel are such brothers is because their thinking is guided by an operative logic of erotic self-origination. In Nietzsche's case, the logic becomes poetic, and in this ambiguously suggestive form, could be disguised and dissimulated—even to Nietzsche himself. It seems to me that the younger Nietzsche had not yet learned to mask his views as much as he did later. There is a youthful ardor to *The Birth of Tragedy:* he reveals what he loves, recklessly—a love and recklessness that has to be seen through many masks later. In the reversal from the sign of unity to the sign of difference, I believe that one can still see the shape of what he loved as ultimate, relative to erotic self-origination.

You will object that Nietzsche in *Ecce Homo* describes *The Birth of Tragedy* as having something of the offensive smell of Hegelianism, as well as indicating his rejection of the artistic metaphysics. But why should we take anything that Nietzsche says at face value? Nothing he says can be taken at face value, on his own admission of being a masked philosopher. "Faces" are always at least "two-faced." The mask cuts two ways. It may hide depth and profundity. It may also perfume the secret odor of "Hegelian" metaphysics that Nietzsche does not want us to smell, or smell out. Nietzsche has taught us only too well how to smell out other philosophers. The nasal metaphor is one that he uses frequently, perhaps too frequently. I find no reason for accepting at "face value" Nietzsche's claim to have discarded the artistic metaphysics. This is where he revealed his deepest ardor as a younger man, an ardor whose youthful naïveté he later sought to conceal. It is always hard to betray or confess one's deepest love, especially when age and the acids of skepticism have corroded one's more innocent faith.

Twilight of an Ideal

I do not forget the differences of Hegel and Nietzsche, in that erotic origin can be thought either in terms of an explicit teleology, or as ateleological. Hegel's self-origination has a teleological thrust—the goal is the self-mediating constitution, through self-othering, of the self-completing whole. With Nietzsche, self-othering seems to be without telos, seems to issue in multiplicity without final unification, unrestricted differentiation without ultimate reintegration. This latter understanding informs the deconstructionist reading of Nietzsche. There is much to the point about this reading, but I think there is more to be said. Explicit disclaimers to the contrary, Nietzsche does not avoid his own telos, a telos that is an equivocal *auto-telos*. Not surprisingly the aesthetic, as supposedly auto-telic, comes in again. What I mean is implied by statements like this: "World—a work of art giving birth to itself!"[24] How does a work of art give birth to itself? Only if there is an *ontological self-origination* that is the very dynamic self-becoming of the process of being itself. We humans find it hard to think of a work of art apart from its origination by an artist. This was true of the early Nietzsche. And a world giving birth to itself?

---

24. *The Will to Power,* trans. W. Kaufmann and R. J. Hollingdale, ed. W. Kaufmann (New York: Random House, 1967), 419; *Der Wille zur Macht* (Leipzig: Kröner Verlag, 1930), 533.

I query: Why do some commentators breathe an audible sigh of relief that Nietzsche gave up, "mercifully," as Nehamas puts it,[25] the language of the world artist? What is the mercy, what is the relief? No explanation is offered. But of course, the embarrassment is the embarrassment of God. Strange shame at a god, when without the slightest chagrin one then continues to gas on about Dionysus. And one must query, given the seeming elision, where does the world artist go? What new form, more merciful, less embarrassing, does it take? Because it does take other forms, but now, as I put it, under the sign of difference rather than identity.

Has the "world-artist" been elided for fear of falling back into the arms of a god, or God? Can one avoid this? I suppose that Nehamas' literary/textual model, applied to Nietzsche's metaphysics of the self-birthing artwork world, would make the world into *a self-writing text, without any writer or author*. A *self*-writing text without any "self" to write the *self*-writing text? What kind of text is that? Instead of thinking thinking thinking (*noēsis noēseōs noēsis*—Aristotle's god, Hegel's god), writing writing writing? What god this: writing writing writing?

Even to say: a work of art giving birth to itself, one notes that it is to *itself* that "it" (whatever this *deus absconditus* is) gives birth. Self-origination is still *self*-origination, and as long as we try to make articulate sense, resort to some such locution seems impossible to avoid entirely. One might say nothing, but that hardly helps. One might say: "origin," or "origination"; but then inevitably one asks, what kind of origin or origination? And then resort to terms like identity and difference, same and other, is unavoidable. Nor will it help very much to write "origin" and then draw a line though it, as Heidegger does with "being." There is no escaping the hard tasking of thinking of origin. The first jolt of the typographical gesture dissolves pretty quickly, and still we metaphysicians are perplexed—both about what appears and what is crossed out, even when it is crossed out.

The work of art that gives birth to itself tries to be its own father, mother and offspring. Is the idea intelligible? It is hard to make intelligible. It is as hard, or as easy, as some of the old ideas of God. This says as much for the old God as for Nietzsche's supposedly new "god." And do not tell me that Nietzsche should not be subject to that kind of "metaphysical" analysis, that to do this is "ontotheology." This gives Nietzsche, and his admirers, a very convenient bolt-hole whenever we ask about the intelligible coherence of his ideas. I cannot avoid thinking that his "god" dresses up in aesthetic/ontological form what metaphysicians of old spoke of as *causa sui*. (Does "writing writing writing" become something like "language languaging language" in Heidegger—somewhat like "world worlds" or "nothing nothings"? He attacks the onto-theological god of *causa sui* but "language languaging language" sounds

---

25. A. Nehamas, *Nietzsche: Life as Literature* (Cambridge: Harvard University Press, 1985), 91.

suspiciously like a kind of *logos* as *causa sui*.) As I mentioned, Nietzsche excoriates this notion of the *causa sui* as showing the deep fear of philosophers, fear of time and origins, their "Egypticism" (*W,* VI, 3, 68; *PN,* 479 ff.). But what Nietzsche denounces in others has an uncanny tendency to haunt Nietzsche again, indeed to be resurrected in a different form. I suppose this is why Nietzsche had to continually leap frog himself, and why in the end, what finally returns is the old familiar, "my own self." It is a hard act to sustain the absolute originality one had proclaimed. His "madness," in a paradoxical enough reversal of perspectives, brings out the point with maximum lucidly. I refer to the penetration of one of his first mad letters (6 January, 1889, postmarked 5 January—*Briefwechsel,* III, 5, 577–78 [Brief 1256]; *PN,* 685–86), that poignant plea to Burckhardt: Bear with me please, for I am new to the business of being a god; "I would much rather be a Basel professor than God." And what is the pathetic destiny of this god? Sentenced to while away the next eternity cracking bad jokes!

Though Nietzsche is now presented as *the* philosopher of difference, it is the circuit of the *same* that is reconstituted in the work of art that gives birth to *itself*. The credentials he offers us for being the philosopher of difference are thus equivocal through and through. For there is no radical creation of the other as other, if the *causa sui* of the world/work of art that gives birth to itself (or even writing writing writing) is all there is. It is the same that is eternally recurring. I cannot enter further into the eternal recurrence of the same here, except to say that it too bears on trying to close the circle and bring the two sides above together—extreme self-affirmation and *amor fati*.

Within the circle, or what is called the ring of eternity, the same might often look like the other or different. But that is *within the circle*. Moreover, Nietzsche is talking about the circle itself, not about what is in it. Plato returns. For Nietzsche is arrogating to himself the powers of the Platonic philosopher as the spectator of all time and eternity. Nietzsche must in some sense, a sense he cannot explain, be able to "see" the circle of the whole, be somehow transcendent to it. Again the evidence of a logic of erotic origination seem to me unmistakable in Nietzsche's vision, and again in a manner which makes Nietzsche a kindred, not only of Schopenhauer, but of Hegel.

I identify a major source of this logic of erotic origination in a tendency to identify theogony and cosmogony in idealistic and pantheistic philosophies that appropriate Spinoza's sense of *causa sui:* It is necessary for God to become; indeed we cannot separate this "self-becoming" from the process of becoming of the world; ultimately the two are the same. This necessary self-becoming exhibits the character of an erotic absolute. How does one find this strain in relation to Nietzsche? One might think of Schelling's appropriation of Spinoza here, and of the fact that Schopenhauer reproduces a number of possibilities already fermenting in perhaps the more idealistic framework of Schelling. The dark other to idealism already shadows Schelling's ambiguously idealistic version of the erotic absolute. Schopenhauer, I recall, speaks directly of the genital organs as the focal point of the will, and what is will but the obscure striving energy that is the primordial ground of all becoming? All willing, he says, arises from deficiency. This is eros as lacking, and as struggling to overcome its lack. This eros here functions as *the* metaphysical metaphor for the happening of being as a process of becoming. This primordial will is a blind, insatiable striving that seeks release in this or that satisfaction, only to find itself in endlessly repeated dissatisfaction. The will-less knowing of art offers episodic release, Schopenhauer says, the saint's release a more final salvation. The erotic origin initially lacks peace, but strives for peace in an erotic struggle that seeks to transcend eros.

Interestingly, while Nietzsche criticizes Schopenhauer for a melancholy attitude to sexual eros, he praises Plato for his "philosophic erotics" out of which developed a new art form of the Greek *agon,* namely dialectic (*W,* VI, 3, 119–20; *PN,* 527–29). Yet Nietzsche also continues Schopenhauer's sense of the darkness of the origin but transforms will into will to power. We have already looked at a clear testimony to the erotic origin in *The Birth of Tragedy,* where through suffering and contradiction, creation and destruction, the primordial One seeks *its own redemption* in the process of becoming.[26] He seems to reject Schopenhauer's will-less knowing and the saint's extirpation of will; he accentuates the process of striving itself, striving without end, intensifies erotic struggle to frenzy, and without any peace at the end such as we find, say, in Platonic eros. I say he "seems," for in fact the "unselving" involved in this makes the extreme willing into a kind of will-lessness: willing everything in *amor fati* is consent to everything, and hence not just willing in the sense of asserting one's own will. The erotic absolute is absolutized under the mythic name of Dionysus; but this absolute seems an orgiastic absorbing god which swallows us and all Apollonian individuation.

I think Nietzsche's description of the world as a "monster of energy"[27] is extraordinarily revealing:

> And do you know what the "world" is to me? Shall I show it to you in my mirror? This world: a monster of energy, without beginning, without end; a firm, iron magnitude of force that does not grow bigger or smaller, that does not expend itself but only transforms itself; as a whole, of unalterable size, a household without expenses or

26. Consult the second last paragraph of Hegel's *Lectures on the Philosophy of Religion* (1827): the whole point of Hegel's philosophy is God's *reconciliation with himself,* through nature and history. God's *self-redemption.* What kind of a God is this that needs to *redeem itself?* If one did not despise the stupidity of such a "God," one might pity it for having to endure what seems to be *its own madness and evil.* See my *Hegel's God: A Counterfeit Double?*

27. *Will to Power,* 549–50; *WzM,* 696–97.

> losses, but likewise without increase or income; enclosed by "nothingness" as by a boundary; . . . as force throughout, as a play of forces flowing and rushing together, eternally changing, eternally flooding back, with tremendous years of recurrence, with an ebb and a flood of its forms; out of the simplest forms striving toward the most complex, out of the stillest, most rigid, coldest forms towards the hottest, most turbulent, most self-contradictory, and then again returning home to the simplest out of this abundance, out of the play of contradictions back to the joy of concord, still affirming itself in this uniformity of its courses and its years, blessing itself as that which must return eternally, as a becoming that knows no satiety, no disgust, no weariness: this, my *Dionysian* world of the eternally self-creating, eternally self-destroying . . . my "beyond good and evil," without goal, unless the joy of the circle is itself a goal; without will, unless a ring feels good will towards itself—do you want a *name* for this world? A *solution* for all its riddles? . . . *This world is will to power—and nothing besides!* And you yourselves are also this will to power—and nothing besides!

To any philosophically sophisticated reader, and Nietzsche has not been blessed with such readers often enough, it is impossible not to hear an echo of the Parmenidean One, the well-rounded circle of truth. Of course, this One has been dynamized by Heraclitean becoming in its eternal arising and dissolving. The self-becoming of the will to power closes into a cosmic circle. Recall the Dionysian faith Goethe incarnated for Nietzsche: "the *faith* that only the particular is loathesome, and that all is redeemed and affirmed in the whole—*he does not negate anymore*" (*Twilight of the Idols,* Skirmishes, 49). What kind of "yes" to the whole is this "highest of all possible faiths" that finds the particular loathesome? Redemption *from* the particular rather than redemption *of* the particular? One also hears in the background of the citation above the voice of Spinoza's One—the Whole, fated, necessary, absolutely determined. One hears in the background the voice of Hegel singing speculative hosannas to the dialectically self-mediating totality. Indeed since the human being is also will to power and nothing else beside, it seems impossible to distinguish the human self from the cosmic circle as will to power and nothing else beside. The beginning and the end is will to power and nothing else besides, and everything seemingly different and other is swallowed back into this orgiastic absorbing god.

In a word, Nietzsche is guilty of the sins he has charged to *messieurs* the "metaphysicians." He is shameless about these sins, indeed seems to be hardly mindful of the fact that he is committing them. Alas, it is easier to take the speck out of "Plato's" eye than the beam from one's own. Do I exaggerate? Well, simply take note of the totalizing claim of Nietzsche's language. Nietzsche may sometimes start out with the rhetoric of "suppose," but by the end he is tempted with being recklessly totalistic. And he succumbs.[28] Hegel is supposed to the totalizing philosopher *par excellence* but his totalism is almost meek and dull compared to the reckless rhapsody of Nietzsche's totalism. You might say, as some commentators have, that Nietzsche was incautious in understanding will to power in cosmological terms, that he should have confined the thesis to human being. But when was Nietzsche ever cautious? He hated caution. Daring he loved—intellectual, spiritual daring. And can you seriously imagine him, like a good considerate scholar, or moderate analyst, saying: The world is will to power—for the most part. Or there is nothing else but will to power—but only here and there, and maybe now and then. Or: let me tentatively suggest the following empirical generalization: the world is will to power; but since all the data is not yet in, we should claim no more than may be so.

No. Nietzsche wanted to legislate. Nietzsche wanted to dictate. He does not say: the human being is motivated, for the most part, by will to power. No. The world is will to power and nothing else besides. We ourselves are this will to power, and nothing else besides. Making a total claim, one must even say, *staking* a total claim, Nietzsche is an extremist. It is all or nothing. And as it turned out, he had rightly divined that it was this lure of the extreme, not reason and argument and evidence, that would win him converts. Nietzsche does not deign to make a case but instead dazzles us with his dancing at the edge. The dancing may begin in frenzy, perhaps even in divine madness, but because the dancer never resolves his equivocity towards the divine, because he can in no way distinguish between dancing full of God and dancing the idol of absolute self-glorification, that is, self-deification, the dancing ends in mad madness. For Nietzsche's self-glorification is self-deification. Like the *causa*

---

28. The previous citation is only one of many where we find the totalizing claims. *BGE*, §13: "Life itself is *will to power*." *GM*, II, sect. 2: "One places . . . 'adaption' in the foreground, that is to say, an activity of the second rank, a mere reactivity. . . . Thus the essence of life, its *will to power*, is ignored." You might object that Nietzsche in *Beyond Good and Evil* (§36) begins an important reflection on will to power by asking us to "suppose." True, but *only* suppose? He goes on to wonder if the *one* will to power is not demanded by "the conscience of method." Question expecting the answer yes. This idea of the one will to power, Nietzsche says, must be pushed to its utter limits. From "suppose" to "must"? Granting the rhetoric of supposition and the look of a hypothetical beginning, the direction overall and end intended is unmistakable: if we can affirm all plurality, Nietzsche says, as "the development and ramification of *one* basic form of the will—namely, of the will to power, as *my* proposition has it . . . then one would have gained the right to determine *all* efficient force univocally as—*will to power*. The world viewed from inside . . . would be 'will to power' and nothing else.—" We end with the very same words as cited from *Will to Power*. As often happens with Nietzsche's rhetoric of "suggestion" and "suppose," an easy-to-miss shift occurs as he insinuates himself into the confidences of his reader, a shift revealed in a move more and more to the strongly *assertoric* mode, and this even though he might also naughtily delight in upending his reader by ending in a "perhaps." Open declamations abound in Nietzsche of the form "*every* philosopher *hitherto* . . ." or "*all* morality till now or *hitherto*. . . ." Other times the transition from "supposition" to "say-so" is more masked.

sui, Nietzsche wanted to create himself. As he said in highest admiration of Goethe: he created himself (*W,* VI, 3, 145 f.; *PN,* 554). Nietzsche willed to be his own mother and father and offspring all together. This is erotic *self-origination,* and like Hegel's absolute, in debt to nothing other, for there is no genuine other; what finally comes home, so spake Zarathustra, is the "self." In fact, finally there is no "self," and what we come home to is nothing.

A question at the end to be put to self-creation: how connect with Nietzsche's stress (in *The Birth of Tragedy*) on the horror of Oedipus' *unnatural deeds*—murder of his father and incest with his mother—as making possible tragic seeing?[29] Would not the will to self-creation, for a finite creature, not also be unnatural? And what must be murdered for this to be possible? In what bed must eros finds its bliss of incest? If that were the only access to *seeing,* we would not have gotten much beyond the evil of being in Schopenhauer, except where he renounced it, here we are urged to intensify it. If art's redemption is inseparable from eros thus intensified, here in the form of will to power willing itself, how distinguish this redemption, beyond moral good and evil, from a self-surpassing into the *evil of being?* And we are supposed to say "yes" to *that?* I pray protection from the promptings of Lady Macbeth who would persuade me to that. Nietzsche sometimes prompted himself the way Lady Macbeth prompted Macbeth. Be hard! I know too that to come to the redeeming of evil one may have to be exposed to the execration of evil, and in this exposure be graced with a "yes" of trust in the ultimate good.[30] I cannot see how Nietzsche's "yes" could possibly be a "yes" to that grace. I renounce any baptismal pledge to Nietzsche's god and his redemption. I ask to be allowed to take my leave and look to an exit to the outside. Or wait in woo, and in a porosity that makes a way, for the "yes" that pours from outside in.

Nietzsche's song and dance continues to bewitch too many, but for us the spell is broken. A different "amen" to the good of the "to be" has woken us from his enchantment. We have ceased to be bewitched. We see with almost unnatural lucidity that there is no rope across the abyss that our will could conjure up and walk. Our will cannot perform that kind of magic. The metaphysical magic that conjures away the otherness between God and man is black magic. Our will must be differently willing for that difference.

---

29. Ernst Bloch makes the pertinent suggestion that metaphysics after Schelling seems to become rather *oedipal.* In "Oedipal metaphysics an original *darkness* or *incognito* is reflected, if not a fantastically contrived *crime.* In this respect, every last investigation of origins is related to the Oedipal form, which treats the incognito basically not just as an unknown of the logical variety, but also as something uncanny, unknown even to itself." *The Utopian Function of Art and Literature: Selected Essays,* trans. Jack Zipes and Frank Mecklenburg (Cambridge Mass.: MIT Press, 1988), 260.

30. See my "Sticky Evil: *Macbeth* and the Karma of the Equivocal," in *God, Literature and Process Thought,* ed. Darren J. N. Middleton (Aldershot: Ashgate Publishing, 2002), 133–55.

7

Art and the Self-Concealing Origin

Heidegger's Equivocity and the Still Unthought Between

HEIDEGGER, ART, FINESSE

One must honor Heidegger for his efforts to keep us mindful, in his singular way, of the question of being, in an epoch when the calculative dominion over beings increases its sway on a daily basis. The univocalization of being, especially characteristic of Western modernity, promises the realization of Descartes' dream of our becoming the masters and possessors of nature. But in the realizing of the promise, the *esprit de géométrie* seems to have progressively replaced the *esprit de finesse,* to such an extent that modes of mindfulness that fall outside the horizon of univocal calculation strain more and more to maintain their importance. The strain might be expressed in a number of forms: for instance, that between "logos" and "eros" or "mania"; or between Enlightenment and Romanticism; or between scientism and aestheticism; or between logocentric philosophy and tragedy; or between systematic univocity and aesthetic equivocity; or between (with a bow to Nietzsche) "Plato" and "Homer," or (with a bow to Kant) between "Newton" and "Homer." To claim that art matters metaphysically means that we must come to the aid of the unheeded finesse. Heidegger, one might argue, is a thinker who asks us to heed.

This above litany reflects also the strains that have engaged us variously. Does not Heidegger have a justified place in that engagement? The answer has to be yes, not only for his reminding us of the question of being, not only for his efforts to further the dialogue of the philosopher and poet, but for his offering us the widely admired meditation "The Origin of the Work of Art." Here we seem to come into our own with respect to the theme of art, origins and otherness. Art—we seem invited to expect—opens us to the more original work of truth, other than the (mimetic) correctness of propositional correspondence, long advocated by more logocentric philosophers. We seem to be promised, through heed to art, an understanding of our participation in this more original, more "creative" work of truth.

How is the promise held out to us by Heidegger, and how redeemed, if it is redeemed? One might ask heed for finesse, but one must have finesse to heed the asking. Has Heidegger finesse—finesse enough? He promises much, but I find something equivocal about his promise, and something equivocal about the redemption of the promise. Given this double equivocity, is it surprising to find reactions at opposite extremes: Heidegger as immeasurably deep in a "metaphysical" sense, Heidegger as a (twentieth century) blowing of Romantic wind; Heidegger as inspired vates, Heidegger as cunning charlatan? Neither view is entirely right, but both are right in some measure, and right because Heidegger appears to promise something of ultimate moment, but the redemption of the promise turns out to be somewhat less than a saving "letting be." Hence our sometime misgiving that we conclude with an anti-climactic "let down."

Many of Heidegger's admirers praise "The Origin of the Work of Art" as something of unprecedented originality. Such claims can be greatly overstated. Given our investigations, the rich complexity of many philosophers' concerns with origin and art can hardly be doubted. This rich complexity is sometimes overt, sometimes implicit, but it is undeniable. Only a defect of philosophical education can blind one to this. Heidegger does exercise a spell, and his admirers fall under the sway of his self-portrayal as thinking "outside" metaphysics, or seeking an other origin prior to philosophy, beyond philosophy. This seems too simplistic, or self-serving. Of course, noting his claim to difference may help us understand the above contrast between admirers and detractors: the first elevate Heidegger in conformity with his own self-portrayal of difference; the second depreciate him, for perhaps the same reason, that is, they can make little sense of his difference and his claims for difference. In my view, if Heidegger were situated more explicitly in the long line of serious philosophical reflection on art, origin, otherness, his difference would appear less singular, and something of the rationale of his engagements might appear more persuasive. Fidelity to that longer line makes it impossible to be either such an admirer or detractor. I would be neither an earnest worker in the heavy industry of Heideggerian scholasticism nor an opportunistic spoiler in an anti-Heideggerian campaign. Heidegger's equivocal stance prompts an other position, not quite between these extremes, but as returning Heidegger to a between at which some philosophers have hinted, some better than others, some more mindless of what they are doing, but, like the sleepers of Heraclitus, still contributing to the work of the logos.

I am interested in the otherness of the origin and what art might communicate of it, and how this challenges ways of philosophical articulation. Heidegger's "origin" seems very indeterminate. If so, how speak of it, since all speech is determination, and if determination, caught in the fixing of determinacy, hence necessarily given over to the temptation of univocity? Can one speak equivocally and keep the indeterminacy open? But to speak equivocally can be duplicitous: dubious in the sense of double, as two-faced. Is there a speech which, while determinate, remains true to the overdeterminate? Clearly poetic speech can be such. Remember Kant's aesthetic ideas: determinate yet more, inexhaustible with regard to univocal fixing. Remember too the imaginative universal of Vico. We must grant some determination but seek determinations alive with an intimation of the overdeterminate: the issue intimates the source. This is especially true of religious communication (and not just poetry). Being religious is more inaugural than being aesthetic. And philosophy? In fact, the way Heidegger speaks about the *unthought* is by way of the *thought* originals—that is, only by the "destruction" of the tradition; and this as a history of the names of being. Why should we not place Heidegger's unthought origin in the company of other efforts to *think* origin? Will we have to conclude that the diversity and *otherness* of that thinking falls outside Heidegger's view, if that history is reduced to "onto-theology" and something like the univocalization of being? What of the recurrent sense of otherness, and here and there, the between?

Given the longer line of reflection on art, origins, otherness, it is impossible to accept without qualification Heidegger's characterization of the "tradition" of reflection on art. I will come to this again, and crucially with respect to the difference of making and creation. Nor in thinking of origin should we be mesmerized by slogans about "metaphysics," as if that dealt with simplistic univocal principles or some big thing, or ultra substance. We need more finesse, whether in agreement with Heidegger, or disagreement. I will engage Heidegger with some of the dominant possibilities with respect to art, origins, otherness, as reflected in the thinkers so far studied. Having first summarized some main themes of "The Origin of the Work of Art," I will ask how Heidegger might be understood relative to Platonic originals, to transcendental and dialectical origins, and the erotic origins of Schopenhauer and Nietzsche. Heidegger has tried to engage all these thinkers in a variety of ways, but not from a more developed metaxological orientation. It is towards this that I move, sometimes circuitously but always with an eye on, or ear for the "yes" to being art allows, and the sense of the ultimate origin that is communicated in the between. True, the theme of *das Zwischen* does appear, on and off, in Heidegger's work, but it is given nothing like the rounded articulation that a fully metaxological philosophy requires. It appears as an operative theme, and is episodically named, but in its fuller dimensions it remains basically *unthought*. Though named, on and off, it remains without a logos. (Heidegger is not the only philosopher for which this holds.) This lack will allow us to give more determinate substance to the suggestion of Heidegger's equivocal promise.[1]

---

1. My development of a metaxological metaphysics has important points of overlap with Heidegger, but the differences are finally more important, and the manner the task of thinking is

THEMES OF "THE ORIGIN OF THE WORK OF ART"

Here is a brief summary of some main points of this essay. A work presenting itself with a more meditative character does not lend itself to easy summary, and I respect that. Nevertheless, the essay is well known, and no claim is made to offer a textual exegesis of its full details. Given our previous explorations, a context is offered for shedding light on it that would not come, even were one to treat it as a sacred text requiring line by line commentary. One could well look at it line by line, and find something both suggestive and questionable in many lines. This cannot be our task here. In being immensely suggestive, Heidegger is also capable of being immensely evasive. I do not think this is just a mask. I do not think the evasion is conspired. It is the equivocal way of the man and his thinking of origin.

Heidegger is concerned with an other origin, more primordial than the beginning that seems to have got under way with Greek philosophy and its canonical concepts of truth, being, thing, work and so on. Philosophy's own origin is defined in its quarrel with poetry, and Heidegger wants to engage the poets differently. Art itself turns out to be an origin. Where lies the emphasis? First on art as origin? Or on origin as giving rise to the work of the art work, as setting forth something of the happening of truth in a primal way? On both, in fact, though these two emphases are not always kept apart. The second sense of origin is clearly most important, since its bearing cannot be confined to art, but concerns the whole of being, and the happening of being as such. It is more ultimate than the first, with bearing on, say, what being religious and being philosophical also effect. Of course, if art is inaugural, Heidegger also names other founding happenings, including the work of the statesman and the thinker. If art has bearing on this primal origin, it has a bearing on the happening of being as such, most intimate with respect to its truth as made manifest to humans. I take this to be at issue in art's metaphysical significance, and of central concern for Heidegger. His hermeneutics of the history of philosophy notwithstanding, variations of a similar theme can be found in some the thinkers already discussed.

To summarize then: Heidegger offers a discussion of thing and work, which reminds us of many overtones in the word "thing" and how rich and diverse they are. Modern thought has a very flat sense of "thing," if it has a sense of things at all. Heidegger, as we know, has devoted a whole study to the

---

envisaged. While this must remain in the background here, the reader should consult what I say about different senses of metaphysical thinking in *BB*, especially chapter 1; also "Being, Dialectic and Determination: On the Sources of Metaphysical Thinking," *The Review of Metaphysics*, 48 (June 1995): 731–69, reprinted in *Being and Dialectic* (Albany: State University of New York Press, 2000), chapter 1; and "Neither Deconstruction or Reconstruction: Metaphysics and the Intimate Strangeness of Being," *International Philosophical Quarterly* (March 2000): 37–49.

question "What is a Thing?"[2] The ontological thereness of things comes to be shown by art. One remembers the will-less release to things beyond instrumentalizing, named as art's "disinterestedness" by Kant and Schopenhauer. There is a celebrating appreciation of what is there as there, beyond serviceable disposability and consumption. It is not a calculative but contemplative comportment. One might say: in the between things show their being as being; art is not concerned with worldless things, since a thing is shown in its world; but its world is also shown in the thing, and art is also a way of showing world in this thing. Heidegger does not quite put it that way, but one cannot forget the traditional language of the universal in the singular. Heidegger wants to avoid that, but looking charitably at the tradition, there is no reason why we cannot also sound the deeper ontological resonances in notions that ostensibly seem to be worn out. What seems worn out may mean that *we*, not they, are worn out.

Heidegger discusses three conceptions of thing: first, that of substance/accidents; second, that of the unity of the sensory manifold; third, that of the union of form and matter. The third receives special mention, since Heidegger wants to locate it in intimate relation with traditional aesthetics. Form and content—these are "the most hackneyed concepts . . ." (*GA*, 5:12; *OWA*, 658). The matter also concerns the more technical sense of making, as the imposition of form on matter, and for some instrumental purpose, carrying thus the hidden risk of an assault of being. Art and things point to an origin deeper than form and content by attending to the being of beings, not simply their use for us. Undoubtedly the notion of making is pervasive in the tradition, and most radically expressed in modernity in the collusion of science, technology and will to power. Heidegger generalizes to the whole tradition from the Greeks, Plato and Aristotle, down to now. He overstates the point surely, in his will to have a totalized picture of the Western tradition as covering over a more primordial origin. Apart from the dubious totalization, he is evasive of certain questions concerning the crucial difference of Demiurgic making and creation, as we will see.

In the second section of "The Origin of the Work of Art," there is a discussion of the work and truth. Here we find the revealing discussion of the Greek temple as opening up a world. (As I said before, there is no Gothic Heidegger here, except perhaps in the silenced background of the world of the shoes of the peasant.) Here he makes claims about world and earth as in polemos. Earth, *Erde*, is grounding but also self-concealing. Without earth, no world, but world has to be won, and on the ground of what both makes it possible, and

---

2. "Der Ursprung des Kunstwerkes," *Gesamtausgabe*, Bd. 5, "Holzwege" (Frankfurt: Klostermann, 1977), abbreviated to *GA;* I will again refer to the English translation of "The Origin of the Work of Art" in *Philosophies of Art and Beauty*, and incorporate references into the text as *OWA*. *What is a Thing?* trans. V. Barton and V. Deutsch (Chicago: Regnery, 1967).

necessarily recedes into its own hiddenness. Earth powerfully suggests the origin as self-concealing in its making possible an opening of world. The theme is Nietzschean, as is the theme of polemos, and I will say more below in relation to the Dionysian origin. With regard to truth, we find the well known contrast of *alētheia* and *orthotes* (correctness). There is truth more primordial than correctness. Heidegger is surely right to point to some such more primordial sense of truth. Whether he does justice to this, or the plurivocal promise of "being true" is another issue (see *BB,* chapter 13). As ever with Heidegger we find great suggestiveness but spiced with such equivocity as to make us wonder if more is promised than is delivered, or can be. His admirers generally seem satisfied with the offer of a promise and will not ask about the promise if it seems to deliver nothing but itself. We ask for more.

In the final section there is a discussion of truth and art, again bearing on the contrast of *alētheia* and more derivative truth. Here we again find discussion of *technē* and *phusis,* and perhaps the most suggestive part of the whole essay bearing on creation as a bringing forth that is not making as technical. But again what is being suggested is inherently equivocal. Heidegger makes a virtue of this. "Truth occurs as such in the opposition of the clearing and double concealing. Truth is the primal conflict in which, always in some particular way, the Open is won . . ." (*GA* 5: 48; *OWA,* 685).[3] I see an unstable tension between the opening as a *giving,* and the human being as a *projecting.* I wonder if, on these terms alone, we can be true to the *release* of art beyond the human being as "projecting." If so, Heidegger remains captive to the deep equivocations of post-Kantian thought we have explored between human originality and the primal origin as other. I will discuss this below, in terms of Heidegger's hints about *creation* and *nothing,* and how he addresses the between.

Finally, there is an appendix in which Heidegger recurs to Hegel's claim about the "end of art." In the next chapter I will take up a significant strand of this theme, where the equivocity bears on the address, less than fully forthright, to the explicitly *religious* dimension of the matter. The present chapter will bring us to that point. Here again Heidegger is not singular in remaining captive to some deep equivocations about being religious of post-Kantian thought.

Heidegger, the Between and Platonic Originals

Heidegger's view of Plato is many-sided. He clearly distinguishes "Platonism" and Plato. He is rather reductive in his questionable "Plato's Theory of Truth,"

3. In this section (*OWA,* 686), the other historical ways of founding truth are mentioned. Such themes are also present in *Introduction to Metaphysics,* and *Beitrage zur Philosophie (Vom Ereignis)* Frankfurt: Klostermann, 1989, *GA,* 65; *Contributions to Philosophy (From Enowning),* trans. P. Emud and K. Maly (Bloomington: Indiana University Press, 1999).

more sophisticated in his discussion of the *Sophist;* and though often the shadow of Nietzsche's cartoon of Platonism is in the background, he gives us a Plato somewhat more fleshed out in the *Nietzsche* book, moving, perhaps wavering between the mimesis of the *Republic,* and the more entrancing thoughts of the *Phaedrus.* Overall the emphasis is on *technē,* demiurgic making, and the final importance of "presence," all contributing to a "Platonism" finally reductively stylized in late essays like "The End of Philosophy and the Task of Thinking," and not absent from "The Origin of the Work of Art."[4] If one could gather the strands together, one might say: the caricatured Plato of Nietzsche shapes implied claims to his own originality, though that claim must be weakened, I believe, if we have a sophisticated view of Nietzsche's *The Birth of Tragedy.* There, many important moves are made which one might call Heideggerian, had not Nietzsche already beaten him from the blocks. But then, of course, did we not also see that Schopenhauer had often beaten Nietzsche from the blocks?

I detect the "Plato" of the negative version of mimesis, the dualism of original and image, coupled with the dualism of *eidos* and instance, placed in an ethos where the ontological milieu of the metaxu is not given due weight, and where mimesis becomes a univocal representationalism, itself intimately tied with the so-called correspondence theory of truth. If we take the metaxu differently (recall, for instance, the nuances of mimesis discussed in chapter 1), we cannot stylize "Plato" quite so. The significance of eros and mania testify to energies of being in the between that exceed "ontic" univocalization, and that shape movements of self-transcending that cannot be accounted for simply in the language of univocal presence. It is true that a crude mimetic model can fix on *orthotes,* or *homoiosis,* and lose the more original sense of metaxological truth. But an art work is more than such a "correct" mimesis. And we must remember, a reminder Heidegger does sometimes heed, that mimesis is more complex than normally granted. This is especially important in relation to the problem of equivocal being, of *being as equivocal.*[5]

Parenthetically I anticipate some very basic issues that extend beyond Plato. This problem of image and original, and the likeness that, in being like to an original, is false, points towards the problem of the difference of *sophist*

4. "Platons Lehre von der Wahrheit," in *Wegmerken* (Frankfurt: Klostermann, 1976), English trans. T. Sheehan as "Plato's Doctrine of Truth," in *Pathmarks,* ed. W. McNeill (Cambridge: Cambridge University Press, 1998). *Platon: Sophistes,* Frankfurt: Klosterman, 1992 (*GA,* 19); English trans. R. Rojcewicz and A. Schuwer (Bloomington: Indiana University Press, 1997). *Nietzsche* (Frankfurt: Klostermann, 1996), 2. vols. *GA,* 6.1 and 6.2; English translation D. Krell and F.A. Capuzzi, 4 vols. (New York: Harper and Row, 1979, 1982, 1984)."Das Ende der Philosophie und die Aufgabe des Denkens," *Zur Sache des Denkens* (Tübingen: Max Niemeyer Verlag, 1969), 61–80; English translation Joan Stambaugh, "The End of Philosophy and the Task of Thinking," *On Time and Being* (New York: Harper and Row, 1972), 55–73.

5. See *BB,* chapter 3 on being and equivocity; on dissembling identity, see the discussion of the orchid and the chameleon, but most especially the human being, the equivocal being par excellence.

and philosopher. Equivocity concerns the semblance, the dissembling of being. Plato is aware that this problem concerns more than a rigid correctness, but something in-between: not true, not false, but the semblance of true: this semblance, to be false, must be true to the original, as a counterfeit must be. This is a strange situation: the semblance of the true accomplishes its *falsity by being true* to the original. With the perfect form of falsity, there may appear no difference to the true. Yet it will be false. How? Not in terms of form alone, but in terms of the movement of spiritual energies, in terms of the good that the eros serves. For instance, the form of mutual hatred might well mimic mutual love: but the good would be served in the second, and despoiled in the first: sameness or difference of form is not the most ultimate truth. This is an aspect of the problem of *counterfeit doubles*.

This great problem also bears on the question of the *good of the "to be."* In his "The Saying of Anaximander" Heidegger avers: "Every epoch of world-history is an epoch of error."[6] This is true, in one respect, with reference to the equivocity of being; error is straying, as being other to the origin; finite being, as other to the origin, comes to be astray. But being astray, means there is a way; and perhaps many ways that are on the way. What I call counterfeit doubling opens perplexity about an original not counterfeit, perplexity unremitting in the measure of the enigma of that original. Heidegger must be true, in some way, to say truly that every epoch is in error. If not, his statement raises suspicions of being a post-metaphysical cousin of the chant of the Wicked Sisters of Destiny in *Macbeth:* "fair is foul, and foul is fair." (Nietzsche has a related difficulty when he tries to say truly: "All is false.") It is important that with Anaximander, to be [as finite] is to be in injustice, relative to the origin, *to apeiron*. This is to subscribe to the ontological guilt, if not evil, of the finite being, and its usurping "to be." Nor is this so very far from Levinas and his *la mal de l'être;* nor from the different forms of "better not to be" we find in Schopenhauer and Nietzsche.[7] It is to lack the affirmation of the good of the "to be," and the thought of the origin as releasing the finite "to be" into its own ontological good. This issue will come back.

To return again directly to mimesis: "correspondence" need not be defined by a fixed one-to-one correlation of univocal image to univocal original; it can be understood to point to hidden reserves, in relation to the appeal and response of truth in the co-responding that takes form in the communicative between. As being is plurivocal, so also is the promise of being true. Heidegger is quite *dualistic,* relative to this plurivocal character of being true. Obsessively, he returns to the doublet of *orthotes* and *alētheia,* in furtherance

6. Der Spruch des Anaximander," *GA,* 5: 338; "The Anaximander Fragment," *Early Greek Thinking,* trans. F. A. Capuzzi and D. Krell (New York: Harper and Row, 1984), 27.

7. There is also an afterlive of Anaximander in Hegel's view of the evil of finite particularity in its logico-ontological necessitation. See *BHD,* chapter 4.

of his more correct view of a more primal "being true" than correctness or correspondence. But there are a plurality of different ways of being true, depending on whether the univocal, equivocal, dialectical and metaxological sense of being is to the fore. I have given a fuller account of this plurivocity in *Being and the Between* (chapter 13). What the original disclosure and opening betokens asks to be articulated in terms of the metaxological between rather than simply in terms of our baptizing it with a name such as "Open." Otherwise, we find it hard to get beyond a kind of indeterminate gesturing towards what is more original, coupled with fear of determinacy, since determinacy seems again to chain us to that derivative correctness, away from which we strain to move. The philosopher must point the way from the derivative to the original, but it is also his vocation to find ways of express mindfulness that articulate the meaning of what is multiply in play *between* the original and the derivative.

The theme Heidegger stresses most often in Plato is that of *eidos,* or Idea. What of dialogue? What of "dialectic," and not at all in a modern idealistic sense? What of the differences of kinds, their otherness, and their weaving together and being carded? What of the question of a "unity" beyond the *eidē,* a "unity" which holds the kinds together? What of a sense of the "not" which is not identical with the "not" distinguishing kinds? What of eros and mania? What of the Good beyond being? Not enough of these—to put it charitably. The Good—all but a mere utility! Come now.

This monoeidetic obsession with *eidos* has repercussions for a related reduction of creation to making: in this view, *eidē* are possibilities that are be actualized, as form is imposed on matter. Heidegger seeks another sense of creation to this making, and rightly. But he pours all previous concepts of "creation" into the mold of this "making," and hence they must fail by contrast with his claim to fidelity to the more original conception. I am not saying you will find this conception in Plato, but Heidegger is disingenuous in molding all forms of creation to this form of "making." Heidegger wants to heed, rightly, the difference of the "what" it is, and the "that it is," and *eidos* can mask the "that it is," in seeming to comprehend it. This is related to Parmenides' *"esti."* I would relate this to our "yes" towards the "to be," an ontologically affirming "yes" that the great art work can offer. A creation more original than making refers to the bringing to be of the "that it is," and of possibility and actuality as more determinately defined. This would refer us not just to creation as the origination of form and matter, possibility and actualization, but to a radical possibilizing source more original than creation itself.

Be that as it may, and I must say more,[8] we could state the matter not quite in Heidegger's terms, if a different attention were given to the *between.*

---

8. See *BB,* chapter 6 on "Origin," and chapter 7 on "Creation"; also my "Hyperbolic Thoughts: On Creation and Nothing." I speak of different senses of transcendence in the next chapter.

Plato does not give us in all explicitness a philosophy of the metaxu, but it is at work, as we see especially when eros is overt. Taking the between differently, *eidos* could be thought otherwise than in crude dualistic terms. To say the least, the self-surpassing of eros, as well as the surplus power of mania, would make us balk at thinking of Plato too simplistically under any rubric of "logocentrism." This would be a univocalizing reduction of Plato's plurivocity. The bind of logos and *technē* is important for Heidegger, given his claim that the traditional sense of logos has its roots in *technē*.[9] We know how the interpretation of Aristotle's *Nichomachean Ethics* shaped decisively the younger Heidegger, and how the place of *technē* is important, relative to *poiēsis, praxis, phronēsis, epistēmē, theōria* and so on. And while the role of *technē* is obviously very important in Plato, there is more there, as there is in Aristotle. But does not Heidegger render us a kind of "Aristotelianized" Plato (the dualistic theory of ideas),[10] as well as an Aristotelianized angle with respect to *technē* and "creation": essence imposed on existence, as form on matter; "creation" bringing possible form to be as this instance: *eidos* as eternal possibility made matter, as *eidos* here present in informed being? If one forgets the between, of course, the whole thing becomes unintelligible. Who forgets it? Plato? I think not. Aristotle? I am not sure. But does Heidegger effect *his own* univocalization while claiming to detect in them the crimping univocity of a more "ontic" presence?

If a logos of univocity determines the intelligibility of the "first" beginning, of course it must obscure the more primal coming to be of creation. Logic and *technē*, derivative from a more primal origin, represented by the art work, take over the between and determine the terms in which origination is thought. One agrees: this can happen, happens all the time. There is something more original than "ontic" presence and determinate manifestation, these being outcomes of a process of determining, more than all determinacy, perhaps even more original than the interplay of presence and absence, of manifestation and hiddenness. More original in this sense: the play of presence and absence, manifestation and reserve happens in the between, but what gives the between to be is neither this interplay nor what eventuates in it. What gives the between is not the between, and even less what eventuates in it, nor the forms of relativity that come to be there. This other source is the origin. As other, it cannot be reduced to the between, the relativities and

---

9. This is hinted at where the instrumentality of equipment is coupled with the form-matter structure, and creation (ex nihilo), obviously not a Platonic notion, is itself assimilated to *technē* (*OWA*, 660).

10. Gadamer makes a somewhat similar point, as well as suggesting that Heidegger never quite got the hang of Plato. *Heidegger's Ways* (Albany: State University of New York Press, 1995), chapter 8. See also Stanley Rosen, *The Question of Being* (New Haven: Yale University Press, 1994), where Heidegger's Aristotelianized Plato is powerfully criticized. Heidegger expends much attention on Aristotle in his discussion of Plato's *Sophist*.

beings within it; and yet as thinkers what we have of mindfulness of that origin comes to us from our being within the between. We must pursue, in and through the between, some sense of this exceeding origin as other. There are different ways to this, of which great art may be one. But the determinate beings and relations must have about them something exceeding determination. Something of the overdeterminacy of the origin as other is communicated in the overdeterminacy of the happening of the between, as well as singular happenings in it that tell of transcendence in a sense excessive to human self-transcendence.

This last point is important, since if the between is univocalized as a Platonic "this world" over against that "other world" of a higher eidetic univocity, we fall all too easily under the spell of Nietzsche's denunciation of the transcendence of the "afterworldsmen." We fall under the spell only because something in us is already hollow enough to fall under hypnosis. We believe we have woken from sleep, but what if we have fallen into a deeper sleep whose dreams mimic wakefulness? Nietzsche's denunciation of "Plato" makes it harder for us to recover a fuller sense of the meaning of transcendence, since transcendence as other, and indeed as higher, seems to be eclipsed in the hubristic overreaching of human self-transcending, itself making its claim on the highest.

Heidegger felt the temptation of the latter, more, he succumbed to it; and even though, after his political disgrace, he became less comfortable with it, his equivocation relative to transcendence as other was never resolved. Could one say that the call of the earth, *Erde,* as a Chthonic origin, held him in an enchantment? He saw well enough the dissembling of the equivocity in "The Origin of the Work of Art"; but the enchantments of equivocity were perhaps preferable to him than the fate of tyrannous univocity, namely, the abandonment of the earth by gods. We are still within the ring of his *sacral politics.* Transcendence *above* was barred—Nietzsche's spell to counter Plato. But transcendence *below*—allowed by Nietzsche's new bewitchment—comes forth from the immanences of the earth, rising up through its singular manifestations, such as the great poet, or the great political leader, or the great thinker of being: Hölderlin, Hitler, Heidegger. This trinity seems to prepare or make an abode for more ultimate transcendence in human self-transcendence in immanence.[11] But have we not learned too well from understanding Schopenhauer differently that, without ethical and religious discernment, from that ground under the underground monsters can spring forth—monsters that mock and malign the unsuspecting Sabbaths of the earth?

Some have claimed that Heidegger's politics were essentially Platonic: philosophers must rule. There is a family resemblance; and there is the fact

---

11. On this, see my *BHD,* chapter 1. What is at play here is also related to what I call erotic sovereignty. More on this later.

that the three classes in Plato's *Republic* seem mirrored in Heidegger's three forms of service in his *Rektoratsrede: Arbeitsdienst, Wehrdienst, Wissensdienst.*[12] But far more important is the fact that Plato's ethical-metaphysical concerns come from a different spiritual world. I find nothing comparable in Heidegger to Plato's discernment concerning the problem of the tyrant, nothing like the Good *epékeina tēs ousias,* nothing like the excessive transcendence of the Good in the dimension of height, and as other to human self-transcendence. All of these significantly temper the temptation to hubristic will to power of erotic sovereignty.[13]

Look even at the "sovereignty" of the divine demiurgy in the *Timaeus.* There is some conformity to Heidegger's claim: the Demiurge looks to the Ideas as paradigms to shape the chaos of matter into a cosmos; and indeed there is a geometry of the divine here which is inscribed in the material world itself. This might seems to anticipate the modern mathēsis of nature, and the image of God as the absolute geometer we find in Kepler and Galileo. Yet despite what looks like overlap, it is extremely important to note that the eikonic making of the world is not motivated by *geometry:* the Demiurge is motivated to create out of a desire to make the world the *most beautiful and good possible.* If I can transport back Pascal's terms, this is a matter of *finesse* and not geometry. In Plato's demiurgic making *geometry serves finesse.* And finesse concerns the discernment of what is most good and beautiful, and the ultimate "yes" to these.

Moreover, demiurgic making comes out of a communicative being that forms for the other, because the forming power is not jealous, or envious. In the *Timaeus* the descriptions we find of the cosmos made are not those of a univocal geometrical figure, but those bearing on a *beautiful work of art:* this is what a *cosmos* is. It is the *aesthetics of being,* rather than the geometrics, that are more ultimately motivating, more moving. The geometrics of being serve the aesthetics—aesthetics here understood with all the metaphysical and religious and ethical weight the "aesthetic" carried in the ancient ethos, not the evacuated "aestheticism" of post-Kantian culture. We cannot disjoin being and the good, as happens in the ethos of modernity: the aesthetics of being call us to appreciate the worthiness of being there, a worthiness to which we can return a celebrating and consenting "yes." Interestingly, this weight of the aesthetic is just what is in question in Heidegger's own claim to overcome "aesthetics." I do not say demiurgic making is the more primal creating, but I do insist on the finesse that exceeds any "ontic" geometrics, that exceeds the univocalizations of being to which geometry without finesse easily tends.

---

12. *Die Selbstbehauptung des deutschen Universitat* (2nd ed. Breslau, 1934), 115 f.; cited in V. Farias, *Heidegger and Nazism* (Philadelphia: Temple University Press, 1989), 104.

13. See *EB,* passim, but especially chapters 10 and 15 on erotic sovereignty.

Heidegger and Transcendental Origins: Imagination and Coming Back to the Between

The theme of original being binds Platonic thought to transcendental thinking in Kant and post-Kantians; and even though a "Copernican Revolution" is claimed with respect to Plato, Platonic themes continue to reemerge in post-Kantian thought. Heidegger appears far less singular when placed in the context of this long concern with original being, and not now seen as merely reductive to ontic determinacy, either in pre-Kantian or post-Kantian thought. He seems singular in returning to a putative pre-Platonic origin to rethink a quasi-"transcendental origin" of a pre-modern sort in a modern/postmodern context: an origin before the origin in Plato; an origin beyond the origin of transcendental self in Kant. He does claim to think the otherness of the origin in more radical terms than the others. Nevertheless, his putative radicality puts him into deep kinship with those he seems to want to surpass: surpass by not surpassing them "metaphysically," but by being other again to "metaphysics."

Heidegger's engagement with Kant is again very diverse, and my remarks primarily bear on how different strands point us back to the between and the thought of origin there. I will mention below Heidegger's views of Kant's aesthetics with reference to Schopenhauer and Nietzsche. In his *Kantbuch* his desire to break with all "subjectivism" is clear. One cannot forget his involvement and eventual break with Husserl: despite his phenomenological "apprenticeship" with Husserl, his early involvement with the question of being, as stretching back into the medievals and the ancients, already contains seeds which must flower into uneasiness with transcendental subjectivity. Husserl's belief that Heidegger had not really gotten beyond the natural attitude, being too infected with a "realistic" side, psychologism, "transcendental anthropologism," reflects, I think, Husserl's own enchantment with transcendental philosophy more than Heidegger's defect of perspicuity.[14] Phenomenology is understood as concerned with the regress *(Rückgang)* to consciousness under the guidance of the question of being. Heidegger always had the metaphysical tradition, ancient and medieval too deeply in his bones not to know that the turn to the self in modern thought, radicalized in transcendental philosophy, could not really do justice to the "is" of the "I."[15] Thus his remark in *Being*

---

14. Yet perhaps in at least the younger Heidegger, there is too much of submission to the view that something "revolutionary" happens with Kant's transcendental philosophy. Of course, that "Copernican revolution" that is not quite Copernican, since it fails to be heliocentric. On this point Plato is the revolutionary, in the exact sense of seeking to revolve the soul, turning it up in the direction of the Sun.

15. See Heidegger's "Mein Weg in die Phänomenologie," *Zur Sache des Denkens* (Tübingen: Max Niemeyer, 1969), 81–90; "My Way to Phenomenology," *On Time and Being*, Joan Stambaugh (New York: Harper and Row, 1972), 74–82. We note his early interest in the question of

and Time on the *cogito ergo sum:* the "is" of the "I am" remains ontologically enigmatic. This is related to the issue of inward otherness. A strong voluntaristic side has been pointed out in the earlier Heidegger, from the stress on resoluteness in *Being and Time,* to the self-assertion of the German university and a people in his *Rektoratsrede,* to his involvement with Nietzsche and the will to power of modern subjectivism. His dialogue with Hölderlin and his granting of the letting be of poetic saying turned him from *that* I. One senses that the turn was equivocal in its success in release from the self-willing self. The enigma of the I in its inward otherness is mixed in with a complex voluntarism in the German tradition from Leibniz, and that we have seen in Kant and his successors. While Heidegger saw more lucidly than these successors the urgency of turning from any imperialism over the otherness of being, we still have to ask to what extent the turn is more an equivocal promise than a truly delivered release.

In his *Kantbuch* we might see an effort to come to terms with the issue of origin in relation to transcendental imagination.[16] This book has been the object of controversy. I think of Cassirer's claim that Heidegger "usurps" Kant. If one were to do something similar to Heidegger himself to wrestle with his studied equivocation, Heideggerians would be instantly up in arms. But, accurate to Kant or not, one has to take seriously Heidegger's philosophical engagement with the *Sache selbst.* The claim is generally: Kant approaches transcendental imagination as primary, the root of the two stems of understanding and sensibility. Moreover, in productive imagination we approach a power at the edge of determinate intelligibility (Heidegger does quite not put it thus). If imagination is productive, it is the forming power and not the form, a prior energy of articulation never exhausted by any determinate articulation. If so, there is something always categorially unmastered about it; as source of origination, the productive imagination points to an inward otherness which resists categorial

---

being from Aristotle (mediated through Brentano, though one notices the mention of Carl Braig and ontology); this is coupled with a complex inheritance from Husserl of certain concerns of transcendental philosophy and its turn to the self, a complex inheritance evident in *Being and Time* in that the first question of being is approached through *Dasein* not the transcendental ego, and yet displacing some of the latter's possible latent ontological functions in a more worldly sense, making us also wonder if a certain privileging of "self" is never completely purged, or if this starting point is enmeshed in (masked) anthropologistic terms, so as to keep us from the full intimate strangeness of being. Fundamental ontology seems like transcendental philosophy turned to the question of being, and in that sense, it reconnects us with something of the ancient sense of "transcendental," as having to do with being itself in its ontological hypercategoriality. Heidegger would be neither modern nor ancient in wanting to have both: let us say, the inward otherness of the human being, and the otherness of being as something more primordial than any entity, including the human being; the belonging together of transcendental "inward otherness" and the hypercategorial ontological otherness of being itself.

16. *Kant und das Problem der Metaphysik* (Frankfurt: Klostermann, 1991), *GA,* 3; English trans. Richard Taft, *Kant and the Problem of Metaphysics* (Bloomington: Indiana University Press, 1990).

determination. Kant allegedly recoiled from the abyss he had opened up. We might put the issue: the originating ground of intelligibility and articulation seems itself to be beyond intelligibility in a categorial sense. Is not this part of the terror before unruly genius in the *Critique of Judgment:* genius, a favored power that is at the origin of form, is not itself a form; genius shows that the origin of determination is more like indeterminate, or overdeterminate power? Heidegger himself makes repeated swipes at genius as a mere subjectivistic puff of shallow post-Kantian aesthetics. In fact, the issue is more complex, and with far reaching ontological implications. Kant, far from being precursor of post-transcendental ontology, evades the ontological issues raised here.

I think the following point is important. Heidegger suggests an ontological interpretation to this original power, and connects it with time. If imagination and time are inseparable, what kind of origin does their originary power suggest? Is there an other origin to originary time? This is *not,* I think, what is at stake when Heidegger talks in a "transcendental-ontological" register of productive imagination and the release of pure time in his *Phenomenological Interpretation of Kant's Critique of Pure Reason.*[17] If there is this other origin, it would not entail a becoming of time, or a becoming in time, but a *coming to be of time itself.* Is there an other to time, as itself the possibilizing power of finite becoming? Is there an origin as other to time that possibilizes the coming to be of time as itself the possibilizing power of becoming? The ancients talked about eternity, and Heidegger dismisses this as the reduced presence-to-hand of the *nunc stans.* What I have just asked about could not be so characterized. It is not clear to me that Heidegger distinguished well enough between "coming to be" and "becoming," and understood well enough that the former suggests something more radically originative than the latter, and to which thinking in terms of time alone could not do justice, since the issue is just the coming to be of time itself. The point has a bearing on *creation* as an original *coming to be* and not just a temporal *becoming.*

An analogous point could be put in terms of original imagination, understood ontologically. One might say: it shows the energy of being that is coming to articulation out of the darkness of the abyssal ground in self. This might sound very Schellingian. If so, to speak thus would also signify an effort to

---

17. See *Phanomenologische Interpretation von Kants Kritik der reinen Vernunft, GA:* 25, 417–18: "The productive imagination is the root of the power *(Vermögen)* of subjectivity, it is the basic, ecstatic constitution of the subject, of Dasein itself. Insofar as out of itself, as has been shown, it releases pure time, and thus contains pure time in itself as far as the possibility is concerned, it is *the original temporality* and thus the radical power for ontological knowledge." I think this is not radical enough relative to the otherness of the root, and more original *being giving to be* of productive imagination itself. Or in terms I sometimes use: our original power in its inward otherness is given to be by an other origin, relative to which the language of temporality raises hesitations, since temporality too is given to be, and hence not absolutely original. The later Heidegger did come to appreciate something of this being given to be.

overcome the subjectivism that transcendental philosophy always risks, but within the context of an immanent development of transcendental philosophy itself. The conditions of the possibility of knowing show the indispensability of transcendental imagination, not simply as a subjective epistemological power, but as the articulation of the power of the "to be," in and through "self." Heidegger, like many thinkers engaged with transcendental philosophy, is intent on a sense of prior unity or synthesis that is not the derivative synthesis which joins together subject and object. The latter is a derivative determination, and to start with it risks being too late for the origin. One can make a derivative synthesis of subject and object, but a thorough consideration of the relation of subject and object, recalls one to a more primordial, presupposed sense of "synthesis." This primordial synthesis cannot be a static unity; it must be an originating source; it must be like the transcendental imagination which, as a unifying power, gives rise to subsequent multiplicities within which we situate the subject-object split, or relation.

Note transcendental imagination is not floating in a void; it is rather the place in the "subject" where, as it were, the under-ground stream of being as original breaks surface. Transcendental imagination as ontological is itself an expression of the articulating energy of being that comes out of the darkness of the ultimate origin into the light of articulate selfhood. It is precisely this fact that allows us to misinterpret it, and give it simply a subjectivistic interpretation. What has emerged into subjective articulation gives the "self" its being for itself, and so we take "self" as a self-subsistent power. It is no such thing. This power is a flower of the ontological power of being. We forget that it has *come to be,* and hence forget that in its being for itself something is communicated of the more ultimate origin, that now, in turn, can become doubly forgotten.

I would stress the deep structural similarities in the mode of regressive procedure we find in Kant, Schelling, Hegel, Schopenhauer, and Nietzsche: the given, everyday world offered to us is articulated in terms of "subject" and "object," but this articulation is not the last word, or the first: this very determinate articulation points back to its own origin in a power what cannot be encapsulated in terms of "subject" or "object." Relative to this determinate difference, the origin is transobjective and transsubjective. Among the idealists, the tendency is to describe this origin in terms primarily borrowed from the "subject" side of this split. Granting complexities, the transdeterminate, the overdeterminate origin is the "transsubject" that includes in its "hyperunity," or "hypounity," the subject-object relation. Recall only the post-transcendental Spinozism of Hegel where the one substance becomes absolute subject, itself not "merely" subjective or objective, but both and more.[18]

18. I say nothing here of the defect of this way of thinking the origin which, because it lacks thought about the agapeic origin, cannot do justice to the giving of being as genuinely other to the origin. See *BB,* chapters 6 and 7, for instance.

Kant hesitated to think this issue through to any absolute unity, remaining in the split between subject and object: so he was, as he said, both transcendental idealist, empirical realist. This doubleness, or remaining in the split, was a defect for the idealists, but it could be given a more positive interpretation as a fidelity to the between, though not philosophically self-conscious as such. I think it is the hint of this possibility in Kant that still attracts many to him. I think it attracted Heidegger, and in some ways reflects his own philosophical strategies. And yet if we are to think origin as demanded by transcendental philosophy, we cannot just canonize the split, and will have to run the risk associated with the idealistic reconfiguration of the between as the medium of the so-called absolute's fulfilled self-mediation: run the risk, ask again about origin, but avoid the ruin that is idealism's counterfeit completion.

The momentum of Kant's thought is to pass further along the "subject" side of considerations. We are brought to the recalcitrant inward otherness, be it in Schelling's ground beyond consciousness, or in Schopenhauer's and Nietzsche's will. If there is an ultimate origin, it cannot entirely yield to either a subjectivistic or objectivistic understanding, putting aside the fact that the subjectivistic legacy has not been entirely shaken off. In all cases, the ultimate origin is beyond the subject-object split, though this split, and their relation is communicated by that origin. Hegel is the odd man out here, in that the other thinkers conclude that the origin is other to thought thinking *itself.* I would say also that the being of the between comes to be as originated relative to an origin that is releasing of finitude in a way not evident in these thinkers.

Heidegger follows a not dissimilar strategy but the result is more far reaching than in the other post-Kantians, because he perceives, with Schelling, that the question of origin cannot be divorced from the most archaic perplexity of the philosophical tradition: Why being and not nothing? First, Heidegger genuinely exploits the fact that Kant's transcendental philosophy is occasioned by the problematic status of metaphysics as a science; he surmises some secret ontological implications of transcendental philosophy, even if not known self-consciously by Kant himself. Secondly, by this move he potentially reopens the philosophical tradition in a way that transcendental philosophy can threaten to close. Think again of the Kantian rhetoric of *revolution,* and the implication of rupture with the past as merely dogmatic metaphysics. The scope of the question of the philosophical *heritage* is widened by Heidegger by his interrogation of being as origin, origin given to the tradition but also forgotten. Finally, if the prior "unity" is spoken of in terms of being, the break with transcendental philosophy concerns present and future, as well as the past, and as I think, it must also bring the question of time itself into question. I mean here too the question of *the other of time,* what the premoderns called "eternity." The transcendental radicalization of subjectivity is tempted with the forgetfulness of being, but if transcendental possibilizing, be it of imagination, or some other power(s), must be interpreted ontologically, the question of being in its *otherness* must arise again, and in the very inward otherness that transcendental reflection reveals at its utmost limit of reflection. The power of being in the self as origin opens towards the power of being as originally other to us, and as communicative in the between of the ultimate origin.

Imagination itself, I would argue, is itself a *threshold power,* a intermediating power that asks us to think, both the irreducible doubleness *between* the self as origin and the ultimate origin, and their communication in the coming to be of that between.[19] There are systematic pointers towards the question of origin in *Being and Time* in the claim that subject and object *already belong* together. The togetherness of the two does not even require the arcane philosophical strategy of transcendental regress: world is always and already constituted by this togetherness. The spontaneous self-transcending of the human being, in its being in the world, is already *with* being. This "being with being" (I do not mean Heidegger's own *Mitsein*) is more basic than the subsequent reflective distancings of subject and object: these are derivations from the already articulated togetherness. Insisting on the ontological significance of this helps us bypass the sterile impasse of modern subjectivism, itself a sign of the attenuation of our more elemental intimacy with being. An abstracted self, uprooted from being, faces down a dimmed down object, flattened in its thereness and made disposable for calculative dominion. If the poet names this original intimacy, the philosopher has to think it again.

In sum: one might claim that the question of original being can be approached from the point of view of the regress to transcendental innerness; or from the point of view of egress into the things themselves with which we dwell in a worldly way. Just as the regress has to be freed from a wrong subjectivism, no matter how elevated its transcendental terms, so the egress has to be rescued from a levelling objectification of being in the world. Original selving must be restored to its ontological grounding; things must be recharged with their original density. This double restoration of self and other asks also for a restoring finesse for their more original relativity, a finesse that may allow some discernment of the origin as giving the relativity that gives the self its originality and things their enigmatic thereness. All this asks us to think the between as the space of plurivocal intermediation of self and other, as a happening of being, of the interplay of beings there, of the singular participation of the human being in this happening; asks us to think, even more radically of the origin of the between which is more than this happening or interplay or singular participation. Heidegger's reflection in "The Origin of the Work of Art" can be seen to participate in that task.

---

19. See my "Religious Imagination and the Counterfeit Doubles of God," *Louvain Studies,* 27:3 (Fall 2002), 280–305. See also the discussion of imagination, aesthetic and religious, in *Philosophy and Its Others,* 83 ff., 111 ff.

HEIDEGGER AND DIALECTIC ORIGINS: ART EXCEEDING HEGEL'S SPECULATIVE SELF-MEDIATION

Heidegger engages Hegel in many places, in *Being and Time,* for instance, extensively with regard Hegel's concept of experience in the *Phenomenology,* less extensively but no less intensively in a variety of remarks in *Identity and Difference.* There is a proximity and a genuine distance: proximity in that each takes the tradition of philosophy with seriousness, even as they think philosophy is more than historical erudition, but an address of the matter itself; distance in that Heidegger does see something about origin that Hegel does not. There is Heidegger's qualified endorsement of Hegel's thesis about the end of art in "The Origin of the Art Work." Hegel's judgment remains in force, though what Heidegger intends by this is different than Hegel, and I think connected with a different sense of origin as self-concealing in its unconcealing. It is noteworthy that in his book on Nietzsche, Hegel's *Lectures on Aesthetics* do not figure prominently in the same way that so many other figures in the history of reflection on art do, such as Plato and Kant. There is much that might be said, but I will connect what I see as Heidegger's sense of the self-concealing origin with this issue of the future of art, and its incognito religious significance.

If Heidegger does seek the between, one might say Hegel does too, but the qualification is: in the latter, we find the speculative self-mediation of the between, in the former, the happening of the between cannot be entirely self-mediated. This follows from a realization of the defect of transcendental philosophy, which is not rectified by speculative idealism, but camouflaged by being transported into a different register. The absolute is still modelled on transcendental subjectivity, thought this now is the One that includes in itself subject-object (S-O): it is Subject (Subject-Object), S(S-O). The determinate difference of subject and object is the self-differentiation of the more absolute subject. The between becomes here the self-differentiation of this One and the mediated self-return via the self-unfolding of its own differences and their being gathered together in the whole that is the true result and is the true. This self-differentiation, I think, does not do justice to the givenness of finitude as finite. There is another difference that is not the speculative ruse of the absolute emerging from initial indefiniteness and passing towards its full self-determination. The difference as difference points to a different origin, something more than determination, but also more than self-determination.

In Heidegger's discussion in *Identity and Difference*[20] his attitude to Hegel as onto-theo-logic emerges clearly. I do not like the blanketing use of "onto-theo-logic" to describe the Western tradition, but it does have its point relative

20. *Identitat und Differenz* (Pfullingen: Verlag Gunther Neske, 1957); English trans. Joan Stambaugh, *Identity and Difference* (New York: Harper and Row, 1969).

to the continued lives and afterlives of Aristotle's god of thought thinking itself that receives its most ambitious resurrection in Hegel's speculative system. This too is "God" as *causa sui:* absolute self-determination. I am in agreement with the *question* put to this god by Heidegger. (Remember, however, a question I posed about "language languaging language" in the last chapter, pp. 203–4.) I would ask if this philosophical god is a counterfeit double of God—all the more difficult a question in Hegel's case, since he claims to give us a philosophical God that does essential justice to everything essential in the God of the religions, especially Christianity. I cannot pursue the point here, though one must consider if Hegel's god is a counterfeit double of God,[21] a question I have pursued elsewhere. But the same question and similar misgiving arise in my mind about Heidegger himself. The sometimes evasive equivocality of Heidegger allows him often to play both side of the street: conservative and revolutionary; destroyer and creator; godless and more godly than the godly; willful and yet more yielding to ultimacy than St. Joseph of Cupertino. Here too with the divine. One senses a mixture of willingness and lacerated lostness, an astonishing gentleness and a furious rage. Perhaps one cannot ask for more with such an ultimately worthy matter of thought. And yet the God beyond the whole possibilizes a different release.

Heidegger's origin still remains very indeterminate. Is it erotic, is it agapeic, is it manic? Is it a counterfeit double of God? Given that many early admirers were theologians, does it mimic God? Is it *Moira,* or destiny? Above gods and mortals, as in Greece? But if like *Moira,* what of *Dikē?* Is it blind? If it gives, how give? For itself? For what is other? Gives as itself good? As beyond good and evil? If beyond good and evil, how beyond? As evil beyond good and evil? As good? As like *Geist,* or Will? If not good, why then for us the exhortation to *Gelassenheit?* Does not "letting be" seem to imply the *worthiness* of being? How well does Heidegger do in articulating this? If the origin is agapeic, why all the talk about *polemos?* Too Greek? And remotely derived from a too scholastic, perhaps even Christian division between Athens and Jerusalem? If so, must one not cut oneself off from some extraordinary thoughts? What if the other origin, is neither Greek nor Jew? Why then does Heidegger's origin have a preference for Greece and Germany as its elected emissaries? Why not Rome? Too instrumental? Would not Hegel agree: Roman religion as the religion of expediency, or "external purposiveness"? Judea? Too much transcendence as other? Too much Christian servility? Would not Nietzsche agree and even Hegel, the modern "Christian" systematizer?

Heidegger seems captivated by the metaphor of the circle, captivating to Hegel as much as to Parmenides. Is the origin of the between an origin beyond the circular whole, if the openness of the between points beyond Par-

21. See my *Hegel's God: A Counterfeit Double?*

menides, not Parmenides before the tradition, but beyond Parmenides and Plato? Beyond demiurgic making and the circular self-mediating whole, and beyond the fourfold of earth, sky, mortals, gods? Moving us towards creation *ex nihilo,* and thoughts not quite found in Athens or Hellenized Germany? But think even of the majestic Roman Pantheon, the building where Rome gathered all the gods of the peoples, later again a space of Christian worship. In the Pantheon the dome's diameter is the same as the height of the overall building, and the dome's radius equals the height of the ways. Thus if the circumference of the dome were extended, it would constitute a perfect sphere which touched the exact centre of the floor.[22] If one stands on that floor, one is not enclosed in any self-contained space, for the opening in the roof, itself circular, is receptive to *the sky beyond the sphere.* The opening lets in the heavens beyond, as they offer sun or rain. This roof open to the sky beyond, so to say, images a pagan sphere that cannot close the circle but like a porous between points to the God beyond the whole, and beyond Heidegger's fourfold. But this God beyond the whole is not just pagan.

What of Hegel's claim that the true is the whole? But consider how for Hegel being is an empty beginning, the most universal and deficient thought determination. This is not the happening of being, and Heidegger has the right of it here. Heidegger is a guardian of astonishment before the "that it is at all" of being.[23] Something full, rich, overdetermined is given in original astonishment at the given happening of being. This is not impoverished immediacy, merely implicit until the dialectical process proceeds further in its self-becoming. There is a logic of self-becoming in Hegel, not a sense which connects radical origin with *coming to be at all.* Heidegger's thought of the origin evinces a mindful rapport with this overdetermination: not indeterminate as merely indefinite but too much, in excess of univocal determination rather than defective in such determinations. Hence the move from this overdeterminate origin cannot be a process towards its self-completion. If origin shows itself in the determinate happenings of the between, there is also something to it that remains in reserve, not only as too much, but as other to those finite determinations that are happenings of being in the between. The origin is not dialectically self-mediating but other. The origin may show itself, but as showing itself it is also self-concealing, indeed for Heidegger doubly concealing, since this self-concealing itself gets concealed by the showing itself, and by the focussing of our attention on what has come into manifestation, rather than on the happening of manifestation as such, and what withdraws into hiddenness even in this happening.

---

22. Renee Ryan insightfully drew my attention to this character of the Pantheon in Rome. John Hymers kept us straight with the calculations.

23. On astonishment as agapeic, perplexity as erotic, and curiosity as tied to determinate cognition, see *Being and the Between,* chapter 1.

If Hegel's speculative logic claims the *Aufhebung* of art and religion into philosophy, this *Aufhebung* is dictated by a view of origin as completely mediating what in the beginning is hidden and merely implicit, as we saw in Hegel's move from symbolic to classical to romantic. This cannot be true, if something excessive to dialectical self-mediation emerges in self-mediation itself, and the infinite inwardness of the romantic. Heidegger does not put it this way, but this inward otherness is certainly a breaking point which asks post-Hegelians to think the other of thought thinking itself. This also means: thinking the other of will willing itself. Heidegger became more aware that the momentum of modern subjectivity leads not just to a rational culmination in Hegel's thought thinking thought, but to a "voluntaristic" acme in Nietzsche's will to power, to will willing will, one might say. If Heidegger was earlier captive to this will willing will in the self-affirming will that decides for itself and chooses itself, he came to later awareness of a defect of this, I would say, as an ontological defection from the full ontological promise of the between, and the human being as an intermediate. The power of art, and poetry in particular, is very important here. The origin cannot be will willing will: something more is given, more like an inspiration communicated from the other; and something more is asked of us, more like the *wooing* that awaits the gift of the gracing word.

In that Heidegger saw this, he has more insight to offer on a point I made before about Hegel: namely, that instrumental *Verstand* and speculative *Vernunft* are too close for comfort, too close for the second to be the releasing and released mindfulness that metaphysics should foster. I mean both are forms of the self-mediating mind, one more instrumental, the other claiming speculative autonomy. In fact, the *same logic* is at work in each: self-determining mind in and through the other: thought thinking itself, and hence not released to the other in a different freedom, or releasing the other into a different creation. Heidegger does not put the point as I do, but the free release of great art always exceeds this speculative logic. I would add that the elemental practice of being religious does too.

Each of these is as little amenable to the speculative *Aufhebung* as the instrumental appropriation, and I mean this regardless of the way Hegelians will try to make the *Aufhebung* innocuous by claiming that art and religion are "preserved." That is *not* the point at issue. What is thus preserved is *not* the most basic matter in question. The philosophical deficiency of this strategy is that it does not understand that more is at play in the situation than can be answered for by any such speculative *Aufhebung* and its dialectical preservation of "otherness." By insisting on talking in that way, we are insisting on missing the point, namely, that there is a release of mindfulness in being aesthetic and being religious that is in communication with the philosophical release of mindfulness, but this communication is not a matter of speculative dialectic. This release has to do with the excess of the origin. The community of the three is to be thought metaxologically rather than dialectically.

Again Heidegger does not put the point that way, but his "suspension" of judgment about Hegel's "end of art" thesis might be seen as pointing towards this different community, where the end as Hegel sees it is now connected with the defection from the deeper sense of origin that a long entrenched orientation to being, be it univocal or dialectical, has simply passed over. Rethinking the other origin entails the reminder of that other origin, and in that reminding, the power of great poetry stands as indispensable. The issue here is not one of historical and cultural self-becoming; it concerns a defection from ontological and metaphysical mindfulness of what is at play in the between and the tokens of the origin communicated there. Science, technology, the will to univocity, be it human reason's will to itself alone, or human will willing itself, all contribute to the metaphysical amnesia of what is there. One might say we are successful and powerful only because we are profoundly superficial. The poet is one who finds a different profundity in and through the surfaces of the between. Heidegger could be more forthright that we must not allow "being religious" also to fall into a fugue state. Heidegger wavers here. We must be more honest about the religious, and the community of the religious and the artistic.

Thus Heidegger's praise for Schelling should be no surprise: he foundered in his thought but there was something superior in his failure than in Hegel's success. The darkness of the night is not here the same darkness that it is for Hegel's absolute knowing: the night in which all cows are black. There are other ways to be in the night, some of which, say, awaken eros. Of course, it is with respect to Hölderlin, and the inaugural power of the poet, that "being religious" comes again. The poet is the namer of the holy. This is a sacred mission. One must not forget this when the end of art is broached. One of the most important considerations here is to remember that everything turns upon being religious. We can easily equivocate on this if we lack the finesse to discern the vocation of the poet. Heidegger was not always as forthcoming about "being religious" as one would like. Hegel might seems less equivocal in bringing art, religion and philosophy together in absolute spirit. But being less equivocal thus is itself equivocal, even more equivocal, if the releasing power of art and religion is reconfigured in terms of a logic of speculative self-mediation. And even more equivocal again, if I am right that Hegel's philosophy finally gives us a counterfeit double of God while claiming a higher speculative fidelity to the absolute original.

Heidegger is closer to both Hölderlin and Schelling, Hegel's friends, and rightly so. One might wonder if he could be a *fourth* "virtual signatory" of that symptomatic fragment: "Earliest system-program of German Idealism" (Marx and Nietzsche might be other virtual endorsers, at least of some lines in it). Except, of course, the focus on ethics in this fragment, also called *eine Ethik* must give some pause, even if the emphases on the aesthetic, on radical creation, on a new mythology, are suggestive. Gadamer revealingly recounts Heidegger in a lecture reading from Schelling's *Freiheitsschrift:* "The *Angst* of life drives the creature from its center." Heidegger added: "Gentlemen, show me a single sentence out of Hegel's work that has such depth."[24]

Relate this *Angst* and being "driven out" to what, on a number of occasions, I called *the sweats*. Art and the sweats have much to do with the erotic origin, and with the night. Hegel's tart dismissal of Schelling is not with argument, but with a quip, perhaps cheap. But even if Schelling's absolute is the night in which all cows are black, we could still ask what sweats come on in that night? Kant did not want to sweat; Hegel seemed to want to sweat but then perks up, well that is done with now, and here we are, all high and dry: no sweat. After Schopenhauer, after Schelling, thinking faces into that night, the ground under the underground of the Cave, where the light of the sun seems not to reach. We face, so to say, the black sun, at the ontological opposite to Plato's bright sun. To face that black sun, to get out of that blackness, the bootstrapping power of Hegel's speculative dialectic looks like conceptual pretence: a shuffle that seems to move but does not move, where logic itself is the rational dream of motion that never gets from the terrible spot. The sweats are not just thought determinations, but the tremors of a shaking in which ontological foundations seem to tremble. To move dialectically from thought determination to thought determination as a therapy for these shakes is comic: conceptual calmness pretends it does not shake, and its intoxication with thought determinations is so intoxicated it mistakes its efforts to steady its shakes for absolute metaphysical sobriety. Is this logic, or a mad madness that thinks itself divine madness, or God's thoughts before the creation of nature and finite spirit? Who is dreaming this dream? Hegel? Thought thinking itself? Or a cunning reason over whose countenance can pass the protean face of the evil genius as much as the good God?

Though Heidegger resisted being situated in any post-Platonic heritage, he can be situated in this post-Hegelian inheritance that will not accept what Hegel wants to pass on, not just because Hegel's achievement is not granted (as with Schopenhauer), but because this achievement brings to mind what is lacking: the perfection reveals the defection. It is as if we see the metaphysical madness of a certain perfected metaphysics. (And is there not a kind of metaphysical madness in not being able to tell the difference between ourselves and God? At the opposite end of the spectrum, is there not an analogous metaphysical madness in our cybernetic age in not being able to tell the difference between ourselves and a computer?) Not only after Kant, but especially after Schelling, Schopenhauer, Nietzsche, we cannot evade this as a seri-

24. Gadamer, *Heidegger's Ways,* 163, also 116 (slightly differently recalled there: "the human being" is mentioned, not the "creature"). Gadamer rightly points out how it is Hölderlin alone who seems to win Heidegger's unqualified endorsement; with others, everything is more double-edged: a yes and a no. On Schelling, *Schellings Abhandlung über des Wesen der menschlichen Freiheit* (Tübingen: Niemeyer Verlag, 1971); *Schelling's Treatise on Human Freedom,* trans. Joan Stambaugh (Athens: Ohio University Press, 1985).

ous question. Metaphysics must call itself into question. This is its nature: to be a perplexity to itself. Aristotle implies our achievements renew their own extreme perplexity, even when we humans are successful. I think this is implied by the image of us being like bats in sunlight. To be as blind as a bat, as we are at the *heights,* means the black sun and the bright are sometimes hard to tell apart. Aquinas might approve (*ST,* I–II, q. 102, art 6, ad 1), in that he approved of Aristotle (*Meta,* Bk II, 1): the uncertain knowledge of higher things is better than the more certain knowledge of lower.

Hegel might endorse speculatively the dialectical coincidence of enlightenment and blindness, but he would reject any *excess* of the light so exceeding us that we are thrown back into the deepest perplexity about the sun's brightness or blackness. Hegel is again an odd man out if we think of Plato, Aristotle and Aquinas as granting a more challenging *equivocity* at what seems the togetherness of opposites, at the highest or deepest level of illumination or ignorance. This equivocity Hegel did not grant in the full measure of its power to make us sweat. Oddly, Heidegger has more in common with these other thinkers, putting aside his stylization of their thought as "metaphysics." I mean his heed to something like such a *constitutive equivocity* in our relation to what is most original or ultimate.

You say Hegel's image—the owl of Minerva taking flight at dusk—indicates something similar? Yes, but only equivocally, and against his more encompassing intention. At dusk the determinate outlines of happening are still somehow visible; and it is the *completed determinacy of day* that Hegel insists on; it is not the *constitutive equivocity between day and night, between the bright sun and the dark.* Hegel's owl sees things in outline, in logical form. Kierkegaard might say: silhouettes without thisness, essences without singularities, the "what" not the "that." What happens after the night darker than twilight falls: absolute night, night alone, *ab-solo?* The Hegelian owl will flutter against absolute night as a *contradictio in adjecto:* there can be no such thing; an absolute night cannot logically be; after all I see shadows moving. To talk about such a night is to talk about it as if it were meaningful; so some light is thrown on it and in it; ergo, absolute night cannot be. How else could I fly by night? But if logic is the realm of moving shadows—and Hegel admits as much—where are we? Are we in the keeping of the ether of God's thoughts before creation, or in Hades; and if the latter, is not Hegel's logic as much in the under-ground, and its dance of shades, as Schopenhauer's will, or Nietzsche's Dionysian origin? What does Heraclitus the Obscure brightly say? Dionysus is the same as Hades.

And one might further ask: Does not constitutive equivocity concern more the play of light and darkness, the astonishing chiaroscuro of being; concern the equivocity of finite being as a happening that is, but that yet might not be; concern whether this double play is dialectically determined to the teleological dominance of the one side of light, as if the other side were, as other to the light, just the light in its own otherness? But what is so logical about that? Would this not be a kind of *miracle,* if darkness is the self-othering of light? And why not then claim the opposite miracle, that light is the self-othering of darkness? Is this, in effect, not what, say, Schopenhauer does? But why chose one miracle rather than the other? Perhaps the miracle has to do with origin as giving creation as a coming to be, despite nothing. For is not the perplexity posed by "absolute night" also the issue of the nothing beyond determinate negation?[25] And why accept all this talk of absolute reason, or will, as if they threw light on one miracle or its inversion; while we then go on quickly to forget the miracle, or magic, of light othering itself as darkness, or darkness giving rise to light? Nietzsche, I surmise, had an intuition that there was something very strange here, and that this strangeness is more intimate to the heart of being than the logic of the idealist, be it "Platonic" or Hegelian. Nihilism, I would say, does not do away with the light but makes the light newly perplexing, newly strange, as if the day itself were a kind of night. The "idealists" will sing through the night, denying the logical possibility of what they are, in fact, enduring, and living through. And so a new instance of an old worry comes back to us: Is the hymn to the panlogist god just another form of whistling in the dark? Whistling, not only to allay the sweats, but in distraction from the enigma of coming to be, and being given to be at all, out of nothing?

Heidegger and Erotic Origins: The Polemos of Equivocal Being and Exceeding Will to Power

Much might be said of Heidegger's great engagement with Nietzsche, perhaps less about his seemingly non-relation to Schopenhauer, but my brief remarks will follow the above and focus on the erotic nature of the origin.

---

25. Will the owl's nocturnal eyes so long for determinate shape that it will give up thought in the black darkness and sit out the night? What if Schelling had already sharpened vision in the night in which all cows are black? Maybe he will be a better guide-bird of night. Hegel's *metaphor* was effective in demolishing Schelling in the eyes of many. Yet this is metaphor; we look for stronger logical argument; as argument it is derisory; it is not an argument; it is a debunking image, a sarcasm. And Hegel is supposed to establish everything by the labor of the concept! Where is the labor of the concept in this sarcasm? Of course, in a number of places Hegel accuses Schelling of being *abstract.* I wonder if Hegel is being droll. Given his own virtuosity with abstractions he fondly calls concrete, one thinks of those gestures of affection when one man gives another a *rough blow* to show how much he likes him. Perhaps what we see after Hegel is the dark night turned against Hegel, his light, one might speculate, generating its own other. His speculative categorization of night as light irritated others, determined others to name night *as* night, and to go into it. As if to cock a snout to self-certain reason and say: Perhaps there are more night things, things frightening and astonishing, in heaven, on earth, and under earth, than are dreamt of in your philosophy, Herr Hegel.

"Polemos is the father of all and the king of all. . . ." Thus Heraclitus again.[26] But note that when Heraclitus claims Dionysus is the same as Hades, he refers to the shameful parts, the phallus the Dionysian worshippers carry in procession, "besides themselves in mania *(mainontai)* and celebrating Lenaean rites" (Fr.15). The eros of the night is not far away.

Comparing Heidegger here with Schopenhauer and Nietzsche, his emphasis falls less directly on night as on what gives light, comes into the light. After all, he speaks of *Lichtung*, and *Offenheit*, and *Anwesenheit* (see "Das Ende der Philosophie und die Aufgabe des Denkens"). Yet his astonishment at this giving of light and the light given, and the concealing of the origin in its unconcealing, militates against any callow enlightenment. He shows some finesse for an elemental equivocity of being, itself inseparable from the creative power of the aesthetic, and the generative power of sources of being beyond univocal determination (see *Being and the Between,* chapter 3). The light given, the giving source, the mystery of this source, make the light itself strange. All of this has bearing on the erotic origin, as reflecting something of the desire to be in and through, and sometimes in spite of, the threat of not being that marks the happening of contingent finitude. Heidegger's feel for the equivocal polemos of being puts him in the same family of erotic origins. He struggled with ambiguities in his own understanding of the role of the creative person in that polemos, and sought to exceed the will to power as the acme of a metaphysics of subjectivity. Yet he remained close to Nietzsche, uncomfortably so, in that his own terms were not discerning enough concerning equivocal being and the erotic origin. In relation to Schopenhauer, Heidegger hides his own equivocity, as I now want to indicate.

Heidegger may speak, after Hölderlin, of the night of the world, the gods having fled. What eros for the gods in that night? What mania from the gods? One does not find much eros in Heidegger, though care, *Sorge* seems to function in partial analogy in human existence. And interesting study would be to ask about the interminglings of *poros* and *penia* in Heideggerian care, and further again what there is of the sleeping divine festivity that offered the original occasion of eros's conception in Diotima's account. Is there enough mindfulness of the divine porosity at the origins of our seeking being? I do not find the high festivity, by comparison with Nietzsche; and no irony, almost nothing of the divine playfulness of Plato. Perhaps this play has to do with a peace of being more divine than the polemos. And how much more would we warm to Heidegger, if he had a few ounces of Nietzsche's glorious mockery, especially self-mockery. Come to think of it, it is astonishing Heidegger picked up nothing of this from that other maestro in philosophy's self-mockery,

---

26. "*Polemos panton men patēr esti, panton de basileus, kai tous men theous edeixe tous de anthrōpous, tous men doulous epoiēse tous de eleuttherous.*" War is the father of all and the king of all, and some he shows as gods, others as men; some he makes slaves, others free. Heraclitus, fr. 53.

Kierkegaard, he from whom Heidegger picked up, took, and not always graciously, so much else. Yet there is a kind of erotic modulation to his sense of the origin in "The Origin of the Work of Art."

Suppose we say: the happening of the "to be" is inseparable from the anguish of the "not to be"; the will to life as desire to be is inseparable from the defect or defecit of being out of which the desire emerges; and both the happening and anguish, the desire and defecit, are themselves happenings that first live us before we live them, as if all originated by a metaphysical necessity, or a fate or a destiny. To whom could we attribute this line of thought? Answer: As much to Schopenhauer or Nietzsche as to Heidegger. Questions then: Is Heidegger as honest about the darkness of *eros turannos* as Schopenhauer? If one were a doctorandus, or a docent who knew nothing of Schopenhauer, and much of Heidegger, and proposed to speak of the dark origin and the theme of will-lessness, would one receive a failing grade for believing that one was near, or in, the Heideggerian homeland? If one were to say that the poet names the holy, and then went on to speak of the redemptive power of art and the saint (you might even speak of the holy, using the Latin *sanctus*), would you be forgiven for thinking that there is no discord between the one and the other? Who spoke about the *Sabbath* of the will? Was not the first Sabbath of being the day of rest from creation when the creation was seen by God as good, very good? Needless to say, if this is to name the holy, it is beyond polemos. Does not the Sabbath name the original *peace* of being?

Nothing is more striking than Heidegger's animus against Schopenhauer as a vulgarizer of Kant. He claims every interpretation of Kant's aesthetic disinterestedness is wrong, blaming Schopenhauer most of all for this. But why does his Eckhartian *Gelassenheit* not quite persuade us from listening to Schopenhauer's will-lessness with less animus? Willing wills will itself not to will. What delicious self-contradiction in this will to be released from will! But one can understand something of its why. "Voluntarism" becomes antivoluntaristic when it is struck by the dark horror of the *eros turannos,* and its temptation to evil will to power. This horror surfaces perhaps in less dissimulating form in Schopenhauer than in Heidegger. I mentioned before Schopenhauer's tendency to speak in rather streamlined dualisms about Plato and philosophical problems, wondering if this provided impetus to Nietzsche and then further to later thinkers also to stylize so the "tradition" in terms of such binary oppositions, now of course to be deconstructed. I find in Heidegger the same tendency to think in doublets: Being/beings, authentic/inauthentic, *orthotes/alētheia,* ontological/ontic, and so on. The deconstruction of the univocity of binary oppositions may itself fall foul of a new form of *equivocal univocity,* even as it presents itself as a renewal of equivocity beyond univocity. Such a pattern of double thinking can produce reversals as much in Heidegger (the famous *Kehre*), as in Schopenhauer and Nietzsche. Reversals from will willing itself to will-lessness (or will willing itself not to will) are not the peculiarity of the despised Schopenhauer.

One of the more dubious effects of this double thinking is evident in the not-so-hidden ingratitude in Heidegger's expressions of gratitude. Am I mistaken in divining a dissimulated superiority in his humble expressions of respect? Think of his use of the doublet: ontological and ontic. I, Heidegger, an ontological thinker, thank the others too ontic, others like Kierkegaard, religious thinker that he was. Do I ontologically usurp the merely ontic? Not I. I, Heidegger, seem to say almost exactly the same thing (say, on *Angst*) as Kierkegaard, but I say it wearing an ontological hat, while he a merely ontic hat. How superior or higher or deeper or more fundamental the same thing seems when you say it wearing an ontological hat! What one can say wearing a fundamental ontology hat is extraordinary when you compare it to the idle chatter babbled by those wearing merely ontic hats. Did I learn that trick from Kant? But I do not learn tricks from anyone. Kant's trick: I cannot quite catch big metaphysical fish using theoretical hooks, but look what I can catch when I use a practical, moral hook. I can catch freedom, immortality, even God. Hats and hooks, it's all in the name. Magic names. Bewitching names. Bewitchment, of course, is a religious category, and intimately tied up with the enchanting powers of counterfeit doubles.

What about Nietzsche's high noon? The polemos of equivocal being is here too, and the struggle of erotic origination in which self-transcending seeks to be its own origin, middle, and higher goal. At the meridian of Nietzschean day, the middle of high noon, I as original coincide with the origin as fate; there are no shadows between us: everything is middle, and there is no middle; everything is difference, and there is no difference. What then is the difference between the shadowless noon and the lightless night?

Recall an important point I made before, however: the shadows cast by the dark origin *only look like light,* but more "truly" they are shadows of darkness: their being true is their being false. This is a very important point to ponder following from Schopenhauer's erotic origin. I wonder if Nietzsche understood this point better than Heidegger. Why? Because Nietzsche tried to do more than gesture to an unthought origin. If the origin is thus erotic, true is false, and false is true, light is dark and dark is light. Thus the Weird Sisters, the Wicked Sisters of destiny, put it in *Macbeth:* "Fair is foul and foul is fair, Hover through the fog and filthy air." *Macbeth* is *the* play of the equivocity of being, and also of *evil daring or will* beyond good and evil.[27] Everything turns not only on the play of equivocity *in* the between, and indeed constitutive *of* the between, but of the good or evil of the origin of the between, and of the communication of that origin that appears to hover in the fog and

---

27. See "Sticky Evil: On *Macbeth* and the Karma of the Equivocal," in *God, Literature and Process Thought,* ed. Darren J. N. Middleton (Aldershot: Ashgate Publishing, 2002), 133–155; also my "Murdering Sleep: Macbeth and Shestov," in *The Tragic Discourse—Shestov and Fondane's Existential Thought,* ed. Ramona Fotiade (New York: Peter Lang, 2003). "Weird": an Old English word for fate or destiny.

filthy air. If there is not a fundamental good to that origin it is hard to justify the release of our amen to being. Then the hurly burly's never done, and the battle's lost even when it's won.

In the "Letter on Humanism" (*GA,* 9: 359; *LH,* 237), Heidegger speaks of evil as the "malice of rage" *(Bösartigen des Grimmes);* also of the not and nihilation; this is not due to no-saying; "nihilation unfolds essentially in Being itself, and not at all in the existence of man . . ." (*LH,* 238). He refers to Hegel and Schelling but does not here discuss their views of negation, and what might distinguish him from them. "The nihilating in Being is the essence of what I call the nothing. Hence because it thinks Being, thinking thinks the nothing" (*GA,* 9: 360; *LH,* 238). Very well, but the equivocation between good and evil, between the "yes" and the "no" is suspended in the silent homogeneity communicated by this sentence: "To healing Being first grants ascent into grace; to raging its compulsion to malignancy."[28] Being is the granting power in the case of grace, as it also is in the case of malignancy. How then distinguish the "yes" and the "no"; or since it is being that is at issue, the good of the "to be," and evil? "Silent homogenity?"—you say. Strange thing to say about such a thinker of difference! Heidegger, Deleuze says, "follows Duns Scotus and gives renewed splendor to the univocity of being."[29] Yet some such splendors are not always splendid. But surely it is self-evident that one would prefer the favor of grace to the rage of malice? Self-evident to common decency, yes; but if common decency is "merely" ontic, and the stress of circumstances brings on real polemos, I mean war, then some will be blinded to self-evident decency and the difference *ontologically* of grace and malignancy blurred. The so-called "ontological difference" will blur ontological difference, relative to the good of the "to be," and our being good in the between.

And one asks: Why should the "quiet power of the possible" (*"die stille Kraft des Möglichen," GA,* 9: 317; *LH,* 196) be *quiet,* and not least if it also rages? How then does it favor? An incognito life of quiet desperation, or worse? How understand the "power of the possible?" It is not finite possibility defined by reference to determinate actualization. Is it ultimate possibilizing power beyond determinate possibility and its actualization?[30] Heidegger here hints at this "beyond," yet there are ways of privileging possibility that make no possibility privileged; ways of thinking difference as difference that end up homogenizing all difference. The sun shines on the good and the evil alike. Yes. Does it then favor evil and good alike? We wonder. Yes, name the

---

28. *GA,* 9: 360; *LH,* 238: *"Sein erst gewahrt dem Heilen Aufgand in Huld und Andrang zu Unheil dem Grimm."*

29. Giles Deleuze, *Difference and Repetition,* trans. P. Patton (London: Athlone Press, 1997), 66.

30. I say more below about this, when discussing creation, coming to be, and nothing. See also the following chapter where I speak of a third sense of transcendence, beyond the transcendence of nature and human being, relative to this hyperbolic possibilizing power as agapeic.

holy and the horror, do not slide around it. But as there is a dialectical *Aufhebung* that so slides, there is a post-philosophical silence that slides too. We cannot be thus quiet. Would we rather the *posse* of the God of Cusanus? Or the living God of Shestov, or Kierkegaard for whom "all is possible." Or the Dionysian god of Nietzsche for whom, it seems "all is false," and it also seems *"Alles ist erlaubt"?* Or the hyperbolic God beyond the whole, origin of agapeic possibilizing? These are different "possibilities." And there are very different ways of allowance, and ways of allowance that allow, that is, favor nothing. If Heidegger hints at the "favor" of being, he does not further deign to give a sign. He does not quite say "fair is foul, and foul is fair," but at least Macbeth came to know and grant that the powers do not give rage and healing homogeneously; they give rage as healing for his evil daring beyond good and evil. Heidegger goes on to invoke (*GA,* 9: 361 ff.; *LH,* 239 ff.) a thinking of being, beyond theory and praxis, that "towers above action and production," yet is humble and marked by "simplicity"(*GA,* 9: 362; *LH,* 240), in the advent of being, and the adventure of thinking.[31] Why does the uneasiness persist that we are being juggled with, that the left hand is taking back what the right hand seems to offer? And do these hands usher us firmly enough towards the Sabbath that frees into the "It is good," or the Witches' Sabbath that ensnares us in the equivocation: "fair is foul, and foul is fair"?

What of Hegel's claim: pure light is the same as pure darkness, a deficient sameness, for pure light and darkness are merely indeterminate? In truth, there are different indeterminacies, some merely indefinite, others overdeterminacies. Hegel fastens on the defect of the indefinite, but it is the overdeterminate that is at stake in thinking of art, origins, otherness. This is known by Nietzsche, and also by Heidegger. But if the equivocal polemos of being means only that fair is foul and foul is fair, the deeper issue bears on the *good of the "to be."* The point is not only the difference of *eros uranos* and *eros turannos,* but also the difference between the good *eris* and the bad *eris* (such as Hesiod indicates in *Works and Days*): the "good *eris*" calls forth the agon that challenges the best excellences of erotic sovereignty, the "bad *eris*" releases merely the waste of destructive war. For there is an evil release. And so the point turns on the "yes" to being, be it called the Sabbath of the will, or *amor fati,* or *Gelassenheit.* What is the release and to what it is released?

We cannot evade the issue of the good of being in terms of the agapeic being of the giving source. If origin is an erotic source, it is unclear how we can see further than a giving that must finally be *for itself,* even if the giving passes through the other. I do not find in Heidegger resource enough to make

---

31. I do not do ethics, Heidegger suggests, I think ethos; less Aristotle, more Sophocles (*GA,* 9: 352–53, *LH,* 231–33). But see *EB* on a metaxological thinking of ethos, and the ethics that follows from this, addressing the question "What is it to be good?" consistent with the metaphysics addressing the question "What does it mean to be?" of *BB.*

sense of being beyond this circle, a circle we found in Hegel and, differently, in Schopenhauer and Nietzsche. He had intimations of that "being beyond," but these intimations are articulated in language not true to the possibility of the good of the "to be," beyond the equivocations of erotic self-origination. Much of it has to do with an evasion of an excessive sense of the good, of an archeology of the good that brings us back *very differently* to "Plato," to despised "metaphysics," to "onto-theology." If one understands the point I am making, these last terms now seem so threadbare as to beggar the philosophical imagination. We risk the *penia* of philosophy but without the fecundity of its eros.

Plato's sun is the good that as excessive light also blinds. To stand in the Nietzschean high noon is to be intoxicated with absolute Dionysian sobriety. This looks like, but cannot be, the blindness of seeing that the Platonic philosopher suffers standing under the sun. Looks like but cannot be, since the sun of Nietzsche is beyond good and evil, and it is not good beyond good and evil. Of course, the hymns sung by Nietzsche make absolutely no sense if there is not some ultimate good, some absolute worthiness to be sung, about this sun. Nietzsche, like Heidegger, was often too busy dissociating himself from what he took to be "Platonism" and "Christianity" to notice enough how the song now sung tends to mimic that which it repels from itself. Dissociation by negative relation, of this there is too much; and not enough granting that the repelled other stands also in the darkness of the light; and not enough granting that in the standing, there is a straining towards the good of the "to be," and not merely in any cheap moralistic sense, all too easy to dismiss cheaply. The "yes" at issue is an ontological, metaphysical one, with immense aesthetic, religious and ethical reverberations. I sometimes wonder if the immensity of these reverberations so *overcame* Heidegger in their "too muchness" or overdeterminacy that the needed discernment of differences and relations that sets them out for articulation exceeded his philosophical and post-philosophical resources.

But let us look a bit more at how Heidegger's interpretation of post-Platonic philosophy on the first beginning binds him closely to Nietzsche who, in the *Birth of Tragedy*, asserts a break and impoverishment of Western culture with Socrates-Plato.[32] Heidegger's related claim about *Seinsvergessenheit* end-

32. Heidegger does not dwell much on *music*, something that joins Schopenhauer and Nietzsche, and perhaps music is closer to erotic emergence than poetry: music is more original than "poetry," in this sense that it points more elementally to the emergence of articulation before the word has steadied into more definite saying. Singing is before saying. So Vico. But there is not much song in Heidegger, no thought singing its other. Heidegger is more like Kant and Hegel here. What if "all art constantly aspires towards the condition of music" (Walter Pater)? Is there something of this in the later Heidegger? Surely there is something of this in Nietzsche's ideal? The musical Socrates. Song is no feeble "Romanticism." And what is more important to the despised Plato than a fitting *paideia* with regard to *ta mousika?* This means that you would have

ing in technology and cybernetic thinking is constant, as is evident in his late essay "The End of Philosophy and the Task of Thinking." There is a continuous arc of unfolding: Platonism is metaphysics, Nietzsche is reversed Platonism, hence still metaphysics, though now of subjectivity and will to power, and this is continuous with metaphysics becoming science and technology, ending in our time in world-dominating cybernetics. Thinking the other origin will entail a recapitulation of the first beginning with Anaximander, Parmenides, Heraclitus.

The first beginning zoned on what happens within the happening of being, not the happening as happening. One might say: first we thought the originated as originated, and forget the originating; now in an other beginning we must think on the originating as originating (giving [as] giving, as I put it); but we must also grant that there is a "side" to the originating as giving that cannot be manifested without remainder in the originated as given; this is reserved by the nature of origination. The difference of the origin as origin and what the origin originates is kept as a difference, kept open. This is close to what I mean by an agapeic origin as giving the between and finite being its otherness as otherness, and hence as irreducible to the origin as originating: origin gives creation, but creation is not identical with origin. *Lichtung* is beyond determinate presence/absence; it absents itself in presenting, and in making presence possible and its interplay with absence. See it thus as opening a space that is a between. But the more original source is reserved: if this is something simple, it is yet a "too muchness" that asks a kind of poverty of the philosopher. The will to univocal clarity would be pernicious: assault on this mystery that strangely possibilizes even this assault.

The origin of the lighting, in giving the clearing, itself withdraws; the light that gives retreats into darkness; we mortals cannot have pure light. This is the chiaroscuro of the play of equivocal being, as I put it. What I think is interesting about Heidegger is how the light itself becomes enigmatic: dark to us, dark in itself. At times here, I see surprisingly the affinity of Plato and Nietzsche, counterparted by an affinity with Hegel that Heidegger does not escape. How distinguish Heidegger and Hegel here? A lighting as process has something *more* than determinacy, but as effected, as "having come to be" it gives a determinate clearing; in this we live. But the origin of the clearing is beyond determinacy in the sense of a determinate world, or even a superentity allegedly god; we can never directly address the origin of the clearing; we can only catch its first rays in the clearing itself; and it is as if the dawn rays are closer to the primal, for the origin itself is dark; or if one were truly to

---

to be a poet, while being a philosopher, and not only have a dialogue with the poet; and this was true of Plato and Nietzsche, these two who for Heidegger are the beginning inversion and inverse end of metaphysics. Heidegger's view becomes of secondary importance when we grant that they *just did it.* I mean sang.

return to the origin one would be overwhelmed, drowned, whether in light or dark is difficult to say.

The metaphor that expresses something of this deeper night of the origin seems to be named as *Erde* in "The Origin of the Work of Art." When Heidegger talks of earth, we naturally think of mother earth, though one does not detect anything very maternal about Heidegger's earth. Is world the son or daughter of earth, or the spouse? Are we back with Oedipal metaphysics such as we mentioned with Nietzsche? If world ultimately derives from earth, be it child or spouse, is there still not here some incestuous relation between origin and offspring or husband? Are we not then dealing with an incestuous erotic *self-mediation of the same origin with itself,* through world, and perhaps through earth, if the mother of mother earth is a deeper self-concealing sub-terranean origin? Try as I might, I do not see here the radical origination of the different as different, the agapeic origination of the other as other, as I would put it. You might say this is the archaic pagan religiosity of the earth. We come from the earth, we go back to the earth, womb and grave, giver of birth and place of last resting. Very well, but among the old gods of Greece, the sons of Gaia were the Titans, among whom Prometheus stood out in provocative contestation with Zeus. Attention has been called to the Promethean strain of Heidegger's "Origin of the Work of Art," especially in its earlier version (see note 47 below). Is Heidegger's Prometheus "a just Prometheus under Jove"? But paganism does not own the earth. And are there not *other* celebrations of the earth that welcomes seeds that fall to it, and in their death give forth a different harvest?

What then is earth? Earth is dark ground, earth is opaqueness; fertility yes, but also as womb, the place where death entombs. *Erde* is not the Platonic Sun, but it does enable growing, and as dark, it is an analogous reminder of a recalcitrant otherness that our minds cannot overreach or comprehend. Like Schopenhauer and Nietzsche, Heidegger wants to go *down,* deeper than the Cave. They go down to rise up, inspired by an origin beyond their individual subjectivity. Is there anything analogous in Plato? He bows to the Olympians, Nietzsche and Heidegger return to the *gigantomachia,* the war of the Titans and the Olympians. (How nice to see you again, Signor Giambattista Vico!)

And eros as daimon midway between earth and heaven? If there is an earth and a world for Heidegger, is there a heaven? And a hell? In our technological age we seem to see only the despoiled earth. (How could the tree of philosophy grow in that ground?) Of another hell he was too stonily silent, for in that nothing there was a nihilating evil exceeding differently his philosophical, postphilosophical resources.[33] Heidegger's Chthonic side reminds us

---

33. In *Einfuhrung in die Metaphysık* (Tübingen: Niemeyer Verlag, 1953), 20; *Introduction to Metaphysics,* trans. R. Manheim (New Haven, Conn.: Yale University Press, 1959), 26 he tells us that naming the Nothing honestly is a hallmark of the metaphysician.

Schopenhauer's will, as his *Kehre* and *Gelassenheit* remind us of the reversal from will into will-less knowing. But if Schopenhauer has a Chthonic metaphysics, he still thinks that an Olympian Platonism contributes to salvation from the darkness of the under-ground. Return to the Chthonic origin would simply be death.[34] Of course, the building of a world enacts a *distance* from earth. We must offer our devotion to Apollo too, hesitations about "logocentrism" notwithstanding. (Recall Kant's *safety* before the sublime.) Heidegger will not be swallowed by earth, he will keep the distance, he will tarry in the difference, staying as close to the origin as possible, intimate with its danger.

As with the Dionysian origin, the danger we again face is that of an *absorbing god* which appropriates the singular self. Remember Nietzsche in the *Birth of Tragedy* and the metaphor of the maternal womb. Are we its issue, or its impregnating partners? If we cannot be sure which is which, are we guilty inevitably of an unnatural act of incest, which Nietzsche claims to be at the source of tragic art? In Heidegger's polemos of earth and world, what is happening? Does the artist issue from earth, or impregnate it, or both; or appear as an issue already pregnant with the conception of its own mother and father? Is the artist then his or her own mother, father, and child? Or a child that impregnates itself and gives birth again to itself? This is Nietzsche again. Is not Heidegger's insinuation of the thinker as somehow giving name to the voice of being implicated in equivocation on all of this? Now challenging being to come to voice, now seeming to receive voice from what is always other, now said to be necessary to being for being to have that voice? Derived from the other source, and yet indispensable to the other source? Derived from what must also derive from it? Hence circulating in an equivocal pattern of mutual derivation and determination that, as equivocal, only hides its ambiguous proximity to Hegel's dialectical origin, self-circulating, self-mediating through its own other? Is not then the creative human being the "owned other" of the (Heideggerian) origin?

If there is anything to these suggestions, we also come again close to thoughts occasioned by Kant's view of genius. For one might suggest a reading of genius as the favored of nature *(Erde),* one foot in the dark unruly underground, one foot in the clearing, the light of articulation. Heidegger is straddled between these two, earth and world. The creator is this intermediate (a point he makes about the poet). The mush of Kant's sensory manifold is like a decomposed version of earth, just as the transcendental ego is an abstract version of genius. And as the transcendental ego has to shed light to

---

34. This is a consideration in Adorno's and Derrida's questioning: a cult of *Blut und Boden,* a nostalgia for some maternal or paternal homeland; certainly words like *ursprunglich* and *eigen* and cognates are pervasive; Heidegger concerned with the otherness of one's own, and less in the otherness of the non-own, a never-to-be-owned otherness, as Derrida seems to be, or an otherness perhaps never to be "en-owned" as the English translation of *Beitrage* of *Ereignis* as En-owning has it.

differentiate this mush, earth in Heidegger needs the creator as the agent of the process of primal differentiation, the creator who is (in) the light though the light is not his, privileged intimate and inaugurator at once. Or should we not say: the artist, the genius, is a pocket of wind released by the fertile compost? But then where is the breath that breathes on the humus and makes it human? Can the compost *breathe itself* as human, breathe on itself and give itself forth as the human creator? Do we not need *another* breath, not of the compost, not of the human and more than a gust of empty? Kant, we recall, was diffident about the unruliness of the genius precisely as dipping down into nature/earth as a dark origin. The polemos of earth and world is won in Kant above the earth in the moral world. In Schopenhauer will as earth comes to clearing above ground in the world as representation. In his polemos of will and representation, genius has a privileged relation to will as dark origin, and as excess to a clearing beyond instrumentalization or *technē:* root in the dark origin, excess as emergent from this, clearing as the intellect who sees in the dark, released beyond will as devouring beings, creative beyond technical instrumentalization of what appears in the clearing.[35]

Polemos, quintessentially a Greek theme, inseparable from an agonistic sense of being, is emphasized supremely by Nietzsche.[36] Though Heidegger does not speak of a Dionysian origin, we cannot help but think of Zarathustra's commandment: Remain true to the earth! (Again how anti-Copernican! If, that is, Copernicus asks us to look away from ourselves to the Sun.) Is world a shaping of chaos in Nietzsche's sense of a creative formlessness? But what shapes the chaos? Does it shape itself? Does earth *shape itself* as world, but through the medium of creative humans, hence the privileged intermediate power of creative humans midway between earth and world? Is this the world as work of art that gives birth to itself, even if through the original intermediation of creative humans? Nietzsche: "The world is to all eternity chaos." But why call chaos such a miraculously self-birthing world—miraculous at the very least because beyond the principle of sufficient reason, which

35. Is this a "post-metaphysical" revamping of genius, projected either into archaic Greece, or into privileged poets like Hölderlin, or the "coming ones," the favored intimates of the "last god" that Heidegger prophesies. The point is not just to object to this, but to make sense of it, and of what Heidegger says and does *not* say but should. I find myself resistant to the insinuations of being unprecedented. He was able, and still is able, to carry out this bluff because few had or have a comparable grasp of the tradition of philosophy, and even fewer, if anyone, had such a one track philosophical mind vis-à-vis "the tradition." Perhaps few, or none (not even Nietzsche, I think) had the strong philosophical will to power, or mania, to impose a new interpretation on "the tradition" as Heidegger; for few equalled him in the strength of philosophical resoluteness or indeed acuity, the *conatus essendi* of his philosophical eros. I do not read "the tradition" through Heidegger's eyes, nor think of metaphysics, or being, or the between, or origin, or the good, or God, as he does.

36. See also Jacob Burckhardt on the agonal age in *The Greeks and Greek Civilization,* ed. O. Murray, trans. S. Stern (New York: Macmillan, 1998), 160–213.

itself is a miraculous birth within this miraculously self-birthing world? Is not a self-birthing world like a pantheistic *causa sui?* Why accept the miracle of this self-birthing world over the miracle of creation by the God beyond the finite whole? One wished Heidegger pushed such questions to their limit. Instead he was bewitched too much by the blur of their tangled equivocities.

You might say: a world is in some measure our building of Apollonian form in or on the original Dionysian formlessness. But what is the status of the form and the formlessness? Are we too then forms of formlessness, hence equivocal beings? Pockets of wind loosed from the compost? A world is true if it remains true to the earth. But how does an equivocal being, such as we are, remain true to being itself as thus equivocal? And since the earth seems self-concealing, to what equivocation of this more original ground are we thus being true? *Every being true then must be false,* it seems, if being is thus equivocal only—and this in no manner which we can celebrate, for what truly *worthy of celebration* is left for us to celebrate? And this applies as much to the thinker as to the poet. To what are we given over when we are released beyond the will willing itself? What again of the good of the "to be"? Is Heidegger shying away from something in all of this? Such questions are overtly precipitated by Schopenhauer's and Nietzsche's erotic origin, but I do not think they are formulated with the same force in Heidegger, perhaps because the equivocity of the self-concealing origin seems justification enough for him to leave the equivocity be, and in a manner evasive of these questions.

We know that Heidegger came to be critical of Nietzsche as the acme of a metaphysics of subjectivity as will to power. No doubt, Nietzsche's admirers will find nuance enough in Nietzsche that does not quite fit this. No one schema will completely fit Nietzsche, since he is so protean. Yet Heidegger is not wrong in recoiling, after his turn, from the ontological tyranny harbored in a metaphysics of will to power. I would say this monstrous possibility is harbored more generally in any erotic origin that has lost its attunement to divine festivity as heralding the agape of being. The trace of this attunement is there in Plato, and there are some traces in the festive Nietzsche also, though Nietzsche cannot be fully true to them philosophically, since his too meager philosophical resources leave his better intuitions in the lurch. But does something similar happen to Heidegger, though he masks the absence of words to say what quite is the issue here? If I am not mistaken there is still too much of the dominance of the agon of erotic sovereignty, hence not enough of the release of the agapeic "yes," hence also not enough of the neighboring of agapeic giving or service.

Consider on that score Heidegger's discussion of truth and art in "The Origin of the Work of Art." It bears on the contrast of *alētheia* and more derivative truth, circles around *technē* and *phusis,* and offers some of the most suggestive remarks on creation as a bringing forth that is not making as technical. While very suggestive, what is being suggested is obscure. Heidegger makes a virtue of this. "Truth occurs as such in the opposition of the clearing and double concealing. Truth is the primal conflict in which, always in some particular way, the Open is won" (*GA,* 5: 48; *OWA,* 685). The emphasis seems more on struggle than on the open as given (by what I would call the giving [as] giving). But is there tension between the opening as a *giving,* and man as a *projecting?* Does not a significant instability come from mingling these languages: the human as *given* its being in an opening it does not produce, and the human as *projecting* itself and its world. The instability is between receiving the gift and projecting one's self and world; between what I would call an ultimate *passion of being,* an ontological receiving, a being given to be, and a *projection of self and its world,* neither of which have been unambiguously released beyond their own equivocal being for themselves. In the polemos as Heidegger describes it, the *passio essendi* of the first seems overtaken by the *conatus essendi* of the second, which in turn is not released beyond itself to a new intimacy with the more elemental passion of being. But it is this last release that the freedom of the art work serves. Heidegger has a glimpse of this, but his way of speaking covers it over, or perhaps *half-covers* it.

Heidegger's polemos is the struggle of erotic sovereignty, modelled on an agon, not on creation as an agapeic giving of an other as other. If there are hints of something like the second, Heidegger does not make clear the difference of this erotic struggle of earth and world, and the agape of creation as giving (as) giving. (Not thought thinking thought, or will willing will, or writing writing writing; but giving giving giving—this is the hyperbole of the agapeic origin.) If our thinking remains within the ethos of erotic sovereignty, we are not as free from the will willing itself as Heidegger might like to think and his admirers believe. The *difference* between this struggle and the serenity of release named by *Gelassenheit* requires terms more agapeic than erotic, but Heidegger has not those terms. We have noted the analogy with ruptures and reversals we found in Schopenhauer and Nietzsche, but try as he might to dissemble strong similarities with his post-Kantian predecessors, the legacy of the will willing itself lives on in Heidegger. And though he knew we must certainly get beyond this, though he knew what it might lead to in Nietzsche, his discussion in "The Origin of the Work of Art" does not, and I suspect, cannot lead us there. I do not mean to deny that there are important hints about what being "there" is, but Heidegger's speech is overlaid with a language that often works against its own best intentions—if these are its intentions—since perhaps he does not want to get there at all. A genuine release would mean, among other things, confession that the language used before was systematically dissembling and that philosophical repentance might be in order; but the thing that turned Heidegger to stone was confession that he might have been wrong, terribly wrong.[37]

---

37. Farias recounts how, after the war, Rudolph Bultmann said to Heidegger that he would have to be like Augustine and write his *Retractiones.* According to Bultmann: "Heidegger's face became a stony mask. He left without saying anything further." Victor Farias, *Heidegger and Nazism,* ed. J. Margolis and T. Rockmore, trans. P. Burrell, D. Di Bernardi, and G. Ricci (Philadelphia: Temple University Press, 1989), 282.

Just one instance: I find Heidegger "squirming" in his *Introduction to Metaphysics* when his later additions try to give a non-"subjectivistic" or non-"voluntaristic" interpretation to earlier statements that, to say the least, are rife with ambiguity on this score. His second thoughts produce a double thinking, where he tortures his original text to make it now say what he now holds, not what he then held. For, after all, the incontrovertible tone of declamatory "say-so" cannot confess now that it then was wrong, for then it might now be wrong too. This would be a reversal, or *metanoia* too far. Instead we get the *half reversal* that oscillates in its own circle of studied ambiguation. The second thoughts become double thinking, reflecting the continuation of equivocity from the first attempt, and sometimes even adding to it with a later layer of further evasiveness. He seems impotent to say, with the splendor of the simple: I confess. Like Hegel, he had a desire to be in the right, and more, to let it be known that he was in the right, even if, in Heidegger's case that meant reinterpreting, not the plain sense, but the immanent equivocities of his earlier views. Is this one of his poisoned gifts to the later practices of deconstructive hermeneutics: not the disambiguation of equivocity but its further sophistication, such that revealing becomes a more evasive concealing?

Origin, Creation, Nothing

Here and to follow further, I offer some reflections on origin, whether revealed in the origination of the art work, or in the giving to be of being, or in the opening of the space of finite being that Heidegger often speaks of in terms of *Lichtung,* though sometimes he does make use of the notion of the between, or *das Zwischen.* Does the unthought origin still remain unthought, as well as the between, even though acknowledged? The difference of demiurgic making and creation is important, for a major evasion here by Heidegger has serious consequences for all the themes above stated.

Heidegger grants that the difference of production and creation, of the craftsman and the divine creator is acknowledged in the world of Biblical faith, but immediately goes on to claim its successful overtaking by a metaphysics of form and matter that is decisive historically, and not least for the transition from the Middle Ages to modernity, and hence for the encroachment and assault on things (*GA,* 5: 15; *OWA,* 660–61). Lots of different things are quickly run together here by Heidegger, with a blurring of essential differences in a confusion, in the sense of a fusing together *(fusio con),* not helpful.

When Heidegger reduces to production the sense of origin throughout the *entirety* of the Western tradition, he is not completely wrong with respect to the Demiurge in one regard, namely the imposition of form and matter. Even here, the other dimensions of what is involved, beyond geometry and *technē,* and having everything to do with the being there of the good, and the religious praise and reverence for the worthy beauty of the gift wrought, on these he is simply silent, and by that silence falsifies what the fuller point is concerning the original demiurgic working of the world as a whole. But he is totally wrong to *insinuate* that creation is just production, as imposing form on matter, in notions like *creatio ex nihilo*. One cannot but think he knew better. If he did know better, one must suspect something disingenuous in his claim. If he did not know better, this is a glaring ignorance of something essential. And whether or not he knew better, the say-so of his totalizing claim about the *entire* tradition of philosophy brings out in us strong demurral. Either Heidegger is ignorant, or willful. If ignorant, it is an inadmissible ignorance. If willful, it hardly concurs with the truth of what is at issue with regard to creation. Given his own theological studies, and some knowledge of Medieval thought, it cannot be simple ignorance. If it is willful, perhaps it is less deliberately bloody minded as driven to its distortions by the need to omit the extraordinary challenge that the notion of creation presents, to philosophy in general, and Heidegger's thought in particular. It leads to a complete obfuscation of the deepest issue, a forgetfulness of creation (on Heidegger's part) not less fateful than the alleged forgetfulness of being.

In elaborating the point, let us consider again the polemos of being, but not forgetting how equivocal Heidegger is, and in ways *both* enabling and hindering to thinking. He is a philosopher of the equivocal in the sense that the univocalizing of being is "deconstructed" by him, and he returns to something like Heraclitus's *phusis* which loves to hide. Indeed the polemos of being reminds us of just this equivocal strife in becoming itself. This equivocal strife does not lead to the dialectical *Aufhebung* of Hegel, where the immanent contrariness of being points beyond to a speculative unity, and hence, one might say, a more absolutizing univocity. Hence the importance of difference as difference. But how dwell in the equivocity of being, if not dialectically? After all, Hegel, no less than Nietzsche, paid homage to Heraclitus by averring that there is not a proposition of his that Hegel does not include in his *Science of Logic*. How dwell mindfully with the equivocity of being, if speculative dialectic is not true, nor univocal mathēsis? I don't think Heidegger ever fully appreciated, much less ever sought to give an adequate articulation to, the metaxological promise of equivocal being. The mystery of being becomes the evasiveness of being, when all we seem to be is nonplussed by the equivocity, and we are disabled to take a step further by worry that we become again entangled in the determinations of univocity and speculative dialectic.

Nature loves to hide. But ask now not only what the hiding is but the *love* and the why of the love of the hiding? Think here in terms of *natura naturans* (nature naturing) and *natura naturata* (nature natured). Nature naturing is manifest in and yet concealed by nature natured; yet we could say nothing of nature naturing without what nature natured communicates. And so we must seek to understand the latter, though the danger is that we forget that it is the communication of nature naturing. The artist is closer to the equivocal process of emergence with nature naturing, but also finds his way, or is given a way, to intimacy with this naturing, by mindful heed to what nature natures. One is, as it were, *in between* nature natured and nature naturing. One of the intimate places of kenning that between is one's own being as coming to middle articulation in the envisagement of otherness that original imagination expresses.[38] Heidegger's noted proclivity to think in terms of doubles, where the one seems to be what the other is not, does not always help us in thinking the *between* as the milieu where one is porous to the other, where one passes into the other, and where the other gives signs suggestive of what the source offers.

But consider further. What happens in the between is the communication of what is other to us, as it is also our transcending to what is other. But the between shows itself as a coming to be that communicates of its origin as other to the between itself. A doublet of nature naturing and nature natured will not do justice to this last difference, in so far as the sense of the origin of both coming to be and what has come to be exceeds the happening of the between itself. It is more hyperbolically other than, not only nature natured, but even nature naturing; hyperbolically other to beings, other to the happening of finite being. Did Heidegger understand this hyperbolically other origin? Tokens are that he did not quite, though again these tokens are ambiguous in that his sense of the other origin is that of an enigma concealed in a riddle. In so far as the terms of his thinking still remains in the Eleatic line of Parmenides, reflected in the recurrence of metaphors of circularity, this hyperbolically other origin does not enter the horizon of his thought.

In fact, this hyperbolic origin enters the horizon of human thought through the hyperbolic notion of *creatio ex nihilo*. This comes from Jerusalem, and not Athens, and Heidegger will say that philosophy is Greek and nothing but Greek, but there is finally a "say-so" about this too, a say-so justifying its evasion by the lessons of history. The same history show us different lessons to the one Heidegger wants to teach, namely, that once this idea begins to dawn on thinkers, thinking itself could not just (arbitrarily) close itself off from this astonishing and perplexing thought. As if one were to say: we are philosophers in this office; you have to go to another office to have such questions addressed; we only make circles here; different circles yes, Parmenidean, Spinozistic, Hegelian, Nietzschean and so on, but nothing beyond circles; we do not dream ridiculous dreams of an origin beyond the whole. As a son of Parmenides, Heidegger strikes me as finally not different to Nietzsche, and also not to Hegel on this score, that is, in terms of his banishment from philosophy of the God beyond the whole, the God of original creation.

This banishment is hard to distinguish from diktat or "say-so." True philosophizing is open to even the seemingly strangest possibilities of thought, and this here is no exception. What would one feel about a philosopher who

38. See note 19, above on imagination as middle; as an original identification of difference in *Philosophy and Its Others,* chapter 2.

said: I only think about these things that "Greek" philosophers thought about, especially early Greek thinkers, and that's that! I think we would have to excuse ourselves politely when the astonishing strangeness of these other thoughts, not quite Greek, strike us as worthy of thought. And indeed the same Western tradition invoked to exile these thoughts evidences thinkers who have dared to let their Greek concepts be shaken by visitors from beyond the sanctioned categories. This would be an agapeic practice of philosophical thinking, genuinely hospitable to this astonishing other beyond thought thinking itself, or will willing itself.

Yet does not Heidegger make significant reference to creation and nothing? "Poetic projection comes from Nothing in this respect, that it never takes its gifts from the ordinary and traditional. But it never comes from Nothing in that what is projected by it is only the withheld vocation of the historical being of man himself" (*GA,* 5: 64; *OWA,* 698; in the German the word is *Dasein*). He exploits the resonance of *Ur-sprung* in terms of an unmediated leap. Every origination and new beginning entails a leap, and not least art.[39] Heidegger's remarks are again suggestive, but if there is a serious omission here relative to creation from nothing, what are we to say? What does Heidegger mean by creation? What is the nature of the origin here and the nature of the nothing? Is it an absolute nothing? And what would this mean? Is it a finite nothing? It certainly seems to be so here. But if so, how avoid something like Hegel's doctrine of determinate negation, and everything it portends regarding the dialectical nature of the origin? This cannot be it for Heidegger, given his claims to think difference, and his studied distancing of himself from Hegel.

And yet Heidegger's philosophy claims to be a philosophy of finitude, and if so, and when the nothing appears, how can the nothing also be otherwise than defined except by reference to the finitude of being? It would be, so to say, the indeterminate "back"-ground before which finitude is fore-grounded, brought forth into its determinate being relative to a source, without which it would not be this being or that being. But how again avoid a dialectical interplay between this original indeterminacy and determinate being? If the nothing is all that there is to give the background to the finite foreground, then there is nothing about it that could *originate or create in the properly ontological respect that is required by the situation. Ex nihilo nihil fit.* Since Heidegger is talking about creation, and hence a coming to be, this possibility cannot do either. There must be another sense of nothing, or another sense of the primal power of being as origin that cannot fit into this way of thinking. But this must mean that the so-called philosophy of finitude itself has to be redone. There is another power that

39. "Art lets truth originate. . . . To originate something by a leap....a founding leap—this is what the word origin means. . . ." "The origin of the work of art . . . is art . . . art is by nature an origin: a distinctive way in which truth comes into being, that is, becomes historical"(*GA,* 5: 65–66; *OWA,* 699).

is not a being within the horizon of finitude, that is not human being as transcending within that horizon, and that is misleadingly vacuous to call "nothing," since it is just the power of creative origination that is here at issue. There would be no issue without this power, and though one is tempted to speak of "nothing" to preserve its difference, thus preserving its difference is equally liable to consign it to a nothing where its difference also is lost. More must be said, and more also because the very being of finitude itself is marked by overdeterminacies of being which offer the signs of this superplus power.

I think the notion of creation *ex nihilo* is a way of trying to name this superplus power. For this power of origination is not nothing, though it be no thing; it is what makes the being of being be; not only possibilizing in the logical sense of formal possibility; but possibilizing in an ontological sense in which the creative power of the possible is at work: *posse* as power to bring to be; not possibility as that formal logical possibility that might be instantiated or not, or that essence that might be, that might not be, depending on some transition from possibility to actuality. There is a more primal sense of original creative power beyond the doublet of possibility/actuality, form/matter, *eidos*/instance. (See the next chapter on what I call third transcendence—T3.) The "not" between the two terms of these doublets points to an even more radical "not," since both the terms of the doublet would not be at all, did not this more primal superplus power give them to be, either as possible or as finitely actual. But it is not that this more radical sense of the "not" *originates* them; rather the primal power originates them; and when it is said "out of nothing," this is not out of *their* possibility; it means that their very possibility is itself originated; it too has come to be. The ontological transition is not from possibility to actuality, but from nothing to finite being via the creative bringing to be of this absolute origin.

Heidegger's dictum is that possibility is higher than actuality. This now appears entirely equivocal relative to the sense of possibility here described, and doubly so relative to the absolute origin as itself giving possibility and actuality to be at all. Ask it this way: Is *posse* "higher" than *esse?* If we think of "*esse*" in terms of superplus power that originally brings to be, we are already speaking of "*posse*" in the radically creative sense at issue. Relative to this hyperbolic sense of "*posse,*" the question of its being "higher" than "*esse*" does not even arise. What can "higher" mean at all relative to this hyperbolic origination? Of course, in finitude there may be possibility higher than actuality, in the sense of the promise of an ontological fullness that given actuality does not presently exhaust. But this is not the sense of possibility that is most primal here. Creation *ex nihilo* is not creation from possibility; it is more radical than that, in so far as this primal possibilizing source is not a possibility, not does it originate higher possibility simply, it gives being to be.[40]

---

40. While the present work was being prepared for publication, Richard Kearney's fine book, *The God Who May Be: A Hermeneutics of Religion* (Bloomington and Indianapolis: Indiana

Does the artist, or art work show some participation in this primal origination? Heidegger equivocally seems to suggest yes. Again it is equivocal because he will not forthrightly address the issues I mention above. He will glance off them and then let up and the most difficult and daring perplexities will be evaded. The issue would be something like this: Suppose this primal original is not something that anything finite could possibly instantiate; for the finite *already is* an issue or creation of this origin; it simply cannot be that origin through its own being alone; this is what it means for the finite to be—*not* to be that origin. And yet as originated, the finite is given to be, and given to be with a difference that is not a mere negative determination, but stands there gloriously with all the robustness of rich determinacy: something rather than nothing. Given to be, it is not the origin, but given its "to be," it is simply, as in relation to the origin. Outside of this relation, it would be nothing. What it is in this difference, it is in this relation. There is for it nothing "outside" that relation; and this relation is just its deepest finitude. But—and this is very important—this relation is what creates an "outside" to the origin in itself, for the relation is inseparable from an agapeic origination as *releasing finitude* into its own difference; and this, even while the being given to be of finitude is held in being as being by this agapeic source. If this is so, finitude cannot be determined purely for itself and in itself. To be finite is to be at all, in this relation to the agapeic origin. But this is *not* the Hegelian mutual determination of source and product. There is an asymmetry in relation to the primal source and what it gives to be. Hence, there is simply no way of dialectically overcoming this otherness, this difference, this transcendence.

Perhaps this is Heidegger's intuition also. But does he understand this difference deeply enough and does he have the resources to help us think it? And if not, are we not always running the risk of falling back into something like the mutual definition of the dialectical origin, in which the origin becomes an empty indeterminacy, a nothing in a more nugatory sense? Heidegger's sense of the indeterminacy of the origin wants to guard against this too, but can he prevent it? Or does he try to prevent it by a kind of strategic silence? How now distinguish this from evasion, when the possible vacuity of that indeterminate source seems to suggest itself? I repeat: we need more than that. Heidegger did not quite know what to do at this point; and partly because he has cut his own legs off at the knee by laming the astonishing

---

University Press, 2001) appeared. Kearney makes more sympathetic use of Heidegger than I do, or can. But he has listened better than Heidegger to the voices of Jerusalem with regard to *eschatological* possibility, an emphasis that complements my emphasis on origins. I offer some remarks in "Maybe, Maybe Not: Richard Kearney and God," *Traversing the Imaginary,* ed. John Manoussakis (Lanham, Md.: Rowan and Littlefield, 2003).

enigma of creation *ex nihilo*. I fear this is a self-incurred paralysis, induced by what I would call "postulatory finitism."[41]

And what further of the question of *finite creativity?* In this respect, there does seem something distinctive about humans as original. To be human as original is not to be the merely possible that is to be actualized; it is to be a power of possibilizing that has its own overdeterminacy, not a mere indefiniteness; the original power of being in this more primal sense seems to have endowed us as capable of bringing something new to be. But this could never be creation from nothing, in the sense of the primal origin. Why? First, there is the gift of the "to be." Second, if the gift is original after the manner of its finitude, our creative powers do not qualify the nothing, but are themselves qualified by the nothing. Hence every effort of ours to be more than nothing, and in a new and original way, is itself qualified by a *constitutive nothingness* that simply is inherent in the being of finitude as such. The original gift, as much as this ontological qualification by our nothingness, always means that *our creation cannot but be in the gift of the more original power of being as other to us*. An ideal of self-creation risks distorting this rich equivocity of the human being—reducing our doubleness to singular self-determining terms, set by us alone.

I do think Heidegger protested against the latter univocalization which also lies at the root of the flattening of the earth into a resource for our serviceable disposability. But did he give the best account of our rich ontological equivocity, and its betokening of the more original source? I do not think so. His account of the finitude of the human being is skewed, as are his suggestion about the more primal original. And the skewing of one cannot be separated

---

41. *Postulatory finitism:* I mean something on the analogy with Kant's "postulatory theism." If you look at life thus, then X. The "if" entails an *als ob*. But why must you look thus? For "postulatory theism" the *als ob* "projects" "God." For "postulatory finitism" the *als ob* refuses to postulate God. But why *that* "project"? What if eros has fallen asleep, into a new sleep of finitude? What of the hyperbolic sleeplessness of eros, impatient even with the *als ob?* When it wakes, it makes it impossible to look at life only within the *Gestell* of the "postulatory finitism." Everything is more perplexing—dark in that sense. But there is no "must" that absolutely determines to postulatory finitism. This last, however, is taken by some as a kind of given which determines in advance every nook and cranny of interpretation. If a kind of "postulatory infinitism" predetermines Hegel, one worries that a postulatory finitism determines Heidegger all along the line. When the postulatory infinitists or finitists start preaching to us with their "must," this is an edifying discourse too far. Why should we listen to their "must," if we have had some intimation of the dimension of the hyperbolic? Everything about the situation makes us fear that the finitism (or Hegelian infinitism, *mutatis mutandi*) is a form of ontological bewitchment, a spell cast by Nietzsche and through Heidegger and his afterlives. These bewitchments can be so effective that we can reach a point where we are like anorexics who stand before the food of life and cannot eat, because the label is misplaced or misread, or simply because it is not the label that is supposed to fit, and what would restore life is passed over, and a form that seems to mimic it is put in its place, but we are dying from malnourishment.

from the skewing of the other. His tongue seems not free to say what his eyes, one feels, should have seen. When "ordinary" people speak ("ontically") of divine genius they are not wrong: they say what they see, even if they do not fully understand what they see or say. But does anyone, finally? Better thus to see and say than to squint and speak as if one has seen otherwise. One might have seen otherwise, but only in certain circumstances is squinting the best way to look.

On Giving and Projecting: An Ill-fated Marriage?

Look again at how it is the language of *projection* that comes back for Heidegger with respect to poetry (*GA,* 5:60 f.; *OWA,* 695).[42] Is projection like the language of subreption, self-mediation through the other, self-affirming through the future superman? With Nietzschean resonance, Heidegger projects the "coming preservers," and heralds the last god.[43] Projection seems to be a "throwing" that goes from me towards something other; it does not *let happen* the otherness as other. Heidegger wants both sides. I think the language of projection will have to be given up. It is too dissimulating as to the meaning of human self-transcendence; it risks falling in the same family of will to power; it distorts the *passio essendi* with its more essential ontological communication of the giving of being. If you ask me, Plato's eros and mania communicate something truer to the happening of poetic saying in the metaxu: to the seeking and to the receiving, to the endeavor and to the gracing. Projection is a crude metaphor, so crude it has taken on an epochal life—it is used so thoughtlessly.

Of course, Heidegger wants to say the human being is first thrown by Being, before he is throwing, projecting. I offer some citations from the *Letter on Humanism* which many commentators see as gathering up many thoughts first sought in "Origin of the Work of Art," especially in the later

---

42. "Poetry as illuminating projection, *Dichtung als lichtender Entwurf*" (*GA,* 5: 60; *OWA,* 695); "Projective saying is poetry, *Das entwerfende Sagen ist Dichtung*" (*GA,* 5: 61; *OWA,* 696).

43. "The poetic projection of truth . . . is also never carried in the direction of an indeterminate void. Rather, in the work, truth is thrown toward the coming preservers, that is, towards an historical group of men. . . . This is the earth and, for an historical people, its earth . . . everything with which man is endowed must, in the projection, be drawn up from the closed ground . . ." (*GA,* 5: 63; *OWA,* 697). This anticipates the prophetic language of the last god guff in *Beiträge.* This throwing as projection still reminds me too much of the futurity of the Nietzschean will that wills itself in willing its future, and that is said to decisively issue the difference to time: It will be so. Projective say-so. Despite all talk of heritage, it is the "future" that seems "redemptive." We risk mixing the worst of "decisionism" with an empty bathos of futurity; for other-future replaces other-world, a saving of the earth assisted in its birth through the creative few. Very Nietzschean, but without Nietzsche's humanizing self-mockery.

version it assumed, and hence putatively released from the self-assertiveness said to mark the earlier Heidegger. I find the matter by no means so evident, and not least with reference to the strife of being itself. "Man is rather "thrown" from Being itself into the truth of Being." "Man is the shepherd of Being" (*GA*, 9: 331; *LH*, 210). "The self-giving into the open, along with the open region itself, is Being itself" (*GA*, 9: 334; *LH*, 214). "Being is illumined for man in the ecstatic projection *[Entwurf]*. But this projection does not create Being. Moreover, this projection is essentially a thrown projection. What throws in projection is not man but Being itself, which sends man into the ek-sistence of Da-sein that is his essence . . ." (*GA*, 9: 337; *LH*, 217).[44]

Put aside the question whether the language of projection is the right way to speak of the *giving* of Being. Let us grant that Being from itself gives, and more primally gives than *Dasein* projects. But this giving of Being is a kind of projection in the case of *Dasein* who is first projected. Are we to conclude then that the human being is Being's self-projection? Why does this remind us of the self-differentiation of the Idea? Or the objectification of the Will? Or the concretion of will to power? And then there is the reversal from throw to counterthrow, *Entwurf* to *Gegen-wurf*. Indeed the "More" is connected to the "throw," and to human being as the "counterthrow" of Being *(Gegen-wurf)* and this counterthrow, "more" than the human being as *animal rationale*, transmutes into the shepherd of Being (*LH*, 221). We ask as we did with Schopenhauer's reversal: What enables it, how does Being possibilize it, if It, Being, is in a throwing and counter-throw? How and what can It *throw back at Itself*, in and through the human being as Its own throw? How does man as the throw back to Being, throw itself back in the released mode of the "shepherd"? Throwing back has all the connotations of the erotic polemos that seems to struggle or be in strife, *as much from one side as from the other*. But then what *giving* can be going on here? If it is the self-giving of Being, it seems as much the strife of Being with It-self, as the giving of Being to *Itself*, as to the human being, or to Itself through human being. Hence this self-giving, in and

44. These are citations from the *Letter on Humanism* in *Basic Writings* (*GA*, 9: 327; *LH*, 207): "Projection" in *Being and Time* is not subjectivistic but is "the ecstatic relation to the lighting of Being. . . ." Thinking this was made difficult by the holding back of the second part of *Being and Time* where "everything is reversed . . . thinking failed" (*GA*, 9: 328; *LH*, 208). Does this mean: I failed? No. Heidegger does not fail—he always had this in mind. Why not say: *my* thinking failed? Not at all: Thinking failed. Remember Kierkegaard's excoriation of the Hegelian's thought without a particular thinker? Hegel: thinking thinks thought. Heidegger: thinking did *not* think. And Heidegger and Sartre? Sartre, Sartre—what can one say? Metaphysics, reversed metaphysics, it's all the one. Are you sure I wrote to him in highly complementary terms, telling him he was my true interpreter? If so, since he did not reply, he has completely banalized my ontological intentions. See also *GA*, 9: 334; *LH*, 214: Being as It gives, *es gibt*, and Parmenides' *esti gar einai:* "The primal mystery for all thinking is contained in this phrase." And *GA*, 9: 331; *LH*, 210: "Yet Being—what is Being? It is It itself. The thinking that is to come must learn to experience that and to say it." What is *It?*

through strife, in and through the throw and counterthrow of the human being, is too close for comfort to the self-mediation of the same we found in Hegel, and the erotic origin we found in Schopenhauer and Nietzsche. The circle is closed again, no matter what inordinate strife goes on inside it. The giving as radical release of difference is not in fact thought—surface appearances notwithstanding. We seem to have a counterfeit double of a self-giving that only *seems* to release the otherness as other. As a seeming giving, this release would seem to be a dissembling giving. And if it is not our projection on being, but Being's self-projection in us, what becomes of the "poverty" of the shepherd in this throwing of Being? Does it not become a vanishing moment in an ecstasis that is finally Nothing?

What to conclude? Heidegger lacks finesse enough for discerning different forms of giving, of self-giving. Not least, the difference of erotic and agapeic giving remains wrapped in equivocity that promises everything, but actually muddies too much. Is difference qua difference in fact thought at all—for all the surface claims notwithstanding? And consider what is said of throwing and the *neighbor*.[45] Heidegger seems tone deaf to the inappropriateness of the language of throwing with regard to neighboring. If you had a "throwing" neighbor you would not think him a very good neighbor—he would be always challenging you in his counterthrow—you would not be able to get along. The "with," the home, would be disrupted by allegedly more authentic polemos. But that is not at all being a good neighbor. The language is all skewed.

I do know that love can be *la guerre tendre*. But think again of wooing a beloved, or a muse. Translate that into the agonistic language of throw and counterthrow. At most you might get a *forced inspiration,* but that is *not* inspiration as true release. Or suppose you had a wife that was counterthrowing in the between all the time; throwing herself at you, as you yourself, already thrown, threw yourself forward, or back again at her, in projecting; she challenging you, you counter-challenging. What *grace* here? What *favor?* What *endowing?* The language of agon is all out of kilter with the language fitting for espousal. The marriage would not last too long, I venture. Difference as divorce would come back very quickly rather than the between as mutual espousal. When one thinks of being espoused between the throw and the counter-throw, one thinks of the wise epigraph Kierkegaard placed at the start of *Concluding Unscientific Postscript:* Better well-hanged than ill-wed.

Faithful Heideggerians may take this as too irreverent. But there is a playfulness that is reverent—reverent in irreverence. Heidegger shows resolute seriousness, dare one say it, a kind of pushy earnestness. But laughter is, can

---

45. "[Man] gains the essential poverty of the shepherd whose dignity consists in being called by Being itself in the preservation of Being's truth. The call comes as the throw from which the thrownness of Da-sein derives. . . . Man is the neighbor of Being"(*GA,* 9: 342; *LH,* 221–22).

be, the piety of questioning. Laughing too is like religion—one man's worship is another man's idolatry. The joke falls on a stony soul. Here is a playful image. Beatrix Potter, the teller of thoughtful tales for children, offers a picture of the counterthrow. I mean the tale of *squirrel nutkin* and the wise owl. Squirrel nutkin is always challenging the wise and silent owl, trying to *provoke* a response. Questioning may be the piety of thinking, but there are different ways of posing the same question, some with the dissembled aggression of provocation, others with the shy reverence of admiration. Questioning that *contests* may claim the form of piety, but is the spirit the spirit of reverence? Not with squirrel nutkin, in any event. Eventually, it is true, the owl wisely did take a nip out of squirrel nutkin's tail, and some lesson was learned. It would be impious to venture any speculation as to whether Being could take a nip out of Dasein's tail. But one might query what lesson might have been learned after the turn. Would we need an "about face"? But do we find rather a "save face"? If so, would it not be as if the challenge of squirrel nutkin all along anticipated that bite, and its provocation all along was a higher form of neighborhood to the wise and silent owl? The piety of your thinking makes you hesitate to accept that? I hesitate too, but then I think, there is something to it. Then again, maybe these musings only betray the anxiety of an ontic animal, a brow-beaten husband of being, or a mere metaphysical mouse. But perhaps really I should learn to speak more "Elfish."

The Still Unthought Between

I finish with some thought about the between, *das Zwischen,* the metaxu. There are a number of betweens, of course: between art and the sacred, between earth and world, between humans and being, the space of Heidegger's fourfold between earth, sky, mortals, divinities. I want to focus more generally on how Heidegger mentions the between. It is not overt in "The Origin of the Work of Art." There is an important naming of it in the *Letter on Humanism,* and also there are references to it in the *Beiträge,* each relevant to our purposes here. I want to reiterate that the language of projection is not suitable to speak about it. If there an openness to the between, this has implications both for the releasing power of its origin, as well as for the forms of release within the between. Neither the primal originating release of the between as the happening of finite being, nor our finite release within the between, is to be called "projection." There is asked of us a plurivocal "being true," in which we need more than a juxtaposition of "correctness" versus *"alētheia."* Art and religion are of great moment in keeping us alive in the porous mindfulness of what this plurivocal "being true" asks of us.

Here is Heidegger's description in the *Letter on Humanism* (*GA,* 9: 350; *LH,* 229):

> Being itself, which as the throw has projected the essence of man into "care," is as this openness. Thrown in such a fashion, man stands "in" the openness of Being. "World" is the lighting of Being into which man stands out on the basis of his thrown essence. . . . Thought in terms of ek-sistence, "world" is in a certain sense precisely "the beyond" within existence and for it. Man is never first and foremost man on the higher side of the world, as a "subject," whether this is taken as "I" or "We." Nor is he ever simply a mere subject which always simultaneously is related to objects, so that his essence lies in the subject-object relation. Rather, before all this, man in his essence is ek-sistent into the openness of Being, into the open region that lights the "between" within which a "relation" of subject to object can "be."

I am in agreement with Heidegger, in the general drift of what he says here, and apart from the language of "throw," but less sure about what remains unsaid, and how this effects what is said. The plurivocal possibilities of the "between" are not at all developed in their fullness in a manner that *Being and the Between* and *Ethics and the Between* at least try to effect. Almost everything remains hidden, and silent in Heidegger's "naming" here of the "between." As already indicated, the language of "throw" is not the right language to heed the finesse of origination and coming to be, nor is "care" sufficiently rich to name the *ontological loves* of the human being, which mingle at least four dominant loves: self-affirming, erotic, filial, and agapeic.[46] "Care" is an anxiety ridden form of eros, and hence not even adequate to this form, to say nothing of the other forms. And this has important repercussions for what art affirms, and not least the form of the "Amen" to being which we have explored diversely. I mention this last, for Heidegger is also to be situated in that concern, hide as he might his fundamental similarities to other thinkers.

But let me refer to another paragraph (203) in *Beiträge* (*GA,* 65: 325–26) where the between again comes up for consideration:

> Projecting-open is the between [Zwischen] in whose openness a being and beingness become differentiatable, so much so that at first only a being *itself* is experiencable (i.e., a being as sheltered-concealed as such and thus with respect to its beingness). Merely going over to essence as ἰδέα mistakes the projecting-open, as well as the appeal to the necessary pre-givenness of a "being."
>
> But how the projecting-open and its essential swaying as Da-sein continue to be covered over by the predominance of *re-presenting,* how one comes to the subject-object-relation and to the I-posit-

46. See *EB,* passim; also my "Enemies" in *Tijdschrift voor Filosofie,* 63, no. 1 (2001): 127–51.

> before-"consciousness," and how then *on the contrary* "life" is stressed—this reaction in the end in Nietzsche is the clearest proof for the *lack* of originariness in his questioning.
> Projecting-open is not to be "explained" but rather is to be transmuted in its ground and abground and in that direction to dis-place humanness into Da-sein and to show humanness the other beginning of its history.

In this set of posthumously published notes, the importance of the art work recurs a lot, as does Heidegger's stylization of the "tradition" of metaphysics beginning with *eidos,* and so on. Heidegger's hyphenations (say, projecting-open) might appear as advances of thought, but sometimes they simply *expose the equivocation* by laying side by side considerations that, while essential, yet exist in a deep tension that is not necessarily addressed just by the two being laid side by side. This is the case here and in other instances. It is as if a man and woman were to marry and to retain both names in a hyphenated or double-barrelled name. Some marriages work out fine with the double hyphenated name, but other marriages conceal the deeper tension by exposing it, even though what is needed is something other again which transforms the couple in hyphenated coupling. The danger of polemos will not miraculously bring forth favor and grace and bestowing just because the two are laid side by side and joined by a hyphen. The hyphen is a gesture towards a between, and perhaps no more than a gesture, but what the between means and needs is more than such a gesture.

That said, Heidegger's characterization of the between as projecting-open is more acute, in that the language of the Open qualifies the language of "projecting," and in that sense perhaps shows, despite Heidegger's self-conscious intentions, hesitations concerning the language of "projection." I just recall that the *Letter on Humanism,* written later, does not show the hesitation overtly, making one wonder if Heidegger missed an opportunity, or did not see what the issue was here. But even with all these qualifications, this is not the way to go. I would say something like this. What we call the between is an ontological given. The origin of the given happening might be called a giving giving; not just a giver, but a giving for the giving, hence not just a once off univocal act, but a continuous origination, where continuous does not here mean the continuity of time but something more like the constancy of eternity, and not a *nunc stans,* if by this we mean to contract this giving giving into a univocal and merely static eternity. The origin as the giving (as) giving is in the dimension of the hyperbolic with respect to the becoming of time, and hence it can be the radical creator of coming to be. The traditional difference of time and eternity, if saved from a falsifying dualistic opposition, is more true to this *difference* than the modern collapse of eternity into time, and the univocal demand on temporality that it do the work of *both time and eternity* (as one suspects about Heidegger).

What the need of *der letzte Gott?* Heidegger suggests that man's belongingness to being and the last god's need *(Bedürfen)* for being come together (*GA,* 65: 414–15). They come together as a strife *(Streit)* between the passing-by *(Vorbeigang)* of god and man's effort to realize himself historically (413). In this strife "the god overpowers man and man surpasses the god" (*der Gott übermächtigt den Menschen und der Mensch übertrifft den Gott,* 415). The god overpowering man: what holy ravishing this? And how humanly surpass or exceed the god, how be *above* here? Violence in this surpassing—and of whom by whom? Not here in any case, "a just Prometheus under Jove." If we find here in Heidegger's language hints of eros and mania, striving and receiving, *conatus* and *passio,* this is *without* the *agapeic porosity* that is allowing of the passage of reverence between the human and the divine unsurpassably above it, and allowing an *other* difference irreducible to any circle wheeling around itself. And is this not how Heidegger describes the last god: no end, but the wheeling around itself of the beginning, *kein Ende, sondern das Insicheinschwingen des Anfangs* (416)? What is this wheeling about itself of the other beginning? A self-wheeling circle ecstatic about itself? But the circle of the god who wheels about itself is echoed back to us from Hegel, as well as Nietzsche, or Parmenides, to name some. And with every such "god" we always wonder if it has wheeled away, into its own closure, from the God beyond the whole, and so also only feigned the passing between the human and divine whose porosity no circle can image or capture, except perfidiously to what was, and is, and always will be, *above* us.

And what if the origin as a giving (as) giving is an agapeic source that releases the between, the beings in the between, and the relativities of beings in the between, including that between the so-called "subject" and "object," self-being and other-being, each in diversely qualified relations within the more primal possibilizing "relation" of relations, the milieu of relativity that is the between? Then we can say about ourselves, and indeed other beings: we are given first, not thrown: created: given to be. The between names a being given to be: there is a coming to be before there is a becoming. The primal coming to be is *of* the between, as given to be by the origin. This is one of the reasons why, in *Being and the Between,* I distinguish origin and creation. The second is not the first; for the first has an otherness that is reserved to itself as exceeding everything finite that is given to be. In religious terms, this is the hyperbolic mystery of God as Godself. The second, creation, as giving the finite between presupposes the otherness of the first; presuppose this origin as agapeic, that is, as releasing creation to be as free for itself. Perhaps one might call the latter, the second, the Open. But certainly origin as giving the opening is not the opening. And opening is not the best word, since it dilutes the radical nature of the "coming to be." If anything, "Open" seems more like a primal becoming, than a primal coming to be. This last would be more like an origination from nothing. (I say "like" in that no unqualified assertion of what it univocally "is" is possible for humans. "Likeness" means a kind of mimetic hyperbole that intimates by excess the hyperbole of the other origin. A mimetic hyperbole participates in creative power after the manner of finite being.) The between is given in this primal coming to be. The between then is the finite happening of being within which the togetherness of beings, and human being's togetherness with being, is made actual. And when we come to ourselves there, we may think we are "projectors"—but this is not original enough, and it is conducive to false being, if we forget that there is a *passio essendi* before there is a *conatus essendi.* Our *passio essendi,* our receiving of being given to be is not a "throw," and our being gifted with *conatus essendi* is not our "projecting."

Perhaps "projecting" alone is too complicit in the language of *conatus,* which becomes a striving to be, or strife, with all the equivocations involved therein, already noted. Heidegger cannot get away from these, nor escape their ensnarement by simply coupling "projecting" with Open by means of a "hyphen." The "hyphen" dissimulates the problem; in fact, merely restates it. We need to give up the language of projection if the *passio essendi* is more elemental, and ontologically primal. It is on the basis of this "being given to be" that we can give ourselves to be, but in gratitude to the first gift, and in attendance on the openness of the between. And, all honor to Heidegger, he is trying to move in this second direction; but his language shows him still entangled in the striving to be, that strives *despite* the *passio essendi,* itself poorly rendered in the language of *Geworfenheit.* The full ontological dimensions of the between, and our being given to be in it, are not fully expressed. The sense of the agapeic origin that would go with this, also is not properly named: the origin of radical coming to be, and not just as a between, but of the between as the happening of contingent finitude, and not just of determinate becoming within the happening of the between.

Remember also that Plato was a thinker of the between, in which different relations such as mimesis, as well as different transcendings, such as eros and mania, show their becoming. But the metaxu also suggests the beyond of the between, named now as the Good. If the excessive origin is agapeic, it is unthinkable without the name of the Good, though we need not confine ourselves only to the Platonic thought of it. Something of the meaning of this Good concerns not this or that good, but the good of the "to be," given to be from beyond the finite "to be." If one connects this with the evil of the "to be" with Schopenhauer and Nietzsche, one begins also to see the connection with nihilism. If the between is an opening as coming to be that intimates its origin from Good, then also the opening to human being as given to be concretizes the "yes" to being as good by the origin. The communication of this "yes" may indeed be plurivocal—beyond univocalization; and equivocal, in that our claim to be for ourselves alone precipitates a polemos in which our claim to be *the good* turns the between into a site of strife between good and evil. But this even more means that the origin of the between is not best described as Open or "projecting." This origin that gives the openness of the between is not projective: not "projecting" itself or an other. The giving as a free releasing is agapeic. This original agapeic giving also releases the primal porosity of being, in which and through which all finite communicability and communication is possibilized and effected. Sub-ject, ob-ject, pro-ject; the first two yes, but also the third is caught in the "overagainstness" that hinders us from thinking the togetherness that makes the overagainstness possible, and the origin that makes the togetherness possible.[47]

I know that Heidegger wants to wed the language of polemos with the language of an intimacy between those in strife. But the language he uses for the second such as bestowing, grace, favor, and so on, cannot be derived from the language of the first. It is rather the other way around: polemos presupposes a more originary peace, without which no true peace will come to be from the accentuation of struggle, or strife, or the apotheosis of self-assertion. Heidegger is in *exactly the same position* as Schopenhauer and Nietzsche on this score. But because of his equivocal language, he creates a surface that can easily fool us, and perhaps even he fooled himself on this score. Everything about this other language has to do with being religious and with coming clean on this. This means waking up from the bewitchments in post-Kantian philosophy, conjured in different ways by Kant, and Hegel and Nietzsche, that suspend us in a metaphysical paralysis concerning the ultimacy of transcendence as other. Great art seems to wake us from this paralysis, and it sometimes does. But often when we make it serve as a surrogate for the silenced transcendence, it less wakes us as holds us faster in the bewitchment again. Heidegger's equivocity between art and the religious evidences for me that he has not genuinely woken from this bewitchment. Or is it that he gives us an odd mimicry of the awakening, a mimesis that plays with the awakening but remains half asleep: one eye open, one eye shut?

Safeguarding our intimacy with this other origin has less to do with an overcoming of metaphysics, as with the porosity of being religious, and with keeping free its passage in a manner that no human, that no epoch, can determine through himself or itself alone. When reading Heidegger, whether on art or other matters, one finds it hard to put away images of being religious. He plays the role, sometimes, one fears, mimics the motions of a kind of high priest. He performs the preparatory ablutions, dons the vestments of the most high celebrant of the mysteries, chants the necessary *introibo,* and then appears to lead his people to a high place of expectation, something is coming, something will come, and then we await for the words of consecration to enact or effect the mystery of transubstantiation, and words are uttered yes,

---

47. J. Taminaux in *Poetics, Speculation, and Judgement* (Albany: State University of New York Press, 1993) has an illuminating discussion of *OWA* where he shows a shift from a more Promethean *technē* in an earlier version to a less self-assertive register in the later version. This is all to the good, I agree, but I think that we are still, at most, only half way there, as it were, and far less near to the truth of the origin than Heidegger's orchestration wants to suggest.

dark words, perplexing words, but no consecration seems to take place, there seems no saving there, there is nothing there. Having been brought close to the mountain top in expectation, we seem *let down:* nothing happens, and we are brought down the mountain, the vestments and sacred vessels must be packed and put away, and we wonder if we have witnessed the counterfeit double of a revelation or communication rather than any real thing. Is something being feigned, something being faked, though its approximation to the real thing makes it difficult to discern as such? Was he priest or magician, vates or charlatan? Did we wake or did we sleep? Where will we find the needed finesse that ostensibly Heidegger seems himself to be offering? A seducer needs finesse. So does a philosophical seducer. But as Socrates the midwife reminds us, there can be mimetic pregnancies that yield a wind egg, a puff of nothing—a counterfeit double of being pregnant with an enigmatically deep message, but nothing seems born. Heidegger has stirred us deeply, but then as Jaspers puts it "he leaves us with empty hands."

And so we come back to our beginning with the above two opposite evaluations: high priest and empty prophet. Both seem right, both seem wrong; right in what they affirm, wrong in that each silences the rightness of the other, and so falsifies the inherent equivocity of Heidegger. The mask is double faced: sometimes the double face is a guardian of finesse about the holy; sometimes it is doubly double-faced and hence just two-faced in a vulgar "ontic" sense. Suppose the face before us has one eye open, one eye shut. Suppose this is a mask, behind which the other face also has one eye open and one eye shut—but these second set of eyes are open and shut on the *opposite* side of the face. Then the mask facing us would seem to see, with one eye open, one eye shut; but in fact, the chiaroscuro of both seeing and being blind would turn out, behind the mask, to be just sightlessness, for none of the eyes that could see would see. What then would the doubly self-concealing source be concealing in revealing itself, in showing its face? How could we decide if Heidegger was less a blind Teresias as bleared by such a self-concealing doubled face? We could not decide simply by listening to Heidegger's own prophesies, or looking at the face he shows, or mask. We would have to see for ourselves, that is, open ourselves to the mystery, or be opened. We would ourselves have to "see," that is, be prophetically blind. But would not this too be madness? And whether divine or wall-eyed, who will tell?

8

Art and the Impossible Burden of Transcendence

On the End of Art and the Task of Metaphysics

The End of Art: Asking Too Much, Asking Too Little

The "end of art" puts Hegel immediately in mind, and his well known proclamation: for us art, on the side of its highest destiny, is now a thing of the past (VA, I, 24, also 23; HA, I, 11, also 9–10). What exactly he means is still disputed. One reason the thesis is controversial, I think, is that in modernity art has been asked to bear a special burden different to other epochs. I will point to a paradoxical position: Too much has been asked of art, with the result that too little, or almost nothing, is now being asked of art. And too little is now asked, because too much was asked—asked in the wrong way.

My title also echoes, while altering, another thinker's words for whom the end of art was important. My original here is Heidegger: the end of philosophy and the task of thinking. Heidegger claimed that the end of metaphysics is in cybernetics, and looked to another beginning in which the thinker would be in dialogue with the poet. The renewal of thinking is bound up with the continued life of art, in the figure of the poet. I find difficulties with Heidegger's claims about the end of metaphysics,[1] and, as we say, ambiguities in the high place offered by him to art.

There seem to be a plurality of ends, or if you prefer, different "deaths" at stake: the end of art, the death of God, the end of philosophy. We are more

---

1. I refer again to *BB,* chapter 1; also "Being, Dialectic and Determination: On the Sources of Metaphysical Thinking," *The Review of Metaphysics,* 48 (June 1995): 731–69; and "Neither Deconstruction or Reconstruction: Metaphysics and the Intimate Strangeness of Being."

familiar with the Hegelian claim of the end of art, and the Nietzschean death of God, but of late the end of philosophy has returned to haunt us. I say returned since, of course, the theme haunted Hegel's time and his aftermath. Our century is not original regarding this provocative theme. For instance, we might see Marx and Kierkegaard as claiming this end: Kierkegaard to make way for religious faith; Marx to clear the path for revolutionary praxis which also will pierce the heart of religion with another stake, the stake of dialectical subversion. It is significant that the death of one is followed or accompanied by the death of another, as if for one to continue the others must continue also, or for one to be re-born the others must also come to life in a new way. Or perhaps each must be rooted in a shared milieu, rich enough in metaphysical and spiritual resources, to nourish the extreme demands each, at its best, makes of the human being. We now seem to lack such a milieu, and the wings of creative venturing which can be birthed there.

Heidegger's proclamation of the poet's task in the wake of the alleged completion of metaphysics can be seen to ask for a *being born again:* metaphysics may die into cybernetics, but thinking asks to be reborn beyond calculative mind, and in dialogue with the naming of the holy, said to be the poet's vocation. Heidegger's poet is not a post-Kantian aesthete, a specialist of aesthetic experience. The poet is sacerdotal. If the thinker thinks being, the poet names the holy. One might say: the poet serves to mediate the blessing of being, the thinker remains attentive to the communication of being. Heidegger sees himself as freeing thought from the prison-house of "theory," but his invocation of the poet as the namer of the holy places us back in the neighborhood of the religious festival, hence closer to the meaning resonating in the ancient word, *theōria*. Heidegger may be right to recall us to this different sense of thinking; but I find questionable the implication that the history of metaphysics is the stifling of this thinking. There is an unmistakable rupture between the premodern and the modern sense of "theory," which tells against any monolinear totalizing of the history of metaphysics.

My point takes shape: something *extraordinary* is being asked of the poet. He is to partner the thinker in one of the most ultimate of enterprises. Heidegger is not original in placing on the artist such a weight of metaphysical destiny. Nietzsche also makes a hyperbolic demand. The end of philosophy in the guise of Socratism might promise a new beginning: the higher artistry of tragic philosophizing. Nietzsche offers a radicalization and transposition of the metaphysical status Schopenhauer attributes to the artist, namely, redeeming us from the bondage to the futile wheel of will, releasing us into the freedom of contemplative, will-less knowing. And of course, the lineage of such ideas goes further back to Schelling's elevation of genius to metaphysical status. This elevation reflects, as well as consolidates, the apotheosis of the great artist in the Romantic reaction to Enlightenment scientism. It is important to makes sense of this apotheosis, not least because we still think in light of it, even though we have grown more acid with suspicion than was common in the youth of Romanticism. In the form it has taken in postenlightenment modernity, this role of the artist is all but impossible to maintain. That is, the artist is to be *the* voice and exemplary manifestation of transcendence. Given the history of the last two centuries, I believe such a role is impossible to sustain outside of some religious representation of the meaning of transcendence. Cut off from this, the claim is not just impossible to sustain, but may produce deformations of the meaning of transcendence, and indeed a kind of violence of human self-transcendence against itself.

Not only is the relation of philosophy to art and religion in question; so also is the relation of the religious and artistic. This relation is deeply equivocal in post-Hegelian culture. That culture often either lacks or rejects the resources of Hegel's dialectical way to deal with this relation. I have argued elsewhere that because Hegel is not lacking a sense for this relation, he might offer better means than many of his successors to shed some light on the paradox I stated above: too much has been asked of art with the result that little or nothing is now asked of art. But Hegel also contributed to that paradox. Why? Because of equivocities in dialectic's relation to religious transcendence and art's otherness. Sometimes overtly, sometimes implicitly, post-Hegelian thought takes a stand in relation to these equivocities. But it is enmeshed in them too, since it exhibits a decidedly equivocal relation to the religious, and to transcendence in religious form. Very differently to Hegel, art is asked to bear the burden of transcendence but within a cultural ethos wherein reference to the energies of the religious remains either muted or transposed or stifled. Art does not die into the religious, there to be sublated; rather the religious "dies" and the nameless afterlife of its transposed transcendence is ambiguously resurrected in art.

I hesitate to speak of our *postmodern* condition, since the word can mean everything and so can also mean nothing. Nevertheless, my point has continuing relevance. Enlightenment critique, Marxist demystification, Nietzschean suspicion and so forth have their postmodern *afterlives*. We remain at best diffident about the religious. While we are less gushing than the Romantics about genius, still a kind of "saving" role is often assigned to art: not religion—only art can "save" us now. While our "comfort levels" with the religious are very low, the same cannot be said for the aesthetic. Could one say that the most impressive of "post"-religious art is, as it were, prayer without praying? Do we not find here too the afterlife of a religion of art, a *masked* religion of art, one that sometimes has to squint through the mask, or wink: one eye open, one eye shut?

The Burden of Transcendence

Why speak of the *impossible burden of transcendence?* The issue is linked to the contested lives, and afterlives, of art, religion and philosophy in modernity.

The issue is not just the prohibition on transcendence as other to us, say, in a Nietzschean fashion, or with qualifications, a Kantian fashion. I do not say that transcendence as other to human self-transcendence is sheerly impossible but there may be a sense of transcendence as other that is impossible to subject completely to the measure of our thought. And yet this other transcendence asks our mindfulness, though it may entail for us an all but impossible challenge. As perhaps Kant glimpsed, we may have to try to think what cannot be entirely conceptualized. But first, it may be helpful to distinguish three different senses of transcendence. It is the third that raised the question of possibility and impossibility.

T1

The transcendence of *beings as other* in exteriority. The transcendence of such beings consists in their not being the product of our process of thinking; their otherness to us resists complete reduction to our categories, especially in so far as they simply are, or have being at all. Their determinate thereness as other and their otherness as being at all gives rise to the question: What makes possible both their possibility, as well as their actuality? What makes possible the possibility of their being at all? This is a metaphysical question about their being there at all: Why beings and not nothing? And what meaning resides in their recalcitrance, as simply being, to our complete conceptual mastery? The possibility of transcendence as *other* to their transcendence is opened by such questions.

T2

The transcendence of *self-being*, or *self-transcendence*. The meaning of possibility is here realized in interiority rather than determined externally. There is possibility as freedom, as self-determination, as the promise of free creativity. To be self-determining suggests a source of determining in excess of objective determination. In addition to the above questions, we must ask also: Is this self-transcendence merely an anomalous overreaching into emptiness, or a genuine self-surpassing towards transcendence as other? This second transcendence of self-being, as suggesting a source of determining in excess of objective determination, is certainly in question relative to the nature and meaning of human "creativity," a notion which figures so prominently in reflection on the place of art in our time. Indeed, self-transcendence and "creativity," despite the indeterminacy of "creativity," indeed perhaps just because of this indeterminacy, are often simply identified with each other. Hence the image of the great artist as the exemplary incarnation of "transcendence," here understood as self-transcendence.

T3

The question is whether there is an original source of transcendence as still *other* to these two senses. This, we might say, would be *transcendence itself,* not as the exterior, not as the interior, but as the superior. Transcendence itself would be in excess of determinate beings, as their original ground; it would be beyond self-transcendence as its most ultimate *possibilizing source.* It would be beyond the ordinary doublet of possibility/reality, as their possibilizing source. It could not be just a possibility, nor indeed a determinate realization of possibility. It would have to be active possibilizing power, in a manner more original and other than possibility and realization. It would have to be possibilizing beyond determinate possibility, and "active" beyond all determinate realization. In excess of determinacy and our self-determining, it would be overdetermined transcendence which, as other, would not be a merely indefinite beyond to finite being.

The question it raises is: If it is not under any finite category of the possible or real, if it is above, *huper, über* them, is it yet the original power to be at its most ultimate? What must this active possibilizing power be, if it is such as to give rise to finite being as *other* to itself; hence also as making possible the finite space or middle for the other two kinds of transcendence; and especially as releasing human self-transcendence into its own free creativity? For the third sense of transcendence could not to be identified with any *projection* onto the ultimate other of the first two senses. Its otherness would have nothing to do with projection. This does not mean we turn our back on first and second transcendence. It does suggest that there is to be no objectification (T1) or subjectification (T2) of third transcendence (T3). But second transcendence (T2), in its ineradicable recalcitrance to complete objectification, is pointed beyond objectness and subjectness to transobjective and transsubjective transcendence (T3).

This third transcendence (T3) has been made especially problematic by a certain development of second transcendence (T2) in modernity, particularly in so far as our self-transcendence has defined itself hugely in terms of its own autonomy. Then a certain logic, rather *bewitchment of self-determination* casts a spell over all our thinking, and the thinking of what it other to our self-determination. Inevitably, third transcendence (T3) becomes endowed with an equivocal position. I want to say that there is a tension, not to say an *antinomy,* between such autonomy and transcendence. This is not just a mere contradiction, but a tension wherein a number of different possibilities for existence and thought take shape. In this equivocal space the traditional respect accorded to third transcendence (T3) from an essentially religious point of view comes under onslaught, and for reasons to which I will come. Yet it is also into that space of equivocality that art is inserted as somehow enabling us to deal with the tension of autonomy and transcendence. In this insertion art comes to assume some of the roles previously accorded to religion. But the antinomy is not resolved. Third transcendence remains mocking and welcoming. Is it possible for art to be the bearer of third transcendence, purely through itself, if it is defined in a cultural ethos wherein the religious urgency of ultimacy has not a major role in shaping the mindfulness of humans?

Third transcendence as other points beyond objectification and subjectification. Do some strains of postmodernism point beyond self-transcendence to transcendence as other? Much is suggested in the many mansions of postmodern thought. The suggestions are sometimes vacillating, indeed with an agonized hesitation to be more forthright relative to third transcendence. But "being beyond" as *trans* might also be *between* subject and object; and so third transcendence may not be absolutely unapproachable through T1 and T2. For these approaches, art and religion are crucial, since neither the languages of objectivity or subjectivity are true enough to the happenings of art and religion. Such happenings are transsubjective, transobjective, but anchored in the sensuousness of the "objective," as well as dynamized in and through the energies of the "subjective." There is here a trans-position: a position that is trans and between: *meta* as *metaxu,* in the double sense of the Greek—"in the midst," and also "beyond, over and above." Such a transposition undoubtedly calls on the artistic as well as the religious, but the former alone is not sufficient, especially if the latter has been put in epochē, so to say. Postmodern aestheticism strikes one as suspended in this epochē (under erasure, so to say). The postmodern interest in Kierkegaard: does it not drift towards treating religion as another aesthetic possibility? The temptation, if we privilege the aesthetic, is that we play an exciting game of peek-a-boo with transcendence as other. Now you see it, now you don't. We play the same game with human self-transcendence. Often again in this half-light, one wonders if transcendence as other has been replaced by human self-transcendence as othering itself: the self as other speaks for the other beyond self, but protects itself thereby from transcendence as other in the more ultimate sense. Does our celebration of the postmodern self/nonself then mask the fear to take the further step needed?

Art may be crucial in carrying self-transcendence and naming transcendence as other, but it can never substitute for religion. As we will see, an impossible burden of transcendence is placed on art by some significant post-Kantian and post-Hegelian thinkers. But the continuing challenge of the antinomy between autonomy and transcendence suggests the need to reconsider the latter, and not just human self-transcendence. The "end" of art, as I will suggest, has something to do with art's *reversal* into aesthetic inconsequence in the wake of this previous imposition on it of this impossible burden of transcendence. If this "end" asks of us a rethinking of transcendence, something of the task of metaphysics is implied, and it is not at all the so-called "end" of philosophy.

ART AND THE "END" OF METAPHYSICS

What here of this so-called "end of metaphysics"? Despite the bad name metaphysics has had of late, the need for metaphysics has not ceased. Sometimes it takes forms that do not officially present themselves with the calling card marked "metaphysics." One of those incognitos is connected to "art."

In modernity we often find a kind of allergy to transcendence. I do not mean human self-transcendence. Clearly the powers of human self-transcendence have been asserted, glorified, divinized, debunked, but never treated with any less than ultimate respect. We take ourselves very seriously, even when we deconstruct ourselves. We have to account for ourselves in every sense: we are mature, autonomous, self-determining beings, and so on and on. We are self-surpassing, self-overcoming beings. Transcendence? I am transcendence!

Whence then the allergy to transcendence as other (T3)? Self-transcendence has been yoked to a model of autonomous self-determination: the self is the law of itself, self-regulating, self-legislating, not only in morality a là Kant, but indeed in aesthetics where the genius is frequently proclaimed as the legislative power who gives, directly or indirectly, the rule to art. But such autonomous determination is dialectically equivocal concerning the place of the other.[2] The other disturbs every effort to make this self-determining autonomy absolute, *ab-solo*. The song of self-transcendence sings to itself over the murmurings of an equivocal attitude to transcendence as other to self.

The equivocity is evident in modern philosophy itself: metaphysics must be absolutely self-determining knowing, justifying itself purely through itself; and if it makes any forays into transcendence as other, it must do so from the standpoint of its own secured and guaranteed autonomy. Traditional metaphysics of transcendent being must fall, if this is the ideal of knowing one sets before oneself. Transcendence as other must be subordinated to self-transcendence, but such a subordination signs the death warrant of transcendence as other, whose real meaning becomes just its meaning for me, not for itself as other. It must submit to me, I do not submit to it, or indeed to anything. I am the Lord.

Kantianism is clearly hamstrung by this requirement it sets itself. Kant had his own desire to open thought to transcendence but the overriding ideal of self-determining knowing (albeit not fully realized for Kant in knowing, but claimed in practical reason) makes him at best equivocal about transcendence as other. This hamstringing of transcendence as other in no way destroys the need for it, as Kant also clearly saw, if again with a divided mind, indeed a bit of a bad conscience, with respect to the ineradicable metaphysical exigencies of the human being.

---

2. On this more fully, see "Autonomia Turannos: On Some Dialectical Equivocities in Self-determination."

Of course, Kant is an extraordinary thinker, and some of the nuances of his views are easily flattened. Hegel is also an extraordinary thinker, but he is representative of this project of autonomous or self-determining knowing. He is dialectically complex, and his philosophy is deeply qualified by gestures towards some conceptually strategic acknowledgement of transcendence and otherness. Yet when it comes down to it, in the end, he is entirely a modern thinker, in that self-determining knowing supplies the meaning of the whole. Where the other is acknowledged, it will be included as a necessary moment of a more encompassing process of self-mediating knowing. This is evident in regard to art, since art always has a residue of otherness, namely, the sensuous otherness of the medium of artistic expression; this is not conquered in art itself. Only in philosophy is this externality entirely overcome, Hegel believes. Even where religious transcendence is noted, it too is yoked to a long and complex dialectic in which finally transcendence is reduced to immanence, and the traces of divine enigma conceptually conquered.

The whole scientistic impulse of Enlightenment did not help here. Any reference to transcendence is seen as the continued residue of a properly outmoded obscurantism. Comte's triadic unfolding from religion to metaphysics to positive science is representative: progressively the signs of transcendence must be transformed into the immanences of determinate positive science, entirely at home with its own conceptualizations of being, and cleverly free from any homesickness for religion or metaphysics. Does the exigence of transcendence vanish? Not at all.[3] Scientism is itself a surrogate project of transcendence: it is human self-transcendence, attempting to divinize its own scientific powers, as the light that the world will recognize as properly its own, and there will be no mystery here, and no mystery beyond this proper light. All will be light.

And yet there is only too much darkness to all this light. We have become more tired of these proclamations of light, when we remember the monsters this light has spawned, and will no doubt continue to spawn. The sweats come in many forms. As the project of modernity unfolds, we find again and again systematic tendencies leading to the devaluation of transcendence as other. The tendencies are to be seen in philosophy, in religion itself (Kant's religion within the limits of reason is exemplary), in hostility to religion (Marx, Nietzsche, Freud), in ethics (utilitarianism and Kantianism, emotivism, relativism), and indeed in art. Nevertheless, it is with respect to art that a *different light* begins to glow. As the light of Enlightenment congratulates itself, a howl of protest arises from the blindness of the human spirit that this light produces. The Romantic protest may have its problems,

3. Even Comte came to acknowledge that: in his foundation of the positivist Church, in his increasing fondness for what he took to be an original fetishism marking early humans, in his belief that our age needed something analogous.

but we still bob in its backwash, if only because we still bob in the dark backwash of Enlightenment.

There is the problem too that transcendence as other seemed to have been conceived in very dualistic fashion. Transcendence as other was up there, or over there, or beyond, all in opposition to down here, and the here and now, and the present. I think this is a flattened way to describe the thinking of transcendence by premodern thinkers; yet there is no doubt that it can easily lend itself to the kind of dualistic opposition that, in turn, can easily lead to the redundancy of transcendence.[4] For if transcendence is so other as opposite, it seems we can finally say nothing of it, and its relevance to life here and now becomes open to critique. There is the added factor that the language of transcendence was often used to buttress the legitimacy of political orders that seem restrictive of genuine freedom; hence religion seems to provide a mere ideological rationalization of the will to power of the rulers. The fuller and more enlightened release of the powers of human autonomy demand the destruction of transcendence. Hence for Marx, the critique of religion is the basis of all critique, the indispensable step to foster a proper revolutionary attitude. Others like Feuerbach, Nietzsche, Freud, Sartre, to name only some, suggest that the destruction of transcendence as other is necessary to release our own powers of self-transcendence, our autonomous creativity. Art will come to share in the same project, in that nothing other than art will be allowed from outside to interfere with the proper fulfillment of its own immanent creativity. The hint of an other will be greeted with irritation, or alarm, as a threat to aesthetic purity and autonomy.

Art and the Need of Transcendence

More could be said, yet despite the allergy to transcendence as other, there *continues* the ineradicable need of transcendence. This continued need is evident even in efforts at the self-absolutization of our own power of surpassing. Transcendence as immanent is not forbidden, but rather spreads over the

---

4. Think how the importance of the sublime in the eighteenth century defined a reaction to the soul-lessness of mechanistic nature; it offered a sense of nature as *other* and *more*. This offering originally emerged in a religious, not merely aesthetic, context. This is the intimation of the excess of T3, in the excess to mechanism of T1. There is the question of divining further the meaning of this intimation. Here the issues of pantheism and panentheism come to the fore. Is this excess of transcendence a beyond of the sort recommended by traditional theism? Or immanent in a manner more congenial to some modern thinkers (albeit moderns dissatisfied with a mechanistic view of nature)? Moderns neither mechanists, nor traditional theists, and who reject what they take to be a dualistic world-picture between creator and creation, such as they ascribe to traditional theism? I think that relative to the excess of third transcendence (T3), God cannot be adequately approached in the language of holistic panentheism.

place of transcendence as other. The argument runs like this: If transcendence is not somehow manifest here and now, that is, immanently, its relevance is questionable; and since metaphysics and religion are under a cloud, and scientific enlightenment will not really meet the exigence of transcendence (making a devalued earth, making it serviceable and disposable for an instrumental reason), a space opens for art to step forth boldly, and stake its claim to epitomize the power of immanent transcendence.

And indeed art *does* seem to be the product of creative power out of the ordinary. It can disrupt and de-familiarize our sense of being. It can refresh our perception. It can help us speak free of the tiredness of dead metaphors. It can allow us to look at creation anew, and indeed to celebrate its worth, in a way science cannot. It can speak to the whole human being, and not just to the instrumentalized intellect. It need not shun the truth of what cannot be brought into the light of scientific truth, especially those perplexing mysteries at the heart of human existence. It can witness to the pathos and ecstasis of the human spirit, opening us beyond already sedimented ways of being, auguring something more, something richer—and not elsewhere, but here now in the here and now. Art is a celebrant of the sensuous, and unlike the supposedly joyless religions of guilt, and their evil eye for the human body, has its pleasure in what nature gives. In a word, art seems to offer a way to meet the need of transcendence without the seemingly dispiriting dualisms of prior religions and metaphysics.

Let me relate the point to Kant's account of genius. Genius, as Kant says, is the one through whom nature gives the rule to art. But if genius gives the rule, he or she is beyond the rules, transcendent in a peculiar way: a source that makes manifest but a source itself hidden in darkness. In modernity genius is often seen as the epitome of creativity and originality. The great artist assumes many of the attributes formerly reserved to deity: someone *sui generis,* not defined through another, marked by extraordinary power, both in making and in vision, a superabundance of overflowing energy that irresistibly finds its mark, perhaps even a status beyond the law, beyond good and evil, as Nietzsche would have it. Nor are we to think in terms of any ideal of moderation: genius is the epitome of creative transcendence, but there is something extreme, over and above, something excessive to that transcendence. Even if the transcendent other is put out of play, the genius can offer an image of transcendence as immanent, as coming to manifestness in human existence. The genius draws up, or draws down, the beyond into the now. He or she makes creative transcendence incarnate. Though Kant is more sober in his language, his sobriety masked intoxicating implications. His readers immediately divined something revolutionary when in the *Critique of Pure Reason* he gave the privilege to the self-activity of the knower in defining nature's intelligibility. The hope of autonomy was held out: we are no longer abject or supine before nature, we are beyond it as free, and free in our power to determine the intelligibility of its being-other. The Romantics might tend to misread Kant, but we should be not surprised that they were such enthusiasts of a writer so severely unromantic on the surface. The privilege of the determining, potentially creative self, all surface appearances notwithstanding, is declared.

There is a further ambiguity; the apotheosis of the self is not all. This self cannot be elevated to a higher status simply in virtue of its human-all-too-human being. The elevation rather takes place in virtue of something excessive coming to manifestation in genius. That is, genius is the revelation in the human being of *something other* than the human, something perhaps greater and more fundamental, more originary and more ultimate. Recall that Kant defines genius as he through whom nature gives the rule to art. It seems that nature is giving the rule, and through the genius (as in T2). It is not that genius (T2), seemingly the elemental and energetic and originative power, is the simple rule-giver; something other is working through the genius. Kant calls this other "nature," and if I am not mistaken it seems to mingle some of the marks of first and third transcendence (T1 and T3 above).

Kant has a quite equivocal attitude to genius, something not always noted as we saw, partly because so many of his commentators themselves are culturally defined by a pregiven proclivity to see the genius as the embodiment of transcendence. They are heirs of Romanticism, even when they make a point of scoffing at the putative excesses of Romanticism. Yet we might see these very excesses as the signs of naïveté. They may also be signs of a more uncalculating honesty. If we now have become more circumspect, we may have also become less spontaneously honest. Genius is made to bear the impossible burden of transcendence, impossible in a manner recognized by religion, impossible in that ultimately transcendence is beyond all human autonomy and self-mastery, precisely because there is always a rupturing otherness of which nothing human can be sovereign master.

Put otherwise, the rhetoric of autonomy and the rhetoric of creative transcendence are not, in the end, seamlessly compatible. The second points to an other dimension that lies beyond autonomy, however glorious and majestic and sovereign. Interestingly, the cult of genius does recognize this, but it also wants to pay its homage to the rhetoric of autonomy. It wants to have its cake and eat it too, when it comes to transcendence. But there comes a point when the rupture of otherness makes it less and less possible to sustain the rhetoric of autonomy.

There is a reversal here: it is precisely the rhetoric of autonomy that guides us towards artistic genius in the modern sense as the epitome of immanent transcendence; but just that epitome leads to the recognition that the absolutization of autonomy is not finally sustainable at all. Properly understood, this should lead to a total rethinking of transcendence. Often, in fact, it leads to a repeated vacillation between autonomy and transcendence, very rarely brought out in its unsustainable equivocality. If autonomy is ultimate, transcendence must be subordinated; if transcendence is ultimate, autonomy can never be absolute.

Did Kant think through the equivocal situation? I do not think he did. He opts for the moralization of the aesthetic and the sublime, and finally it is the destiny of pure moral autonomy that has to place genius, and the sublime, in its order of things. Kant also contributes to the equivocal situation to the extent that art is aestheticized; it is said to be autonomous vis-à-vis religion and ethics and science, though this autonomy is finally abrogated by Kant himself, though not by the aesthetic followers of more Romantic strain. This autonomy reflects the modern division of functions into separate areas: we might call it a plural autonomy; yet the ideal of total autonomy generates its own *aporia,* in that the relation to the other always comes back to haunt autonomy. (A certain devaluation of being is in the background of this aestheticism.) Like the eclipse of transcendence as other, the insistence on autonomy in the first instance has also to be reconsidered. The separation of art is in the end a compromised separation, full of fatal equivocation.

What of the use of Kant's views for postmodern purposes, not in accord with his more moralizing aim? In the tension between Enlightenment and Romanticism, a way is followed to a *deconstructed version* of the Romantic side: Romanticism without Romanticism. Does the aestheticization of the sublime have the seriousness of Kant's moralization? If modernity is defined by a double process of objectivizing and subjectivizing, should we not rather call postmodernism "hypermodernism," as a continuation of *being between* Enlightenment and Romanticism? It is neither one nor the other, undecided between them; and yet it is both, since in not being one or the other, it is both a repudiation and continuation. It reflects a culture of autonomy become uncertain and critical of itself, indeed agonized about itself. If a sense of an other emerges, it is an indeterminate other or self. One hesitates to call it third transcendence (T3). Self-determination reaches into the roots of self and finds the other to self, and yet this other is thought within an ethos of now agonized self-determination. So we vacillate about the more radical sense of third transcendence (T3) and release to the other. If the antinomy of autonomy and transcendence is mirrored in Enlightenment and Romanticism, it is also mirrored in their postmodern *promiscuity*. And despite the fact that our agonized self-determination wrings its hands in uncertainty, this other fact stands massively before us: self-less, impersonal technology reduplicates its spiritual deficiency in the narcissism of the self absorbed in itself.

To return to the more immediate aftermath of Kant: The anointing of art is not just the prerogative of the few. The entire culture lays its hands on. The cultured despisers of religion make art and culture into surrogate religion. There is nothing more striking than the religion of art in the nineteenth century. This is not at all like the *Kunstreligion* of the Greeks with which Hegel deals. True, there was widespread yearning for the Greeks, supposedly not stained by the shame of the Christians, living in unself-consciousness unity with nature, within themselves, and with their others in society. But *Kunstreligion* is first of all religion, and not art in the modern sense at all: it is religion in which the formative powers of art are deployed to their utmost to present plastic images of the divine, and in a manner that has been thought, and with some right, to be unsurpassable.[5] The religion of art in the nineteenth century is first and foremost art, set apart from religion as previously understood. Of course, in both art and religion the exigence of transcendence is at work. It is not that there is not an artistic side of religion or a religious side of art. But after Kant art, considered in as purely as aesthetic fashion as possible, assumes the characteristic of a devotion and piety.

The cult of the genius is only one aspect of it, the genius as emissary of the divine. Recall the sometimes noted comparison of the opera house to the temple: the museum as church. (True, there are museums now that flirt with the image of the fun-house.) An academic goes to a conference in a strange city; come Sunday morning, we do not inquire where the local church is; we ask directions to the local museum, there to pay our obeisance to the god of art. One is to make touch with the holy. The art work is transcendence made flesh. Ironically there is something religiously archaic in this aesthetically advanced behavior, for the museum, after all, is the temple of the Muses, and who knows what spirits haunt that temple, and what wooing might still be called forth there. Sometimes too museums remind one of pilgrimage sites of the middle ages. The pilgrims come in crowds to gaze in wonder at the famed exhibits, while the cardinals of the art church, the curators of the great museums, vie with each other to secure the most prestigious shows.

Of course, the quasi-absolutization of art is invaded by, even as it in turn invades, the commercial market.[6] There is something quasi-religious about the way the market instrumentalizes this aesthetic quasi-absolute: art objects become fetishes because of contact with the genius, like relics of saints in previous ages, or pilgrimage memorabilia like medals, scapulars, crosses, rosaries, or other scraps and shreds that have had some chain of contact with the "presence," and on whom the aura of the sacred rubs off. It is not quite the contagion of enthusiasm that the rhapsode in the *Ion* communicates, as the magnet charges the rings that hang from it. I think rather of Picasso signing the table napkins, and just that signature turning them into valuable commodities. Art is holy but it is also cash. I think of Salvador Dalí, in later life, signing *empty sheets* for cash. (*Avida Dollars:* André Breton's brilliant rebaptism of Salvador Dalí.) Some have seen this (as well as, seemingly contradictorily, his surreal somersault from "sacrilege" to "mysticism") as a "sell-out," or a "betrayal." But there is a kind of *lethal consistency* in it. Again: Asking too much of art becomes asking nothing much at all—as long as you have the holy signature of the genius. Or now—the celebrity!

---

5. This point is crucial to an understanding of Hegel's thesis of the "end" of art; see my "Art and the Absolute Revisited."

6. See *PO,* chapter 2 on the cult of novelty, and art as commodity.

We might even be tempted to settle for more splinters under the skin of good sense, such as elephant dung pictures of the Mother of God, or lights going on and off in a room—recent works crowned with the prize honoring the name of the great Turner. A dishevelled bed with soiled underwear and assorted accoutrement of the boudoir was *not* awarded the prize, and one cannot but marvel at what discernment and delicatesse had to be mustered to make that aesthetic judgment. But let us not be too snide: If one goes to any popular place of holy pilgrimage, there the hucksters spring up, like weeds after rain that breaks the drought. Weeds spring up with the flowers; they choke their bloom. These tares are not thrown onto the bonfire but turned into lucrative exhibits.

Equivocating between Art and Religion

We must notice more than the commercial exploitation, or the kitsch of this religion. Art must have intrinsic value before it is instrumentalized, value for itself before it is utilized. If the second dominates, the first is violated or corrupted. This can happen with eros and love too, and at the extreme pornography is the corruption. Philosophers too are erotic beings, and the early forms of eros are sometimes the most ardent. Thus at the opposite extreme to commercial exploitation, philosophers have invested art with an extraordinary aura of high seriousness: something about art approaches the absolute. I repeat: We need not deny that art, so far as it is spiritually serious, is bound up with the enigma of transcendence. Nevertheless, some of the thinkers to whom I will now refer, either deny, or are equivocal about, its relation to other carriers of our sense of transcendence, such as metaphysics, or religion. Because of the perceived demise of traditional religion, because of the perceived bankruptcy of spirit deriving from a merely scientistic enlightenment, because of an intimation that the apotheosis of reason in the high noon of idealism was not enough and that metaphysics in idealistic form seemed at an end, art gets conferred with extraordinary powers. It becomes *the* metaphysical activity.

Let me detail the matter relative to some important thinkers, and with respect to three major points: the extraordinary value ascribed to art; the equivocation on the religious; the diverse workings of the unnoticed antinomy of autonomy and transcendence.

First Point

Significant instances are not hard to find where the artist is elevated into all but a mouthpiece for the absolute. The hesitancy in Kant's attitude to genius dissolves, and the restraints he would impose on genius are seen as rationalistic timidities. Thus the fact remains that Hegel *does* accord art a position at the highest level of absolute spirit. I underscore this absoluteness. Schelling is even more insistent: something about art is higher than philosophy: art brings the whole human being to the absolute standpoint, whereas philosophy brings only the conceptual mind. Here Schelling has more successors than Hegel. This is connected with a diffidence about the supreme claims Hegel makes for reason, and the belief that there was an *other to reason* that his idealism made too recessive. In the tension between Enlightenment and Romanticism, the Romantic side seems to win out: something other to reason is seen as the very ground of reason. Romanticism is the truth of Enlightenment: the dark origin of creativity, exemplified in the great artist or work, shows the manifestness of this transcendence, and not scientific nor philosophical reason.

This Schellingian line of inheritance, as we might call it, might be connected to Schopenhauer. Though he hated Hegel, there are resonances not anathema to Hegel's view. I mean the sense that while art, religion and philosophy are others, they are *familial* others. There is an other to reason, will, but this is without goal, hence threatens a merely futile striving; art allows us to contemplate it, hence releases us from bondage to it; and most especially does music offer a direct revelation of the will itself; it is the privileged metaphysical art. For Hegel and Kant poetry is the supreme art, but with Schopenhauer music takes that place. I mention this because the issue of the *other of reason* is here crucial. Something is communicated in music which seems of absolute moment, but this cannot be captured in discursive thinking, or the determinate objectifications of language. Music is its own "language," or the direct expression of the will itself. Despite significant divergences, a kinship with Hegel is not lacking in the way art, religion and philosophy count as exemplary in the family of ways of expressing what is ultimate. Thus the religious saint has a supreme function in releasing us from the futility of the will, and on occasion Schopenhauer suggests an idea of philosophy as like the conceptual counterpart of art: the self-knowledge of the will itself which rises above will to free contemplative knowing. As with Schelling, so with Schopenhauer the philosopher too must have the touch of genius.

Nietzsche stands in this line of inheritance of deconstructed and deconstructing idealism. Very evidently in his *Birth of Tragedy* the genius is important, thought it is not only the human genius, but the *world-genius,* the world-artist. As we saw, for Nietzsche the only possible theodicy is an aesthetic theodicy—a view though modified, never repudiated. The artist, the tragic artist stands superior to the philosopher who inhabits the safe lowlands where pedestrian thought creeps furtively along. Dialectic is rabble, as he put it; tragic art is high, noble, it is above, able to look down at the darkness of what is below. Again the other of reason is disclosed here, in that the "below" is a dark and fearsome abyss, the knowing of which brings unbearable suffering. Art is the vehicle of this dark rooted transcendence, called the primal One in the *Birth of Tragedy,* later less theologically called will to power. There is no doubting that the human creator is the medium of this power other than itself.

Art never loses its supreme redemptive function for Nietzsche. And "redemption" is the word, nothing less will do. The supremacy of music here again indicates the turning over of Enlightenment and the showing of the dark origin. If art has metaphysical significance, music is the very singing of that significance. It is not enough to speak that significance, it has to be sung. Thought might not only have to think what is other, thought might also have to sing its other.

There is much I must pass over in silence here. I can only mention again Heidegger's according the poet an extremely high place as the namer of transcendence, and the power of art to bring us into proximity with the origin. So also in the grim fallen world of Adorno, what little consolation he finds, he finds in art, and most of all in music. Rorty comes close to being the chirpy caricature of the whole thing, *sans* metaphysical pathos: the strong poet and utopian revolutionary are offered as signs of hope for human creativity, but without subtle enough hermeneutical self-consciousness or *esprit de finesse*. Rorty: the Andy Warhol of recent American philosophy—though more earnest than Andy. At least Andy made sure to wink: one eye open, one eye shut!

(Parenthetically: One wonders if Andy Warhol was superior in not taking himself with the seriousness Richard Rorty now does, all appearances notwithstanding. Andy was getting away with it, and winking as he did. Is Rorty getting away with it, but not quite winking? The wink is a small gesture communicating honesty about something not there. But this might seem too uncharitable with so much moral earnestness. My apologies: Rorty does say somewhere that "truth" is what your colleagues let you get away with. Still I do divine a disguised temptation to the "religious" here. I mean that in his mission to edify, Rorty has now become a secular preacher, albeit in the services of a certain form of liberalism. One wonders if this preaching, qua preaching, is more absurd even than the preachers of old, for they believed there was some ground in truth to their homilies. Rorty denies that—"ground in truth"—to accept that would be like asking someone with a sweet tooth to suck lemons. And yet he expects us to listen to his sermons. But as with Nietzsche's groundless "Amen," there is no true basis ultimately in being for the consolation of art or for preaching. The concerned last man is in the ascendent, having learned a trick or two from Nietzsche himself. Listening to these postphilosophical homilies, my mind sometimes wanders, and I wonder if in the past the travelling hypnotist might answer to that line of work. We went happily to the performance of the hypnotist, both desiring to fall under his spell and dreading it. And we did see leprechauns up trees when we left the hall. But on waking up later, we had a good laugh at the nonsense of it all, and maybe the good laugh at the nonsense was the point of significance of it all. But Rorty has become serious and solemn about the nonsense of it all—which is the truth, if what he says is true—which, of course, it cannot really be, if what he says is true. And don't say: "But that is rhetoric!" Do you think I don't know that. Besides, what other kind of "refutation" could there possibly be, if what rhetoricians like Nietzsche and Rorty say is "true"? Can you "argue" your way awake from a spell?)

Second Point

This concerns the equivocity on the religious. It helps to keep in mind the Hegelian view of *Kunstreligion,* and its *non-aestheticized* sense of art. After Hegel I find a vacillation between a Kantian aestheticized sense (connected with the univocalized separation of art, religion, science, and so on, into specialized divisions), and a perhaps more archaic view which sees a kind of promiscuous equivocity of religious and art (the two are impossible to separate univocally). I think that what Schelling means by great art cannot be univocally separated from his other great concern, namely, myth. Myth is the art of God, so to say. And the reason we need a philosophy of mythology is that God reveals himself differently in different epochs through the myths, that is, the systems of religious images that particularly relate to the ultimate origin of being, and destiny. All of history is a kind of religious art and the temporal manifestation of its plural forms. I divine here some anticipations of a Heideggerian historicized view of the epochal mittences of being. Indeed, a somewhat analogous point might be urged relative to Hegel's three epochs of art, the symbolical, classical, romantic, which are also three epochs of gods or the divine.

In Schopenhauer, the tone of reverence for the artist borders on the religious, or pseudo-religious, and this despite his self-avowal as an atheist. An atheistic aesthetic, so to say, would be entirely too crude a view of the work of transcendence in art and religion. Schopenhauer obviously rejects lock, stock and barrel the whole system associated with a moralized God. Yet so many of the things he says are full of religious, quasi-religious resonances, and not only in relation to religions from the orient, as he was not shy in granting. Perhaps one might say of Schopenhauer that he was one of the first of the philosophers who displayed a kind of *atheistic religiousity*. It is the darkness of the origin (his interpretation of transcendence in the sense of T3) that replaces a sense of the origin as good. His view of will as this blind, ugly, senseless, needy energy made it impossible to think of the ground of things in conventional theistic terms. The other of reason here assumes a face more like Descartes' evil genius. Art, religious, philosophy are efforts to escape the evil of the evil genius; to be is not to be good; to be is evil. Schopenhauer's prayer: Art, religion—deliver us from this evil!

In Nietzsche by contrast, there is a counter celebration of a more affirmative power in will. I must confine myself to my main point: Nietzsche's view of art is essentially religious. I am not talking about Christian or Jewish religion but the tragic art of the Greeks. Such an art is not at all like the modern aestheticized view of the post-Kantian. It is art as a kind of *Gottesdienst,* a divine service. The god served is not Yahweh or Jesus but Dionysus. Nietzsche is a votary of Dionysus; as is his image of the great artist. Hence here too, as we find in Schelling, we cannot separate the artistic and the mythic. This is clear in so far as it is not I qua empirical individual that produces art. Art comes to be through singular individuals (the genius as *Übermensch*) who are destined to be the outstanding manifestation of the truth of being as will to power. What is at issue is not only the artist giving birth to the art work, but the world itself as an art work giving birth to itself; and then within the world as art, the human artist as speaking, singing this process of coming to birth, coming to be, even in all passing away. We very easily mistake the complexity of Nietzsche, since the heat of his denunciation of Christianity is so blasting that we think of him as radically anti-religious. Yet if we look carefully at his view of art, the carrying of transcendence he asks of art makes little sense without invoking the religious, as a nonindividualistic art of the ultimate, itself as will to power.

Can one make a somewhat related point about Heidegger? He had a tormented relation to religion, and his sometimes hostile attitude to Catholicism might make one expect antagonism to religion; but the fact that Hölderlin is his chosen interlocutor is full of ironies and resonances. There are unstated elective affinities here, not least in that Hölderlin—after all, Hegel's friend, and between whom there was more genuine warmth than between either and Schelling—turned to poetry rather than conceptual dialectic in response to the bankruptcy of Enlightenment modernity. Hölderlin is a poet of the vanishing of the gods and the harbinger of a new coming. There is nothing "aesthetic" about him at all. The dialogue of poet and thinker makes no sense outside of an honest naming of the religious.

Why do I smell equivocation on the religious all over the place? One longs perhaps to name transcendence, but fears to do so lest one be accused of being out of joint with the times; as if, in the end, one could not quite get clear of the Enlightenment that one also despises. I ventured elsewhere that Heidegger is a kind of closet Comtean but *in reverse*, a kind of inverse positivist: he laments the fall from the gods to cybernetics, but he accepts, as the destiny of the West, something like this positivist move from religion/theology, through metaphysics, to positive science (see *BB*, 38–44). He wants to do an end run behind not only Christianity, but also classical Greek philosophy, and the purer pre-Socratics await beyond the goal line. Much of this reminds one of Nietzsche's attitude to Socratism and "theoretical man" in the *Birth of Tragedy*, though more ponderously and turgidly handled. I wonder again if we might be better served by the eyes and ears of a Vico, with his feel for the family relations of the poetic and the religious.

I find in Adorno a *strangled* religious impulse. Though he calls upon the messianic theme, invokes the light of redemption, in the evil world of fallen instrumental reason the only stray ray of light coming to us seems to be from art. Rorty produces the chirpy caricature of the whole thing. He is a kind of cardboard Comtean who has grown old and tired and jaundiced with positive science. There is no need for "redemption," just a little bit of consideration will do. It is as if philosophers should learn to say: "Have a nice day!" I say nothing against politeness, but there is here the absence of any urgency of ultimacy.

All that stuff is regressive fundamentalism. True, there are one or two traces of an atrophied religious sense.[7] Rorty cleverly shuffles forward into the dying of the light, though he thinks that the dying of the light is an advance in enlightenment. In the end he can give no satisfactory reason for the direction of his clever shuffling. He has to use rhetoric to make the religious other feel shamed about his "preferences." This is an old Enlightenment tactic to convert the other into the cultural despiser of religion. Rorty is more understated than, say, Marx, or Nietzsche, but this is only because the latter were moved by surrogate transcendence and their own urgency of ultimacy. Rorty wants nothing to do with the latter. Hence instead of the Marxist roar or Nietzschean curse against religion, there is a bleat of culturally condescending superiority: "It is not to our taste"—supposing one could *smirk* in saying this.

Third Point

What of the antinomy of autonomy and transcendence? First think of Kant and Hegel as offering us different models of autonomy or self-determination. Kant's notion of the self-legislating moral will is perhaps the most radical effort to define autonomy in contradistinction to heteronomy, which carries nothing but negative connotations, as we see in the *Grundlegung*. Hegel is more dialectically sophisticated than Kant, since he includes reference to the other, *to heteron,* in his definition of self-determination: rational autonomy becomes absolutely self-determining when, though it transcends towards the other, it yet incorporates this other as a moment of its own self-determining. I have been suggesting that the otherness of third transcendence (T3) resists these understandings of autonomy or self-determination. Art can serve to bring to mindfulness this other transcendence. But it cannot do so on its own, if not already dwelling within an ethos wherein the communications of third transcendence are given some names. Religion is the way these names take form in finitude.

I find again a deep tension, sometimes indecision concerning how both autonomy and transcendence are to be accommodated. The general thrust of modernity is to subordinate the second to the first. But one might claim that art, as bringing transcendence to mindfulness, tells against this, and indeed relativizes the superior claim of autonomy. If the above thinkers are followers of Kant, it is a modified Kant of the *Critique of Judgment* they follow, not Kant of the *Critique of Practical Reason*. Art is the other more metaphysically significant. (Schiller is one of the first *hybrids:* he mixes the Second and the

7. See Richard Rorty's essay "Trotsky and the Wild Orchids," in *Wild Orchids and Trotsky—Messages from American Universities,* ed. Mark Edmundson (New York: Viking, 1993). I find the preaching at its most overt in Rorty's *Philosophy and Social Hope* (Harmondsworth: Penguin, 1999).

Third Critiques, morality and art). A move is prepared in Kant, though he would not make this, since moral autonomy is unconditional for him, and nothing else. His discussion of genius harbors the antinomy: genius seems the epitome of autonomous human creativity, yet in the genius something other is coming to manifestation, and this is not in the control of the genius at all, certain not initially; the genius is not first master but medium, and then master so far as he or she forms what is given from a source that cannot be called his or her own. The genius is a "self" that is not self-possessed, since what she or he reveals none can possess, for it is a gift given from a source of transcendence beyond human mastery. Kant calls this source "nature," but his reflection does not go much further than calling for the proper education of the genius, lest this other drive him to excess and madness.[8]

Hegel seems to address this antinomy, but in a manner that hides the antinomy, or equivocates dialectically about it, since he thinks in terms of a more inclusive dialectical self-mediation through the other; hence the *difference of transcendence itself* (T3) is shortchanged, indeed counterfeited. Transcendence is not at all an Hegelian word, and where there is any suggestion of it, it seems predominantly associated with a dualistic *Jenseits*. We see it in his attitude to the unhappy consciousness, but also in his attitude to the sublime and the symbolic. Nor is there anything such as I would designate as a post-Romantic symbol. The ultimate is imaged in terms of a self-transcendence that looks like an erotic origin that becomes itself in and through its own other. Transcendence as other (T3) is assimilated to a comprehensive forms of self-transcendence (T2), at home with itself through its own self-becoming in and through its own other. There is no agapeic origination or creation of an other as irreducibly other.

Here too I detect some vacillation between the aesthetic and the religious. In his *Aesthetics* Hegel is equivocal about the aesthetic as "for itself" in distinction to the "religious." He is not fully clear about the issue at stake. Why? Is there an acquiescence in contemporaneity and art as for itself, an acquiescence that followed by others, like the Romantics, leads in directions to which Hegel could not acquiesce? His understanding of the religious might potentially exceed many of his contemporaries, though this is not at all the case with

8. Kant renders self-transcendence (T2) as autonomous self-legislation. Some forms of the sublime suggest the excess of nature's otherness (T1); there is also an intimation of the excess of T2 (the supersensible in the human), but finally autonomy is safeguarded from any heteronomy and any breakthrough of transcendence as other (T3) aborted. Genius points to the excess of T2, with intimation of the excess of T1; and each with intimation of the excess of T3. The first excess is then domesticated by the discipline of taste, the second by moral duty, the third by religion within the limits of reason alone. In a nutshell with Kant: Apollo makes a *triple eunuch* of Dionysus. In my view, this means that human autonomy ceases fully to be self-transcendence as self-transcending. Any self-surpassing *passes back* to the self surpassed, who thus is more basically insistent on determining *itself*, rather than opening to what is beyond. Hegel gives a more dialectical version of this circulation of self-surpassing around to the self surpassed, in and through the other surpassed.

respect to the representation of transcendence as other (T3). Finally, he too is a cheerleader for the cultus of self-determining being, offering a holistic logic not adequate to transcendence as other, or God beyond the whole.

Schelling's claim about the need and superiority of genius reflects a tilting towards the *self as medium of transcendence* rather than as Kantian autonomous agent. A word Kant repeatedly used for the genius is "extravagance" and this for him is a deeply derogatory word. The point about transcendence is evident in Schopenhauer, in so far as a will-lessness is endorsed: not the good will of Kantian morality, but a kind of excess of intellect in the genius that finally reverses and releases will from itself into will-less knowing. This will-less knowing transcends moral will, all moralizing, yet is more true to the ultimate will which is not a good will at all, more evil than good, though beyond good and evil in the moralized sense. I think Nietzsche divined the need to affirm transcendence rather than autonomy. He is like Schiller in mixing "art" and "morality" in a will to power that is artistic, but that is also the supreme legislator, like Kant's will. Everything about Nietzsche Kant would have hated as "extravagant," and yet there is an astonishing convergence of the two in this emphasis on sovereign self-legislating will. For Nietzsche the latter is not moral, but artistic. The great artist embodies the art of creating new values and imposing them on reality. The supreme legislator is the medium of transcendence as will to power, he is not the autonomous moral subject.

Consider again what Nietzsche claims about his own experience of "inspiration"—the most profound in millennia, undergone as a fated necessity which overflows with excess, and not a false step from start to finish. *Zarathustra* came to him: something else spoke through him, all he had to do was write it down. And yet Nietzsche is very Kantian in emphasizing the self-activating subject. He develops Kantian insights about the dynamic knower, and concludes that reality is an interpretation; but he radicalizes the Kantian claim and then makes the self a construct too, and in this step begins to dissolve the active Kantian self. Our autonomy to create turns into the fact that we are ourselves created, constructs. It is interesting to think this way of what he suggests in the *Birth of Tragedy:* not simply that we are artists, but that *we as artists are first and foremost works of art*—worlds of the world-artist. Autonomy seems to dissolve in face of this other transcendence, and yet there is a kind of aesthetic Kantianism too: the superior artist as supremely legislative, self-legislative and legislative for others too. There is as much an aestheticization of the supreme autonomy of the legislating moral will of the *Critique of Practical Reason,* as a radicalization of the exemplary artistic genius of the *Critique of Judgment.* The genius may be the one through whom nature gives the rule; but now this rule-giver is "nature" personified, singularized; the gap between self and other, self-transcendence (T2) and transcendence itself (T3) vanishes in creativity. I become the One, I become the ultimate other. The difference of autonomy and transcendence dissolves. I am now absolute autonomy, I am absolute transcendence. Why am I a destiny? The question finds its answer in something reminiscent of a kind of aesthetic Hegelianism: the poet-philosopher is absolute. I, Nietzsche, am God.

Heidegger, I think, chooses an indeterminate transcendence over autonomy. Between the earlier and later Heidegger there is an ambiguity between self-transcendence (T2) and transcendence as other (T3), an ambiguity never entirely eradicated, though the later tilt is towards a somewhat indeterminate sense of transcendence as other. In *Being and Time* there is still a "voluntaristic" resolute self that reminds us of the Kantian legislative will, but this stress on the self-asserting self becomes progressively diminished. He might not put it as I do, but clearly transcendence is supreme over the claimed autonomy. Though in the case of singular humans like great thinkers, artists, political statesmen (again see "The Origin of the Work of Art"), one wonders if for Heidegger the gap of the I and transcendence is diminished. Thinker: I am the voice of being—Heidegger. Poet: I am emissary of the holy—Hölderlin. Leader or statesman: I am the destiny of the German *Volk*—Hitler. If in the early Heidegger the singular great individual is tempted to say, I am transcendence, in the later Heidegger, some indeterminate transcendence as other is more ultimate than self-transcendence.[9]

I do not find in Adorno sufficient metaphysical depth to deal with the antinomy. In our time the alienated artist almost inevitably is made to serve the instrumental world of serviceable disposability, but what room is there for the genuinely free artist, and in the name of what kind of transcendence would he create? Adorno is silent. If there is transcendence, perhaps it is finally beyond all images, like Yahweh, and hence the highest image of transcendence is no image of transcendence. No image is the image. But then we must distinguish different silences. There is a world of a difference between the silence that is full of the divine and the silence of the evil that strangles all self-transcendence. And neither again is the silence of the confused human being who simply does not know what to say, to say nothing of the silence of the timid thinker.

Rorty seeks to want to hold on to some form of enlightened autonomy. He dabbles in waters that overwhelm the secular pieties of that autonomy. One thinks of a child playing with what (to change metaphors) he hardly knows is fire; or perhaps the child is only seeming to be playing with fire; he really wants it that nice people would be nice and considerate and not horribly cruel. This way of wishing for a nice day imparts the kiss of death to metaphysical seriousness. A Rortian might smirk again at the last phrase, but one would have to say: Is someone here just not getting it?

Art and an Other Transcendence?

Can I state an overall point? One detects a movement that first accentuates autonomy, and then "deconstructs" it, and then further, in that "deconstruc-

9. On this in relation to Heideggerian historicism, see *BHD,* 43–55.

tion," gives witness to the workings of an *other* transcendence beyond sovereign self-transcendence. It is not at all transparent what that other transcendence is; nor that art can be its privileged bespeaker, or emissary or shepherd. Clearly, there are different interpretations of it: *Geist,* will, will to power, being. These tends to be forms of erotic transcendence, none is fully agapeic transcendence in the sense I define. Though there is a breaking out of the closure of autonomous self-determination, something of the *modern privilege of self-mediating being* shadows these notions of transcendence as other. They continue to show some equivocality about transcendence as other, and cannot get completely clear of a self-transcendence that ends up finally defined as "for itself." A transcendence that is not a self-transcendence for itself remains to be thought more fully. This other transcendence I call agapeic transcendence.

What if such transcendence as other has to be given a certain priority over autonomy and self-transcendence? Then we must raise questions that bring us into the neighborhood of the religious. We must ask if the religious transcendence, stifled by enlightenment, constrained by moralistic autonomy, substituted for in different disguises in art, some of them profane if not outrightly atheistic, ought not to step out of its incognito, or at least be allowed to stammer its own name once more. The antinomy of autonomy and transcendence points us in this direction, and with less of the vacillating equivocity that we see in the last two centuries. I linked the "end" of art with the paradox: too much was asked of art such that now almost nothing is asked of it. But it is not that we ought not to ask much of art, but we ought not to displace onto its shoulders the task of being *the* carrier of transcendence. The "end" of art is its collapse under the burden of being the privileged speaker of transcendence, and the emergence of new metaphysical perplexity in the impossibility of repressing the question of transcendence as other, other to self-transcendence.

The task of metaphysics includes the thinking of this unthought transcendence as other. This is inseparable from a rethinking of religion, and the community of art, religion and philosophy. The religious itself is inseparable from what in *Philosophy and Its Others* (chapter 3) I call the urgency of ultimacy. Every mode of human being marked by spiritual seriousness is in some way marked by this urgency of ultimacy. I say urgency, and in different respects: urgency as flaring up in our being unbidden; urgency as an urge coming to us as if were from behind our back; urgency in that an exigency emerges that is not optional—it has to be faced; urgency in that our time to face it is finite—we do not have forever; urgency as energizing our self-transcending as search for the ultimate as transcendence other to us.

I say ultimacy, but there is here some indeterminacy, or overdeterminacy. What the ultimate is remains in question, and this indeterminacy, better, overdeterminacy has to be interpreted. This I do not deny at all. Quite the contrary, this is one of the unavoidable tasks of metaphysical thinking, urgently unavoidable. This is one lesson I take from the unfolding above indicated: self-transcendence remains enigmatic; but this enigma opens into the deeper enigma of transcendence as other. This opening raises an essential perplexity, one we cannot definitively answer in univocal terms, one we can never entirely dispel, though our thinking of it may lead to a deeper mindfulness of the matter at stake. The question of transcendence as other, beyond definition in terms of self-determining autonomy, arouses the question of the origin such as enables human origination but which is not itself identical with human origination, and which is not to be assimilated to any image of origination as *self*-determining being. Genuine origination suggests the agapeic creation of what is other as other.

I would offer now, however, these qualifications to the language of the "urgency of ultimacy." A temptation with the language of urgency is to misunderstand it in terms of some human self-activity, whereas it is more immediately intimate with the *passio essendi* than the *conatus essendi*. The urgency of ultimacy emerges into form from the *passio essendi,* though it is given form by us in terms of our *conatus essendi,* and so shaped with some more definite directionality towards what we consider as ultimacy. But before all that, there is the primal porosity of being. Our being religious is perhaps our most elemental participation in that porosity. Of course, in itself the porosity seems like nothing, and yet it is the fecund opening source of all possibilizing. We fill its seeming emptiness with a variety of determinate practices of life, or determinate forms of being religious, such as, for instance, this institutional shape or that. The more elemental sense of being religious is not this or that determinate form, but has to do with the primal porosity. Determinate forms of life can hide it, can clog it, as indeed they can also keep free its openness for passage between us humans and the divine. We live in it, we live it, but live it so that we block it, congest it. Often to come to know of it again, to be visited with it more nakedly again, is like a return to zero. This return to zero unweaves the forms of *conatus essendi* falsely claiming ultimacy, restores the energy of self-transcendence to the *passio essendi,* and opens us again to the porosity of being. This return to zero can be an interface between us and the more original source(s) of creativity.

The creative artist lives too on that interface. The artist who waits in woo knows something of this nothing; knows something of the breakdown of the self-evidences of taken for granted determinacies; knows something too of expectation beyond determinacy, and self-determination; knows something of breakthrough in which the energy of creation streams again. The streaming we sometimes call inspiration, and the artist is nothing: nothing but passage; nothing as intimate with the primal porosity; nothing yet creative medium of agapeic origination; nothing and yet promise of agapeic mindfulness of all that is; a creative between—between nothing and God.

This promise of agapeic mindfulness is connected to the fact that the articulations of the artist are plurivocal. Some artists are more plurivocal than others, Shakespeare obviously, Dostoevski, Joyce, but think of Dickens. He named himself "The Inimitable," and yet he was the absolute mimic. We know this, his histrionic nature. In his writing room in later life, he was surrounded by mirrors, and he would rush from his desk to the mirrors and into them makes faces, and then return to his desk and furiously write. A stroke of the pen and a singular character appears in all striking singularity. What was this amazing power to bring to be? Everything and nothing. Dickens was an extraordinary porosity become creative—creative in the word that offers us a world full of unique singulars, deliciously named: Pecksniff, Mrs. Gamp, Uriah Heep, Chuzzlewit, Pickwick, Miss Havisham, Gradgrind, Ebenezer Scrooge, Edwin Drood, the list stretches and stretches.

The poet has no identity, Keats said, but this is the porosity of being taking creative form as imagination. Negative capability? More than that, more than negative, more the agapeic power to create, to enter the life of another, to release another into its singular otherness with a life of its own. Shakespeare had this, Dickens, others too. If it calls for some agapeic mindfulness, this not only is intimate with the *passio essendi* of the artist-creator but is also a *compassio essendi* which is with the singularly intimate life of others. This is a love that is creative, and a love of what is created, a love that exposes itself to what is mean and small and hateful, and even in that exposure it is yet a love. William Trevor is a contemporary writer who astonishes and moves us with this agapeic mindfulness taking imaginative form. We hear it calling too with the works of great musicians, like Mozart, when they disappear in the sounding of the music itself. No god need be named, but some music is so mysteriously intimate with the porosity of being that we are awakened beyond ourselves, as if released into a kind of praying.

Do some of the figures previously discussed make approaches to the issue of transcendence as other? If so, these approaches suggest a certain lack of full lucidity about the antinomy between autonomy and the transcendence, and a certain restraint caused by the religious equivocation. If we face the latter, we must engage the community of art, religion and philosophy, and not in a manner which replaces the second with an *ersatz* ultimacy. Such a replacement leads to a falsity or hollowness in the whole. I am not denying that a merely dualistic religiousness runs into an impasse in sustaining its vision of transcendence, nor that scientistic enlightenment is bankrupt, indeed nihilistic, and also that idealistic reason, just in seeming to be a consummation, really produces a reversal in which the monsters of nonreason are loosed. Nor am I denying a metaphysical meaning to art. I am denying that art alone can be made to bear an unbearable burden of transcendence. Though great art can have something absolute about it, we must guard against a false absolutization of art. There is a big difference, and we need finesse not to distort the matter. Alone art cannot offer the sanctuary wherein the seed of spirit can survive the uprooting storm of nihilism.

Certainly Hegel did say: art and philosophy are divine services too, *Gottesdiensten*. Nor need we dismiss Heidegger (even granting hesitancy about his meaning) when he said that only a god can save us. But art cannot be the *sanctus sanctorum* in which the burden carried by religion, science and metaphysics can be sustained, and renewed. Art can be a carrier of transcendence, only if these others are themselves in robust spiritual shape. Its health rises or falls by its sustenance in community with these its others. If these are sick, it cannot be their cure. More likely than not its claim to be the cure will be a new infection through which the anorexia of art itself will come about. Art is not the remnant which will save the rest. The impossible burden of transcendence is God. Without the religious, we collapse under the burden.

If the human soul has wings or must grow wings, is it as if philosophers have been trying to fly with one wing, or perhaps none at all? (I make no mention of philosophers content to crawl or plod or slouch or hop.) What if we are sustained by two wings all the time, even though we deny that one of the wings (religion) is a wing, or that it has any right to contribute to our elevation? Cut it off, however, and the other wing (art), by being overtaxed in bearing us aloft, will lose its strength. Then we cannot prevent our tilt and plunge. Art on its own, overtaxed, asking too much of it, means art weakened, and then nothing much can be asked of it. Not only transcendence as other (T3), but self-transcendence (T2), its urgency of ultimacy, proves an impossible burden. What then? Let the other wing be what it is, let it keep its strength by being used, by flying. Might thought fly on the strength of such wings? Is this one of the tasks of metaphysics at the "end" of art?

Born Again beyond Aestheticism: Art and Being Religious?

I come back to the three "deaths" mentioned at the outset. If there is a death of one, it is symptomatic of sickness in the community of them all. Hope of resurrection of one calls for hope of resurrection of the others. Is there any one that has greater power? After long consideration, I see that religion has power that neither art or philosophy has: it is most intimate with the primal porosity, the *passio essendi,* and the urgency of ultimacy; it serves to move transcending for the many and not just the few, and hence it is more crucial to the culture of a community, and its pervasive spiritual well-being or feebleness. The religious is the more democratic art of the ultimate, imaging a culture's divination of original being, sustaining publicly this divination by ritual practices, even while rooted secretly in often unarticulated intimations of transcendence as other. And while in the intimacy of the soul it keeps open the porosity between the human and the divine, yet it also issues in ethical life that publicly enacts its most secret love of what is ultimate.

The matter does not proximately concern any sectarian, or ecclesiastical or institutional form of the religious. Institutional form is not unimportant, since it concretizes the communal shape of a religious inspiration. This last is the issue, though again there may be an intimacy more primal than this proximity.

One might ask: Is not inspiration inseparable from the primal porosity and the *passio essendi?* Is it not perhaps the artistic counterpart to what in religion is the showing of the divine or revelation? Do not eros and mania, and their shaping of our original self-transcending, reveal something of our utmost promise in the between, but as moving from the finitude of the middle to the boundaries of the between, between what is human and transhuman? On that boundary the intermediating powers of being aesthetic and being religious join, but as facing beyond themselves, and by being addressed by what exceeds them. The greatness of art always renews our astonishment and perplexity about the original and the ultimate. What are the ultimate sources of origination? Can we fully vouch for them in terms of human originality? Is not human originality itself a created originality? We are *passio essendi* before we are *conatus essendi,* passion of being before striving to be. We are first created, before we create. If so, what is the more ultimate source of originality? The issue at bottom is the interpretation of originality and ultimacy in terms of human self-transcendence or in terms of transcendence as other, or the communication between these two.

I would say this last: great art intimates something of this communication. It keeps unclogged the primal porosity of our being in the between. But the most overt name for the worldly form of this communication is religion. At its most fundamental and intimate this communication has everything to do with the *passio essendi* out of which the urgency of ultimacy springs. Religion in that sense is closer to the womb of origination: there is an ontological immediacy of the communication of ultimacy, felt as urgent in the human to whom it is shown. This, of course, has to be mediated: religious communities and their art, and indeed human art, can shape the form of this showing. Art is religious to the degree it is inspired, and this even though the divine be silent in a deep incognito. Inspired art is prophetic in more senses than one: it images what is and what is to be; and in this, it also images what has been aborted in the given promise of original being. Truthful to what is, it seeks fidelity to what is to be; in this it may know also the grief of the stillborn beauty, in what was and what is.

If there an intimacy with the origin, this origin is excessive to our self-transcendence. So far the intuitions of the post-Hegelians are not wrong. Origin is not the abstract indeterminacy of the Hegelian beginning, driven then forward in its own self-becoming. It is agapeic origin. This is a name with many religious resonances. It is not defined by a metaphysics of dualistic opposition, nor the dialectical logic of a progressive teleology, nor finally the a/logic of a deconstructive a/teleology. The latter too has not seen deeply enough into the difference of the erotic and agapeic origin (as we saw with Nietzsche, and Heidegger). Great art offers an imagistic concretion of agapeic origination.

If the religious is the most intimate, closest to the origin, as taking on worldly form, it is the most universal in potential—and this despite the particularisms of sects that would arrogate this universal promise primarily to themselves. The incognito of the religious today is revealed in the felt pull of this promise of the universal. The promise remains relatively *indefinite,* and the universal struggles to show itself in the forms of determinate community. A sign of this: diffidence about the institutional, a diffidence often motivated by religious scruples. And yet the communal, hence mediately the institutional, is ingredient in the fuller communication of the ultimate.

We live in a culture of autonomy in which the religious as naming transcendence as other is made one lobby among other, or driven to the margins, or sent underground. By contrast, I suggest the religious porosity between human and divine is the grounding happening in the most intensive and extensive sense: Grounding happening, in which occurs the communication between original human self-transcendence and ultimate transcendence as the other origin. Most intensive, in that it is most intimate to the unfathomed being of the human being. Most extensive, in offering the most embracing largesse to human creativity: the enabling gift out of which our own powers are allowed to be shaped and to shape themselves. A culture which acknowledges such ultimate gift is a religious culture. All culture is religious in that regard of being impossible without the ethos of the primal gift of being as original. This is given to the human, but not initially given by the human, but given as enabling the self-becoming of human powers to the utmost of their creative promise.

This matter is primarily one of ethos: not of this or that specialized activity within the ethos (art, religion, philosophy as specialities). I mean ethos relative to our sense of the ontological milieu of ultimate value. Our current reconfiguration of the ethos is dominated by objectification, subjectification, instrumental mind, freedom as autonomy that has difficulty with the other, and so forth. The "end" of art is not due simply to a "reflective" culture. While there are many factors, what is dominant in the ethos of a culture is crucial. In this instance, if a certain objectifying orientation degrades the soil on which wonder flourishes, the debilitating effects on art, religion, and philosophy will not be far behind. "Thought," of course, can play a part in all of this, especially a certain univocalizing instrumentalism that wills to eradicate the equivocities of being. Dialectical thinking is not immune from this temptation, not all practices of philosophy are. Such practices of philosophy are complicit with degrading the ontological milieu which, though equivocal, is yet full of promise. Not surprisingly also, such philosophies often turn out to be enemies of religion. By contrast, the full ontological weight of great art brings us back to the ethos: arrests us to the mystery of what it is to be; and is hence a happening of original religious astonishment and perplexity before the ultimate. In the desert of instrumentalized being (itself produced by our reconfiguration of the ethos), it guards a reverence that is metaphysical. It images an agapeic mindfulness that listens to voices that speak beyond the dry raspings of devalued being, voices that sing of the secrets of the always sacramental earth.[10]

---

10. *EB* explores, among other relevant issues such as the different forms of freedom (Part III, *passim*), the question of ethos (chapter 1), as well as the religious community of agapeic service (chapter 16).

Some of the above thinkers might be seen in this light, though they do not see themselves so. Are they always helpful enough in attending to the incognito of the divine? The way some of them name art adds another layer of possible misidentification, when the religious is left to languish in the equivocity of its post-Enlightenment feebleness. What of Hegel? The fact that he names all three, art, religion and philosophy, as forms of absolute spirit is important, given the subsequent equivocations, especially in relation to art and religion. Nevertheless, I would reformulate his way of treating this triad. The otherness of the origin (T3) is not to be reduced to the dialectical holism of transcendence made immanence. In Hegel, human self-transcendence and transcendence as other are symmetrically mediated with each other, such that each becomes a moment of a more encompassing, total process of self-transcendence, which is no transcendence finally, since the transcending finds itself again in what initially seems other. Transcendence as other is entirely mediated in the total process of thought's self-determination in which self-transcendence is total self-mediation through its own others: T3 is modelled on a dialectical variation of T2; and so the irreducibility of the otherness of the origin is slighted.

In that respect, my sympathies are with some of the post-Hegelians who divine this otherness of the origin to total self-mediation. The powerful nature of the Hegelian self-mediation of the whole often occludes this sense of original transcendence beyond the whole; and yet this otherness erupts in different guises, say the inward otherness of the inspiration of genius, the astonishment before the "that it is at all" of nature (T1) in experiences of the sublime, or in religious joy, or fear and trembling, or the sweats, before the unmastered and unmasterable originality of God. That said, though Hegel's more forthright naming of the religious makes him an ally in bringing the issue into the open, his dialectical equivocation on divine transcendence as other always risks an extraordinary *counterfeiting of God*.[11] The equivocities of post-Hegelian culture on the religious, and its request that art bear the burden of transcendence, finally help less than one might have initially expected.

There is a pluralism of manifestations of ultimacy. The agapeic origin sources the pluralism of creation. There is no determination to one form of manifestation to the exclusion of many; or indeed to the inclusion of many within one and one only form. That the origin is agapeic enables the happening of communication which is inherently pluralistic: to create is to glorify the pluralism of creation, not to reduce its manyness to one essential form. Art, religion and philosophy are articulations which approach ultimacy in its originality. Instead of the *Aufhebung* of art into religion and religion into philosophy, I would stress the space *between* each, as the place each is enabled to be, by the origin, each in its difference and communication with the others, and

11. I have argued this more fully in *Hegel's God: A Counterfeit Double?*.

with the origin. The origin enables the spaces of the between and possibilizes sameness and otherness in an open community. This open community, relative to transcendence/difference, cannot be described in terms of dualistic opposition; relative to sameness, cannot be captured in univocal monism, nor either the dialectical self-mediation of One, understood in a kind of Hegelian sense; nor again is it a deconstructive equivocal many—for difference thus totalized is indistinguishable from total identity. It involves what I call a metaxological intermediation of different sources of transcendence; even though the ultimate transcendence (T3) is the hyperoriginal that hyperbolically possibilizes, without univocally determining, the promise of the other transcendences (T1, T2).

Religion *lived* is our being in the porous happening of communication between ultimate transcendence (T3) and finite transcendences (T1, T2). Religion *reflected* in its truth is (metaxological) philosophy which understands that *to be is to be religious,* namely, to have one's being in the happening of the between by virtue of the ultimate giving of the agapeic origin. Among the tasks of metaphysics, after the "end" of art, is to search this truth of the *metaxu*. Being true to that task asks us to be mindful of how art matters metaphysically. Can this task be faithfully discharged without constant honesty concerning the truth of being religious?

Our revels are not now ended: not now, perhaps never. The dream is not over. There are dreams that drowse, half waking, half lost, in the sleep of finitude. But there are dreams of art, religion, and philosophy that call to waking beyond such sleep, waking again to an absolved porosity of being in which we hear a guardian calling: no more a dissembling amen to being; no feigned Sabbath of thought; no more counterfeit doubles of God. Vexed and balmed, we are searched and asked: Are we no more than a gust of nothing? Or more, much more than an extravagance of empty?

Index

absolute, 13, 127; absolute whole, 94, 95, 99, 103, 89, 102; and Hegel's aesthetics 152; and death, 158
absolute knowing, 94, 112–13, 158, 213
absorbing God, 118; and Dionysus, 205–6, 243
Adorno, Theodor, 3, 99, 243n, 280, 282, 286
aesthetic, aesthetics, ix–xi, 2, 4, 5, 12, 15, 24, 29, 38, 39, 50, 117–19, 126, 220, 221, 223, 235, 271, 273n, 284; and religion in postmodernism, 162
aestheticism, 209, 270, 276
aesthetic ideas, 72–77, 82, 84, 140
afterworldsmen, 124, 219
agape/agapeic, 8, 17, 48, 49–51, 94, 108, 109, 113, 126, 127, 238n, 250, 262, 287; and origin, 155, 191; and willing, 161; and the good, 162; and creation, 199; agapeic service, 245
agon, 205, 239, 246, 256
alētheia, 214, 216, 236, 245, 257. *See also* correctness, *orthotes*
amor fati, 191, 193, 196, 204. *See also* fate
Anaximander, 141 153, 159, 160, 168, 188, 241; and Hegelian self-mediation, 175
angst, 231f., 237
antinomy, 10, 130; of autonomy and transcendence, 269f., 276, 278, 283, 287, 289
apatheia, and Kant, 75
Apollo, Apollonian, 68, 77, 104, 111, 243, 245, 284n. *See also* Dionysian
Aquinas, St. Thomas, 6, 49, 61
Aristophanes, 35, 104, 106, 170
Aristotle, 13, 25–27, 31, 36, 76, 112, 161, 218, 221n, 228, 223, 239n, *Nichomachean Ethics,* 218; as father to Hegel, Schopenhauer, Nietzsche, 144; *deinos* and *eleos,* 168
architecture, 115–30
art, ix–xi, 1–17, 4, 9, 16, 24, 29, 31, 35, 36, 119, 120–26, 230 f., 236, 250, 257, 258, 262, 267ff., 271, 273, 276, 278, 280f., 289, 291ff.; artwork, 246, 247, 252, 277; end(s) of, 231, 265–94; paradoxical position of in modernity, 265, 267, 287; burden of transcendence, 267–71, 275, 287, 289, 293; and religion, chapter 8 *passim,* 267, 276f.; as incognito of metaphysics, 271; as incognito of religion, 287, 291
Aschheim, Steven, and Nietzsche, 185n
astonishment, 3, 23, 30, 32, 94, 107ff., 112–13, 229. *See also* wonder
Athens, 228f., 249
Aufhebung, 122, 239, 248, 293
Augustine, St., 108, 110, 122, 246n
autonomy, 10–11, 12, 17, 130, 269–74, 276, 278, 283f., 285–89, 292

Bach, J.S., 48
Bacon, F., 47
Bataille, G., 40, 182n
beauty, 5, 29, 39, 49, 50, 66, 67, 122, 125, 247, 291; and Plato, 151; and ugliness, 158; and truth, 159; and willing, 159

beautiful soul, 96, 128
beginning, 241, 250; Hegel's concept of, 229, 291
being, 2, 19, 24, 27, 31, 32, 49–51, 211, 212, 220, 223, 224, 226, 231, 236, 238f., 241, 244, 247, 251, 254f., 257f., 260, 270, 274, 274, 281f., 286, 292; agape of, 245; worthiness of, 228; determinate, 250; chiaroscuro of, 233, 241, 263; original power of, 253; forgetfulness of *(Seinsvergessenheit),* 225, 240, 248; univocity of, 238, 248; equivocity of, 235, 237, 245, 248; and the evil of being, 162
bewitchment, 262, 269
Beckett, Samuel, 131
between, xi, 4–5, 11, 12, 13, 23–24, 26–29, 31–35, 36, 40, 41, 42, 216ff., 221, 225ff., 237, 241, 244n, 247, 257ff., 270, 288, 291, 293f.; and demiurgic making, 49ff.; Kant and the between, 53ff.; between Enlightenment and Romanticism, 57ff.; and transcendental origination, 60ff.; genius as intermediate, 71ff.; and Hegel, 87ff.; and Gothic cathedral, 129–30; and Heidegger, chapter 7 *passim;* promise of, 230. *See also* metaxological
Bloch, Ernst, 208n
Braig, Carl, 221n
breakdown, breakthrough, Kant and sublime, 84–86; and monstrous architecture, 123
Brentano, Franz, 221n
Breton, André, 110, 161, 277
Bruno, Giordano, 165
Bultmann, Rudolf, 246n
Burckhardt, Jakob, 244n; and Nietzsche 204

Caliban, 142, 156
care *(Sorge),* 235, 258
Catholicism, 116, 121–25, 282
causa sui, 203–4, 228, 245
Cave, the, 14, 21, 22, 23, 31, 42, 54, 71, 166, 168, 203–4, 207–8, 219 223, 232, 242; and second underground, 131–33
Cavell, Stanley, 43, 193n
Chartres Cathedral, 30, 126
chaos, 220, 244
Christ, Jesus, 104. *See also* Jesus
Christianity/Christian, 2, 24, 30, 104, 117, 124, 127, 228, 281f.; post-Christian inwardness, 150–51
circle, 240, 249, 260
classical artform, 98, 101–3, 120
Coleridge, S.T., 21, 43
coming to be, 223, 224, 226, 229, 234, 258–61
community/communication, 4–5, 8, 10, 12, 15, 23–24, 27–30, 32, 34, 36, 40–41, 43, 45–49, 50, 129, 186, 262f., 289f., 291f., 293f.
compassio essendi, 150, 161, 289. See also *passio essendi*
Comte, Auguste, 2, 272, 282
conatus essendi, 10, 13, 15, 38, 43, 244n, 246, 260f., 288, 291. See also *passio essendi*
concealing, 214, 235, 245, 247
Copernican revolution, 53, 54, 60–61, 76, 221n; and Nietzsche, 189
correctness, 257; and mimesis, 37. See also *orthotes*
counterfeit/counterfeit, 10, 13, 14, 16, 30, 35, 48, 123, 150, 293. *See also* double
counterthrow *(Gegenwurf),* 255
creativity/creative/creation, 3, 5–6, 7–11, 21, 29, 31, 35, 128, 214, 217, 219, 232, 236, 241, 245, 250, 260, 273n, 274f., 280, 284, 288f., 293; *Genesis,* 6, 26; and Hegel, 95ff.; self-creation, erotics of creation, 157, 194, 197–98, 200ff., 208; and otherness, 167, 176–77, 187; and will to power and Nietzsche, 173, 193, 194; *ex nihilo,* 184, 248f., 251, 253; creative power, 235, 274; finite, 253; agapeic, 288. *See also* mimesis/imitation, demiurgy/demiurgic making
Cusa, Nicholas of, 170, 239
cybernetics, 241, 265f., 282

Dalí, Salvador, 160; Avida Dollars, 277
Danto, Arthur, 67n6, 90, 97n7

Deleuze, Gilles, and will to power, 184n; and Heidegger's univocity of being, 238
demiurgy/demiurgic making, 5–6, 29, 35, 49, 49–51, 247, 248. *See also* creation
Derrida, Jacques, 111, 184–85, 243n
Descartes, René, 19, 24, 30, 31, 281; and *cogito,* 55, 112; and genius, 75; post-Cartesian modernity, 25, 31, 93, 175; Cartesian clarity and distinctness, 174, 195; and *mathēsis* of nature, 181
destiny, 265, 281, 285
determination(s), determinacy, 210, 221, 227, 241, 252, 268, 269, 288
dialectic/dialectical, 8, 13, 15, 26, 36, 39, 42, 87–91, 94–96, 108–13, 115, 117, 122, 126, 127, 128, 217, 230, 231, 232, 292f.; and Hegel, 171; and Plato 171; and Dionysian, 188ff.; and Heidegger, 227ff.
dialogue, 217, 266; Platonic, 36ff., 171–72
Dickens, Charles, 288f.
difference, 227, 237f., 240, 241, 242, 244, 248, 249n, 252, 256, 259, 293f.
Dionysius/Dionysian, 13, 14, 15, 68, 75, 77, 83, 84, 111, 134, 141, 153, 154, 159, 160, 167–68, 172, 183, 184, 187–91, 196, 197, 199, 206, 235, 239, 240, 243, 245, 281, 284n
Diotima, and eros, 41, 156, 191, 235
disgust, and art, 67
distinterestedness of art, 138–39
divine, the, 228, 260, 286, 290ff.; incognito of, 293
Don Juan, 109, 151
Dostoevski, Fyodor, 288
doubleness, double, 249, 253, 263; double thinking, 236ff., 247; counterfeit double, 216, 226n, 228, 231, 256, 263, 294
doublets, 236ff., 249, 251, 269
dualism, 7, 8, 9, 11, 12, 24–26, 28–31, 31–32, 34, 38, 40, 42–43, 111, 126–28, 146–47, 216, 273, 273n, 289, 291, 294
Duns Scotus, 238
earth *(Erde),* 124–26, 213, 214, 219 242, 243ff., 253, 254n, 257, 292. *See also* world, fourfold
ecstasis, 41, 43, 48, 122, 127, 256
ego, transcendental, 221n, 243
Egypt, 99, 100; and Nietzchean "Egypticism" 204
eidos, 215, 217, 218, 219, 251, 258f. *See also* Idea
Ekhart, Meister, 236
elemental, xi, 4, 39
Eldridge, Richard, 43
Elfish, and fundamental ontology/philology, 176; Squirrel Nutkin, 257
Emerson, R.W., 32, 43, 90, 193n
Enlightenment, ix, 4, 12–14, 40, 58, 62, 64–66, 72, 74, 78, 79, 83, 88, 89, 107, 113, 209, 266f., 273, 276, 278ff., 282f., 287, 289; and Kant, chapter 2 *passim;* and Hegel, 87ff. *See also* Romanticism
equivocal/equivocity, x, 3, 7, 9, 16, 25, 28, 33, 35–37, 39, 40, 117, 124, 215–17, 219, 233, 236ff., 243, 247f., 252, 256, 259, 261f., 269, 271, 275f., 278–77, 289, 293; and Nietzsche, 191
eris, 239
eros, 11, 12, 14, 16, 21, 22, 24, 28, 29, 31, 34–40, 41, 45, 47ff., 57, 73, 85, 88, 108, 117, 127, 209, 215, 239, 242, 244, 253n, 254, 260f., 278, 291; and Platonic middle, 34–40; Platonic, 150; and Schopenhauer, 150, 155, 161; *eros turannos,* 134, 150, 152, 155, 156, 157, 165, 167; *eros uranos,* 150, 156; and creation, 199; and sovereignty, 239, 245f.; and origins, 200–2; and Heidegger, 234ff.
eternity, 25, 121, 124, 223, 225. *See also* time
evil, 157, 158, 162, 237ff., 240, 285f.; and Nietzsche, 182, 208

Farias, Victor, 246n
fate, 196. See also *amor fati*
Faust, 151
Feuerbach, Ludwig, 21, 194, 200f., 273

Fichte, Johann Gottlieb, 3, 54; and Schopenhauer, 142
finite/finitude, 6, 8, 11, 121, 225, 227, 235, 247, 249ff., 257, 260f., 269, 283, 291; horizon of, 251. *See also* infinity
Foucault, Michel, 182n
fourfold (earth sky mortals gods), 229, 257
free, freedom, 56, 70, 72, 155, 230, 237, 274, 292
Freud, Sigmund, 200
fundamental ontology, 221n, 237
futurity, and Nietzsche, 182n, 192

Gadamer, H.G., 96, 218, 231–32
Gaia, 242
Geist, 73, 81, 96, 98–100, 102–3, 124, 126, 129, 143, 145, 147, 189. *See also* spirit
Gelassenheit, 228, 236, 243, 246
genius, and Kant, chapter 2, *passim;* as intermediate, 71ff.; and taste, 72; and Hegel, 96ff.; and Schopenhauer, 138ff.; and Nietzsche, 195, 198–99; and Heidegger, 243ff., 266f., 271, 274f., 277ff., 284f., 293; evil genius, 232, 281; divine genius, 254; post-metaphysical genius, 244n
gift, giving, givenness, 214, 227, 246, 247, 250, 252, 254–57, 259f., 262, 292; agapeic giving, 245f., 256; and Schopenhauer, 149; of grace, 160; of good, 166
God, 5–6, 10, 49, 58, 61, 74, 82, 100–1, 104, 117, 125, 127, 142, 157, 162, 186, 194–95, 200–1, 203–4, 220, 227, 229, 231ff., 237, 239, 244n, 253n, 281, 285f., 288, 294; and sublime, 80; and Hegel, 157; and Plato 169; as impossible burden of transcendence, 290; death of, 265; absorbing god, 243; hyperbolic (beyond the whole), 239, 245, 249, 260
god(s), 235, 241, 282; "last god," 244n, 260; guff, 254
Goethe, Johann Wolfgang von, 121; and Schopenhauer, 143; and Nietzsche, 206
good, 5, 29, 39, 48, 49–51, 157, 166, 217, 220, 237ff., 240, 247, 285; excessive, 240; beyond being, 217, 220; archeology of, 240; beyond good and evil, 228, 239, 274, 285. *See also* evil
Greece/Greek, 29, 116, 117, 120, 124–26, 238, 256, 259, 262; and the Platonic Idea, 159
guilt, 216, 274

Hardy, Thomas, 131
Hegel, G.W.F., ix, 3, 11, 12, 13, 14, 15, 19, 29, 39, 42, 49, 224, 227f., 232f., 234n, 239, 240, 241, 243, 247, 252, 253n, 255n, 260, 262, 267, 272, 282f., 284, 286, 289, 293; and Ideal and Idea, 13, 56, 78, 86, 100, 117, 145, 146–47; and absolute spirit, x, 99, 102, 103, 152, 231, 278, 293; and creativity, 63n, 96, 154; and *Geist* (spirit), 81, 96, 98–100, 102, 103, 120, 143, 145, 147, 152, 189; and sublime, 86, 119, 126; and "end" of art, 88, 89, 112, 113, 119, 120–21, 127, 231, 265f., 277n; and genius, 91, 96, 97; and the epochs of art, 98, 99, 105, 117–18, 120–22, 230, 281; and symbolic, classical, romantic art-forms, 99, 101, 102, 104–6, 109, 117–18, 120–22, 124–26, 127, 173, 281; and *Kunstreligion,* 276, 281; and transcendence, 115, 117, 272; and architecture, 115–30; Gothic cathedral, 13, 116–17, 118, 120–26, 127, 130; and post-Hegelian era, 112–13, 128, 267, 270, 291, 293; and Schopenhauer, 142–48; and the need to know, 145–46; and concrete universal, 146; and *Verstand/Vernunft* distinction, 146–47; and *Begriff* (concept), 146; and Aristotle, 146; and bad infinity, 151, 152; and desire, 152; and healing, 152; and absolute, 152, 158, 167; and music, 153; and poetry, 153; and will, 155; and freedom, 155; and God, 142, 157; and beauty, 159; and origin, 166, 189,

194; and becoming, 174; and dialectic, dialectical self-mediation, 175, 179, 188; and Nietzsche, 144, 179, 188, 189–90, 201–3, 207; and historicism, 144; absoluteness in art, 152; and *eros turannos,* 152; and *Phenomenology of Spirit,* 227; Spinozism of, 224; and being, 229; and logic, 230, 232f.; true as the whole, 229, 272; and *Aesthetics,* 284; and *Gottesdienst,* 289
Heidegger, Martin, 3, 9, 11, 13, 15, 16, 29, 50, 53, 54, 74, 86, 90, 92, 111, 112, 113, 117, 124–26, 127, 130; chapter 7 *passim,* 280ff., 286, 289, 291; and metaphysics, 148, 180n, 183; and nothingness, 153; and art, 154; and Schelling, 172–73; and sameness/difference, 184–85; and will to power, 184n; prophesying, 192n; and language, 203; "The Origin of the Work of Art," 209, 210, 211, 212–14, 236, 242, 245f., 250, 254, 257, 262n, 286; *"What is a Thing?"* 213; "Rector's Address," 219, 222; "Saying of Anaximander," 216; "End of Philosophy and the Task of Thinking," 215, 241; *Kant and the Problem of Metaphysics,* 221, 222; *Being and Time,* 221f., 226, 227, 255n, 286; "My Way to Phenomenology," 221n; *Phenomenological Interpretation of Kant's Critique of Pure Reason,* 223; *Identity and Difference,* 227; and Nietzsche, 227, 241, 259, 262; *Contributions to Philosophy,* 192n, 243n, 254n, 257f.; "Letter on Humanism," 238, 254f., 256, 257, 259; *Introduction to Metaphysics,* 242, 247; *Plato's Theory of Truth,* 214; voluntarism of, 222, 230, 236, 286; turn *(Kehre),* 222; and genius, 241; and projection, 246, 254–59; as priest or prophet, 262f.; as masked thinker, 263; and *es gibt,* 255n; and shepherd of being, 255f.
Hell, 242
hermeneutics, 212, 247
Heraclitus, 41, 180, 195, 210, 233f., 241, 248
Hesiod, 239
Hermes, 181
Hitler, Adolf, 123, 219, 286
Hölderlin, Johann Christian Friedrich, 88, 102, 219, 222, 231, 235, 244, 282, 286
holiness, 158
holy, the, 231, 236, 238, 277. *See also* poet
Homer, versus Plato, 115, 116, 166, 169, 186; and Newton, 75
human, human being, 238n, 253, 255, 266, 270f., 274f., 279, 281, 287, 291f.; human body 274
Hume, David, and reason versus passions, 165
Husserl, Edmund, 111, 221
hyperbole/hyperbolic, 5–6, 8, 15, 40, 126
hyphen, hyphenation, 259, 261

Idea, and Plato, 11, 14, 23, 25, 30, 73, 147–48, 153, 160, 217, 218, 220; Platonic Idea, 136–37, 140, 142, 144, 145, 146, 147–48, 154; and Kant, 12; and Hegel, 12, 74, 117, 146–47, 189; and Schopenhauer, 74, 144, 146, 153, 154, 160; and Nietzsche, 74, 146, 153, 194–95; and Heidegger, 74; and participation and metaxu, 23ff. See also *eidos*
idealism, 224, 225, 227, 234, 278
idiot/idiotic, 3, 35, 38; and Nietzsche, 177
idol/idolatry, 16, 129
imagination, 67, 69–70, 72–74, 77, 223, 225f., 249n; and Kant, 67ff.; and sublime, 81; transcendental imagination 222–24
imitation. *See also* mimesis, creativity
immanence, 8, 9, 10, 11, 37, 39, 116, 127, 272, 274. *See also* transcendence
indeterminacy, 223, 239, 250, 252, 287, 291
infinite/infinity, 112, 113, 121, 127, 128; and Hegel, 152

inspiration, 34, 43, 45, 116, 288, 290f.; and Nietzsche, 197. *See also* mania, porosity

Janaway, Christopher, 134
Jaspers, Karl, 9, 263; and foundering, 172
Jerusalem, 228f., 251n
Jesus, 281. *See also* Christ
Job, 85, 168, 169, 175
Joseph of Cupertino, 228
Jove, 167, 181, 242, 260
Joyce, James, 19, 288
Judaism/Jews, 86, 100

Kant, Immanuel, 1, 3, 9, 11, 12, 15, 16, 31, 209, 211, 221, 222, 224, 232, 236, 237, 268, 272, 275ff., 279, 283ff.; and genius, ix, 11, 12, 41, 57–59, 62–66, 68, 70–76, 79, 91, 145, 194, 223, 243f., 271, 274f., 278, 284f.; and Ideas, 12; and sublime, 12, 81ff.; and nature, 47, 55, 56, 73; and beauty, 66, 67, 122; and music, 35, 78, 240n; and imagination, 67, 69–70, 72–74, 77, 93; and discipline of taste, 68, 69, 70, 72, 79, 194; on limits of knowing, 88; on autonomy, 284f.; and dualism, 12, 224f.; and prayer, singing hymns, 78; and God, 58, 82; and aesthetic formalism, 140; and the sweats, 147, 196, 231; as father of Hegel, 143, 145; as father of Schopenhauer, 143, 145, 150, 154; and will, 155; and origin, 165, 194; and Nietzsche, 167; and transcendental self, 189; and aesthetics, 221, 271, 277, 281; and Heidegger, 221ff., 236, 262; post-Kantian era, 246; practical reason, 271
Keats, John, 289
Kearney, Richard, 111n, 251n
Kierkegaard, Søren, 54, 107, 109, 112, 233, 236, 256n, 266, 270; and Schopenhauer, 142; and Don Juan, 151; *Concluding Unscientific Postscript*, 256
King Lear, 157
Kline, George L., 182n, 192n
Kunstreligion. See also Hegel

laughter, Plato and Nietzsche, 169; and Heidegger, 256–57
Leibniz, G.W., and Nietzsche, 175
Levinas, Emmanuel, 20, 216; and evil of being, 111; and ethical thinking, 161–62
liberalism, 280. *See also* Rorty
light, 233f., 235, 241, 244, 283. *See also* sun
logos/logoi, 4, 23, 36, 45, 209ff., 218; and Schopenhauer, 153; and Nietzsche, 174; and idealism 175–76
love, 16, 47–48, 258, 278; and Hegel, 157
Lukacs, Georg, 143n
Lyotard, J-F., 82n12

Macbeth, 208, 216, 237, 239
MacIntyre, Alaisdair, 132n
madness, 78, 79, 232, 284; and Kant, 76ff.; and Schopenhauer, 160; and Nietzsche, 197; and Dalí, 160; and Heidegger, 263
mania, 8, 11, 12, 16, 21, 22, 24, 29, 31, 34, 37, 40–49, 51, 57, 73, 85, 108, 209, 215, 228, 235, 254, 260f., 291. *See also* inspiration, madness
Mann, Thomas, 131
Manzoni, Piero, 67
Mao, Zedong, 123
Marx, Karl, 3, 9, 29, 90, 182n, 200, 266, 267, 272f., 283
matter and form, 217, 219, 247, 251
metaphysics, 211, 221, 225, 230, 233, 240f., 242, 245, 255n, 274, 278, 290f.; task of, 265–94; end of, 271–73; Oedipal, 242; Chthonic, 242f.
Merda d'Artista, 67, 79
metaxological, metaxu, x, 4–5, 8, 11, 20–21, 22–24, 26–29, 36, 38, 39, 41–42, 47, 48, 55, 56, 60, 113, 130, 166, 168, 171, 194–95, 215, 217, 218, 221, 230, 247, 277, 254, 257, 270, 294; and Plato, 194. *See also* between

mimesis, chapter 1, *passim;* and Platonic middle, 31ff.; and Kant, 67ff., 215, 216, 261f. *See also* imitation and creativity
modernity, 4, 7, 9, 10ff. 16, 24, 29–30, 33, 35, 37, 38, 117, 212, 220f., 265ff., 269, 271f., 273n, 274f., 282f., 287
Mozart, Wolfgang Amadeus, 289
Müller-Lauter, W., on wills to power, 184n
Muse(s), the, 10, 47, 277
music, 34–35, 47, 48, 78, 240n, 280; and Kant, 77–78, 153, 240n; and Schopenhauer, 146, 149–50, 153, 240n, 279; and Hegel, 153; and Nietzsche, 153, 240n, 280; and Heidegger, 240n

nature, 9, 10, 24, 29–30, 55, 77, 115, 120, 122, 238n, 244, 248, 273n, 274ff., 284; and genius, 60ff.; and Kant, 61ff.; and sublime, 80–86; *natura naturans* vs. *natura naturata,* 248f.
Newgrange, 118
Newton, Isaac, 64, 175, 209; and Homer, 75; Newtonianism 60, 62, 71, 73, 79, 80, 81
Nicholas of Cusa, 170, 239
Nietzsche, Friedrich, chapter 6 *passim;* 3, 8, 11, 13, 14, 29, 40, 42, 43, 62, 65, 66, 73, 74, 78–79, 84, 86, 90, 93, 102, 109, 124, 209, 211, 216, 224, 227f., 232, 235, 237, 239, 242, 244, 246, 248, 253n, 259ff., 267f., 274, 279f., 285f., 291; and Schopenhauer, 8, 31, 141, 143, 144, 145, 159, 182n, 188–89, 191, 194, 195, 215, 225, 236, 245, 262, 266; and origins, 92, 134, 151, 159, 160, 165–208, 237, 239, 245, 256; and paganism, 8; and philology, 174–76, 180–81; and Plato, 5, 14, 20, 29, 31, 44, 46, 154, 166–72, 219, 241; and Hegel, 144, 179, 188, 189–90, 201–3, 231; and Kant, 167; and tragedy, 35, 168, 243, 279, 281; and *das Ureine,* 183–84, 184n, 193, 200, 201; and poetry and philosophy, 75, 169–73; and nihilism, 10, 48, 151, 153, 161, 234; and inspiration, 197; and self-creation, 194, 197–98, 200–2, 208; and Apollo/Dionysus, 8, 13, 14, 15, 68, 77, 141, 153, 159, 160, 167–68, 172, 183, 184, 187–91, 196, 197, 199, 206, 233, 239f.; and "yes," 134, 160, 199, 208; and will to power, 8, 10, 14, 15, 30, 48, 111, 146, 160, 169, 170, 173, 178, 184, 184–85n, 197, 205–6, 207, 230, 236, 281f.; and religion, 186–87, 201–2, 272f., 283; and God, 200, 201, 203; and Nietzschean deconstructionism, 134, 148; and desire, 151–52; and music, 153, 178; and Idea, 153, 154; and genius, 153, 198; and eros, 154, 191, 208; and Heidegger, 159, 183; and Romanticism, 160; and horror, 161, 168; and compassion, 161; and Schelling, 167; and Socratism, 168; and becoming, 174; and Leibniz, 175; and genealogy, 178–79; and dialectic, 179, 181; and ethics, 178, 180; and metaphysics, 182–83, 184; and futurity, 182, 182n; and aesthetics of origin, 182–87; and sameness/difference, 184–85, 204; and humor, 185, 192, 192n; and masks, 167, 185–86, 188, 190, 191; and *Übermensch,* 190, 191, 195, 254, 282; and *amor fati,* 191, 193, 196; and madness, 192, 204; and Idea, 194; and evil, 208; redemptive power of art, 280; *Birth of Tragedy,* 215, 240, 243, 279, 282, 285; *Thus Spoke Zarathustra,* 285
night, 231–35, 237, 242
nihilism, 153, 161, 162, 234, 289; and Schopenhauer, 133–34
noon, high noon, 237, 240, 278; and Socrates, 46; and Nietzsche, 196
nothing/nothingness, 214, 242, 250ff., 256; and Heidegger, 153
Nussbaum, Martha, 39

Oedipus, and Schelling, 208n
One, the, *das Ureine,* 183–84, 184n, 193

ontological difference, 238
onto-theology, 211, 227, 240
open, openess, 214, 235, 246, 247, 259, 260ff.
origin, 1–17, 21–24, 37, 49–51, 55, 89–91, 95, 109–13, 115, 117, 127, 214, 216, 219, 224f., 235, 241, 250, 252, 281, 291, 293f.; and Schopenhauer, 131–33, 141, 147, 151, 152–53, 154, 155; darkness of origin, 162, 165, 237, 244, 279f.; Dionysian origin, 197, 233, 243f.; hyperbolic origin, 249, 259; agapeic origin, 224n, 228, 239, 241f., 246, 252, 260ff., 284, 291, 294; dialectical origin, chapter 3 *passim,* 243, 252; erotic origin, chapters 5 and 6 *passim,* 200ff., 228, 234, 235, 237, 239f., 245, 256, 291; radical origin, 229, 234; excessive origin, 230, 261; self-concealing origin, 245, 263
origination/originality, 1–17, 40–51, 127, 274
original(s), and images, 25ff.; Kantian originals, 67ff.; primal, 252f.; Platonic, chapter 1 *passim,* 211; original power 269
orthotes (correctness), 214ff., 236. See also *alētheia*
other, otherness, 1–17, 22, 26, 28, 29, 117, 129, 226, 241, 242, 246, 249, 254, 272, 275f., 283f., 285, 293; and idealism, 137–38; origin and Plato, 166; and words, 174–75; and creativity, 176–77
overdeterminacy, overdetermination, 211, 219, 223, 229, 239, 240, 251, 269, 287
Owl of Minerva, 233

pagan/paganism, 8, 229, 242
panentheism, 273n
pantheism, 112
Pantheon, Roman, 229
Panofsky, Erwin, 122
Parmenides, 217, 228f., 241, 249, 255n, 260; and *esti,* 158
participation, 25ff.
Pascal, Blaise, 13, 220
passio essendi, 10, 13, 15, 16, 23, 35, 38, 43, 47, 78, 246, 254, 260, 288f., 291; and Schopenhauer, 149. See also *conatus essendi,* porosity of being
Pater, Walter, 248
perplexity, 216, 225, 232, 234, 252, 253n, 265, 288, 291
philology, and Nietzsche, 174–76, 180–81; and Vico, 181
philosopher(s), 209, 219, 241, 249f., 278, 286, 290
philosophy, 231, 267, 272, 279, 282, 289, 292f.; end of, 265f., 270; transcendental, 221, 221n, 224, 225, 227
Picasso, Pablo, 96, 109, 227
Pinkard, Terry, 142n
Plato/Platonism, 13, 14, 19–51, 209, 216, 218, 220, 221, 233f., 236, 240–43, 245; *Timaeus,* 5, 29, 49, 50, 75, 220; *Symposium,* 21, 35, 36, 39, 49; *Phaedrus,* 35, 36, 39, 41, 42, 43, 44, 46–47, 48, 49, 215; *Republic,* 34, 35, 39, 44, 45, 215; *Ion,* 43, 44–46, 48, 75, 277; *Laws,* 28; *Theaetetus,* 23; *Parmenides,* 26; *Phaedo,* 28, 39; *Sophist,* 33; *Apology,* 22, 45; and mimesis, 11, 20, 21, 24, 29, 31–35, 37, 38, 40, 44–45, 51, 55, 195; and creation, 5–6, 26, 29, 195; and image/original, 11, 20, 23–31, 31–35, 36–38, 41–49, 50, 92, 93, 215; and metaxu, 21–22, 55, 89, 218, 261; and participation, 23–31; Platonic dialogue, 22, 28, 35, 36, 41–49, 170; poetry and philosophy, 19, 22, 44–45, 46; Platonic dualism, 20, 21, 28–31, 34, 38; Platonism and Neoplatonism, 90, 154–55, 195; time and eternity, 49; demiurgic making, 5–6, 49, 49–51; and Kant, 53, 54, 73; and play, 235; Hegel and the Idea, 96, 99, 102, 103, 223; Platonic Idea, 136–37, 140, 142, 144, 145, 146, 147–48, 154, 159, 195; Schopenhauer and the Idea, 140, 142, 144, 145, 147–48, 154; and Nietzsche, 5, 14, 20, 29, 31,

44, 46, 146, 166–72, 204, 206, 209, 219; Heidegger's misreading, 29, 214; and Demiurge, 5, 35, 49, 49–51; and mania, 40–49; and Cave, 131; and Good, 131, 132; and eros, 150, 152; and desire, 151, 152; and philosophical reason, 152; and origin, 166; and God, 169; Plato as father of Schopenhauer, 150; music, 240n
Paul, Jean, and Hegel and Schopenhauer, 143
plurivocity, 216, 217, 226, 257f., 261, 288; and philosophy, 170–73
poet, the, 209, 219, 226, 231, 240n, 245, 265f., 280, 286, 289; as namer, 231, 236, 266, 280, 282
poetry, 10, 20, 22, 44, 77, 78, 211, 254, 279, 282; and Kant, 77–78, 153; and Schopenhauer, 144; and Hegel, 153; and Heidegger, 212
polemos, 214, 235, 237, 243f., 246, 248, 255, 259, 261f.
Pornography, 16, 278
poros, 156, 191, 208, 235
porosity of being, 3, 10, 12, 13, 16, 17, 44, 58, 84, 125, 127, 257, 260, 262, 288ff., 291f., 294; and sublime 84–86; and Schopenhauer, 149–50. See also *passio essendi,* inspiration
posse, 251
possibility, the possible, 217, 239, 251, 258, 268f.
postmodernity, 1, 2, 7, 10, 16, 20, 24, 35, 40, 221, 267, 270, 276; and religion, 162
postulatory finitism, 253
postulatory theism, 253n
Potter, Beatrix, Squirrel Nutkin, 257
praxis, 218; revolutionary 266
prayer, 48, 127, 289
projection, 214, 246, 250, 254–59, 261f., 269; and Ideas, 153. *See also* subreption
Protestant/Protestantism, 121–23, 124–26
Prometheus, 7–8, 90, 167, 242, 262n; under Jove, 242, 260
Pyramids, 118

questioning, piety of, 257

Raphael, and Nietzche, 199
reason/*Vernunft,* 40, 44, 230, 278f., 282, 289; cunning of, 232
relics, 277
religion, ix–xi, 3, 4, 13, 35, 129, 230f., 240, 257, 262, 266f., 269f., 273n, 274–77, 286, 289–94; Biblical, 86, 247; and postmodernism, 162; and Nietzsche, 178, 186–87, 201–2; and art, chapter 8 *passim*
Rimbaud, Arthur, 108
romantic/romanticism, ix, 2, 31, 40, 43, 57–58, 66, 72, 74, 83, 84, 87, 88, 90, 91, 104, 107, 128, 209, 210, 240n, 266f., 272, 274ff., 279, 284; between Enlightenment and Romanticism, chapters 2 and 3 *passim;* and inwardness, 151; and formlessness, 159; and Nietzsche, 160
romantic artform, 98, 103–7; and architecture, 120–21; and Schopenhauer, 140. *See also* Enlightenment
Rorty, Richard, 132n, 280, 282f., 286
Rosen, Stanley, 218n
Rossini, Gioacchino, Hegel and Schopenhauer's admiration for, 143

sacred, x, 129; sacred space, 115, 118
saint, the, 141, 149, 234
Saint Peter's Church, 123n
Sabbath/sabbatical, 239; of the will, 155–58, 236; and earth, 219; witches', 239; of thought, 294
Sartre, Jean-Paul, 255n, 273
Scheler, Max, 119n
Schelling, Friedrich Wilhelm Joseph von, 3, 13, 21, 43, 63n, 65, 74, 81, 88, 92, 111, 223, 223ff., 231, 234n, 266, 279, 281, 285; *Indifferenzpunkt,* and Schopenhauer, 137, 141, 142, 145; relationship with Tieck and the Schlegels, 143; and artistic perfection, 152; and will, 155; and otherness, 167; and failure, 173; and idealism, 204; and appropriation of

Schelling, Friedrich Wilhelm Joseph von *(continued)*
Spinoza, 204; and the Oedipal, 208n; "night in which all cows are black," 231f.
Schiller, Friedrich, 283, 285
Schlegel, Friedrich van, 43; the Schlegels and Romanticism, 143
Schopenhauer, Arthur, 11, 13, 14, 15, 21, 40 66, 72, 79, 86, 131–63, 211, 224, 232, 234f., 237, 242, 246, 261, 266, 279, 281; and Ideas, 74, 140, 146, 148–49, 153, 154, 160; and Will, 8, 14, 84, 131, 132, 135, 141–42, 144, 145, 147, 148–50, 154, 155–58, 160–61, 205, 236, 279; and dark origin, ix, 81, 92, 111, 219, 237, 244, 245, 281; and Plato, 31, 140, 144, 147–48; and genius, 43, 140–42, 145, 149, 153, 157–58; and music, 78, 149–50, 152–53, 240n, 279; and Hegel, 96, 136–38, 142–48, 158, 279; and eros, 131, 135, 150, 152, 155, 157, 205, 256; metaphysical significance of the art work, 132, 144, 145, 146, 148; and Nietzsche, 133–35, 145, 159, 160–61, 182–83, 183–84, 188–89, 191, 205, 215, 236, 262; and pessimism, 133–34; and nihilism, 134; and Kant, 135–36, 137, 138–40, 141, 145, 221; and idealism, 135–38; and Schelling, 137, 141, 142, 145; and release of will, 142, 155–58, 236, 285; and Fichte, 142; and historicism, 144; and the universal, 144; and world, 145; and metaphor of artist, 144–45; and the need to know, 145–46; and allegory, 146; and dualism, 147, 148; and will and rationality, 147–48; and Heidegger, 148, 262; and "ordinary" person, 149; and desire, 151–52; and logos, 153; and Sabbath, 155, 158; and beauty, 159; and horror, 161; and compassion, 161; and sufficient reason, 162
self-consciousness, 176; and Nietzsche, 196
self-determination, 10, 11, 40, 127, 128, 189, 228f., 253, 271, 272, 276, 283, 285, 288
Self-mediation, 225, 227, 242f., 254, 272, 293, dialectical, 230, 284
self-transcendence, 219, 226, 237, 254, 267f., 273, 286f., 291–93
seriousness, and Heidegger, 256
serviceable disposibility, 253, 286
Shaftesbury, Earl of, 7–8, 90
Shakespeare, William, 288ff.; *King Lear,* 157; *Macbeth,* 208
Shaw, George Bernard, 131
Shelley, Percy Bysshe, 21
Shestov, Lev, 239
silence, 171–72, 248, 252
Silenus, and Schopenhauer, 150
Socrates, 3, 22, 23, 35, 39, 41, 42, 43, 45–47, 48, 54, 75, 84, 102, 104, 112, 263, 266, 282; and Socratism, 168, 169–70, 171
song, 126, 173. *See also* music
Sophocles, 239n
space, 8, 11, 12, 13, 29. *See also* sacred space
Spinoza, Baruch, and Schelling's appropriation of, 204
spirit, 189. See also *Geist*
Speer, Albert, 123
Stoic/Stoicism, 75
strife *(Streit),* 260ff.
Sturm und Drang, 57, 76
subjective/objective, 224, 227, 230, 258, 260, 262, 270, 292
subjectivism, 221f., 224, 226f.
subjectivity, 241f, 245, 258; transcendental, 221, 227
sublime/sublimity, 123, 126, 273n, 276, 284; and Kant, 80–86, 122; and Hegel, 86, 119, 121, 122, 124, 125
subreption, 86, 93, 153, 158, 189–90, 194, 254; and Kant, 83ff.
sun, sunlight, 233, 240, 244; black sun 232f.; Platonic 242
surrealism, 110, 161. *See also* Breton, Dalí
sweats, the, 131–32, 231–34; and Kant, 84–85, 147, 196, 231; and Hegel, 87–88, 91, 107, 110, 147; and

Schopenhauer, 131, 147, 231; and Nietzsche, 196; and Hume, 165; and Heidegger, 232
symbolic artform, 98–101, 284; and architecture, 120–21

Taminaux, Jacques, 262n
taste, 68ff., 283, 284n. *See also* genius
technology, 241, 276
temporality, 223n, 254
Teresias, 263
"that it is," 217, 293
theodicy, 175, 186
theōria, 219, 266
Thomas Aquinas, St. *See also* Aquinas
thought/thinking, 238, 292; task of 265; thought thinking itself, 225, 228, 230, 232, 246, 250
throw, thrown, 255–58, 261
Tiantan Park (Temple of Heaven), 118, 123n4
Tieck, Ludwig, and Romanticism, 143
time, 49, 124, 225. *See also* eternity
Titans, 102, 181, 242
"to be," the, 217, 224, 236, 238, 252; evil of, 261; goodness of, 239, 245; "not to be," 236
Tolkien, J.R.R., 176
Tolstoy, Leo, 131
Tongeren, Paul van, 184n
tragedy, 35, 209; and tragic wisdom, 150; and tragic art-life, 167ff.; Nietzsche as tragic philosopher, 173; Nietzsche's tragic vision, 188, 191
transcendental, 8, 12, 53, 55, 60ff., 221; and Kant, chapter 2 *passim;* and Hegel, 82ff.; and Schopenhauer, 136ff.; Heidegger, 221–27; transcendental self, 221
transcendence/transcendences, chapter 8 *passim,* x, 3, 6, 7, 8, 9, 10, 11, 12, 13, 16, 33, 34, 37, 39, 40, 85–86, 115, 117, 120, 122, 124, 126, 127, 128, 129, 238n, 249, 251f., 262, 267, 268ff., 274, 278f., 282f., 287, 294; and Gothic cathedral, 122ff.; first transcendence (T1), 268ff., 273n, 275, 293f.; second transcendence (T2), 268ff., 275, 284, 284n, 285f., 290, 293; third transcendence (T3), 251, 269–72, 273n, 275f., 281, 283–87, 291–94; religious, 267, 272, 285f., 287; creative, 274f.; immanent, 274f., 293; agapeic, 287; enigma of, 288; allergy to, 271, 273; exigence of, 272, 274, 277
Trevor, William, 289
truth, 214, 215, 217, 237, 245, 257, 280; correspondence theory of, 215ff. See also *alētheia, orthotes*
Turner, William (Turner Prize), 278

understanding/*Verstand,* 222, 230. See also *Verstand*
underground, 21; Schopenhauer and second underground, 131–33; and Nietzsche, 166. *See also* Cave
unhappy consciousness, 116, 126, 128
univocal/univocity, 3, 7, 22, 23–31, 25, 27, 28, 32, 33, 34, 35, 36, 37, 38, 40, 42, 45, 217ff., 231, 235f., 248, 253, 259, 260f., 281, 288, 294
universality, 291; imaginative universal, 19; and participation, 25ff.; as incognito of the religious, 291f.; concrete universal, 144, 146. *See also* Idea

vagina monologues, 67
Van Gogh, Vincent, x, 124–26
Verene, Donald, 19
Verstand/Vernunft, 122, 129, 130, 146–47
Vico, Giambattista, 19, 73, 211, 240, 242, 282; Nietzsche and logicism, 181

Wagner, Richard, 131, 189
Warhol, Andy, 280
Weimar, and aesthetic culture, 143
Weird Sisters, 237
will, 246, 250, 255, 266; will to power, 146, 160, 169, 170, 173, 178, 184, 184–85n, 230, 236, 241, 245, 254f., 273, 279, 281f.; will to life, 236
Whitehead, Alfred North, 182
Winckelmann Johann Joachim, and Hegel, 143; and Schopenhauer, 143

Wittgenstein, Ludwig, 137
whole, 117, 121, 127
wonder, 1, 112–13, 292
wooing, 10, 16, 47–48; and inspiration, 230, 277, 288
world, 214n, 226, 242, 245f., 257f.; moral world (Kant), 244. *See also* earth

Yahweh, 281, 286

Zarathustra, chapter 6, *passim,* 153, 244
Zeus. *See* Jove
Zwischen, das, 211, 247, 257f., 211, 247, 257ff.

Printed in Great Britain
by Amazon